Backroad Mapb

MW00682302

Mapbooks

Southwestern Alberta

Table of Contents

www.backroadmapbooks.com

Backroad Mapbooks

DIRECTORS
Russell Mussio
Wesley Mussio
Penny Stainton-Mussio

ASSOCIATE DIRECTOR
Jason Marleau

VICE PRESIDENT
Chris Taylor

COVER DESIGN & LAYOUT
Farnaz Faghihi

COVER PHOTO
Trent Ernst

PRODUCTION MANAGER
Brett Firth

PRODUCTION
Andrew Allen
Shaan Desai
Tara Dreyer
Farnaz Faghihi
Colin Holdener
Jason Marleau
Grace Teo
Dale Tober

SALES /MARKETING
Jason Marleau
Chris Taylor

WRITERS
Trent Ernst
Russell Mussio
Wesley Mussio

National Library of Canada Cataloguing in Publication Data

Ernst, Trent
Backroad mapbook : southwestern Alberta : your complete outdoor recreation guide / Trent Ernst. -- 2nd ed.

At head of title: Mussio Ventures presents.
Includes index.
ISBN 1-894556-28-3

1. Recreation areas--Alberta--Maps. 2. Alberta--Maps. I. Title. II. Title: Southwestern Alberta.

G1166.E63E76 2004   912.7123'4   C2004-901300-9

Published by:

Backroad Mapbooks

5811 Beresford Street
Burnaby, BC, V5J 1K1, Canada
P. (604) 438-3474   F. (604) 438-3470
E-mail: info@backroadmapbooks.com
www.backroadmapbooks.com
Copyright © 2004 Mussio Ventures Ltd.
Updated 2005

Acknowledgements

This book could not have been compiled without the help of a tremendous team of individuals working for Mussio Ventures Ltd. This is a hat's off to Trent Ernst for digging up countless new recreational opportunities. Combined with the talented people at Mussio Ventures Ltd., Andrew Allen, Shawn Caswell, Farnaz Faghihi, Brett Firth, Colin Holdener, Chris Taylor, Dale Tober, Grace Teo and Heather Yetman, we were able to produce the most comprehensive guidebook for Southwestern Alberta.

In our efforts to update this book we have come across a number of people who have contributed invaluable knowledge. To all the people who work and volunteer in tourist information booths, thank you. Without the information you provided, we probably would have got lost. Ditto to all those folks in the outdoor stores and bike shops. You helped us find our way. Thanks to Kris Nelson, from the Cochrane Kayak Club, who helped us revise the paddling section and mark prominent features on the maps, to Dave at Tread Softly (www.treadsoftlycanada.com), who provided suggestions on Crowsnest Area trails, to Steve Donelon, who helped with Kananaskis Country Trails, and Yvette Choma who fielded all sorts of questions about the Bighorn Backcountry.

To all the people in the various levels of government who provided information on activities. There are too many of you to name, and, far too often, we forgot to ask for it anyway. Thank you. A special note of thanks to all those fish and wildlife types, especially Brian Lajeunesse in Canmore and Rob Watt in Waterton, who answered question after nit-picky question about fishing in their respective areas.

This book wouldn't have been as interesting without the many pictures that we have collected. Thanks to all the people who posed for us. A special note of thanks goes to Darrell Ford at Chateau Lake Louise for getting up so early to go canoeing, just so Trent could take pictures. Also thanks to Cory Brightwell ("Yellow kayak dude") and friends, to Randy and Joe (Bow River anglers), and especially to the Renshaws (John and Karla), who suffered our company, and our constant picture taking on the Crypt Lake hike. And to all those people whom we bumped into and asked "Hey, do you mind if we take a picture?" This book is better for your kindness.

Thank you also to all the people who sent us emails to tell us updated information on their favourite areas, be it road changes, new trails, or species of fish that can't be found in certain lakes. We could not have done this without you all, and your help is appreciated. And to all of you who we may have forgotten to mention, but who have provided input into making this the best mapbook on the market, we are grateful for your help and support.

Finally we would like to thank Allison, Devon, Jasper, Nancy, Madison and Penny Mussio for their continued support of the Backroad Mapbook Series. As our family grows, it is becoming more and more challenging to break away from it all to explore our beautiful country.

Sincerely,

Russell and Wesley Mussio

Help Us Help You

A comprehensive resource such as **Backroad Mapbooks** for Southwestern Alberta could not be put together without a great deal of help and support. Despite our best efforts to ensure that everything is accurate, errors do occur. If you see any errors or omissions, please continue to let us know.

Please contact us at:
Mussio Ventures Ltd.
5811 Beresford St, Burnaby, B.C. V5J 1K1

Email: updates@backroadmapbooks.com
P: 604-438-3474 toll free 1-877-520-5670 F: 604-438-3470

All updates will be posted on our web site:
www.backroadmapbooks.com

Disclaimer

Mussio Ventures Ltd. does not warrant that the backroads, paddling routes and trails indicated in this Mapbook are passable nor does it claim that the Mapbook is completely accurate. Therefore, please be careful when using this or any source to plan and carry out your outdoor recreation activity.

Please note that traveling on logging roads, river routes and trails is inherently dangerous, and without limiting the generality of the foregoing, you may encounter poor road conditions, unexpected traffic, poor visibility, and low or no road/trail maintenance. Please use extreme caution when traveling logging roads and trails.

Please refer to the Fishing and Hunting Regulations for closures and restrictions. It is your responsibility to know when and where closures and restrictions apply.

Backroad Mapbooks

Southwestern Alberta Mapkey

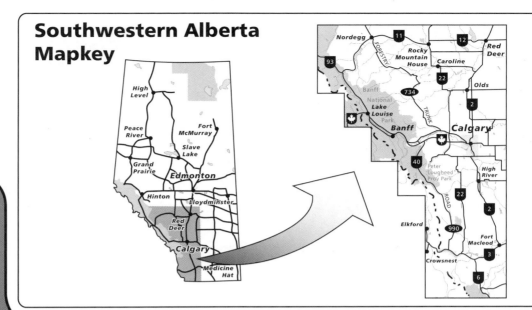

Welcome to the second edition of the Backroad Mapbook for Southwestern Alberta.

The Backroad Mapbook for Southwestern Alberta covers a large area that is bound by the David Thompson Highway to the North, Highway 2 to the east, and British Columbia and the United States to the west and south, respectively.

This is an area of dramatic contrast—where the prairies butt against towering mountain peaks, and the temperature can vary almost 80 degrees Celsius between summer and winter. It is also an area of incredible beauty. There are few roads more dramatic than the Icefields Parkway in Banff, few hikes as breathtaking (in more ways than one) as the Crypt Lake hike in Waterton, and few campsites as nice as the ones you will find on the shores of Kananaskis Lake in Peter Lougheed Provincial Park.

The Backroad Mapbooks have had a history of doing substantial changes and updates to the book and we are very confident you will be amazed by the improvements found within this book. The first part of the book is devoted solely to the reference section. It is easy to see that this section has been expanded. People will find more lakes and streams to fish, more parks to visit, more areas to paddle and even places to look for wildlife.

In addition to the writing, the map section has also changed substantially. We have added three new maps to include the many roads and activities around Red Deer. Another prominent feature is the clarification of paved roads. Now people with RV's and cars will know which roads they will find much smoother travel on. We have also spent countless hours updating the road and trail systems as well as adding new recreational features such as new provincial parks and wildlife viewing areas.

Looking for someplace to go fishing? We have write-ups on over 200 streams and nearly the same number of lakes. Paddling? We have described this area's best rivers and lakes for canoeing and kayaking. Hiking? There's more trails listed and described here than you could probably hike in a lifetime. And the list goes on…

The Backroad Mapbook is much more than a set of maps. It is an explorer's guide. The maps and writing will let you dream of places not so far away. So sit back and enjoy what we have to offer.

How to Use this Mapbook

The Backroad Mapbook is a truly unique product. No other source covers Southwestern Alberta with as much detail for information on outdoor recreation activities as this book.

The mapbook is simple to use. There are two main sections in the book, a reference section and the maps. If you know the activity you are planning, you simply turn to that section and find the activity you are interested in. We cover a broad range of outdoor activities that can be enjoyed year round when spending time outdoors.

Reference Section Features

The reference section found in the guide includes information on backroads, lake and stream fishing, hunting, paddling routes, parks, multi-use trails (hiking/biking, and ATV trails), wildlife viewing and winter recreation. Countless hours have been spent in researching this book, making it the most complete compilation of outdoor recreation information you will find on the region anywhere. This information can be enjoyed by anyone who spends time in the great outdoors.

Index and Map Key

If you are planning a trip to a specific area or site, you should consult the **index** at the back of the book to find the appropriate reference page or map. You can also use the **map key** to find a general area you want to explore. Individual write-ups on paddling routes, parks, trails, etc. can be found through the index or by searching the appropriate reference section. Most write-ups are written in alphabetical order. Due to the number of large parks that are destinations in themselves, we have grouped these listings in alphabetical order under the individual park.

Map Features

Looking at our maps you will notice they highlight all sorts of recreational opportunities as well as the backroad/logging road and trail systems in the area.

Recreational Features

You will find the maps mark points of interest, paddling routes, parks and conservation areas, trail systems and even wildlife viewing opportunities. Both **snowmobile trails** and **long distance trails** are highlighted with a background colour to aid users in tracking these systems. Hunters and anglers will also be happy to see that we have included the **Management Units** on the maps. The big green number notes the zones while the boundaries are marked with a faint green border.

Road Features & Map Legend

By combining city and rural roads with current forestry and logging road maps our maps are designed for people wishing to get outdoors. However, they very detailed and the myriad of logging roads in addition to the various trail systems can be confusing. We provide a **map legend** at the start of each section of the maps to illustrate the region we cover as well as how to decipher the various grades of roads and symbols used on the maps.

UTM Grids & Longitude and Latitude

Another interesting feature on our maps is the small numbers provided around our map borders. The blue numbers and thin blue line represent UTM Grids (datum NAD 1983; projection Transverse Mercator), while the black numbers represent Longitude and Latitude reference points. Although both can be used by GPS users, the UTM Grids are more accurate for land-based travel. We must emphasize that these are for reference only. This generality is because of the scale of the maps and we have to consult several different sources to create the maps.

Area Covered

The Southwestern Alberta mapbook has been laid out in a manner most accessible to the average user. All maps run north to south parallel to the side borders and east to west parallel to the top and bottom borders. The maps start at the southwest corner of the region and end at the northeast corner. The scale of this mapbook is 1:200 000, this means that 1 centimetre is equal to 2 kilometres. Each page represents approximately 38 kilometres east to west and 50 kilometres north to south for a total area of 1,900 km².

Special Note On Backroad Travel

Generally, Southwestern Alberta has a well established road system that provides access to many outdoor activities. However, some farming and logging roads are restricted to public access. Be sure to pay attention to road signs and please do not trespass. The roads marked by thinner black lines and the deactivated roads/trails shown by thin dashed lines on our maps can be explored by off-highway enthusiasts (4x4 and ATV's) as well as trail users. However, people who do venture off the main roads should have good navigational skills and a way to track where they came from.

Updates

Although the Backroad Mapbook Series is the most detailed and up-to-date resource available for backcountry travel, it must be noted that it is only a planning and access guide. We have gone to great lengths to ensure the accuracy of this book. However, over time, the road and trail conditions change. If you do notice a discrepancy, please let us know by calling 1-877-520-5670 or emailing us at updates@backroadmapbooks.com. All updates are posted on our website under the individual book page information.

If you are a GPS user, we welcome you to submit us your tracks and waypoints. These tracks will be used to help put together a Digital Edition of the maps in this book. Finally, backcountry travellers will have a reliable and up to date map set to use in association with a GPS unit.

We invite you to let us help you explore this vast area of Alberta. But we ask that you go prepared to deal with emergencies and always respect private property.

Russell and Wesley Mussio: Founders of Backroad Mapbook Series

Freshwater Fishing
(Lake, River and Stream Fishing)

The Eastern Slopes of the Rockies offer anglers the chance to experience some truly magical angling. From pristine streams to high alpine lakes, there is some truly glorious scenery in this region that serves as a spectacular backdrop to some great fishing.

Because this area has the highest population in the province, regulations are very tight, to protect the fishery. During the 1980s and 1990s, the amount of fishing pressure on the lakes and streams of the Eastern Slope increased significantly, to the point that many of these once great fishing streams and lakes were not producing well. As a result, numerous regulations were developed, including an almost complete bait ban in streams (see regulations for current exemptions), strict possession limits (zero for bull trout in all Alberta waters), size limits (minimum 35 cm/14 inches for cutthroat and rainbow caught in streams, except where noted, and minimum 30 cm/12 inches for rocky mountain whitefish), winter closures for streams (as well as catch-and-release only in fall), and, as of 2004, barbless hooks will be mandatory across Alberta.

Some rivers or lakes are closed to fishing, most notably all streams and lakes within the White Goat Wilderness, Siffluer Wilderness and Ghost River Wilderness Areas. If you don't see a lake or stream listed here, check the regulations; it may be closed. Of course, it may also just be barren, an all-too-common occurrence. In the Rockies, there are many lakes that are too shallow and too high to support fish. Farther away from the mountains, most of the lakes are either too shallow or too alkaloid to sustain a fish population.

The province-wide catch limit is five trout and char per day, with a maximum of one golden trout, two grayling or three lake trout going towards that total. The limit for mountain whitefish is five per day. Catch limit for all streams is two trout per day. There are many streams and rivers that are catch and release throughout the year. As always, check the regulations.

In addition to the closures listed here and in the sportfishing regulations, Alberta Sustainable Resource Development reserves the right to declare emergency closures during times of extremely low water. When in doubt, contact the nearest Fish and Wildlife office.

We have listed the National Parks lakes under a separate section at the end. This is because fishing in National Parks is a different beast than fishing elsewhere in the province. No, the fish are the same, but the regulations governing fishing are different. The lakes are no longer stocked, (meaning that all lakes with fish in them have to be self-sustaining), and you will need a special license to fish. Check with Parks Canada for more information. Regulations can be downloaded from www.parkscanada.gc.ca.

Lake Fishing

Alberta has some of the highest fishing pressure in the country. There are an estimated 350,000 anglers, but there are only about 800 lakes across the entire province with naturally occurring fish populations—plus another 300 or so stocked lakes—to choose from. That works out to nearly 400 anglers per lake. (In comparison, Saskatchewan has an estimated 94,000 fish-bearing lakes, with an average of two anglers per lake.) Of course, most of the fish-bearing lakes are in the north, while most of the population is to the south, which puts an even greater pressure on lakes and rivers in Southwestern Alberta.

Seasonal water temperatures usually determine the quality of fishing. Generally, after the ice melts in the spring, fish are feeding near the surface and are the easiest to catch. As summer approaches, the fish retreat to deeper waters to avoid the algae bloom and the warmer waters. At that time, the fishing success generally suffers. Then, by fall, the water temperatures drop again and the fish return to the surface for better fishing success.

In most low elevation lakes below 1,200 m (4,000 feet), fishing is best in mid April to June and again in September and October. Higher elevation lakes offer good fishing through the summer months. Do not expect ice-off until June (or sometimes later) for high elevation lakes.

Below we have included the fish species found in each lake along with the recent stocking information. Generally speaking, the stocked lakes provide a much better fishery but the fish are usually quite small.

Abraham Lake (Map 26/C1–33/E5)
Abraham Lake is Alberta's longest man-made lake, and is easily accessed by the David Thompson Highway (Highway 11), which runs along the lake's western shore. At the south end of the turquoise lake is the Kootenay Plains Natural Area as well as two campgrounds (Two O'clock Creek Recreation Area and Cavalcade Campsite). Also near the lake is the David Thompson Resort, which offers full facilities. The lake contains brook trout, cutthroat and rocky mountain whitefish (to 1 kg/2 lbs) as well as some large bull trout (to 5 kg/10 lbs). The odd lake trout and rainbow can also be caught. The best time to fish is in fall through to ice up, and the best places to try are near the Bighorn Dam at the north end of the lake or at one of the creek estuaries. Keep in mind that there is a size restriction for the cutthroat and rainbow trout (greater than 30 cm/12 inches) and a bait ban on both the lake and its tributaries. The lake is subject to strong winds.

Alford Lake (Map 28/F2)
This small lake, found just north of the Tay River Recreation Area, holds stocked brook trout. The trout are up to about 15 cm (6 inches) when they are put in the lake, and can grow to about twice that size.

Allen Bill Pond (Map 16/D7)
This tiny pond is home of the Allen Bill Pond Recreation Area, a small picnic site. The pond is located next to Highway 66 and each year it is stocked with rainbow (between 20–30 cm/8–12 inches). In addition to rainbow, the pond is home to some small brook trout and rocky mountain whitefish. Camping is nearby at the McLean Creek and Elbow River Recreation Areas.

Allstones Lake (Map 33/D6)
This small lake is accessed by the Allstones Lake Trail, a 2 km (1.2 mile) one-way trail leading from Highway 11 near the shores of Abraham Lake. The lake contains occasionally stocked brook trout that are best taken by spincasting a lure with bait. A two trout limit is in effect.

Aster Lake (Map 10/D4)
A remote, high mountain lake near the BC boundary in Peter Lougheed Provincial Park, Aster Lake holds stocked cutthroat to 20 cm (12 inches). The lake is a 10 km (6.2 mile) hike from the parking lot at Upper Kananaskis Lake.

Barrier Lake (Map 15/F4)
Barrier Lake is located on the shores of Highway 40 southeast of Canmore. It contains brown trout to 1.5 kg (3 lbs), rocky mountain whitefish to 1 kg (2 lbs) and a few small brook trout. The lake is a man-made expansion of Kananaskis River and is best fished by trolling or spincasting.

Barnaby Lakes (Map 2/A2)
The Barnaby Lakes are comprised of Barnaby Lake and Upper and Lower Southfork, which are drained by Barnaby Creek into the Castle River. The high altitude lakes hold some gorgeous golden trout that can grow to 1.5 kg (3 lbs) in size, but they are usually under 30 cm. The lakes are reached by travelling about 20 km south of Beaver Mines on Secondary Highway 774 and then hiking to the lakes. Since there is a bait ban, fishermen usually restrict themselves to spincasting or fly fishing. Please note that there are several other fishing restrictions on the lake including a 40 cm (15 inch) minimum size restriction, no fishing from November 1 to July 15 and a closure of the outflow and inflow creeks.

Bathing Lake (Map 2/E3)
This small lake is found along the Shell Waterton Gas Plant Road leading from Highway 6. The lake has rainbow trout, which can reach 1 kg (2 lbs) in size. There are no motorboats allowed on the lake so the principal fishing methods are fly fishing and spincasting.

Beauvais Lake (Map 2/D1)

Set in the foothills near Pincher Creek, Beauvais Lake Provincial Park is a popular destination with campers, swimmers, and of course, anglers. The lake is reached off Secondary Highway 775 and contains rainbow and brown trout. Ice fishing tends to be the most productive of all the fishing methods. There is a boat launch at the west side of the lake but bear in mind the powerboat restriction (less than 12 km/h).

Bear Pond (Map 7/G3)

Bear Pond is one of a handful of lakes in Alberta that has been stocked with Arctic Greyling. The lake is located by a short, steep 1 km hike from Secondary Highway 532 and is catch and release only. The feisty greyling can get up to 45 cm (17 inches) if they are not winterkilled.

Bearspaw Reservoir (Map 17/B3)

Behind Bearspaw dam, the Bow River slows down to create this narrow reservoir. The lake is shallow, but with a number of deep channels. It holds rocky mountain whitefish and some large lake trout (to 4.5 kg/10 lbs).

Beaverdam Lake (Map 3/D6)

Beaverdam is a large, shallow, man-made lake. It holds some small brook trout, but fishing here is generally poor. Another option is **Little Beaverdam Lake**, a man-made lake between Paine and Beaverdam Lakes that holds a fair number of brook trout, which will get to 30 cm (12 inches).

Beaver Mines Lake (Map 2/B2)

Set beneath the imposing Table Mountain, this popular lake contains rainbow to 1.5 kg (3 lbs) as well as a few bull trout. The fishing, although steady during the spring and fall, tends to be best during ice fishing season. There is a 12 km/h speed limit for powerboats, which can launch from the Beaver Mines Lake Recreation Area at the south end of the lake.

Big Iron Lake (Map 7/G3)

Big Iron Lake is found past Bear Pond (see above). It is 3 km (1.8 miles) from the road to the lake, which is occasionally stocked with Arctic Greyling. The fish like to hold in cooler, often deeper water, which can make shore fishing difficult, especially in the heat of summer. As with Bear Pond, the small lake is catch and release only and subject to winterkill.

Birch Lake (Map 29/B3)

Birch Lake is a small lake found north of Burnstick Lake that is stocked odd years with brook trout. The fish can grow to 1 kg (2 lbs) in size and are best caught by spincasting and fly fishing since the lake is hard to troll.

Bovin (Blue) Lake (Map 2/D4)

Reached by the Drywood Creek Trail, this sub-alpine lake is a good option if you want to catch many small brook trout. The fish can be caught from shore or by belly boat using a small lure with bait (worm). The spring and fall are the best times to try but the lake has no inflow or outflow and the water level can fluctuate dramatically, harming the fish population.

Burmis Lake (Map 5/B6)

This tiny lake is located about 11 km east of Blairmore off Highway 3, between the highway and the Crowsnest River. There is a day-use area at the lake together with access to the Crowsnest River. The lake offers small, stocked rainbow. If you are a fly fisherman then the best time to try is during the Stonefly hatch. Please note that the lake is too small to be marked on our maps but is found, as you might expect, near Burmis.

Burns Lake (Map 11/A4)

Burns Lake is a 16 km (9.9 mile) hike from Secondary Highway 546. The last little way up to the lake is steep, and most people are not willing to make the journey. But the intrepid backcountry angler will have a chance to try for one of the cutthroat that grow to 1.5 kg (3 lbs). The big ones are few and far between, but there are lots of smaller fish to keep you occupied.

Burnstick Lake (Map 29/A3)

Located off Secondary Highway 584, this large lake has pike to 2.5 kg (5 lbs), perch to 0.5 kg (1 lb), walleye and a few brown trout. It is catch and release for walleye. Most fishermen try spincasting near the weed beds for best success.

Burstall Lakes (Map 10/C1)

The Burstall Lakes are a series of lakes found 2 km west of Mud Lake via the Burstall Pass Trail. Expect to find cutthroat trout to 30 cm (12 inches)

and the odd dolly varden (not bull trout). If you do find a dolly, contact the Fisheries Biologist at the Alberta Sustainable Resource Development office in Canmore at (403) 678-5508 (ext. 263). The lakes are open for angling year-round.

Butcher Lake (Map 2/E3)

A man-made lake found about 5 km (3 miles) west of the Shell Waterton Gas Plant, Butcher Lake holds brook trout to 30 cm (12 inches).

Carnarvon Lake (Map 11/B7)

Carnarvon Lake is located near the BC and Alberta boundary in the Don Getty Wildland. It contains good numbers of cutthroat, which can grow to 2 kg (4 lbs). Access to the lake is via an 8 km (4.9 mile) one-way hike from the Cat Creek Recreation Area off of Highway 40. The trail can be difficult, if not downright dangerous, when wet. There is a limit of two cutthroat per day at the lake.

Chain Lake Reservoir (Map 8/C2)

Home of a popular provincial park, the lake provides some fairly good fishing for rainbow that reach 2.5 kg (5 lbs) but average under 0.5 kg (1 lb). There are also brook, brown, bull and cutthroat trout and rocky mountain whitefish in lesser numbers. Full camping facilities are found at the provincial park as well as boat launch and other amenities for the fishermen. The reservoir is one of the best family fishing lakes in the foothills.

Chester Lake (Map 10/C1)

Chester Lake contains stocked dolly varden to 4 kg (8 lbs) and is one of the 2 or 3 lakes in Alberta that contains dollies. Dolly Varden. It is rumoured that some may have made their way downstream to Mud Lake and it is because of this escapement that the Alberta Sustainable Resource Development may be opening the lake to harvesting of these deep holding fish in the future. Check the current regulations.

Chief Hector Lake (Map 15/F2)

Found on the Morley First Nations Reserve, this is a shallow lake that would be subject to winterkill if it were not for the aeration. But the rainbow do survive, and thrive. The good news is they can get to 9 kg (20 lbs). The bad news? Because the lake is on the Morley Reserve, it is a private lake, which means you will have to pay to fish here. The lake is also catch and release only.

Chinook (Allison Reservoir) Lake (Map 4/E4)

Easily accessed off the Allison Creek Road, this small lake offers some decent fishing for rainbow to 1 kg (2 lbs) as well as for a few brook and cutthroat trout. The lake is usually stocked each year and has a popular campground. Since there is a powerboat restriction, fishermen tend to fly fish or spincast from a float tube or from the shore. However, they didn't cut down the trees along the shore before creating the reservoir and there are a lot of snags to make shore fishing an exercise in frustration from some locations.

Cochrane Lake (Map 3/D2)

Cochrane Lake is a shallow lake subject to winterkill. There are a few northern pike that survive the winter, and grow to about 5 kg (11 lbs).

Coleman Fish and Game Pond (Map 4/E4)

This small man made lake (too small to show on our maps) is located west of McGillvray Creek, across from the entrance to the gun range. The pond contains good numbers of stocked rainbow to 1.5 kg (3 lbs). Fly fishing or spincasting from shore works, but bringing a float tube or canoe will improve your success.

Commonwealth Lake (Map 10/B1)

This lake is occasionally stocked with cutthroat trout. It is not a popular lake since access is by bushwhacking and shore fishing is difficult. But for those willing to bring a float tube, cutthroat to 40 cm (16 inches) await.

Coral Lake (Map 32/G6)

This tiny sub-alpine lake is found within the Bighorn Wildland Recreation Area. It is reached by a long hike up the Coral Creek Trail from Highway 11 near Abraham Lake. The lake is seldom fished because of its difficult access but it does contain the highly sought after golden trout. There is a bait ban in affect at the lake as well as a limit of one trout over 40 cm (15 inches).

Cow Lake (Map 35/G6)

This large lake has perch that grow to 1 kg (2 lbs) and every so often, a couple hundred large (60 cm/24 inch) rainbow are dropped in the lake. The trout are quickly fished out while the perch are best caught by spincasting the weed beds and shallows. The lake offers camping and a boat launch on the north end.

Crane Meadows Ponds (Map 16/B4)

Found on the south side of Highway 68 on Sibbald Creek, these beaver ponds (to tiny to mark on our maps) hold a fair number of small rainbow and brook trout. Accessing the ponds is difficult without waders, and shore casting is nearly impossible.

Crowsnest Lake (Map 4/D5)

Found on the north side of Highway 3 about 8 km (5 miles) west of Coleman, this cold water lake is one of the few lakes in Alberta that is stocked with lake trout. The lake also has rainbow trout, and rocky mountain whitefish that tend to grow to about 1 kg (2 lbs) as well as a few cutthroat trout. A good boat launch is offered at the southwest end of the lake and camping is found at nearby Island Lake.

Dipping Vat Lake (Map 3/D3)

This small lake is located to the east of Secondary Highway 800, near Hill Spring. A powerboat restriction (less than 12 km/h) is in place. The lake holds fairly large rainbow that can reach 2.5 kg (5 lbs) in size, although the average fish tends to be less than 0.5 kg (1 lb). Fly fishing and spincasting are the mainstays of the fishery.

Eagle Lake (Map 18/G5)

Eagle Lake is located a few kilometres southeast of Strathmore off the Trans-Canada Highway (Highway 1). The warm water lake has pike (to 12 kg), walleye (to 3 kg) and small perch. Spincasting the shallows is quite productive but remember the two fish limit. Overall, the lake is 11.8 square km, has a maximum depth of 4.9 metres and a mean depth of 2.6 metres. There is a campground and a boat launch at the lake.

Elbow Lake (Map 10/G3)

It is a steep 1 km hike from Highway 40 up to this small lake at the summit of Elbow Pass along a popular hiking trail. The lake contains mostly brook and some cutthroat trout to 30 cm (12 inches). Shore fishers will do best from the north side of the lake.

Emerald Lake (Map 4/D5)

Located south of Crowsnest Lake on the south side of Highway 3, this small lake is surprisingly deep. In fact, it is the deepest lake in the area, deep enough to support a few lake trout. The lake also contains a few brook and rainbow trout, but the most common species is cutthroat trout. There is an electric motor only restriction on the lake.

Emerson Lake (Map 13/A5)

This small lake is located on the eastern outskirts of the town of High River. The lake has a few rainbow to 0.5 kg (1 lb) taken on a fly, with bait or by spincasting. Don't count on too much success.

Entry Lake (Map 26/B1)

This small lake found just north of Landslide Lake contains a few cutthroat to 30 cm (12 inches).

Frank Lake (Map 5/A6)

Frank Lake is actually just a widening of the Crowsnest River caused by the Frank Slide. It offers a good area to belly boat but be forewarned that there are many underwater obstacles. The lake is accessed off of Highway 3 and contains surprisingly large rainbow (to 4 kg/8 lbs) as well as cutthroat (to 1 kg/2 lbs) and rocky mountain whitefish (to 1 kg/2 lbs) that are all caught by fly fishing or spincasting. Note that the regulations for Frank Lake are the same as for the Crowsnest River (seasonal closures and limits).

Fortress Lake (Map 15/D7)

This small, high alpine lake is set in the shadow of the Fortress, and is reached via a 4 km (2.4 mile) trail from the Fortress Ski Area to the south. The lake is not ice-free until July and is home to a fairly good population of cutthroat trout.

Galatea Lakes (Map 15/C7)

The Lillian Lake Trail takes anglers to Lillian Lake, a distance of 6 km (3.7 miles) from Highway 40. From there, you will have to try and find the faint footpath up to these two lakes that hold cutthroat to 40 cm (14 inches).

Gap Lake (Map 15/D4)

This lake is located right next to Highway 1A to the west of the Bow Valley Provincial Park. There is a picnic area and a place to hand launch small boats at the lake. The lake contains brook trout (to 0.5 kg/1 lb), a few brown trout (to 6 kg) and rocky mountain whitefish (to 2.5 kg/5 lbs). At the time of writing this book, the lake holds the world record for the largest rocky mountain whitefish (2.55 kg or 5 lbs 10 oz), which was caught in 1991.

Gap Pond (Map 5/A1)

This tiny pond is found next to the Forestry Trunk Road, just south of Dutch Creek. The pond is stocked with rainbow trout, which can get to 1.5 kg (3 lbs), although most are much smaller.

Ghost Lake (Map 16/B2–D1)

Ghost Lake is a large lake next to Highway 1A, and is part of the Bow River. It is 121 square km and has a maximum depth of 34 metres and a mean depth of 14.5 metres. The lake is best trolled for brown trout (to 2.5 kg/5 lbs), lake whitefish (to 5 kg/11 lbs), lake trout (to 13.5 kg/30 lbs) rainbow (to 2 kg/4 lbs) and rocky mountain whitefish (to 1.5 kg/3 lbs). Access to the shores of the lake is limited due to the Stoney Indian Reserve but there is a campground and boat launch available.

Gleniffer Lake (Map 30/B3)

Gleniffer Lake is found south of Spruce View, and was formed by the Dickson Dam on the Red Deer River. It is a big lake, covering 17.6 square km that is best fished by trolling or spincasting in the spring. The lake has brown, cutthroat and rainbow trout, northern pike, rocky mountain whitefish and walleye. Any walleye caught in the lake or the tributaries must be released. The Dickson Dam Recreation Area provides camping on the northern shores of the reservoir and there is a boat launch on the lake. For an alternative, try the **Dickson Trout Pond**, a small pond next to Gleniffer Lake. This pond is stocked annually with rainbow and also has a boat launch.

Glenmore Reservoir (Map 17/D5)

Found in the heart of Calgary, this reservoir of the Elbow River has a few brown trout (to 2.5 kg/5 lbs), perch (to 0.5 kg/1 lb), pike (to 5 kg/11 lbs) and rocky mountain whitefish (to 1 kg/2 lbs). Fishing tends to be very slow throughout the year, with spincasting being your best bet. The reservoir is 3.84 square km and has a maximum depth of 21.1 metres and a mean depth of 6.1 metres. No powerboats are allowed on the reservoir but there is a boat launch for non-motorized boats.

Goat Pond (Map 15/B4)

Goat Pond is found a couple kilometres north of the Spray Lake Reservoir off the Smith-Dorrien Road. It has fair numbers of brook trout, lake trout and rocky mountain whitefish. Trolling, fly fishing and spincasting all work, although there are a lot of snags, and shore fishing can be frustrating.

Goldeye Lake (Map 33/G3)

Goldeye Lake is accessed off Highway 11 west of Nordegg and offers camping. The lake is stocked annually with rainbow, which can grow to 2.5 kg (5 lbs) in size. There is an electric motor only restriction at the lake.

Grassi Lakes (Map 15/B3)

A pair of small lakes found just south of Canmore, the Grassi Lakes contain a few brook trout between them. Access is along a short hiking trail.

Grizzly Lake (Map 2/A4)

The long (16 km/10 mile) hike/horseback ride in scares off a lot of people. But for those willing to make the effort, the lake holds good numbers of stocked brook trout to 1 kg (2 lbs) in size. A bobber and worm or casting a lure with bait (Deadly Dick and worm) are your best bets, although fly fishing near the outlet stream can work well, too.

Grotto Mountain Pond (Map 15/D4)

This small pond, (too small to be marked on our maps), is found next to Highway 1A near the Grotto Mountain Picnic Area. The pond offers fly fishing and spincasting for brook trout, rocky mountain whitefish, rainbow and brown trout. Most of the fish in the pond are small.

Gull Lake (Map 37/F2)

Gull Lake is a large, shallow (maximum depth of 8m/26 ft) lake located 14 km west of Lacombe on Highway 12. It is a popular recreation retreat because it has nice sandy beaches, eight full service campgrounds and clear water. Northern pike, to 10 kg (22 lbs) and walleye are the most sought-after fish in the lake. The best place to fish for northern pike is in the weed covered shallows at the north end of the lake. Extensive stocking of the walleye occurred in 1987-1989 but the population has dropped to the point that catch and release is only allowed. Lake Whitefish were stocked in the late 1970s and the population has built up to the point where the fish can be caught fairly easily. Other species available at the lake include burbot (ling cod), yellow perch and several other course species. Be forewarned that the lake, which is 80.6 square km in size, is exposed to heavy winds throughout the summer.

Harlech Fish Pond (Map 34/C2)

Found on the south side of Highway 11 about 8 km east of Nordegg, this tiny pond provides reasonable fishing for small, stocked rainbow. The rainbow are best caught by spincasting, bait fishing and fly fishing from shore or a belly boat. A picnic area is at the lake.

Headwall Lakes (Map 10/D1)

The route to Headwall Lakes starts from the Chester Lake parking lot. After crossing Headwall Creek, an indistinct, easy-to-miss trail branches off to the left and follows the creek up to the small lakes. Both lakes hold cutthroat to 30 cm (12 inches), and are easy to fish from shore.

Hogarth Lakes (Map 10/C1)

A pair of crystal clear lakes found northwest of Mud Lake (head west along the Bustall Pass Trail, then take a right past Mud Lake), these two lakes contain cutthroat to 40 cm (16 inches). Fly fishing works well.

Island Lake (Map 4/D5)

Highway 3 provides good access to this lake, which is found next to the community of Crowsnest. The lake has stocked brook trout as well as native cutthroat and rocky mountain whitefish. The fishing can be fairly good throughout the spring and fall by fly fishing or spincasting, although shore fishing is not as productive as actually getting out on the water in a boat. Occasionally, anglers will find rainbow in the 4 kg (9 lb) range, but 1.5 kg (3 lbs) fish are more common.

Jackfish Lake (Map 34/G2)

This small lake (2.39 square km) is located next to Highway 11 and has brook trout, pike, walleye and perch. The brook trout are best caught at the outflow creek by spincasting, while the walleye must be released if caught. Camping and a boat launch are provided at the Jackfish Lake Recreation Area.

Kananaskis Lake, Lower (Map 10/E3)

Found in the heart of the Peter Lougheed Provincial Park, Lower Kananaskis Lake is accessible by a good paved road (Kananaskis Lake Trail) and offers several camping and picnic sites. Trolling is the most productive method of fishing this lake, which holds bull trout (to 5 kg/11 lbs), cutthroat (to 1 kg/2 lbs), and rainbow (to 2.5 kg/5 lbs). In fact, the lake holds the record for Alberta's largest bull trout taken in the mid-1980s, a whopping 8.14 kg (17 lbs, 15 oz). Please note that Northwest Bay and Smith-Dorrien Creek

are closed to fishing to protect spawning bull trout. Also, there is a bait ban on the lake.

Kananaskis Lake, Upper (Map 10/E4)

Upper Kananaskis Lake is arguably the prettier of the two Kananaskis Lakes. However, the fish are usually smaller, due to fluctuating water levels. The lake holds rainbow, which can get to 2.5 kg (5 lbs). 2001 was the first time the lake was stocked with bull trout and these fish have grown to 45 cm (18 inches). They were stocked again in 2003 along with cutthroat trout (for the first time). Although a trail circles the lake, shore anglers usually fair better near the mouth of the Upper Kananaskis River. Folks with boats have more options, and can try trolling the many bays or around the islands

Kesler Lake (Map 2/G5)

Located just north of the boundary of Waterton Lakes National Park, this small lake holds small rainbow trout. Access is along a faint angler trail.

Lake of the Falls (Map 26/A1)

This remote lake sees few anglers as it is about a 20 km (12.4 mile) one-way hike in. Those that venture in will find plenty of small cutthroat and some large bull trout, taken primarily on lures. You cannot keep bull trout and the possession and size limit of cutthroat is two fish, which must be 30 cm (12 inches). There is a bait ban in affect.

Lake of the Horns (McPhail Lake) (Map 11/B7)

This tiny hike-in lake is found at the headwaters of McPhail Creek and is set in a spectacular rocky bowl. The lake offers good fishing for cutthroat to 2 kg (4 lbs) caught by bait fishing, spincasting or fly fishing throughout late spring to fall. The bottom of the lake drops quickly making shore fishing relatively easy. A two trout limit applies. Another option is to fish the series of beaver ponds, right below the lake.

Lake Rae (Map 10/G3)

This small lake is found south of the Elbow Pass Trail. The small lake is open year-round, with a catch limit of two...if there are any fish here at all.

Landslide Lake (Map 26/B2)

The shortest access to Landslide Lake is by following the trail starting off Highway 11 in Kootenay Plains Wildlife Sanctuary. This alternate route is shorter than the Pinto Lake Trail option. Once you reach the lake, you can expect good fishing for cutthroat taken by spincasting or fly fishing. Please note that there is a two trout limit.

Lees Lake (Map 5/B7)

This lake is found on the east side of Secondary Highway 507 about 3 km south of Highway 3. It is a very popular lake, containing rainbow, which are best caught by spincasting or fly fishing. The lake has prolific hatches, and lots of food allowing the trout to grow quickly (up to 1.5 kg/3 lbs). A power-boat restriction (more than 5 km/h) applies at the lake.

Lillian Lake (Map 15/D7)

Lillian Lake is a tiny sub-alpine lake reached by hiking the Galatea Creek Trail about 6 km (3.7 miles) from Highway 40. Since snow remains on the trail until late June, the fishing season for the small cutthroat begins in July and ends in October. The cutthroat come readily to a fly, small lure or bait. There is a two trout limit in place.

Loomis Lake (Map 11/A6)

Loomis Lake is a tiny lake that is reached by the trail off Highway 40. The 11 km (6.8 mile) hike along an old logging road deters many. However, the surprisingly large cutthroat (to 2 kg/4 lbs) makes the lake well worth the effort to visit. A two trout limit applies.

Lost Guide Lake (Map 27/B5)

A long hike along the Lost Guide/Canyon Trail from the Onion Lake Road accesses this tiny sub-alpine lake. Anglers seldom visit the lake except on horse. It contains good numbers of small cutthroat, which are stocked on a semi-annual basis. A two trout limit is in affect.

Lys Lake (Map 2/B4)

Lys Lake is a remote, rarely visited lake found 8 km (5 km) along a horse trail that follows the outlet creek. The small lake has good shore fishing for rainbow to 40 cm (15 inches), using spincasting gear.

Margaret Lake (Map 21/E6)

A 4wd road along the north side of Waiparous Creek accesses this small, shallow lake. The lake is subject to winterkill, so it may be hard to catch a rainbow after a cold long winter. There is an electric motor only restriction on the lake.

Maude Lake (Map 10/C2)

Located in Peter Lougheed Provincial Park, this seldom-visited lake is reached by a 15 km (9.3 mile) hike along the Maude-Lawson Lakes Trail from the dam on Lower Kananaskis Lake. The small cutthroat in the lake come readily to most trout flies and small lures (with bait). A two trout limit applies.

McLean Pond (Map 16/D7)

McLean Pond is found next to the McLean Creek Trail (2wd access), just south of Highway 66. The stocked pond offers fair fishing for brook trout and rainbow by spincasting, bait fishing or fly fishing. A day-use area is located next to the lake (McLean Pond Recreation Area).

Michele Lake (Map 25/G2)

Few fishermen sample the waters of Michele Lake because it can only be reached by a long, difficult hike up the Cline River and then bushwhacking up Waterfalls Creek. The lake is said to have good fishing for golden trout that reach 1 kg (2 lbs) in size. However, the outflow and inflow creeks are closed to fishing in order to help spawning. Also, there is a bait ban, a one trout limit, a limited season (August 1 to October 31) in addition to a size restriction (greater than 35 cm/14 inches) on the lake.

Mitchell Lake (Map 35/G7)

Mitchell Lake is accessed by Strubble Road and is home of the Mitchell Lake Recreation Area, a camping and day-use facility. The lake is stocked annually and has rainbow that grow to 0.5 kg (1 lb). For best results, try fly fishing or spincasting the shallows in the early spring or late fall. An electric motor only restriction is in effect at the lake.

Mount Lorette Pond (Map 15/F5)

This tiny pond is found off Highway 40 south of Barrier Lake. It contains some small brook trout and rainbow that can be caught by bait fish or spincasting from shore. A network of trails have been developed around the lake to allow access to the physically challenged.

Mud Lake (Map 10/C1)

Located just west of the Smith-Dorrien/Spray Trail, this lake contains cutthroat trout to 30 cm (12 inches), bull trout to 50 cm (20 inches) and whitefish to 30 cm (12 inches). There are also rumours that dolly varden (the close cousin to bull trout), which were stocked in Chester Lake, have made their way downstream to this lake. If you do find a dolly here, contact the Fisheries Biologist at the Alberta Sustainable Resource Development office in Canmore at (403) 678-5508 (ext. 263).

Nordegg Ponds (Map 33/G2)

These two small ponds, located a few kilometres north of Nordegg on the Forestry Trunk Road, are stocked annually with rainbow trout. The shallow ponds (too small to mark on the maps) frequently suffer from winterkill.

Obstruction Lake (Map 32/E3)

This high elevation lake is found in the Bighorn Wildland Recreation Area and is seldom fished due to its remote location. The lake is stocked semi-annually and holds cutthroat to 1.5 kg (3 lbs) taken by fly fishing or spincasting. There is a two fish limit and the fishing season runs from July 1 to October 31. However, the outflow and inflow to the lake are closed to fishing.

Odlum Pond (Map 11/A6)

A tiny tarn at the head of Odlum Creek, this pond produces small cutthroat (the odd one does reach 30 cm/12 inches). A 12 km (7.5 mile) return trail follows the creek up to the lake.

Oldman Reservoir (Map 5/F6)

The Oldman Reservoir is the catchment area for the Three Rivers Dam, which was built in the late 1980s. The lake is extremely nutrient rich given that some very productive farmland was flooded by the dam. As a result, the fish grow to nice sizes. There are stocked rainbow (over 40 cm/15 inches), bull trout and cutthroat (to 2 kg/4 lbs) as well as brown trout (to 2.5 kg/5 lbs). Shore fishing is slow, but if you find the right spot you can have some luck. However, most people troll.

Paine (Payne) Lake (Map 3/C6)

A large reservoir just south of Highway 5 near Mountain View, Paine Lake has good fishing for stocked rainbow. The fish grow quickly (to 2 kg/4 lbs) in the shallow, nutrient rich waters. Spincasting from shore or trolling are both effective methods.

Palmer Ranch (Map 3/C3)

Pay for fishing? You mean, over and above the cost of a license? Well, yeah, some people do, especially considering that the rainbow in the small, spring-fed ponds on this private ranch can get up to 72 cm (28 inches). The owners allow only one party per day on the ponds, which keeps the pressure off the fish, and increase your chances of bringing home a trophy fish. Since it is a private lake it is not marked on our maps.

Peppers Lake (Map 27/F2)

Peppers Lake offers a nice campground and a series of trails to explore. For the angler, it contains brook trout to 1 kg (2 lbs) and is stocked most years. The brook trout are best caught by spincasting a lure with bait in the spring. There is an electric motor only restriction on the lake.

Phillipps Lake (Map 4/D4)

No, you don't need both a BC and Alberta fishing license to fish in this lake that straddles the divide between the two provinces; either license will do. This lake contains cutthroat trout up to 0.5 kg (1 lb) in size as well as some cutthroat. The lake is best accessed from the BC side of the boundary. A rough road from Crowsnest Provincial Park provides access, although you can also hike 3 km (1.8 miles) from the east end of Crowsnest Lake along a gated road.

Phyllis Lake (Map 29/A1)

Phyllis Lake is accessed off Secondary Highway 591 west of Caroline. The lake has a few brown trout as well as a bigger population of rainbow. Fly fishing and spincasting are the preferred methods of fishing. The rainbow are stocked annually and there is an electric motor only restriction at the lake.

Picklejar Lakes (Map 11/C5)

A total of four tiny lakes are found at the headwaters of Picklejar Creek in a gorgeous sub-alpine basin. The lakes are reached by a series of trails from Highway 40 and have a self-sustaining population of cutthroat, which can be taken on a fly or with a small lure. Fishing is closed from November 1 to June 30 and there is a two trout limit. Fish caught in the creek must be released.

Pine (Ghostpine) Lake (Map 31/F2)

Pine Lake is one of the few lakes in this area that holds fish; therefore, it sees a lot of fishing pressure. There are a number of campgrounds, many with boat rentals, to explore the 7 km (4.3 mile) long lake. Shore fishing works well for yellow perch, but you will have to get out onto the lake to have a chance at hooking one of the northern pike (to 9 kg/20 lbs) or walleye (to 3.5 kg/7 lbs) that inhabit the lake. Of course, you will have to let the walleye go, as they are catch and release only. You can keep up to three pike over 63 cm (25 inches). Try working near the weeds with a big spoon or night crawler.

Pinto Lake (Map 25/E1)

Pinto Lake is located in the Bighorn Wildland Recreation Area and is reached by trail. The lake is currently closed to fishing in order to preserve the bull trout population.

Police Outpost Lake (Map 3/F7)

Since this lake is quite shallow it is subject to winterkill and it is recommended to check with your local tackle store to determine whether the lake is worth fishing before heading out. It contains brook and rainbow trout, which grow rapidly, and can get up to 2 kg (4 lbs). A nice provincial park offers full service camping and a boat launch. The lake can get reedy, and a boat will help your chances of catching a fish (and not just snagging reeds). A powerboat restriction (maximum boat speed 12 km/h) is in place on the lake.

Quarry Lake (Map 15/B3)

This so-called lake is actually a flooded rock quarry near Canmore. The lake contains stocked arctic grayling to 30 cm (12 inches) that take well to flies. The lake is catch and release only.

Rainy Ridge Lake (Map 2/A4)

Remote access to the lake ensures excellent fishing when you arrive, although word is getting out about this spectacular destination. It sits beneath the mountains of the Continental Divide and offers golden trout to 1 kg (2 lbs) that can be caught using a fly or lure. The lake is best accessed by a 4 km (2.6 mile) hike off of an old logging road that continues south from the West Castle Ski Area. There is a second, longer trail that leads to the lake, although the only advantage with this route is that the trailhead is easier to find off the Middle Kootenay Pass Trail. Nearby Upper Rainy Lake, often confused for this one, holds no fish. Neither do Rainy Lakes, which are found south of Rainy Ridge Lake. There is a bait ban on the lake as well as a one trout limit (40 cm minimum size). Also, the tributaries and outlet creek are closed to fishing.

Rawson Lake (Map 10/E4)

Rawson Lake is found in the Peter Lougheed Provincial Park south of Upper Kananaskis Lakes. A short trail leads from the Upper Lake Trail to Rawson Lake. It is a 5 km (3 mile) hike to the lake, but with cutthroat getting up to 2 kg (4 lb), it sees heavy pressure. Please note that fishing season runs from July 16 to October 31, all fish must be released and there is a bait ban in affect at the lake.

Ribbon Lake (Map 15/D7)

Ribbon Lake is located at the headwaters of Ribbon Creek. The lake, which is accessed by a perilous 10 km (6.2 mile) hike up (and we do mean up; the last couple kilometres are steep and exposed, and can be dangerous in wet weather) from Highway 40, has many small cutthroat. The fish take readily to most small lures and trout flies. The lake is frozen until mid June so it is best to fish from late June until ice up in late October. The lake has a primitive campground on its shores and has a two trout limit in place.

Rocky Children's Pond (Map 36/A5)

Located on the outskirts of Rocky Mountain House, this small pond is stocked annually with rainbow. Fishing at the pond is restricted to children only and there is a day-use area next to the pond. Bait fishing and spincasting are the methods of choice.

Rummel Lake (Map 15/C7)

Found just outside the northern boundary to Peter Lougheed Provincial Park, this tiny lake is accessed by a rough trail up Rummel Creek. The lake offers good fly fishing and spincasting for small cutthroat in the spring and fall. The fishing season runs from July 1 to October 31 and there is a one trout limit (greater than 40 cm/16 inches) and a bait ban.

Running Rain Lake (Map 11/A6)

An undeveloped 2.7 km (1.7 mile) trail begins opposite the beaver dams on Highway 40 and follows the creek to Running Rain Lake. The lake sees few anglers, due to its remote location, and as a result offers good fishing for small cutthroat (to 40 cm/15 inches). Spincasting and fly fishing have equal success. A two trout limit is in affect.

Scarpe Lakes (Map 2/B4)

It is a 3 km (1.8 mile) one-way hike from the junction of the Scarpe Creek and Castle River to the Southernmost Scarpe Lake, if you can make it the junction. Some years, you have to hike up to 15 km (9.3 miles), as the road gets washed out, rebuilt, and washed out again. The stocked lakes contain rainbow to 1 kg (2 lbs) that are caught by fly fishing, bait fishing or spincasting. There is a limit of two fish per day. The South Lake is easier to get to

and holds slightly bigger fish (many of which are actually rainbow-cutthroat hybrids) than the West Lake. Consequently, it sees more anglers. North Lake holds no fish.

Shunda (Fish) Lake (Map 33/G3)

Shunda Lake has fair fishing for rainbow (to 2 kg/4 lbs) best caught by fly fishing or spincasting. It is stocked with rainbow and is home of the Fish Lake Recreation Area. An electric motor only restriction applies to the lake. Due to the easy access, ice fishing is also popular.

Sibbald Lakes (Map 16/D3)

The biggest of the Sibbald Lakes is only 5 m (15 feet) deep at its deepest, and, as you might expect, is subject to winterkill, which keeps the number and size of fish down. The lakes are located just south of the Trans-Canada Highway, and offer slow fishing for small rainbow and a few brook trout. No motorboats are allowed on the lakes.

Sibbald Meadows Pond (Map 16/A4)

On the north side of Secondary Highway 68, this popular stocked pond has lots of room for fly casting. Expect to find rainbow and brook to 30 cm (12 inches).

Smuts Lake (Map 10/B1)

This tiny, hike-in lake is found below Mount Smuts. It is open all year, but you can only keep one cutthroat trout larger than 40 cm (15 inches).

Sparrows Egg Lake (Map 10/E3)

One of a group of lakes that occupy the marshy valley bottom between Highway 40 and the Kananaskis Lakes Trail, this small lake is a 2 km (1.2 mile) hike from the Elkwood Campground. It contains stocked rainbow to 2.5 kg (5 lbs) and cutthroat to 2 kg (4 lbs). The catch and release only lake is prone to winterkill.

Spillway Lake (Map 10/E2)

Spillway Lake is located right beside the Smith-Dorrien/Spray Road just past the north end of Lower Kananaskis Lake. It contains some rainbow trout. The water is shallow and clear, so it is easy to see the fish. They can see you, too, and are easily spooked.

Spray Lake Reservoir (Map 15/B6)

Spray Lake Reservoir, in Kananaskis Country, is easily accessed by the Smith-Dorrien/Spray Road south of Canmore. The south end of the lake borders Banff National Park and there are several campgrounds and day-use areas nearby. This is a good-sized lake, over 20 km (12.4 miles) long, and is subject to strong winds. It offers reasonably good fishing for lake trout (to 8 kg/18 lbs), cutthroat (to 1 kg/2 lbs) and rocky mountain whitefish (to 1 kg/2 lbs). The lake has a boat launch and is best trolled during the early spring and the late fall.

Stenton Lake (Map 15/C2)

Access to this small lake at the head of the South Ghost River involves a rather long drive up and around to the South Ghost Trailhead, and then a 10 km (6.2 mile) hike up the South Ghost Trail. Because of this relatively difficult access, few anglers make the trek. Those that do will find stocked cutthroat to 45 cm (18 inches). You can keep one, as long as it is over 40 cm (16 inches).

Strathmore Children's Pond (Map 18/G4)

Located on the east side of the town of Strathmore, this small pond offers bait fishing and spincasting for small rainbow. The pond can only be fished by children and no powerboats are allowed.

Strubel Lake (Map 35/G7)

Strubel Road to the southeast of Strachan provides access to this small lake. There is a day-use area at the lake and camping at nearby Mitchell Lake. Strubel lake has stocked rainbow that can grow to 2.5 kg (5 lbs). The fish are best caught by bait or spincasting in the early spring or late fall. Please note that there is a powerboat restriction (less than 12 km/h) in effect.

Swan Lake (Map 28/C1)

Swan Lake still holds the Alberta record for the largest brown trout, an 8.2 kg (17 lb, 9oz.) fish caught in 1991. In addition to big browns, the lake holds large lake trout (to 5 kg/11 lbs) and pleasantly plump pike (to 10 kg/22 lbs).

However, don't expect to catch many fish, as the numbers are very low. The lake offers camping at the recreation area but is subject to many restrictions. There is a bait ban and a powerboat (less than 12 km/h) restriction in effect and the lake is closed from January 15 to June 15.

Sylvan Lake (Map 37/C5)
This large lake (42.8 square km) is easily accessed by Highways 11 and 20. The lake is home of two provincial parks (Jarvis Bay and Sylvan Lake) and is bordered by the town of Sylvan Lake to the south. It has a maximum depth of 18.3 m and a mean depth of 9.6 m, while offering fishing for lake whitefish and perch (to 1 kg/2 lbs), pike (to 10 kg) and walleye (to 3 kg/6 lbs). Fishing for the perch and pike is best in the winter and there is a catch and release restriction on walleye.

Talus Lake (Map 10/G2)
Open year-round, there is a limit of two cutthroat at this tiny, hard to access lake.

Tay Lake (Map 28/F2)
Tay Lake is stocked annually with rainbow that grow to 1 kg (2 lbs). The lake is reached by a short trail and has an electric motor only restriction.

Three Isle Lake (Map 10/C3)
To reach this small sub-alpine lake, take the Three Isle Lake Trail beginning on the northern shores of the Upper Kananaskis Lake. Because of the 10 km (6.2 mile) one-way hike, the lake sees few fishermen. Fishing is very good for small cutthroat on a fly or with a lure. Camping is provided at the east end of the lake and there is a two trout limit in affect.

Tombstone Lake, Lower (Map 10/G2)
Named after nearby Tombstone Mountain, which in turn was named for the distinctively shaped rocks near the summit, this lake contains lots of small cutthroat to 30 cm (12 inches). It is a 10 km (6.2 mile) hike in to the lake. Nearby Upper Tombstone Lake holds no fish.

Twin Lakes (Map 35/G4)
Twin Lakes are found to the east of Secondary Highway 756 and just south of Crimson Lake. There is a provincial park campground and boat launch on the west lake while the east lake is restricted to electric motors only. The west lake has perch and pike and is noted for its deep, clear waters. The east lake has pike available during spring run-off.

Waterton Reservoir (Map 3/C3)
Waterton Reservoir has a few slow growing pike (to 5 kg/11 lbs) as well as brown trout and rocky mountain whitefish (to 2 kg/4 lbs). Since the lake is rather unproductive, fishing success tends to be quite poor. You will have better luck fishing one of the creeks or rivers that flow into the reservoir (try Drywood Creek or the Waterton River).

Watridge Lake (Map 15/A7)
Located a short walk from the Mt. Shark Trailhead south of Spray Lake, Watridge Lake contains good numbers of cutthroat to 4 kg (8 lbs). Fly fishing or spincasting from a float tube works best, as shore casting is difficult.

Wedge Pond (Map 15/E7)
Found right next to Highway 40 north of Limestone Mountain, this small pond was recently stocked with grayling. The pond has a bait ban and catch and release restrictions in place.

Whiteman Pond (Map 15/B3)
This tiny pond has brook and lake trout as well as rocky mountain whitefish. The pond is easily accessed by the Smith-Dorrien/Spray Road southwest of Canmore.

Window Mountain Lake (Map 4/E3)
Access to this gorgeous lake, set below Mount Ward, is by a 2 km (1.2 mile) hike from the Allison Creek Road. The lake provides good fishing for rainbow to 1 kg (2 lbs) as well as some smaller cutthroat with fly fishing and spincasting working equally well. The possession limit is two.

Stream Fishing
Although there are some good fishing lakes, southwestern Alberta's best fishing is usually in the rivers and streams. The major rivers of the southern foothills are the Waterton, Castle, Crowsnest, Bow and Oldman River. Each of these rivers has small tributary streams, which also provide good fishing. Throughout the year, each of the rivers has good hatches of stoneflies, mayflies and caddis flies. There are other insect hatches as well, all providing good nymph and dry fly fishing throughout the summer months.

In most rivers, the spring runoff begins to peak in mid May and continues through to the end of June. Often times during runoff the rivers are very difficult to fish because they are murky and too high. Therefore, it is best to wait until the end of June to begin fishing. In any event, the fishing regulations in place now prevent fishing in the Eastern Slope streams and rivers until April 1, June 1 or June 15 depending on the area.

The Eastern Slope Region is divided into four watershed units, two of which are covered by this mapbook. Streams in Eastern Slope Watershed Unit 1 are open from June 16 to August 31 for summer catch and keep, while streams in Eastern Slope Unit 2 are open from April 1 to August 31. The fall catch and release season runs from September 1 to October 31 for both units.

The rationale for these seasons is that in the winter, the fish tend to concentrate in larger holes in the rivers and are easier to catch. In the fall and spring, the various species spawn and are also easier to catch. These closures hope to limit over-harvesting during these times.

For fly fishers, the main dry flies to use are the Adams, Royal Coachmen, Elkhair Caddis, Blue Winged Olive and Pale Morning Dun. The best nymphs and streamers are the Black or Golden Stone Fly, the Pheasant Tail, the Golden Ribbed Hare's Ear or the Woolly Bugger (black or olive colour).

Alford Creek (Map 28/F2-29/A2)
Alford Creek is a tributary of the Clearwater River. It has brook trout (to 0.5 kg/1 lb), brown trout (to 2 kg/4 lbs) and rainbow (to 1 kg/2 lbs). It is easily accessed by Secondary Highway 591 and offers good fishing throughout the year, but is catch and release from September 1 through March 31.

Allison Creek (Map 4/E4)
Allison Creek is a tributary of the Crowsnest. It contains brook, cutthroat and rainbow trout, which tend to be small but can reach 0.5 kg (1 lb) in size. The creek is easily accessed by the Allison Creek Road.

Baptiste River (Map 34/E1-35/C1)
This small river is found to the north of the North Saskatchewan River and is open for fishing from April 1 to October 31 with a two trout and five whitefish restriction. A number of secondary access roads off Highway 11 provide access to the river, as does the Valentine Trail and Aurora Trail. The river contains brook trout (to 0.5 kg/1 lb), brown trout (to 1 kg/2 lbs), bull trout (to 2.5 kg/5 lbs), pike (to 2 kg/4 lbs) and rocky mountain whitefish (to 1 kg/2 lbs). The river is open from April 1 to October 31 for fishing.

Bateman Creek (Map 16/B4)
Bateman Creek has brook, bull, cutthroat and rainbow trout. It drains into the Jumpingpound Creek near Old Buck Mountain and is accessed by Secondary Highway 68.

Bearberry Creek (Map 29/A6-E7)
The Bearberry flows into the Red Deer River at Sundre. It holds rocky mountain whitefish and bull trout.

Beaver Creek (Maps 5/G1-6/C5)
Beaver Creek gets its name from the extensive network of beaver dams along the creek. Those beaver dams are often stocked with cutthroat and rainbow trout, which grow to 0.5 kg (1 lb).

Beaver Creek (Map 7/G5-8A4)
Beaver Creek is a tributary of the Livingstone. It holds plenty of small cutthroat, which grow to 0.5 kg (1 lb) in size. The creek is catch and release only and accessed by trail from the Forestry Trunk Road.

Beaver Mines Creek (Map 2/B1-5/D7)
A tributary of the Castle River, this creek contains brook, bull, cutthroat and rainbow trout as well as rocky mountain whitefish. For the cutthroat and rainbow, a 30 cm (12 inch) minimum size limit is in place.

Belly River (Map 3/C7-G1)

This medium size river has many deep pools to sample as it flows through Waterton National Park from Montana and continues in a northeast direction past the Blood Indian Reserve. The river and its tributaries are open for catch and release fishing from June 16 to August 31, upstream from Secondary Highway 800. Downstream from the 800, the river (not the tributaries) is open from June 16 to October 31. Also, rocky mountain whitefish can be caught (using maggots) and kept from Aug 16 to October 31. As a result of the strict regulations, the river has good numbers of pike to 4.5 kg (10 lbs), bull trout to 2 kg (4 lbs), rainbow trout to 1 kg (2 lbs), rocky mountain whitefish to 1 kg (2 lbs) and cutthroat to 0.5 kg (1 lb). There are reports of a few brown trout and Montana grayling in the river but do not count on catching one of them. Fly fishing and spincasting are the preferred methods of fishing. Remember, if you are planning on fishing inside Waterton National Park, you will need a special license, and the regulations are different. Check before you fish.

Bighorn River (Map 33/A6-E4)

The Bighorn River, which is open from June 16 to October 31, drains a large area of the Bighorn Wildland Recreation Area into the North Saskatchewan River north of Abraham Lake. It is best accessed along most of its length by trail from Crescent Falls. The river contains brown and cutthroat trout as well as rocky mountain whitefish (all to 1 kg/2 lbs) and bull trout (to 2.5 kg/5 lbs) below Crescent Falls. Above the falls, smaller cutthroat inhabit the waters so it is difficult to catch fish that you can keep (greater than 30 cm/12 inches). Below the falls, the cutthroat must be a minimum of 35 cm (14 inches) to keep. Camping is offered at the Crescent Falls Recreation Area.

Blackstone River (Map 33/A1-E1)

This river contains bull trout to 2.5 kg (5 lbs) as well as cutthroat and rocky mountain whitefish to 1 kg (2 lbs). It is reached by secondary roads off the Forestry Trunk Road and Chungo Road and trail for the more remote sections of the river within the Bighorn Wildland Recreation Area. The river and its tributaries are limited to catch and release fishing to preserve the stocks and upstream from Mons Creek (including Mons Creek), the river is closed to fishing. The best camping is at the Blackstone Recreation Area off Chungo River.

Blairmore Creek (Map 4/G4)

This creek contains brook, cutthroat and rainbow trout but finding a legal sized fish (35 cm/14 inches) could be difficult, as the fish tend to be very small. You will find more rainbow near the confluence with the Crowsnest, while cutthroat are more common upstream.

Blindman River (Map 37/C1-38/A5)

The headwater of this slow moving river are found to the west of Gull Lake. The river contains pike and walleye, but the walleye must be released if caught.

Boundary Creek (Map 3/F7-G7)

North of Police Outpost Provincial Park, the creek flows into Alberta, does a quick loop, and the heads back into Montana. The creek holds pike that reach 2.5 kg (5 lbs) in size. Spincasting a lure is your best bet, although fly fishing for pike is becoming a popular pursuit.

Bow River (Maps 13, 14, 15, 16, 17, 18)

The Bow River is a very good fly fishing river and is considered one of the best in Western Canada. It is easily accessed along Highway 1 and 1A from Calgary to Banff. Numerous campgrounds and other facilities line the river. South and east of Calgary the river can be accessed from various highways and backroads. The fishing in this section of the Bow is as good or better than anywhere on the river, especially if drift fishing.

Since the conditions change daily, it is best to be prepared to fish anything from dry flies to nymphs or streamers. Dry flies work best when you see the fish rising. As a general rule, if you want to dry fly fish anytime throughout the summer, then try just after sunrise and near dusk. The river has numerous hatches that fly fishers can try and match including caddis flies from mid May to mid September, grasshoppers and flying ants from July to September, Trico from the end of August to the end of September. The best flies for the river are the various Adams patterns, caddis fly imitations and a multitude of nymph imitations. Patterns of choice include the Blue Winged Olive from mid April to mid May, then again from mid August to mid October, the March brown in the first three weeks of May and the Pale Morning Dun from mid June to the end of July. The Bow River is heavily regulated, so check regulations before heading out. Remember that the upper section of the Bow River is in Banff National Park, and a National Park Permit is required to fish this section.

Brazeau River (Map 32/C6-F1)

The Brazeau River forms the boundary between Jasper National Park and the Bighorn Wildland Recreation Area. To reach the headwaters, you must hike from Highway 93 on the Nigel Creek and South Boundary Trails for at least 20 km (12 miles) one-way. As a result, there are few fishermen that sample these waters. Also, given that the Brazeau River is dammed (north of this mapbook), there are only a few small cutthroat near the headwaters making fishing less than inviting above the dam. Please note that in this book (or upstream from the Forestry Trunk Road), the season is from June 16 to October and the cutthroat must be greater than 30 cm (12 inches) to keep.

Bruin Creek (Map 8/A6-7/G6)

Bruin Creek is a small creek, which holds small cutthroat that may reach 30 cm (12 inches). The creek is catch and release only, and can be accessed by bushwhacking off the Forestry Trunk Road.

Burnt Timber Creek (Map 21/B5-F2)

Burnt Timber Creek has brown trout, bull trout and rocky mountain whitefish that grow to 1 kg (2 lbs). There are also smaller brook and cutthroat trout found in the creek. Camping is available at the Burnt Timber Recreation Area.

Buster Creek (Map 35/E4-G2)

Buster Creek was stocked with brown trout in 1997. It flows past the northern border of Crimson Lake Provincial Park before flowing into the North Saskatchewan River.

Canary Creek (Map 26/G2-27/B2)

Canary Creek flows into Hummingbird Creek near the headwaters of the Ram River drainage. The creek has cutthroat to 0.5 kg (1 lb).

Canmore Creek (Map 15/B3)

Canmore Creek is a short creek that runs from Grassi Lakes into the Bow River. There has been a recent effort to control brook trout (which are not native to the system), and reintroduce cutthroat, which are. In addition to the cutts and brookies, you will find brown trout and whitefish. The fish are small, usually in the 25-30 cm (10-12 inch) range.

Canyon Creek (Map 16/A7-C7)

Canyon Creek contains good numbers of brook trout, plus a few cutthroat and bull trout. An Elbow River tributary, the lower reaches are easily accessible by road while the upper reaches are accessed via trail or bushwhacking.

Canyon Creek (Map 36/A2)

This Canyon Creek crosses Highway 22 north of Rocky Mountain House and offers fishing for brook, bull and cutthroat trout. All but the brook trout must be released.

Carbondale River (Map 1/E1-5/A7)

This productive river is best accessed via the Adanac Road. The river provides fishing for bull, cutthroat and rainbow trout as well as rocky mountain whitefish. There is also a rainbow-cutthroat cross that is said to inhabit the river. Above Lynx Creek, all cutthroat and rainbow that are kept must be greater than 30 cm (12 inches). That's okay, because the fishing is much better below Lynx Creek. Camping is available at the Lynx Creek Recreation Area.

Carnarvon Creek (Map 11/C7)

Carnarvon Creek is part of the Highwood River drainage, which means that it is catch and release only for brook, bull, cutthroat and rainbow trout. The Carnarvon Lake Trail follows the creek for most of its length providing access to many of the small pools.

Castle (South Castle) River (Map 2/D4-5/F7)

The Castle River produced the largest Alberta cutthroat some years ago, but do not count on catching another record fish, as most cutthroat tend to be small. This is a small volume river, but it drains a large area north of Waterton Lakes National Park, eventually flowing into the Oldman River near Highway 3. The upper reaches are accessed via the Castle River Trail, while the lower sections can be accessed by several main arteries (Highways 3, 507 and 774). Other fish include bull and rainbow trout as well as rocky mountain whitefish. The bull trout can reach 2.5 kg (5 lbs), whereas other fish tend to be under 0.5 kg (1 lb). Upstream of the confluence with West Castle River, the river is known as the South Castle, and the cutthroat and rainbow must be 30 cm to keep.

Cat Creek (Map 11/D7)

Cat Creek flows into the Highwood River just west of the Highwood Junction on Highway 40. The creek has brook, bull, cutthroat and rainbow trout but has several restrictions. Check the regulations before heading out.

Cataract Creek (Map 7/D2-11/E7)

Cataract Creek is so named because of all the small falls along its length. It has brook, bull, cutthroat and rainbow trout as well as rocky mountain whitefish. The creek is accessed off the Forestry Trunk Road (Hwy 940). As a tributary of the Highwood, there are special restrictions. Check the regulations before heading out.

Chambers Creek (Map 35/C3)

A tributary of the Baptiste River, this small creek offers some big fish. The elusive brown trout are rumoured to reach 1.5 kg (3 lbs) and northern pike have tipped the scales at 6 kg (13 lbs). There are also smaller brook trout and whitefish (to 0.5 kg/1 lb).

Clear Brook (Map 9/C3)

Anglers looking for small brook, brown, bull and rainbow trout will not be disappointed in this meandering stream. The creek is open for fishing year-round, but is catch and release from September 1 to March 31.

Clearwater River (Maps 26-29, 36)

This large river drains a large area northeast of Banff National Park and eventually flows into the North Saskatchewan River near Rocky Mountain House. The river contains a wide variety of sportfish including brook trout (to 0.5 kg/1 lb), brown trout (to 1 kg/2 lbs), rocky mountain whitefish (to 1 kg/2 lbs), bull trout (to 3 kg/6 lbs) and pike (to 5 kg/11 lbs). Other than for its headwaters, located in Banff National Park (and governed under a different set of regulations than the provincial regulations), the river is easily accessed by highways or good logging roads. Many fishermen work the lower reaches of the river by floating down the river in a float tube, sampling the various pools and rapids along the way. Tributaries upstream of Timber Creek (Map 27/F5), as well as Timber Creek itself, are permanently closed to fishing. The Banff section of the river is rarely fished, as it takes at least two days to hike to, or a day's horseback ride.

Cline River (Map 25/F1-33/C7)

The Cline River drains Pinto Lake into Abraham Lake. The river is accessed by the Pinto Lake and the Whitegoat Trails along most of its length. It contains bull trout (to 2 kg/4 lbs), rocky mountain whitefish (to 1 kg/2 lbs), and brook trout (to 0.5 kg/1 lb) below the canyon and cutthroat (to 1 kg/2 lbs) above the canyon. The cutthroat must be 30 cm (12 inches) to keep and the river and its tributaries are closed to fishing from November 1 to June 15.

Coal Creeks (Map 11/E5)

Both the North and South Coal Creeks flow into the Sheep River near the Sandy McNabb Recreation Area. The creeks offer bull, cutthroat and rainbow trout and can be accessed by one of several trails.

Colt Creek (Map 34/A1-B1)

Colt Creek is part of the Upper Nordegg watershed and has brook trout and bull trout.

Commonwealth Creek (Map 10/B1)

Commonwealth Creek flows into Smith Dorrien Creek and contains stocked cutthroat to 30 cm (12 inches).

Cottonwood Creek (Map 2/G5-3/A6)

Cottonwood Creek flows east out of Waterton Lakes National Park, then turns south, flowing back into the park just before it flows into the Waterton River. The creek contains brook, brown and rainbow trout. Highway 6 crosses the creek about 4 km (20.5 miles) north of Waterton River, providing the best access point.

Cougar Creek (Map 11/B2)

A tributary of the Elbow River, this creek is accessed by bushwhacking off the Big Elbow Trail. It offers good numbers of brown and cutthroat trout.

Cow Creek (Map 5/C4-D5)

Cow Creek is accessed off Highway 22 north of Lundbreck. While the river can be muddy, especially during run-off, it contains fair numbers of cutthroat, brown and rainbow trout. Most people focus their efforts near the Oldman River Reservoir.

Cow Creek (Map 35/G6)

Cow Creek has brown trout that can reach 2 kg (4 lbs) but tend to average much smaller. The beaver dams were stocked in 1995, improving fishing in recent years.

Coxhill Creek (Map 16/A5-B4)

This creek is best accessed by the Tom Snow Trail. It has brook, bull, cutthroat and rainbow trout.

Cripple Creek (Map 27/B1-34/C7)

Cripple Creek is a main spawning tributary of the North Ram River. Accessed off the Forestry Trunk Road, the creek contains lots of cutthroat, which are smaller but easier to catch than in the Ram.

Crowsnest River (Maps 4-5)

The Crowsnest River is a world-class fly fishing river, due in no small part to its crystal clear waters, beautiful scenery and amazing fishing. The river flows east from chilly Crowsnest Lake to the Oldman Reservoir with 13 major tributaries along the way. Lundbreck Falls, some 40 km (25 miles) south of Crowsnest Lake, marks the only barrier to fish migration on the river. As the general rule, the larger fish are found west of the falls where you will find rainbow, whitefish and brown trout and the occasional bull trout. Above Lundbreck Falls, you will catch the odd brook and cutthroat trout, but the main species are rainbow and whitefish.

For fly fishermen, there are a number of mayfly hatches (try a Blue Winged Olive) that begin in mid April and continue as late as the end of October. However, most of the hatches occur in June through July. There are also caddis fly hatches that run from June to the end of October. Equally, the stonefly hatches occur pretty much year-round. Grasshoppers become prevalent in August through the end of September whereas ant hatches begin in the middle of July until the end of September. From June to early July a size 4 stonefly can be deadly. In August, use a size 14 Adams or Blue Upright. Other trout flies that work at varying times through the year include the Royal

Coachman, Wooley Bugger, Royal Wulff, beadhead nymphs, any midge or black gnat imitation. Please note that the river is heavily regulated depending on the section you plan to fish (e.g. bait bans, closures, size restrictions), so it is well advised to check the regulations before heading out.

Cutoff Creek (Map 27/F4-28/A3)
This small creek has brook trout (to 0.5 kg/1 lb) and brown trout (to 1 kg/2 lbs). The Cutoff Creek Road provides good access to most of the creek.

Daisy Creek (Map 4/G2-5/A3)
Daisy Creek is best accessed off the Forestry Trunk Road near the Racehorse Creek Recreation Area. If you are looking for larger trout then this is not the creek to try. It contains mainly bull and cutthroat trout but there are a few rainbow in the system.

Deep Creek (Map 8/A6)
As a tributary of the Livingstone River, Deep Creek is catch and release only. Despite the difficult access from the Forestry Trunk Road, most of the cutthroat in the creek tend to be small.

Dogpound Creek (Map 22/C7-30/A6)
Dogpound Creek begins in the hills above Bottrel and flows all the way to the Little Red Deer River west of Olds. The creek contains northern pike in the lower reaches as well as brown trout, brook trout and rocky mountain whitefish in the upper reaches. The work done to improve the spawning habitat in the 1980s has dramatically improved the trout fishing.

Drywood Creek (Map 2/D4-3/B3)
Drywood Creek is a small creek reached by Highway 6 south of Pincher Creek. The creek offers a variety of fish species including brook, brown, bull, cutthroat and rainbow trout as well as rocky mountain whitefish. The odd bull trout reaches 2.5 kg (5 kg) in size whereas the other fish species can grow to 1 kg (2 lbs), although the average much smaller. There is a small pond on the creek near the Shell Waterton Gas Plant that holds brook and rainbow trout. The plant has suffered some chemical leaks in the past, and eating fish in the pond or below is not recommended.

Dungarvan Creek (Map 2/G5-3/B4)
While a portion of this creek is in Waterton Lakes National Park, most of it lies out of the park, and is easily off Highway 6. The creek holds small rainbow.

Dutch Creek (Map 4/E1-5/A1)
Dutch Creek contains bull and cutthroat trout as well as rocky mountain whitefish. It is reached from the Forestry Trunk Road north of the Little Stone Ranger Station. A rustic campground can be found at the bridge over the Forestry Trunk Road.

Dyson Creek (Map 11/D4)
Offering brown and rainbow trout, this creek can be accessed by several trails including the Green Mountain Trail.

East Stony Creek (Map 22/E4)
East Stony Creek has brook trout, brown trout, pike and rocky mountain whitefish. The brook trout are the most numerous and tend to be small. Brown trout were stocked in the beaver dams in 1997.

Elbow River (Map 11/A1-17/E4)
From its beginning east of Kananaskis Lakes, the Elbow flows in a northeast direction and is followed by Highway 66, 22 and 8 all the way to Calgary where it drains into the Bow River, after a brief stop in the Glenmore Reservoir. The upper reaches of the river contain small brook trout, brown trout (to 2 kg/4 lbs), bull trout (to 1.5 kg/3 lbs), cutthroat (to 1 kg/2 lbs), and rocky mountain whitefish (to 1 kg/2 lbs). Above Elbow Falls (Map 16/C7), the trout must be 30 cm (12 inches) to keep if they are caught in the main river or one of the tributaries (except Quirk Creek, which is a catch and release stream, open from June 16 to October 31). Below Elbow Falls to Canyon Creek, the river is closed to fishing. From Canyon Creek to Glenmore Reservoir, fishing is open from June 16 to October 31, there is a five fish limit for whitefish and there is a bait ban (except a limited maggot season). Below Glenmore Reservoir to the estuary, fishing is closed from October 1 to November 15, the trout must be greater than 35 cm to keep and there is a bait ban (except for a limited maggot season). In the lower reaches near Calgary, there are brown trout (to 2 kg/4 lbs), cutthroat (to 1 kg/2 lbs), rainbow (to 2 kg/4 lbs) and rocky mountain whitefish (to 1 kg/2 lbs). Most tributaries offer reasonably good fishing.

Elk Creek (Map 27/C3-F2)
Elk Creek is open from April 1-October 31 and offers fishing for brown trout and bull trout on a catch and release basis. The Forestry Trunk Road provides good access along most of its length.

Entry Creek (Map 26/A2-B1)
This small volume creek drains Lake of the Falls into the Cline River. It contains small cutthroat and bull trout.

Etherington Creek (Map 7/D1)
A tributary of the Highwood River (check regulations for restrictions), Etherington Creek has brook, brown, cutthroat and rainbow trout. It is accessed by the Forestry Trunk Road and offers camping at the Etherington Creek Recreation Area.

Evan-Thomas Creek (Map 15/F7)
Evan-Thomas Creek has brook, brown and cutthroat trout in the trail accessed upper reaches. In summer, the lower reaches near Highway 40 tend to be dry.

Fall Creek (Map 34/G7-35/A6)
Fall Creek has cutthroat above the falls and brown and cutthroat trout as well as rocky mountain whitefish below the falls. The Ram Trail and several mining roads provide access to the creek.

Fallentimber Creek (Map 21/D5-29/E7)
Fallentimber Creek stretches from the Forestry Trunk Road to the Red Deer River near Sundre. The creek offers fishing for brook and brown trout (to 1 kg/2 lbs), bull trout (to 1.5 kg/3 lbs) and rocky mountain whitefish (to 1 kg/2 lbs). Check current regulations for closures and size restrictions.

Fish Creek (Map 17/A7-F6)
Most of the activity on this creek occurs at the provincial park in south Calgary. Despite this, the better fishing is found near the headwaters south of

Highway 22. Fish Creek holds brook, cutthroat and rainbow trout as well as rocky mountain whitefish.

Fisher Creek (Map 11/E1-12/A1)
A tributary of Sheep River, Fisher Creek has cutthroat, rainbow and rocky mountain whitefish.

Flat (Trap) Creek (Map 11/D5-G6)
Flat Creek is accessed by the Flat Creek Trail along most of its length. The creek contains brook, cutthroat and rainbow trout as well as rocky mountain whitefish.

Ford Creek (Map 16/A7)
An Elbow River tributary, Ford Creek contains good numbers of brook trout, plus a few cutthroat and bull trout. A trail follows the creek upstream from Highway 66.

Gardiner Creek (Map 1/G1)
A tributary of the Carbondale River, this trail access creek contains bull and cutthroat trout. The latter occasionally grow to 30 cm (12 inches).

Ghost River (Map 21/A6-16/C1)
Ghost River drains Lake Minnewanka and the Ghost Lakes in Banff National Park before flowing eastward through the foothills eventually draining into Ghost Lake on the Bow River. The lower reaches of the Ghost River are accessed by the Forestry Trunk Road, while the upper reaches are accessed by a long trail. The river contains rainbow, brook trout, brown trout and rocky mountain whitefish, which can all grow to 1 kg (2 lbs) but are generally under 30 cm (12 inches). Please note that fishing is closed in the Ghost River Wilderness Area.

Gold Creek (Map 5/A3-5)
Gold Creek flows through the town of Frank before draining into the Crowsnest River near Highway 3. It is a catch and release fishery for bull, cutthroat and rainbow trout as well as rocky mountain whitefish. The creek also holds some brook trout, which can be kept if caught (to a limit of two). Small rainbow and cutthroat can be found in the smaller tributaries such as Morin and Green Creeks.

Grand Valley Creek (Map 16/E1-22/D7)
This creek drains into the Bow River to the west of Cochrane and provides fishing for small rainbow and rainbow-cutthroat cross. The best fishing is near the creek estuary.

Grizzly Creek (Map 2/A2-4)
This tributary of the South Castle River is about 13 km (8.2 miles) long, but the fishing is only really any good for the first kilometre or so as it flows out of Grizzly Lake, where you will find small cutthroat. After that, the creek is very steep and fast, with few holes for fish to hang out in. It is also possible to fish near the confluence, where the fishing is basically the same as in the South Castle.

Harold Creek (Map 21/G4-22/C5)
This tributary of the Little Red River has brown trout, which must be released if caught. Secondary Highway 579 provides good access to most of the creek.

Highwood River (Map 11/A6-13/A1)
Highwood River begins in Kananaskis Country near the BC-Alberta border and flows eastward into the Bow River north of High River. The river contains brook, cutthroat and rainbow trout as well as rocky mountain whitefish, which all grow to 1.5 kg (3 lb) but tend to be under 40 cm (16 in). There are also some larger bull trout (to 3 kg/6 lbs) in the big pools. From the headwaters to the Kananaskis Country boundary, the river and all tributaries (except Storm Creek) are open to fishing from June 16 to October 31 and all trout must be released except brook trout, which have a limit of two. There is also a bait ban (except a limited maggot season). Within 500 m of the Bow River, fishing is open year-round and you can keep up to two trout greater than 40 cm in size from June 1 to March 31 as well as up to five whitefish. Remember, these restrictions are subject to change, so check the regulations before heading out.

Hummingbird Creek (Map 26/G2-27/B2)
Hummingbird Creek flows into the Ram River at the Hummingbird Recreation Area. It holds cutthroat to 0.5 kg (1 lb). Onion Lake Road provides access to mouth of the creek, while the Hummingbird Creek Trail follows the creek up to its source.

James River (Map 28/B7-29/F5)
The James River flows eastward from the boundary of the Bighorn Wildland into the Red Deer River north of Sundre. It has brown trout and rocky mountain whitefish that reach 1.5 kg (3 lbs) in size, but average much smaller. There are also the occasional bull trout to 2.5 kg (5 lbs) in the larger pools as well as northern pike and rainbow trout. The best fishing is found west of Secondary Highway 584.

Joyce River (Map 33/G5-34/A6)
Joyce River is a short river that drains into the North Ram River. It is accessed by hiking the Joyce River Trail off the Forestry Trunk Road. The river has good numbers of small cutthroat. However, fishing is catch and release.

Jumpingpound Creek (Map 16/A6-G2)
This creek flows northward and drains into the Bow River at Cochrane. The creek contains fair numbers of small brook, bull, cutthroat and rainbow trout as well as rocky mountain whitefish. To maintain the fish stocks, the creek and its tributaries are closed from November 1 to June 15 and are catch and release only the rest of the year, except for brook trout (limit of two) and rocky mountain whitefish (limit of five from June 16 to August 31).

Kananaskis River (Map 10/E2-15/F3)
Kananaskis River flows northward from the Kananaskis Lakes into the Bow River. The river is easily accessed along most of its course by the Kananaskis Trail (Highway 40). The fishing is fairly spotty, but with patience you may be able to catch a brook trout, cutthroat trout or rocky mountain whitefish (all to 1 kg/2 lbs). For the river and its tributaries (except Smith-Dorrien Creek) from the headwaters to Highway1, fishing is closed from November 1 to March 31 and all cutthroat and rainbow must be over 30 cm (12 inches) to keep. From Highway 1 to the Bow River, fishing is open year-round, but on a catch a release basis (except for brook trout and rocky mountain whitefish).

Lasthill Creek (Map 36/A3-37/A5)
Lasthill Creek is a slow moving creek east of Rocky Mountain House. It is accessed by Secondary Highways 598, 761 and 766 and contains a few pike. The bigger tributaries, **Horseguard Creek** (Map 36/E5-E7) and **Lobstick Creek** (Map 36/B1-F5), also hold pike.

Lee Creek (Map 3/E7-G5)
Lee Creek is a tributary of the St. Mary River that has its headwaters in Montana. The creek flows into Alberta east of Waterton, and there are various roads that access the creek as it flows north and east to meet up with the St. Mary, off our maps. The creek contains small rainbow and cutthroat, as well as some rocky mountain whitefish.

Lick & Dry Creeks (Map 35/A7-C7)
These two small creeks join to flow into Prairie Creek at the Prairie Creek Recreation Area. The contain brook trout, brown trout and rocky mountain whitefish.

Limestone Creek (Map 28/B3-B5)
A tributary of the Clearwater River, Limestone Creek has brook trout and rocky mountain whitefish.

Little Bow River (Map 9/G3-13/A4)
The Little Bow River drains to the northwest into Highwood River near the town of High River. The river offers reasonably good fishing for small brook, brown, bull and rainbow trout in the upper reaches and some pike (to 4 kg/9 lbs) and perch (to 0.5 kg/1 lb) in the lower reaches.

Little Elbow River (Map 10/G2-11/B1)
This small river has fair numbers of cutthroat and rainbow trout (to 0.5 kg/1 lb) and bull trout (to 1.5 kg/3 lbs). The upper reaches of the river are accessed by the Little Elbow River Trail whereas the lower reaches are accessed by the Elbow Falls Road (Highway 66).

Little Red Deer River (Map 21/G5-30/D2)
From its beginnings near the Forestry Trunk Road, the Little Red Deer River drains in a northeast direction to Highway 22 near Cremona and eventually meets the Red Deer River west of Innisfail. The river contains brook trout (to 0.5 kg/1 lb), brown trout (to 1.5 kg/3 lbs), bull trout (to 3 kg/6 lbs) and rocky mountain whitefish (to 1 kg/2 lbs) in the upper reaches and some brown trout

(to 1 kg/2 lbs), pike (to 2.5 kg/5 lbs) and walleye (to 3 kg/6 lbs) near the estuary. The river is best fished by spincasting a small lure or spinner or by fly fishing a sinking nymph pattern. Please note that the river and is tributaries are catch and release upstream from Cottonwood Road (Township Road 352 on Map 30/C3).

Livingstone River (Map 7/G3-8/A7)

The Livingstone River is a popular foothills river, which forms the main artery of the upper Oldman River system. The river and its tributaries have a good population of cutthroat trout and rocky mountain whitefish. The river is open for fishing (catch and release only) from June 16 to October 31. The river parallels the Forestry Trunk Road until it flows into the Oldman River. If you want to camp overnight, try the Livingstone Falls Recreation Area.

Lookout Creek (Map 33/E1)

A tributary of the Blackstone River, Lookout Creek is accessed by the Chungo Road and contains brook, brown and cutthroat trout as well as rocky mountain whitefish.

Loomis, McPhail and Odlum Creeks (Map 11/B6)

These small creeks are tributaries of the Highwood River and are catch and release fisheries for brook, brown, cutthroat and rainbow trout. They are reached by walking or biking the trails leading from Highway 40.

Lost Creek (Map 1/G1)

Lost Creek has bull and cutthroat trout that are usually quite small (less than 30 cm/12 inches). South and North Lost Creek meet and then flow into the Carbondale River.

Lost Creek (Map 7/D3)

Lost Creek holds small brook trout. The creek runs into Cataract Creek and can be accessed by trail off the Forestry Trunk Road (940).

Lynx Creek (Map 1/G1-4/F6)

A tributary of the Carbondale River, Lynx Creek contains cutthroat trout, which must be greater than 30 cm (12 inches) to keep. The upper reaches of this creek are best accessed by Lyon's Creek Road, while the lower reaches are best accessed by the Adanac Road.

Lynx Creek (Map 27/B1-D1)

This Lynx Creek is found north of Ram Falls on the Forestry Trunk Road. It has cutthroat to 2 kg (4 lbs) but most of the fish tend to be much smaller. However, the cutthroat must be greater than 40 cm (16 in) to keep.

McGillivray Creek (Map 4/F4)

McGillivray Creek runs through the town of Crowsnest and then into the Crowsnest River. The creek contains cutthroat and rainbow trout.

Medicine River (Map 30/D2-36/G1)

This slow, meandering river is easily accessed by a series of section roads as well as Highways 11, 12 and 54. The river contains a small population of northern pike (to 5 kg/11 lbs), walleye (to 3 kg/6 lbs), brown trout (to 1 kg/2 lbs) and rocky mountain whitefish (to 1 kg/2 lbs). Only pike are found in the mid to upper sections (to the west of Sylvan Lake) with the remaining fish species inhabiting the waters near the estuary. Please note that there is a bait ban on the river and all walleye and brown trout that are caught must be released.

Mill Creek (Map 2/D1-5/B4)

Mill Creek is best accessed by Secondary Highway 507 and the road to Gladstone Valley. This is a tributary of the Castle River, and provides fishing for brook, bull, cutthroat and rainbow trout as well as rocky mountain whitefish from June 16 to October 31. It is catch and release for everything but brook trout.

Mist Creek (Map 11/A4-5)

Mist Creek is another catch and release fishery for brown, cutthroat and rainbow trout. The Mist Creek Trail, which begins off Highway 40, provides good access along most of the creek.

Moose Creek (Map 16/B5)

Accessed by the Tom Snow Trail, Moose Creek has brook, bull and cutthroat trout.

Mosquito Creek (Maps 8/D1-9/F2)

Eventually joining the Little Bow River, this big creek begins in the foothills west of Nanton. It has brook, bull, cutthroat and rainbow trout.

Nanton Creek (Maps 8/G2-9/A1)

Nanton Creek joins Mosquito Creek just north of Nanton. The creek has northern pike up to 2 kg (4 lbs) in size.

Nice and Easy Creeks (Map 34/D5-D6)

These two small creeks have a small number of tiny cutthroat. The North Fork Road provides access to the lower sections of Nice Creek.

Nordegg River (Map 33/G1)

Nordegg River is found north of the town of Nordegg and is open for fishing from April 1 to October 31. The headwaters can be reached from the Forestry Trunk Road whereas most of the other parts of the river can be reached by an extensive network of logging roads. The river contains brook trout (to 0.5 kg/1 lb), bull trout (to 2.5 kg/5 lbs) and rocky mountain whitefish (to 1 kg/2 lbs) in the upper reaches. The lower reaches, which are found north of this mapbook, contain pike, walleye and brown trout.

North Ram River (Map 26/E2-34/F7)

The North Ram River begins to the east of the Kootenay Plains Natural Area and drains into the Ram River further east. Like the Ram itself, the North Ram is known for its great cutthroat trout fishing. It is a catch and release only freestone river, with cutthroat up to (and greater than) 50 cm (20 inches), although those are certainly the exceptions. The river is 50 km (31 miles) long, most of which is only accessible by trail, although downstream of where the Forestry Trunk Road crosses the North Ram, the North Ram Road parallels the river for close to 20 km (12 miles).

North Raven River (Stauffe Creek) (Map 29/E1)

Accessed by Highway 54 and Secondary Highway 761, this river holds pike (to 4 kg/9 lbs) and brook trout (to 1 kg/2 lbs), but it is best known for its brown trout (to 2.5 kg/3 lbs). The river is catch and release from April 1 to June 15 and from September 1 to March 31. During the other parts of the year, all brown trout under 40 cm (16 inches) and brook trout less than 30 cm (12 inches) must be released. Because of the strict regulations, the river is now considered one of Alberta's best fishing rivers for brown trout.

North Saskatchewan River (Maps 25-26, 33-36)

The glacier fed North Saskatchewan River is one of the largest rivers in Alberta. It begins in the northern section of Banff National Park and flows in a southeastern direction past Rocky Mountain House, through Edmonton, and on through the provinces of Saskatchewan (where it is joined by the South Saskatchewan River) and Manitoba before draining into Hudson's Bay. Most of the section of river covered by this book is easily accessed by Highway 93 and Highway 11. Above Abraham Lake (Map 26/C2-25/C1), the river is silty, and fishing can be slow. Below Abraham Lake, the river provides a good fishery for brook, brown, bull and cutthroat trout as well as rocky mountain whitefish. There are also some pike and walleye near Rocky Mountain House. To fish the walleye, it is best to cast towards the front of the large holes on the river since the walleye tend to congregate in that area. Any one of a number of spoons or plugs tends to work (Rapala, Big Lindy, Shadlings or Thundersticks). Cutthroat and rainbow must be greater than 30 cm (12 inches) to keep when fishing above the Bighorn Dam (Map 33/E6). From the Bighorn Dam to Highway 22/39, the river is closed from November 1 to March 31 and there is a limit of two trout and five whitefish.

Oldman River (Maps 5, 6, 7, 8)
The headwaters of the Oldman River are found near the BC border in the Beehive Natural Area. The river flows to the southeast and eventually past Fort McLeod. Near the headwaters, the river is fast flowing and has a number of trout species such as brown, bull, cutthroat and rainbow. Near Fort McLeod, the river meanders through farmland making it better for brook trout, northern pike and walleye. Rocky mountain whitefish are also resident in the river. Please note that the river and its tributaries are heavily regulated (e.g. closures, catch and release, gear restrictions), so you should check the regulations before heading out.

Onion Creek (Map 26/G1-27/B2)
Onion Creek drains into Hummingbird Creek and has cutthroat to 0.5 kg (1 lb). The Onion Lake Trail provides access to the creek.

Oyster & Pasque Creeks (Map 7/E4)
Like the dozen or so tributaries of the Oldman River, these small creeks are rarely fished. Most people focus on the Oldman itself, but if you are looking for something a little different, a little less popular, these tributaries are a good option. However, if you are looking for trophy fish, or even keepers, they are not a great place, as most of the cutthroat are below legal size. There are, however, lots of them, plus a few bull trout, too.

Panther River (Map 20/C4-21/C1)
Although the headwaters of the Panther River are in Banff National Park, most of the fishing occurs outside the park near its estuary with the Red Deer River. The estuary is next to the Forestry Trunk Road where spincasting and fly fishing for bull trout (to 1.5 kg/3 lb), cutthroat (to 0.5 kg/1 lb) and rocky mountain whitefish (to 1 kg/2 lbs) can be productive.

Pekisko Creek (Map 7/G2-12/D6)
Pekisko Creek flows into the Highwood southeast of Longview. Highway 22 provides the best access to the creek, which contains bull and rainbow trout as well as rocky mountain whitefish. It is a catch and release fishery for trout, although you can keep up to five whitefish.

Picklejar Creek (Map 11/B5)
Picklejar Creek drains the Picklejar Lakes and offers a catch and release fishery for brook, brown and cutthroat trout. The Picklejar Recreation Area is home to a day-use area near the estuary.

Pigeon Creek (Map 15/D4)
The Skogan Pass Trail parallels Pigeon Creek for much of its length, but most of the fishing occurs close to the Trans-Canada Highway. This is a low volume stream that holds a few brook and brown trout as well as whitefish to 30 cm (12 inches). In dry summers, the creek has been known to dry up completely.

Pincher Creek (Map 2/D3, 6/A6)
Despite being ravaged by a flood in 1995, Pincher Creek is still considered one of the best fishing streams in the foothills. This creek runs through the small town of Pincher Creek before joining the Oldman River. The creek contains rocky mountain whitefish as well as bull, cutthroat and rainbow trout that can all grow to 1 kg (2 lbs). Although the fish are generally quite small, you can only keep two cutthroat and/or rainbow and five whitefish that are greater than 30 cm (12-inches).

Pocaterra Creek (Map 10/F3)
Highway 40 parallels Pocaterra Creek for part of the distance it flows from Highwood Meadows to the Kananaskis River. It holds a fair number of small cutthroat, bull and rainbow trout.

Prairie Creek (Map 16/B7)
Prairie Creek, like most tributaries of the Elbow River, contains good numbers of brook trout, plus cutthroat and bull trout in much fewer numbers. Highway 66 crosses the creek, but to get upstream, you will have to follow the Prairie Creek Trail on foot or by bike.

Prairie Creek (Map 28/A1-36/A6)
Prairie Creek is a large, slow-moving creek that flows into the Clearwater River south of Rocky Mountain House. The creek and its tributaries offer fairly good fishing for brook trout (to 0.5 kg/1 lb), brown trout (to 2 kg/4 lbs), bull trout (to 2.5 kg/5 lbs) and rocky mountain whitefish (to 1 kg/2 lbs). Between Vetch and Swan Creeks (Map 35/G7), Prairie Creek is closed from September 1 to March 31 and catch and release during the rest of the season. Also, downstream from the North Fork Road (Map 35/E7), the main creek, but not the tributaries, is catch and release.

Priddis Creek (Maps 16/E7-17/A7)
This is a small tributary draining into Fish Creek that offers fishing for a few rainbow scattered amongst the beaver dams. Highway 22 provides good access to the creek.

Ptolemy Creek (Map 4/D6)
Ptolemy Creek joins the Crowsnest River north of Highway 3. It contains small cutthroat that are mostly below legal size (35 cm/14 inches).

Quirk Creek (Maps 11/C1-16/B7)
An Elbow River tributary, Quirk Creek contains good numbers of brook trout, plus cutthroat and bull trout in much fewer numbers.

Racehorse Creek (Maps 4/G1-5/A1)
Racehorse Creek joins the Oldman River north of Coleman and can be accessed by the Forestry Trunk Road. It contains bull and cutthroat trout as well as rocky mountain whitefish which all tend to be quite small. Both the **North Racehorse and South Racehorse Creeks** (Maps 4/F2-5/A1) are tiny extensions of the main creek that contain numerous small cutthroat (less than 30 cm/12 inches in size). The tributaries can be accessed by the Allison Creek Road.

Ram River (Map 26/G6-35/B5)
Access into the headwaters of the Ram River is extremely limited except by a long trail (South Ram River Trail). Below Ram Falls (Map 27/D2) and downstream from the Forestry Trunk Road, access to the river is via the Allenby Trail. Towards the lower reaches, where the river flows into the North Saskatchewan River, good access is provided to the river via the North Fork Road. The river has some big cutthroat, some of which are rumoured to grow to a monstrous 60 cm (24 inches). The big cutthroat reside upstream of the falls. Below the falls, you will find bull trout, cutthroat trout and rocky mountain whitefish (all to 2 kg/4 lbs or more). Various sections of the river (and its tributaries) are catch and release so check the regulations before you head out.

Ranger Creek (Map 27/B4)
This trail access creek is a Ram River tributary that contains small cutthroat in good numbers.

Raven River (Maps 28/F4-30/A3)
The Raven River is a heavily regulated river with fair fishing for brown trout (to 2 kg/4 lbs), rocky mountain whitefish (to 1.5 kg/3 lbs), and brook trout (to 1 kg/2 lbs). There is also said to be a few large pike and walleye towards its confluence with the Ram River. It is a catch and release fishery from April 1 to June 15 and from September 1 to October 31. During the rest of the year, all brown trout and walleye under 40 cm (16 inches) must be released. Further, all trout and whitefish must be released from the beginning of April to June 15.

Red Deer River (Maps 20, 21, 22, 27, 28, 29, 30, 37, 38)
The Red Deer River is a major river, with its headwaters at Red Deer Lakes in Banff (Map 20/A3). The river flows in a northeastern direction, draining a large area east of Banff. From Dickson Dam (Map 30/C2) downstream to the Tolman Bridge, there is a good brown trout population because of the

catch and release regulations that were introduced in 1992. Good fishing for brown trout is also offered in the upper reaches of the river west of Gleniffer Lake. Other species in the river include rocky mountain whitefish (to 1.5 kg/3 lb) and some walleye. Please note that upstream from the Forestry Trunk Road (Map 22/C1), the river and its tributaries are closed from November 1 to June 15 and are catch and release for the rest of the year. Below the Forestry Trunk Road, the river is closed from November 1 to March 31, has a two trout and five whitefish limit and is catch and release for walleye.

Ribbon Creek (Map 15/D6)
Ribbon Creek flows from Ribbon Lake, past Kananaskis Village, and into the Kananaskis River. It holds a few brook, brown and cutthroat trout.

Rice Creek (Map 8/C4)
Crossed by Highway 22 just south of Chain Lakes, this small Willow Creek tributary has lots of small rainbow.

Ridge & Spears Creeks (Map 8/A5)
Tributaries of the Livingstone, these catch and release creeks hold lots of small cutthroat. The odd fish can grow to 0.5 kg (1 lb) in size.

Rock Creek (Map 5/B5)
Rock Creek contains cutthroat, rainbow and rocky mountain whitefish. The Crowsnest River tributary is best accessed by Highway 3 about 6 km west of Lundbreck.

Rocky Creek (Map 10/F1-15/E7)
Rocky Creek has brown trout and flows into the Kananaskis north of the Eau Claire Recreation Area.

Rough Creek (Map 34/E6-35/A4)
Rough Creek and the smaller Meadows Creek offer fishing for has brook and brown trout. Rough Creek also contains rocky mountain whitefish and is easily accessed by the North Fork Road before it flows into the North Saskatchewan River.

Savanna Creek (Map 7/E4-G4)
Savanna Creek contains small cutthroat that must be released if caught.

Screwdriver Creek (Map 5/C7)
Screwdriver Creek is found near Beaver Mines and offers fishing for a few small bull trout, cutthroat and rainbow trout. Most of the fish in the creek cannot be kept because they are smaller than the 30 cm (12 inch) size restriction.

Sheep River (Maps 11/A4-12/G2)
Named after the animals that often grace the slopes of the upper reaches, this river flows through the Turner Valley before draining into the Highwood River. The river offers fishing for brook, cutthroat and rainbow trout as well as rocky mountain whitefish (all to 1 kg/2 lbs). There are also some large bull trout (to 5 kg/11 lbs) in the deeper pools. Within the parks, the cutthroat and rainbow must be greater than 30 cm (12 inches) to keep and the fishing season runs from June 16 to August 31. Downstream, the river is open from June 16 to October 31, the trout limit is two and the whitefish limit is five. The river serves as a major spawning area for bull trout and rainbow from the Bow River.

Shunda Creek (Map 33/G2-34/E3)
Highway 11 follows most of the creek providing great access for the brown trout (to 1.5 kg/3 lbs) as well as brook trout and rocky mountain whitefish (to 1 kg/2 lbs).

Sibbald Creek (Map 16/A4)
Sibbald Creek is easily accessed by Highway 68 and offers small brook, brown, cutthroat and rainbow trout.

Smuts Creek (Map 10/C1-15/B7)
Okay. Let's get the name out of the way first. General Jan Christian Smuts was Prime Minister of South Africa in the first half of the twentieth century. So the name isn't rude. The creek contains lots of small cutthroat (to 30 cm/12 inches), and the occasional bull trout or whitefish. There are also worries that stocked, non-native dolly varden are making their way into the system from Chester Lake (see Chester Lake write-up). If you do find a dolly, contact the Fisheries Biologist at the Alberta Sustainable Resource Development office in Canmore at (403) 678-5508 (ext. 263).

Spray River (Map 10/A1-15/A7; 14/G2-15/B7)
Spray River flows north into and out of the Spray Lakes Reservoir, eventually draining into the Bow River at the town of Banff. The river contains brook, cutthroat and rainbow trout as well as rocky mountain whitefish. Anglers willing to hike above the reservoir will find cutthroat, while below the reservoir, you will start finding a few brown trout in addition to the other fish species. Most of the lower reaches of the river are accessible by the fire access road (hike/bike) linking Banff and the reservoir.

Spring Creek (Map 12/E3)
Spring Creek flows into the Sheep River west of Okotoks and offers brook and brown trout.

Star Creek (Map 4/E5)
Star Creek drains into the Crowsnest River west of Coleman. It contains brook, bull and rainbow trout, which all tend to be small.

Stimson Creek (Maps 8/A2-12/D6)
Stimson Creek is easily accessed by Highway 22 and Secondary Roads 532 and 540. The creek contains rainbow (to 1 kg/2 lbs) and small cutthroat. The best fishing is near the estuary. As a tributary of the Highwood River, it is catch and release for trout.

Stony Creeks (Map 28/F4-29/B4)
Stony Creek is a marshy creek with many beaver dams that were stocked with brook trout in 1997. Above Burnstick Lake, West (Upper) Stony Creek produces very well for small brook trout. The Lower Stony holds a few brown and whitefish as well.

Sturrock Creek (Map 33/E2)
Sturrock Creek is a tributary of the Blackstone that is reached by a spur road off the Chungo Road. The creek offers fishing for brook trout, brown trout, cutthroat and rocky mountain whitefish.

Sullivan Creek (Map 11/E5-12/A5)
This creek has brook, brown, cutthroat and rainbow trout as well as rocky mountain whitefish. You can keep up to five whitefish, but the creek is catch and release for all trout. A logging road leads along most of its length.

Swale Creek (Map 34/A1)
Swale Creek drains into Colt Creek, which in turn flows into the Blackstone River (north of this book). Swale Creek holds brook trout and brown trout.

Swan Creek (Map 28/B1-35/G7)
Linking Swan Lake with Prairie Creek, Swan Creek has numerous beaver dams that offer good fishing for brook and brown trout.

Teepee Pole Creek (Map 28/C6-G5)
Teepee Pole Creek has brown trout, brook trout and rocky mountain whitefish. It is a tributary of the James River.

Tershishner Creek (Map 33/D5)
Tershishner Creek drains into the north end of the Abraham Lake. It has brook trout to 0.5 kg (1 lb) as well as rocky mountain whitefish to 1 kg (2 lbs) and bull trout to 2 kg (4 lbs).

Three Sisters Creek (Map 15/B4)
The Three Sisters are one of the most prominent landmarks around Canmore. This creek runs up the valley between those mountains and Mount Lawrence Grassi. The lower reaches are accessible by road just east of Canmore, while the upper reaches are not really accessible except by bushwhacking. The creek contains some brook and brown trout.

Threepoint Creek (Map 11/D1-12/C2)
Threepoint Creek is a spawning tributary for Bow River rainbow and is the largest tributary for the Sheep River. There are also brook, brown and cutthroat trout and even rocky mountain whitefish in the creek. For cutthroat and rainbow trout, the fish must be greater than 30 cm (12 in) in size to keep.

Tod Creek (Map 5/B3-D6)
Tod Creek drains into the Crowsnest River, right before the Crowsnest flows into the Oldman Reservoir. The creek has cutthroat, brown and rainbow trout as well as rocky mountain whitefish.

Tough Creek (Map 3/D7)
This creek has its headwaters in Waterton, but quickly flows out of the park to meet up with Lee Creek. Rough Creek contains small rainbow and cutthroat, as well as some rocky mountain whitefish.

Trout Creek (Map 34/E4)
Trout Creek has brook and brown trout as well as rocky mountain whitefish. It is reached via the Trout Creek Road and several mining roads.

Turnbull Creek (Map 22/B3-4)
Turnbull Creek flows into Harold Creek, which flows into the Little Red River. It holds catch and release brown trout.

Vetch Creek (Map 35/C7-G7)
Vetch Creek drains into Prairie Creek and has brook and brown trout as well as rocky mountain whitefish.

Vicary Creek (Map 4/F3-G1)
Accessed by the Forestry Trunk Road north of Coleman, Vicary Creek is a tributary of the Racehorse Creek. It has a few small rainbow and lots of cutthroat.

Ware Creek (Map 11/E2)
Ware Creek flows into Threepoint Creek and has cutthroat and rainbow trout as well as rocky mountain whitefish.

Wasootch Creek (Map 15/F6)
This Kananaskis River tributary has small brown trout.

Waterton River (Map 3/A6-6/G7)
The Waterton River flows east and north from Waterton Lakes National Park, through the Waterton Reservoir, and then off these maps, to join the Belly River. Between the park boundary and the reservoir, the river holds some large fish (including bull trout and pike to 6 kg/13 lbs). The most common catch is rainbow trout (to 1.5 kg/3 lbs), although you will also find brown and cutthroat trout and whitefish.

Welch Creek (Map 36/D1-G2)
This Medicine River tributary also holds northern pike. The creek can easily be accessed off the Leedale Road.

West Castle River (Map 2/A4-2)
The West Castle River is a catch and release river that is open from June 16 to October 31. It holds plenty of cutthroat and rainbow to 45 cm (18 inches), as well as bull trout to 3 kg (6 lbs) and whitefish. Secondary Highway 774 parallels the river for a ways, but the upper reaches are only accessible by a rough 4wd road/trail.

Whiskey Creek (Map 16/F7-17/A7)
This is a small tributary draining into the headwaters of Fish Creek that offers a reasonably good fishery for rainbow. Most fishing takes place near the creeks crossing with Secondary Highway 762.

White Creek (Map 8/A7)
White Creek is a tributary of the Livingstone that holds catch and release cutthroat.

Wilkinson Creek (Map 7/E2)
Wilkinson Creek drains into Cataract Creek, and contains brook trout. Most of the creek is reached off the Forestry Trunk Road. It is catch and release for all trout.

Willow Creek (Map 8/A2-C3; 8/C3-6/G2)
A good fishing stream, the upper reaches of this creek holds plenty of small rainbow, bull and brook trout. The creek flows into, then out of, the Chain Lakes Reservoir before meandering all the way to the Red Deer River near Fort McLeod. You will find bigger fish closer to the reservoir.

Wind Creek (Map 15/D4)
A tributary of Pigeon Creek, this small creek holds a few brook and brown trout as well as some whitefish. These fish are small (to 30 cm/12 inches) and there are not a lot of them. The main creek is easily accessed off the Centennial Ridge Trail, while West Wind Creek requires bushwhacking to access it.

Yara Creek (Map 21/C1)
Yara Creek is easily accessed of the Forestry Trunk Road north of the Red Deer River Recreation Area. It has brown trout and rocky mountain whitefish.

National Parks

The following is a comprehensive listing of lakes and streams found in the National Parks of Southwestern Alberta. Anglers will find that the lakes and streams are no longer stocked, which may result in slower fishing for generally larger fish. Also unique to National Parks is the fact they are governed under their own regulations and you will need a special license to fish. Check with Parks Canada for more information. Regulations can be downloaded from www.parkscanada.gc.ca.

Banff National Park

Due to its sheer size, there are a lot of lakes and streams to sample within Banff National Park. Although, the easily accessed water bodies see a lot of pressure there are many remote lakes that see few anglers and contain good numbers of fish. Add in the natural beauty of the Rocky Mountains and you can see why Banff is an excellent fishing destination.

Alexandra River (Map 25/A3-D2)

Located by trail north of the Saskatchewan River Crossing, this short river flows into the North Saskatchewan River. The river contains some bull trout, lake trout and rocky mountain whitefish best caught by fly fishing or spincasting. The river is hard to reach as you have to ford the North Saskatchewan River, and like most rivers in the area it is heavily silted, which means poor fishing, especially during summer.

Altrude Lakes (Map 14/A1)

These two small lakes are found next to Highway 93. The lakes have small cutthroat with the lower lake producing the most fish. Spincasting, bait fishing or fly fishing from shore or a belly boat work.

Altrude Creek (Map 14/B1)

The Trans-Canada Highway (Hwy 1) crosses the creek at its junction with Highway 93. The creek has small cutthroat near the estuary with the Bow River.

Arnica Lake (Map 14/A1)

Arnica Lake is reached by trail (Arnica Trail) from Highway 93 and is home to a rustic campsite. The lake holds some good-sized cutthroat but is usually not ice-free until July.

Baker Creek (Map 20/A4-A6)

Baker Creek is a Bow River tributary that drains Baker Lake. The creek has brook, bull and cutthroat trout with the best fishing found near the Bow Valley Parkway (Hwy 1A). The upper reaches of the creek are accessed by trail.

Baker Lake (Map 20/A4)

This lake is reached by a 12 km (7.4 mile) hike up the Skoki Valley, or via the longer Baker Creek Trail. The lake holds good-sized brook and cutthroat trout. If you are not having any luck here, try nearby **Little Baker Lake,** which holds slightly smaller versions of cutthroat. **Tilted Lake** is right next to Little Baker Lake, but holds few, if any, fish.

Black Rock Lake (Map 14/B2)

Black Lake is reached by the Shadow Lake Trail up Redearth Creek and then a trail along Pharaoh Creek. An alternative route is to park near the end of Sunshine Road and hike up the Healy Pass Trail. The lake holds cutthroat to 30 cm (12 inches).

Block Lake (Map 20/C6)

Accessed by a long, difficult hike/climb up the Cascade River Valley from Lake Minnewanka, getting to this lake is recommended only for experienced climbers. Those who make it will find cutthroat trout to 40 cm (16 inches). The lake was once stocked with Quebec Red Trout, but there have been no reports of these trout for years.

Boom Lake (Map 19/G7)

Getting to Boom Lake involves a 5 km (one-way) hike from Highway 93. The lake has rainbow as well as cutthroat.

Bow Lake (Map 19/C1)

Located next to the Icefields Parkway (Hwy 93) north of Lake Louise, Bow Lake is not quite the headwaters of the Bow River (that would be the Bow Glacier), but for most people, it is close enough. The lake has bull trout, lake trout and rocky mountain whitefish. Despite its proximity to Highway 93, the lake still produces well throughout the ice-free season by spincasting or fly fishing. Try the outflow to the Bow River at the south end of the lake for best success.

Bow River (Maps 14-15)

The upper section of the Bow River is in Banff National Park, and a National Park Permit is required to fish this section. For a complete write-up of this famous river see the stream fishing section of this book.

Bourgeau Lake (Map 14/D2)

It is 7 km (4.3 miles) from the Trans-Canada Highway (Hwy 1) to the lake itself. The lake holds brook trout to 30 cm (12 inches).

Brewster Creek (Map 14/E2-G5)

Hiking/horse trails follow Brewster Creek almost all the way to its headwaters, providing good access to the creek. The creek is home to small bull and cutthroat.

Bryant Creek (Maps 14/G6-15/A7)

Bryant Creek, which flows into the south end of the Spray Lakes Reservoir, holds cutthroat and whitefish to 30 cm (12 inches) and bull trout to 60 cm (24 inches). The latter two species are found only in the lowest sections of the creek. This creek is accessed by trail only.

Carrot Creek (Map 15/B2)

Carrot Creek is a Bow River tributary that crosses the Trans-Canada Highway (Hwy 1) just inside the Banff boundary. A trail heads up the creek, but your best chance for success is near the confluence, as most of the fish in Carrot Creek swim up from the Bow.

Cascade River (Map 20/E6-15/A1)

The Cascade River flows into and out of the west end of Lake Minnewanka and is home to brook, bull, cutthroat and rainbow trout as well as rocky mountain whitefish. The best fishing is for the cutthroat in the upper reaches of the river. There is good hiking/biking access along most of the river via the Cascade Fire Road.

Chephren Lake (Map 26/A6)

This lake is reached by trail from the north end of Waterfowl Lakes on the Icefields Parkway (Hwy 93). The lake has small cutthroat and rainbow trout caught by spincasting or fly fishing. Camping is provided at the south end of Waterfowl Lake.

Cirque Lake (Map 26/A6)

This lake is reached by the same trail used to access Chepren Lake. The silty lake has small cutthroat and rainbow trout caught by spincasting or fly fishing.

Citadel Lake (Map 14/E4)

This small lake is found just south of the Citadel Pass off the Citadel Pass Trail. The trail doesn't actually pass the lake, or even get within eyeshot, so very few people visit the lake. Those who do will find rainbow trout in the 30-35 cm (12-14 inch) range.

Clearwater River (Maps 26-27)

The Banff National Park section of this large river sees few anglers due to the distance involved to hike-in. For a complete write-up see the stream fishing section of this book.

Consolation Lakes (Map 19/G7)

These gorgeous lakes are located 3 km (1.8 miles) from the Moraine Lake parking lot. During times of high grizzly activity, you will have to travel in groups of at least six people for safety. The lakes hold brook trout to 30 cm (12 inches), while the lower lake has a few cutthroat, too.

Copper Lake (Map 14/B1)

Located just a short ways from the Trans-Canada Highway (Hwy 1), Copper Lake offers good (but not great) fishing for rainbow to 40 cm (16 inches).

Corral Creek (Map 19/G5)

Corral Creek flows into the Bow River south of Lake Louise. The creek, which is best fished upstream from the estuary, has bull, cutthroat and rainbow trout.

Cuthead Creek (Map 20/E5)

Cuthead Creek is a tributary of the Cascade River, and holds bull and cutthroat trout. The creek is reached by the Cascade Fire Road.

Cuthead Lake (Map 20/E5)

Cuthead Lake is reached by the Cascade Fire Road then an undeveloped trail up Cuthead Creek. The lake has bull and cutthroat trout, which are easily caught by spincasting and fly fishing from shore or a float tube.

Deer (Pipestone) Lake (Map 19/G2)

This lake is found about 2 km (1.2 miles) south of Fish Lakes. There is no trail to the lake, but you should be able to pick out the route in. The lake has lots of cutthroat to 40 cm (16 inches), which take readily to a fly.

Devon Lakes (Map 26/F7)

A long approach makes getting to these lakes difficult. Still, people make the trek, hoping to find one of the big lake trout or bull trout that inhabit the lake (it also holds less than monstrous cutthroat and rocky mountain whitefish). Most will be disappointed, as the lake was over fished in the past. You will still find fish in okay numbers, but not to the size and numbers they were historically.

Egypt Lake (Map 14/B3)

Egypt Lake is reached by the Shadow Lake Trail up Redearth Creek and then a trail along Pharaoh Creek. An alternative route is to park near the end of Sunshine Road and hike up the Healy Pass Trail. The lake contains brook and cutthroat trout. In the summer, it may be tough to find a place to cast from at this popular lake.

Elk Lake (Map 20/F7)

Elk Lake is reached by hiking up the Cascade Fire Road to the Stoney Creek Campsite and then heading south. An alternative route is to walk the Elk Pass Trail from the Forty Mile Trail. The lake contains cutthroat trout to 45 cm (18 inches).

Forty Mile Creek (Map 14/G1-20/E7)

Forty Mile Creek flows into the Bow River within the townsite of Banff. The creek has bull trout, brook trout and cutthroat but is closed to fishing near the town. It is best to hike up the Forty Mile Trail from the end of Mount Norquay Road to sample some of the larger pools.

Forty Mile Lake (Map 20/E7)

After a 20 km (12 mile) return hike up the Forty Mile Trail from the top of Mount Norquay Road, anglers wishing to get to this lake must bushwhack

their way up a small creek that drains the lake. Those who make it will find brook trout to 30 cm (12 inches).

Ghost Lakes (Map 15/D1)

The Ghost Lakes are located at the east end of Lake Minnewanka and are reached by boat or trail. The lakes have a few bull trout, lake trout and rocky mountain whitefish but do not offer great fishing. The best place to try is in the narrows between the lakes.

Glacier Lake (Map 25/E4)

Glacier Lake gets murky during hot weather because of the glacier run-off. As a result, fishing for the rocky mountain whitefish and lake trout is best during the spring and late fall. The lake is accessed by hiking from the Saskatchewan River Crossing off Icefields Parkway (Hwy 93) some 15 km (9 miles) one-way.

Haiduk Lake (Map 14/B3)

Haiduk Lake is accessed by following the Hawk Creek Trail from Highway 93 or the Shadow Lake Trail from the Trans-Canada Highway (Hwy 1). The lake holds some fairly large cutthroat trout, to 1.5 kg (3 lbs).

Hector Lake (Map 19/D2)

Located in Banff National Park, this large lake is reached by a short trail off Highway 93. However, the hike involves crossing the Bow River. The lake, which has a rustic campsite on the eastern shores, offers fishing for brook, bull and rainbow trout as well as rocky mountain whitefish. If fishing is slow, you may wish to venture to **Lake Margaret**, which offers good numbers of small cutthroat taken by spincasting or fly fishing.

Herbert Lake (Map 19/F5)

Herbert Lake is a small lake sandwiched between the Icefields Parkway (Hwy 93) and the Bow River just north of Lake Louise. The lake contains a few small brook trout and cutthroat best caught by spincasting a small lure. Less than a kilometre to the south is **Little Herbert Lake**, which holds a few rainbow.

Howard Douglas Lake (Map 14/E4)

This small lake is found 6 km (3.6 miles) from Sunshine Village on the Citadel Pass Trail. The lake holds plenty of small brook trout, but the odd fish grows to 30 cm (12 inches) or larger.

Howse River (Map 25/F6-G3)

The Howse River is a major tributary of the upper North Saskatchewan River. A hike/ horse trail follows the silty river to its source. Due to the water clarity, you will find slow fishing for bull trout, whitefish and, oddly enough, lake trout.

Isabella Lake (Map 26/C7)

Isabella Lake is the only lake or stream on the Siffleur River system that is open to fishing. Access to the lake is along the Dolomite Creek Trail, and you will need at least a day to hike the 24 km (14.9 miles) to the lake. Once you get there, expect good fishing for rainbow that average 30 cm (12 inches) but often get much bigger. The lake also holds bull trout to 60 cm (24 inches).

Johnston Creek (Map 14/C1-20/B5)

Johnston Creek flows into the Bow River east of Castle Mountain and is accessed along its entire length by the Johnston Creek Trail. There is decent fishing for bull and cutthroat trout in the pools above the Inkpots (Map 20/D7) since the crowds begin to thin out after the first falls. You will want to get above Johnston Canyon, anyway, before trying to fish the creek.

Johnson Lake (Map 15/A1)
Johnson Lake is open to fishing, but most anglers take a pass on this poor fishing lake. There are a few rainbow and brook trout.

Lake Annette (Map 19/F6)
This small lake is set beneath Mount Temple in the Paradise Valley. It contains a few cutthroat and rainbow to 30 cm (12 inches). It is not worth making the trip just to fish the lake, but if you are making the trip, it is worth fishing. Shore fishing is difficult, but not impossible.

Lake Gloria (Map 14/G7)
The lovely Lake Gloria (Glorious Gloria?) is accessed by following the Bryant Creek Trail from the south end of Spray Reservoir and then heading southwest on the Wonder Pass Trail. Gloria contains fair numbers of cutthroat to 1.5 kg (3 lbs), but shore fishing can be tricky.

Lake Helen (Map 19/C1)
It is a 6 km (3.6 mile) hike to get to this alpine lake set high above the Icefields Parkway (Hwy 93). The lake holds brook trout to 30 cm that take well to flies.

Lake Katherine (Map 19/D1)
The 8.1 km (5 mile) trail to Lake Katherine climbs up to Helen Lake, over a ridge (at 2500 m/8125 ft) and down to Lake Katherine, at 2373 m (7712 ft), climbing 575 m (1869 ft) to the ridge. Basically, you will need to put in a bit of work to get to this pretty alpine lake. You may have to do a bit of work to catch one of the cutthroat trout that inhabit this lake, but it is worth it, as they can get to 50 cm (18 inches). Fly fishing works well.

Lake Louise (Map 19/F5)
Arguably one of the best-known lakes in the province, let alone the country, Lake Louise is known for its turquoise waters and dramatic mountain scenery. It is not, however, known for its fishing. It does contain whitefish to 30 cm (12 inches) and bull trout to about twice that size, but only the most persistent angler will have any success.

Lake Merlin (Map 19/G3)
A small, high elevation lake, Merlin Lake is accessible by foot along a rough trail from the Skoki Valley. The last section involves scrambling up a scree slope to access the hanging valley the lake is set in. Because of its high elevation, the lake is not free of ice until July. It contains brook trout to 30 cm (12 inches).

Lake Minnewanka (Map 15/A1-D1)
Lake Minnewanka is a large murky lake located east of the Banff townsite. It is considered to be one of the top ten lakes in the province for trophy lake trout, which can get to 20 kg (45 lbs). You will also find bull trout (to 4 kg/8 lbs), rainbow (to 1.5 kg/3 lbs) and rocky mountain whitefish (to 1 kg/2 lbs). The fishing can be very slow in summer but if you can get deep, you do have a chance to catch those big lakers. Fishing starts to heat up in the fall, but just as it gets good, the lake closes (September 3). Unlike other lakes in the park, motorized boats are allowed on the lake so it is best to bring a boat and try trolling or spincasting near one of the tributaries. There is a bait ban in effect.

Leman Lake (Map 10/A1)
Leman Lake is located by hiking the trail leading south along the Spray River from the reservoir. It does hold small trout.

Louise Creek (Map 19/F5)
Louise Creek drains Lake Louise into the Bow River and is easily accessed by the main road to the town of Lake Louise. Bull and cutthroat trout can be found in the deeper pools.

Luellen Lake (Map 20/B7)
Luellen Lake is accessed by following the Johnston Creek Trail from the Bow Valley Parkway (Highway 1A). A rustic campground is located at the lake, which is populated with a lot of good-sized cutthroat that reach 50 cm/20 inches on occasion.

Marvel Lake (Map 14/G7)
Marvel Lake is accessed by following the Bryant Creek Trail from the south end of Spray Reservoir and then heading southwest on the Wonder Pass Trail. It is 15 km (9.3 miles) from the trailhead to the lake, which means that packing a belly boat is a bit of a proposition (heaven forbid you try carrying a canoe). But because the lake is so big (4 km/2.4 miles long and 75 m/230 ft deep), fishing from the shore often does not produce. If you do try from shore, try around the inflow/outflow streams. Part of the lake is closed to angling year-round. Nearby **Lake Terrapin** does hold cutthroat to 40 cm (16 inches), but the silty water and shallow, weedy area around the shoreline make fishing here almost more hassle than it is worth.

Mistaya Lake (Map 26/A6)
The Mistaya River flows into, then out of Mistaya Lake, which is hidden from the Icefields Parkway (Hwy 93) by a screen of trees. Accessed by trail from Waterfowl Lakes, few people make the trip, preferring to sample the good fishing at Waterfowl Lakes. Mistaya Lake can produce well for cutthroat to 30 cm (12 inches).

Mistaya River (Map 25/G3-26/B7)
The Mistaya River (Mistaya translates as Grizzly) runs from Peyto Lake north through Mistaya Lake, Waterfowl Lakes and into the North Saskatchewan River. The river is never more than a few hundred metres from the Icefields Parkway (Hwy 93) for its entire length. However, the fishing is average in the fall, and even worse during summer.

Moraine Creek (Map 19/G7)
Moraine Creek drains Moraine Lake. It contains brook and cutthroat trout.

Moraine Lake (Map 19/F7)
If you are looking for sheer scenic beauty, it is hard to beat Moraine Lake. Even better, the lake is accessible by road. Anglers, however, will have to take consolation in the scenery, because their chances of pulling one of the few cutthroat or bull trout from the lake are poor, although certainly not non-existent. Fly fishing or spincasting from shore can work, as can fishing from a canoe, which are available for rent at the lake.

Mud Lake (Map 19/G5)
Located near Lake Louise, this small lake is reached by a short trail leading up the Pipestone River from Trans-Canada Highway (Hwy 1) near the Tourist Bureau. The lake can be fished from shore or belly boat for small brook and cutthroat trout. Spincasting seems to produce the best.

Mummy Lake (Map 14/B3)
Mummy Lake is reached by the Shadow Lake Trail up Redearth Creek and then a trail along Pharaoh Creek. An alternative route is to park near the end of Sunshine Road and hike up the Healy Pass Trail. The lake is home to a small population of cutthroat that reach a nice 35 cm (14 inches) in size.

Mystic Lake (Map 20/E7)
Mystic Lake is accessed by either following the Forty Mile Trail from the Mount Norquay Road or the Johnston Creek Trail from the Bow Valley Parkway (Highway 1A) and then walking the Mystic Pass Trail. The lake, which holds bull and cutthroat trout, is surprisingly popular despite the 19 km (11.7 mile) trek in.

Norman Lake (Map 25/E2)
Norman Lake is reached by hiking along the Pinto Lake Trail for about 6 km (3.6 miles) one-way from the Icefields Parkway (Hwy 93). The lake has small brook trout best caught by casting a small lure with bait.

North Saskatchewan River (Maps 25-26, 33-36)
The glacier fed North Saskatchewan River is one of the largest rivers in Alberta. The section found in Banff National Park is not known as a great fishery as the water is silty. For a complete write-up see the Stream Fishing section of this book.

O'Brien Lake (Map 19/G7)
O'Brien Lake is not a big lake, but it holds plenty of good-sized cutthroat, some of which can get up to 50 cm (20 inches).

Owl Lake (Map 14/G7)
Owl Lake is accessed by following the Bryant Creek Trail from the south end of Spray Reservoir and then heading southwest on the Marvel Pass Trail. There are brook trout to 1.5 kg (3 lbs) in the lake as well as smaller cutthroat.

Panther River (Map 20/C4-21/C1)
The headwaters of the Panther River are in Banff National Park. If you wish to fish this section (accessed by a couple long trails off the Bow Valley Parkway or from Bighorn Wildland Recreation Area), you will need a National Park Fishing Permit. For a complete write-up see the Stream Fishing section of this book.

Peyto Lake (Map 26/B7)
Peyto Lake is accessed by a steep 2 km (1.2 mile) one-way trail leading down from the viewpoint on the Icefields Parkway (Hwy 93). The lake holds fair numbers of cutthroat best caught by fly fishing or spincasting from a float tube. If you are fishing from shore, the outlet and inlet streams are the best place to try. Fishing is best just after the ice is off the lake, and again in fall.

Pharaoh Creek (Map 14/B2)
All of Egypt drains into Pharaoh Creek, or at least, all of the Egyptian-themed lakes found south of Sunshine Village. The creek holds small cutthroat and brook trout.

Pharaoh Lake (Map 14/B3)
Pharaoh Lake is reached by the Shadow Lake Trail up Redearth Creek and then a trail along Pharaoh Creek. An alternative route is to park near the end of Sunshine Road and hike up the Healy Pass Trail. The lake holds some cutthroat trout to 30 cm (12 inches).

Pipestone River (Map 19/F1-G5)
Pipestone River flows in a southern direction into the Bow River near Lake Louise. The Pipestone River Trail leads from the Trans-Canada Highway (Hwy 1) near the Tourist Bureau to the headwaters offering a chance to test your luck for the cutthroat trout to 30 cm (12 inches) and bull trout to 50 cm (20 inches). The best place to fish is in the large pools downstream from the canyon.

Ptarmigan Lake (Map 20/A4)
Ptarmigan Lake is reached by the Skoki Valley Trail from the Lake Louise Ski Area and has a few small brook and cutthroat trout. The lake is prone to high winds, making fishing, especially fly fishing, difficult. The lake is usually not ice-free until July.

Rainbow Lake (Map 20/E6)
A small lake set in a bowl just north of the Forty Mile Summit, Rainbow Lake contains lots of rainbow trout, some of which will get to 1.5 kg (3 lbs). Access to the lake is via a difficult 30 km (19 mile) hike up the Forty Mile Trail from the top of Mount Norquay Road or by a 40 km (25 mile) hike up the Cascade Fire Road from Lake Minnewanka.

Red Deer Lakes (Map 20/A3)
The two lakes that make up the Red Deer Lakes are accessed by long trail up the Red Deer River or by trails to the south and west. The eastern most lake has brook trout whereas the western most lake has brook and cutthroat trout. Both lakes are fairly shallow and subject to winterkill.

Redearth Creek (Map 14/B2-D2)
Redearth Creek drains into the Bow River near the warden cabin on Redearth Creek Road. The creek contains brook, bull, cutthroat and rainbow trout with the best fishing being in the canyon near the estuary.

Redoubt Lake (Map 20/A4)
Redoubt Lake is reached by trails leading up Baker Creek and Redoubt Creek from the Bow Valley Parkway (Highway 1A). The lake has small cutthroat trout and mostly small brook trout, although occasionally you will come across a monster (to 60 cm/24 inches). The lake is usually covered by ice until July.

Rockbound Lake (Map 20/B7)
Rockbound Lake is reached by trail up Silverton Creek from the junction of the Trans-Canada Highway (Highway 1) and the Bow Valley Parkway (Highway 1A). The trail climbs steeply up to the lake, which holds some good-sized brook trout and cutthroat.

Sawback Lake (Map 20/E7)
Sawback Lake is reached by a difficult 30 km (19 mile) hike up the Forty Mile Trail from the top of Mount Norquay Road or by a 40 km (25 mile) hike up the Cascade Fire Road from Lake Minnewanka. A rustic campground is at the lake. For those willing to put in the effort, the lake has cutthroat to 2 kg (4 lbs).

Scarab Lake (Map 14/B3)
Scarab is reached by the Shadow Lake Trail up Redearth Creek and then a trail along Pharaoh Creek. An alternative route is to park near the end of Sunshine Road and hike up the Healy Pass Trail. You will find a few cutthroat trout to 1.5 kg (3 lbs).

Shadow Lake (Map 14/B2)
The shadow cast on Shadow Lake falls from Mount Ball, which towers above the lake. Some anglers might argue that the shadow is the result of the fact that this lake does not hold as many fish are others in the area. Access to the lake is via a 14 km (8.6 mile) hike along the Shadow Lake Trail. It contains good-sized cutthroat, brook and rainbow trout caught by spincasting, bait fishing or fly fishing from shore or a belly boat.

Siffleur River (Map 26/D3-E7)
The headwaters of the Siffleur are reachable by trail. In fact, the entire river is accessible by trail, but only the portion within Banff is open to fishing (although none of its tributaries are). It is a pretty river, with a lot of small bull trout and whitefish. For many, the quality of fishing is not worth the long hike in along the Dolomite Pass Trail

Skoki Lakes (Map 20/A4)
Of the two Skoki Lakes, only Myosotis Lake (the lower lake) has fish in it. But the fishing is slow, and often fruitless as there are only a few rainbow left in the lake. While not above treeline, Myosotis Lake has an open shore, with lots of casting room.

Smith Lake (Map 14/B1)
Smith Lake is reached by a short trail (1 km one-way) leading south of the junction of Highway 1 and Highway 93. It contains cutthroat and brook trout. The lake was once known for large cutthroat, but they have mostly been fished out.

Stony Creek (Map 20/G6)
Stony Creek is a tributary of the Cascade River. There is a backcountry campsite at the confluence, which is about a 15 km (9 mile) trip up the Cascade Fire Road on foot or by bike. The Dormar Pass Trail provides access to the upper reaches of the creek.

Sundance Creek (Map 14/G2)
This creek flows into the Bow River just west of the Banff townsite. The creek has a series of beaver dams that hold good numbers of brook trout. The creek is best accessed by the Cave and Basin Road from Banff.

Taylor Lake (Map 19/G7)
The cutthroat trout that populate the waters of Taylor Lake average 30 cm (12 inches) in size. It is a 6 km (3.6 mile) hike to the lake from the Trans-Canada Highway (Hwy 1).

Tower Lake (Map 20/B7)
A small lake on the way to Rockbound Lake, Tower Lake holds a small population of small cutthroat.

Twin Lakes (Map 14/A1)
These two small lakes are best reached by trail from Highway 93. An alternate route is to park next to the Altrude Creek Bridge near the junction of

Highway 1 and 93 and hike the steep trail to the two lakes. Both lakes have small cutthroat with the lower lake producing the most fish. Spincasting, bait fishing or fly fishing from shore or a belly boat works. A rustic campsite is found at the north end of the upper lake.

Two Jack Lake (Map 15/A1)
This small lake is located just south of Lake Minnewanka and has cutthroat, lake and rainbow trout as well as rocky mountain whitefish. Spincasting and fly fishing in the spring and fall is your best bet. The lake is home to a campground and sees heavy fishing pressure.

Vermilon Lakes (Map 14/F2)
In the Bow Valley just west of Banff, there are a series of three small, shallow lakes that offer slow fishing for small rainbow, and brook trout. The lakes are reached by Vermilon Lakes Drive.

Vista Lakes (Map 14/A1)
These small hike-in lakes are reached by the Arnica Lake Trail from Highway 93. The lakes have small cutthroat that can be caught by spincasting, bait fishing or fly fishing from shore or a belly boat.

Waterfowl Lakes (Map 26/A6)
These two lakes—actually, they are widenings of the Mistaya River caused by glacial silt—see a lot of fishing pressure, due in no small part to the large campground here. The lakes hold cutthroat and brook trout to 30 cm (12 inches).

Jasper National Park
The southeastern corner of Jasper National Park is caught on Map 32. For more information on fishing in Jasper, check out the Backroad Mapbook for Central Alberta.

Brazeau Lake (Map 32/C4)
Brazeau Lake is found within the southern reaches of Jasper National Park and is accessed by a long hike along the Nigel Creek Trail. Overall, the hike (one-way) from Sunwapta Pass off the Icefields Parkway (Hwy 93) is about 19 km (11.8 miles). A number of wilderness campsites are located near the lake, including Brazeau Lake Campsite at the southeastern end of the lake. The lake contains a fair number of small rainbow best taken by spincasting or fly fishing.

Waterton National Park
Tucked in the southwest corner of the province (and this book), Waterton National Park is home to a good selection of lakes and streams to sample. Many of the smaller lakes have limited shore fishing options so packing in a belly boat or canoe is a worthwhile endeavor.

Akamina Lake (Map 2/E7)
Also known as Little Cameron Lake, this pretty lake is a 0.5 km hike from the Cameron Lake parking lot. Like Cameron Lake, Akamina Lake holds brook and rainbow trout, both to 30 cm (12 inches). Shore fishing is difficult, as shallows extend far out from shore.

Alderson Lake (Map 2/F7)
This tiny lake is accessed off the Carthew Summit Trail, between Cameron Falls and Cameron Lake. The lake contains small cutthroat that can be caught by spincasting, fly fishing or bait fishing. Packing in a belly boat is helpful, although shore fishing is possible.

Belly River (Map 3/C7)
The short stretch of this river that flows through Waterton National Park is easily accessed by the Chief Mountain Highway (Hwy 6). For a complete write-up see the stream fishing section of this book.

Bertha Lake (Map 2/G7)
Containing good numbers of small rainbow, this small lake is located in a hanging valley reached by a steep trail from Cameron Falls in Waterton National Park. There are primitive campsites at the north and south end of the lake. Both shore fishing and casting from a belly boat both produce, although the shore is brushy in places.

Blackiston Creek (Maps 2/D6-3/A4)
Blackiston Creek contains a few brook, brown, bull, cutthroat and rainbow trout as well as rocky mountain whitefish. Your best bet is below the Crandell Campsite.

Buffalo Creek Ponds (Map 3/A6)
Located near the Bison Paddock, just off Highway 6, these small Beaver Ponds on Buffalo Creek are difficult to fish due to the brushy shoreline. Ardent anglers will find a few rainbow and brook trout.

Cameron Creek (Map 2/E7-G7)
This creek, which drains into the north end of Upper Waterton Lake, has rainbow and brook trout. Since the road parallels the creek, good access is provided along the entire 16 km (9.9 mile) creek, although accessing some canyons is difficult and dangerous to fish.

Cameron Lake (Map 2/E7)
This lake is located on the BC/Montana border, and is reached by following the Akamina Parkway to its end. The lake holds rainbow and brook trout, both to 1.5 kg (3 lbs), that are best caught by fly fishing/ spincasting in the spring or ice fishing in the winter. Shore fishing is not productive (although you can try near the outflow stream), so it is best to bring a float tube or canoe, and troll. The lake is usually icebound into June.

Carthew Creek (Map 2/G7)
The creek has brook, bull, cutthroat and rainbow trout as well as rocky mountain whitefish. It drains into Cameron Creek near the north end of the Upper Waterton Lake.

Carthew Lakes (Map 2/G7)
These tiny lakes are accessed along the Carthew Summit Trail from Cameron Falls or from Cameron Lake. They are found 2 km west of Alderson Lake, in a high alpine basin. The lakes contain small cutthroat that can be caught by spincasting, fly fishing or bait fishing. Packing in a belly boat is helpful, but shore fishing is easy at these alpine lakes, although high winds can hamper casting. The middle lake offers the best fishing.

Crandell Lake (Map 2/G6)
It is a short hike to this tiny lake, from either the Red Rock Parkway (2 km) or the Akamina Parkway (1 km). The lake offers fair spincasting and fly fishing for small brook and rainbow trout, especially early in the season.

Crypt Lake (Map 3/A7)
Located just north of the USA border, this tiny lake is reached by an 8.1 km (5 mile) one-way trail leading up Hellroaring Creek to its headwaters. Since

the trailhead requires a boat across Waterton Lake, and there is no camping at the lake, you will have to hike in, fish, and hike out in a day. Given the remote access, fishing for cutthroat (30-40 cm/12-14 inches) is good throughout the late spring and into the fall. The water is so clear you can see the fish. Then again, they can see you, and are easily spooked. Spincasting and fly fishing from shore or a belly boat works. The lake is not usually ice-free until July.

Goat Lake (Map 2/E5)
Goat Lake is a small lake found a 7 km (4.3 mile) hike from the Red Rock Canyon Parking Lot. The lake holds plenty of small, but shy cutthroat. The water is clear, which helps make the fish spooky.

Lineham Lakes (Map 2/E7)
A series of three tiny lakes, reached by a very steep—and sometimes perilous—trail up Lineham Creek from the Akamina Parkway, the Lineham Lakes are some of the prettiest lakes you will ever see. And because of the rough access, few anglers ever go, which means the fishing is pretty hot, too. The lakes hold plenty of small cutthroat caught by spincasting, fly fishing or bait fishing. Packing in a belly boat is helpful, but you can still shore fish. The lakes are often iced up until mid July.

Lone Lake (Map 2/D6)
Lone Lake is a hike-in lake found near the BC border. The tiny lake is reached by a 13 km (8 mile) one-way hike beginning at Red Rock Canyon. The lake contains small cutthroat, but the forested shoreline makes shore fishing difficult, although not impossible. Packing in a belly boat is helpful.

Maskinonge Lake (Map 3/A6)
This lake is found at the junction of Highway 5 and 6 and is actually a large marshy widening of Waterton River. The lake is only about 1 m (3 feet) deep, but still holds northern pike to 6 kg (13 lbs). For best results, try spincasting the shallows near the inflow and outflow areas in spring. Surprisingly, fly fishing can produce well, too.

Rowe Lakes (Map 2/E7)
There are three lakes that make up this cluster. Fishing the lower lake for brook trout is spotty at best, and non-existent in the upper lakes.

Twin Lakes (Map 2/D6)
Located an 11 km (6.9 mile) hike from the Red Rock Canyon Parking Lot, these two small lakes are perfect fly fishing lakes. They hold plenty of small brook trout, although the fish in the Upper Lake are usually a bit bigger. The Upper Lake also holds a few rainbow to 40 cm (15 inches).

Upper Waterton River (Map 3/A6)
The upper section of Waterton River (just inside the park border) has some great fishing, especially the 2 km (1 mile) stretch between the middle and lower lake. There are some pike near Maskinonge Lake, but it is better known for bull, cutthroat and rainbow trout, which grow to 1 kg (2 lbs) in size. There are also rocky mountain whitefish that can grow to 1 kg (2 lbs). The river is open to angling year-round.

Waterton Lakes (Map 2/D4, 3/A4)
Perhaps the most popular fishing destinations in the park, there are three lakes: Upper, Middle and Lower Waterton Lakes. The Upper and Middle lakes are renowned for their excellent lake trout fishing. Many of the lake trout exceed 9 kg (20 lbs), and up to 1.2 metres (4 feet) long. It is best to fish near the season opening in May or again into late July through to the fall. Most fishermen troll big Flatfish, Rapalas or Kwikfish on a deep troll using a downrigger. Jigging with such lures as Buzz Bombs seems to be effective as well. In terms of the fishing depth, you can catch the lake trout anywhere from right under the surface (in spring and fall) all the way to the bottom (in summer) so a depth sounder would be helpful and fishing your lines at various depths would also be of assistance. The lakes also hold rainbow (to 3 kg/6 lbs), cutthroat (to 1.5 kg/3 lbs), brookies (to 2.5 kg/5 lbs), bull trout (to 5 kg/11 lbs) and rocky mountain whitefish (to 1.5 kg/3 lbs). The Lower Lake (also known as Knight's Lake) is shallower than the other two, and there are fewer (and smaller) lake trout. However, the Lower Lake does hold northern pike. It is possible to fish all three lakes from shore, especially around inlet creeks. Boaters should be wary that the Waterton Lakes are subject to significant winds and very choppy water.

Backroad Attractions

Forming the backbone for backcountry travel in Southwestern Alberta is the Forestry Trunk Road. For some strange reason, the Ministry of Highways changed the road numbering of the northern part of this secondary road to 734. Now the Forestry Trunk Road has three different numbering systems to confuse backroad travellers. Regardless, this road offers a great variety of activities and trails to explore.

Highway travellers will also find several highways that will rival the scenic and recreational values of any in the world. The Icefields Parkway through Banff hardly needs any introduction while many consider the David Thompson Highway (Highway 11) to be an outdoor recreationists dream highway. Not to be outdone is the Crowsnest Highway (Highway 3), which bisects the southern portion of our mapbook. This is another hotspot for outdoor recreation, tinged with a historical flavour.

Branching from the Forestry Trunk and the highways are roads of all shapes and sizes. Many of these can be driven by vehicle, many cannot. Those that cannot are often converted to trails. There are off-highway vehicle areas (unheard of in a national park), cross-country ski systems, hiking, biking and horseback trails as well as unmarked routes leading to spectacular vistas. Southwestern Alberta has a history of resource extraction activity, and many of the trails follow old exploration and logging roads, seismic lines and animal paths. Although they usually provide easy travel, the routes can be somewhat confusing and hard to follow as they interweave with other old roads and trails.

Cars or RV's can travel many of the secondary roads, most of which are paved or hard packed gravel. The paved roads are shown on the maps as thicker black lines with a white fill. Thicker black lines mark the better gravel or main roads. Branching from the main roads are side roads and trails. These routes, marked by thinner black lines and dashed lines on our maps, should be left to the off-road enthusiasts and trail users.

Although we have done our best to classify the road systems on our maps, road and trail conditions can change very quickly. Weather, the status of road systems and the degree of maintenance can all affect the road systems. During industrial hours (6am to 6pm) or at times of extreme fire hazard, logging and rural roads may be closed to the public. Other roads may be gated to protect equipment in the area. Add in low or no road maintenance in some areas and backroad travellers better pay attention.

Our website, http://www.backroadmapbooks.com/bmupdates.htm, has updates on access issues, as well as any new or changed information. If you try to go somewhere and find that things have changed from what we've written, please, send us an email and let us know. As always, we encourage comments, stories and pictures from our readers. Please drop us a line.

BACKROAD TIPS

GENERAL TRAVEL:

- AS THE POPULARITY OF BACKCOUNTRY TRAVEL INCREASES, THERE IS AN EVEN GREATER RESPONSIBILITY TO TAKE CARE OF THE AREAS WE LOVE, BE SURE TO TAKE ALL GARBAGE WITH YOU AND LEAVE ONLY FOOTPRINTS.

- IF YOU PLAN TO TRAVEL THROUGH REMOTE AREAS IT IS IMPERATIVE THAT YOU LEAVE A DETAILED ITINERARY WITH FRIENDS OR FAMILY

- COLD TEMPERATURES, WETNESS OR EVEN WIND CHILL CAN CAUSE HYPOTHERMIA. WETNESS IS PERHAPS ONE OF THE MOST UNDERESTIMATED CAUSES OF HYPOTHERMIA.

DRIVING BACKROADS:

BE CAREFUL WHEN TRAVELING THESE ROADS, AND FOLLOW THESE SIMPLE SAFETY GUIDELINES:

- KEEP YOUR HEADLIGHTS ON AT ALL TIME.

- DRIVE AT OR UNDER THE SPEED LIMIT. TRAVEL SLOWER WHEN THE ROADS ARE WET, OR WHEN YOU KNOW THERE IS A GOOD CHANCE OF ENCOUNTERING AN INDUSTRIAL VEHICLE.

- FOLLOW TRUCKS AT A SAFE DISTANCE. DO NOT PASS UNLESS YOU ARE SURE YOU CAN MAKE IT. EVEN THEN, IT IS NOT A GOOD IDEA.

- SLOW DOWN WHEN MEETING OTHER VEHICLES. THIS WILL HELP SAVE YOUR WINDSHIELD, AT THE VERY LEAST. IF YOU ARE MEETING A LOADED LOGGING TRUCK, PULL OVER TO THE SHOULDER AND STOP.

- AVOID ACTIVE LOGGING AREAS.

- NEVER DRIVE OFF HIGHWAY VEHICLES LIKE ATVs AND DIRT BIKES ON PAVED ROADS OR MAIN LOGGING ROADS.

Paddling Routes
(Lake and River Paddling)

The mountains of Southwestern Alberta are known for their natural beauty and pristine wilderness. What better way to explore the peace and tranquility of the mountains than by paddling one of the small wilderness lakes or a meandering river? On the other hand, whitewater paddlers will find spectacular runs that rival any whitewater opportunities in the world.

As the mountains turn to foothills and then to prairies, there are still paddling opportunities. The rivers are slower moving, and the lakes are often home to numerous birds and other wildlife.

Lake Paddling

There are many, many lakes in Southwest Alberta. While not all of them lend themselves to easy paddling, (some are shallow and reedy, some are over a day's walk from the nearest road) almost all of them can be paddled. What follows is just a handful of the many lakes in the area that lend themselves to easy paddling.

Abraham Lake (Map 26/C2–33/E5)
Abraham Lake is a big lake at the edge of the mountains, and, like most big mountain lakes, it is subject to strong winds, especially during the middle of the day. The lake also has a number of shallow rock ledges that can cause difficulty. However, it is a beautiful lake that is easily accessed off Highway 11.

Barrier Lake (Map 15/F4)
Barrier Lake is located next to Highway 40 just south of the Bow Valley Provincial Park. There is a boat launch at the Barrier Lake day use area that is shared with anglers. This is a man made lake, so watch out for submerged hazards.

Beauvais Lake (Map 2/E1)
Set in the foothills near Pincher Creek, Beauvais Lake Provincial Park is a popular destination with campers, swimmers, anglers and paddlers. The lake is 3 km (1.8 miles) long and is easily circumnavigated in a few hours' easy paddle. There is a boat launch and dock near the campground.

Beaver Mines Lake (Map 2/B2)
Set beneath the imposing Table Mountain, this small lake is easily circumnavigated in a few hours. There is a 12 km/h speed limit for powerboats on the lake, which keeps their wake down for paddlers. There is a boat launch and dock, as well as camping.

Burnstick Lake (Map 29/A3)
Located off Secondary Highway 584, Burnstick Lake is a fairly large lake that is subject to strong winds. The lake is also home to an abundance of bulrushes and water lilies. This is a popular bird watching area and there is a campground at the east end of the lake.

Cameron Lake (Map 2/E7)
Located in Waterton National Park, this small lake is s subject to high winds, but is small and relatively sheltered. Grizzly bears are common sights along the lakes southern end (which is actually in Montana). There are canoe rentals at the lake.

Chain Lakes (Map 8/C3)
Chain Lakes Provincial Park rests along the southeast side of the lake and offers paddlers and anglers a boat launch and dock. The lakes are long and narrow, and are usually calm enough to paddle.

Chinook (Allison Reservoir) Lake (Map 4/E4)
Easily accessed by the Allison Creek Road off Highway 3 northwest of Coleman, this small lake is open to canoes, kayaks and small powerboats. There is a boat launch, camping area and dock.

Cow Lake (Map 35/G6)
This large lake is accessed by Secondary Highway 752 southwest of Rocky Mountain House. It is a fairly shallow lake, with a campground and boat launch at its west end.

Crimson Lake (Map 35/G3)
Crimson Lake forms the hub of the popular Crimson Lake Provincial Park. As you would expect in a provincial park, there are lots of amenities. The lake can be circumnavigated in a day, and is a good place for bird watching.

Glenmore Reservoir (Map 17/D5)
The Calgary Canoe Club uses this reservoir for training. There are canoe rentals at the reservoir and the best access is south on 24 Street S.W. from Glenmore Trail (Highway 8).

Jackfish Lake (Map 34/G2)
This small lake (2.4 square km) is located next to Highway 11 and is a popular fishing lake. There is a boat launch for paddlers to use.

Kananaskis Lakes (Map 10/E3)
Found in the heart of the Peter Lougheed Provincial Park, the two Kananaskis Lakes are accessible by paved road, and both have good boat launches. The Lower Kananaskis Lake is more exposed and subject to higher winds. Canoeists might want to stick to the upper lake, but kayakers should have no trouble. Watch out for submerged trees and rocks.

Keiver's Lake (Map 24/D1)
Keiver's Lake is a small lake located off Secondary Highways 583 and 806. The lake sports a recreation site, and, while there is no developed launch, it is possible to hand launch a canoe.

Lake Louise (Map 19/F5)
Arguably one of the best-known lakes in the province, let alone the country, Lake Louise is known for its turquoise waters and dramatic mountain scenery. Chateau Lake Louise rents canoes and the lake can be circumnavigated in a few hours.

Lees Lake (Map 5/B7)
This small lake is found on the east side of Secondary Highway 507 about 3 km (1.8 miles) south of Highway 3. It offers opportunities for bird watching and fishing. There is a boat launch, but paddlers will be happy to know powerboats are limited to 5km/h.

Lower Waterton Lake/Maskinoge Lake (Map 3/A6)
While the other two Waterton Lakes are deep and windy and best left to big powerboats, Lower Waterton Lake is a great place to explore by canoe. A shallow channel (sometimes too shallow) connects this lake with Maskinoge Lake. Both lakes are shallow and warm, with lots of reeds around the edges that make them good bird watching areas.

Mitchell Lake (Map 35/G7)
Mitchell Lake is accessed by Strubble Road and is home of the Mitchell Lake Recreation Area, a camping and day-use facility. There is no boat launch, but hand launching a canoe or kayak is easily accomplished. Anglers will find that the lake is stocked annually with rainbow.

Moraine Lake (Map 19/F7)
If you are looking for sheer scenic beauty, it's hard to beat Moraine Lake. The lake is well sheltered by a stand of towering mountains, and doesn't get too rough, although storms can blow up quickly in the high mountains. There are canoe rentals at the lake, which is accessed by a paved road.

Outpost Lake (Map 3/F7)
Located near the Canada/USA border, this smallish lake is a good place to paddle. There is a boat launch, and plenty of birds to watch.

Paine Lake (Map 3/C6)
This lake, found just east of Waterton National Park on Highway 5 (then south on a backroad) offers good paddling and lots of bird watching opportunities. There is a boat launch and camping at the Paine Lake Recreation Area. Watch out for powerboats.

Pepper's Lake (Map 27/F2)

Pepper's Lake is a small lake located just off the Forestry Trunk Road and within eyeshot of the Rocky Mountains. It is a pretty lake to paddle but most people who make the trip come to fish. There is a campground on the lake as well as several trails and cutlines in the area to explore.

Sibbald Lake (Map 16/B4)

Sibbald Lake is a small shallow, clear lake. Despite its size, the lake is rarely rough and offers good canoeing.

River Paddling

Below we have described the major river routes throughout Southwest Alberta. For each river, we have included the put-in and take-out locations. The length of each run, the season and general comments are also provided. To grade the rivers, we have used a modified version of the International River Classification System, popularized by Stuart Smith. The grade of a route describes the overall difficulty of a river, while specific features are given the designation class. A river might be classified as Grade II, but there might be a waterfall that should only be run by expert kayakers. In this case, the river would be described as a Grade II run, with a class IV waterfall.

In addition, some runs may be given two grading numbers. This is due to a couple factors. The first is that not everyone agrees on the rating of a river. More commonly, though, the difficulty of a river varies with the amount of water flowing. So a river that merrily babbles along as a Grade II paddle in late summer may be a lot harder to deal with in spring run-off. So, when a run is rated Grade II/III, most of the times it means that in higher water, the run is more difficult.

Grade I: Novices in open canoes or kayaks. Riffles and small waves with virtually no obstruction.

Grade II: Intermediate paddlers. Maneuvering is required. Medium rapids, channels can be clearly spotted without scouting.

Grade/Class III: Advanced Paddlers. Rapids can swamp open canoes. Waves are unpredictable. Scouting should be done before approach. Skilled maneuvering is required.

Grade/Class IV: Expert paddlers; closed canoes and kayaks only. Long, challenging rapids with obstructions requiring maneuvering. Eskimo roll ability is recommended. Good swimming skills. Scouting required.

Grade/Class V: Professional Paddlers; closed canoes or kayaks only. Scouting always required. Long, violent rapids through narrow routes with obstructions. Eskimo roll ability essential. Errors can be fatal.

Please remember that river conditions are always subject to change and advanced scouting is essential. The information in this book is only intended to give you general information on the particular river you are interested in. You should always obtain more details from a local merchant or expert before heading out on your adventure. A good resource is Stuart Smith's Canadian Rockies Whitewater.

Belly River (Map 3)

The Belly River begins in Waterton National Park and leads in a northeast direction past the Blood Indian Reserve and east of our maps. The best paddling is in the foothills in the national park and just north of its boundaries.

Put-in: Highway 6 Bridge (Map 3/C7)

Take-out: Highway 800 Bridge (Map 3/D4)

This is a 30 km (18.6 mile/5–6 hour) Grade II run that begins in Waterton National Park and cuts across country to highway 800. The first part of the paddle leading to the Highway 5 bridge is more for the scenery than the challenge. However, there are some tight corners with rapids and logjams waiting for the unsuspecting person. Below the Highway 5 bridge, the river narrows and picks up velocity creating plenty of whitewater and rapids for 6-7 km. Eventually, the river mellows out over the final 4 km to the take-out.

Put-in: Highway 800 Bridge (Map 3/D4)

Take-out: Highway 505 Bridge (Map 3/F2)

This section of the Belly River is an easy 30 km (18.6 mile/5–6 hour) Grade II early season (May-June) paddle. It is mostly an easy paddle with few rapids and obstacles as the river passes through prairie farmland. A portage around the weir on the Waterton Reservoir outflow (Map 3/E3) is necessary.

Bighorn River (Map 33/E4)

From Crescent Falls, this paddle stretches 6 km (3.7 miles/3.5–5 hours) to Highway 11. The paddle is a tough Grade III route in low water and Grade IV in high water. It leads through a V-shaped canyon with one waterfall that must be portaged and five others that can be paddled, but only by experienced kayakers.

Bow River (Maps 14-17, 19-20)

The Bow River is a large volume river draining in an eastward direction from Banff National Park. Most of the river can be paddled by canoe without much unexpected danger. The dramatic scenery in the Bow River Valley makes paddling the river truly a lasting experience.

Put-in: Lake Louise (Map 19/G5)

Take-out: Redearth Creek Picnic Site (Map 14/D1)

This section starts from the bridge over the Bow River about 3 km (1.8 miles) south of the Lake Louise Interchange on the Trans-Canada Highway. This Grade II paddle takes you 40 km (24.9 miles) to the Redearth Creek Picnic Area. It is a fast flowing stretch of water with two short rapids, plenty of standing waves and an abundance of back eddies. At the put-in, there are some Class II rapids, which can be avoided by putting your canoe/kayak in about 1 km downstream from the bridge. The river shifts frequently throughout its course and there is the occasional sweeper waiting around a corner to overturn or injure an unsuspecting paddler. The water level remains high enough to paddle most of the year because the river is glacier fed. Mount Temple, which looms to the east, offers a spectacular backdrop.

Put-in: Redearth Creek Picnic Site (Map 14/D1)

Take-out: Banff Townsite (Map 14/G2)

Below the Redearth Creek Picnic Site, the Bow River becomes more exciting as it passes through the Redearth Creek Rapids, which are rated Class II (Class III at low water), and should be scouted. Once through these rapids, the river slows down and begins to braid. You must take-out before you hit Bow Falls, which should not be attempted.

Put-in: Below Bow Falls (Map 14/G2)

Take-out: Canmore (Map 15/B3)

This section of the Bow is a gentle Grade II paddle. The Trans-Canada Highway parallels the river all the way.

Put-in: Bear's Paw Dam (Map 17/B3)

Take-out: Calgary Zoo (Map 17/F4)

Give yourself about five hours to complete this easy 21 km (13 mile) paddle. To reach the put-in, drive past Bowness and go to the end of the barricaded road, which takes off to the west. The paddle takes you through the heart of Calgary and away from the crowded shoreline. As you pass by a number of parks, you can see numerous fishermen lining the shores as well as the waterfowl that is common to the area.

Burnt Timber Creek (Map 21/E2–F1)

Burnt Timber Creek offers a 10 km (6.2 mile/1.5–2 hour) Grade II paddle from the Burnt Timber Creek Bridge on the Forestry Trunk Road to the last bridge over Stud Creek on the Stud Creek Road. The run is a small volume paddle highlighted by many boulders, bends and small drops.

Carbondale River (Map 1/G1–5/A7)

Carbondale River is a small foothill river flowing into the Castle River. From the bridge near the Lost Creek confluence to the junction with the Castle River is a Grade II+/III paddle extending some 13 km (8 miles/3–4 hours). Since the channel is quite constricted, there are some tight corners and obstacles to maneuver around. The run begins with several Class II/II+ rapids created by a series of rock ledges. Then, several kilometres along the run are some tough Class III/IV ledges and drops found in a small rock-faced canyon. The river breaks out of the canyon, but continues through a narrow valley with numerous Class II rapids all the way to the confluence with the Castle River.

Castle River (Maps 2, 5)

Castle River is a medium sized river that drains an area north of Waterton National Park into the Oldman River. The section of the river downstream of the West Castle River confluence has some challenging stretches of whitewater worth trying:

Put-in: Highway 774 Bridge (Map 2/A1)

Take-out: Red Castle Falls Recreation Area (Map 2/A1)

This section of the Castle is a challenging 7 km (4.3 mile/2 hour) Grade II/II+ paddle culminating above the falls. The river offers numerous Class II rapids created by sharp corners, boulder gardens and small rock ledges.

Put-in: Red Castle Falls Recreation Area (Map 2/A1)

Take-out: Riverside Ranch (Map 5/D7)

This 24 km (5-6 hour) section is rated Grade II paddle in low water and Grade III in high water. The paddle begins at the Red Castle Falls Recreation Area below the Class IV/V falls (or above the falls if you dare plunge the 2 m/6 ft into a boiling hole). Downstream from the falls is a 4 km (2.4 mile) long Class II/III whitewater section created by numerous ledges and channel constrictions guaranteed to challenge even the best paddlers. From there, the river drains into an open valley with the occasional set of Class II rapids before entering a Grade II/III canyon. You can shorten the paddle by stopping at the Secondary Highway 507 bridge. You can also take out above the canyon. The ranch is private property, and you will need permission to cross the land.

Put-in: Riverside Ranch (Map 5/D7)

Take-out: Secondary Highway 510 bridge (Map 5/E5)

This is a 11 km (3-4 hour) Grade II paddle beginning at the bridge on the Riverside Ranch Road to the east of Secondary Highway 507. The river flows into an open valley, offering the occasional Class II/II+ rapids created by some rock ledges and constricted channels. If you are looking for more excitement, or if you are too shy to ask for permission to put in at Riverside Ranch (it is private land, so do ask), you can put in above the canyon. This will add 1 km to the trip, as well as an exciting grade II+/III+ section with some class III/IV+ rapids.

Clearwater River (Maps 27, 28, 29, 38)

The Clearwater River is a medium sized river that drains from Banff National Park into the North Saskatchewan River at Rocky Mountain House. There are three different paddling routes to choose from.

Put-in: Elk Creek Recreation Area (Map 27/G2)

Take-out: Cutoff Creek (Map 28/A3)

This section of the Clearwater River is a 21 km (4 hour) Grade II paddle that gets quite braided as it flows through the foothills. There are some small rapids, sweepers and logjams along the run, particularly around the corners. Towards the end of the run, the river drains into a single channel with the occasional small rapid.

Put-in: Cutoff Creek (Map 28/A3)

Take-out: Forestry Trunk Road Bridge (Map 28/D4)

Paddlers looking to cherry pick the exciting bits of this run may wish to take-out at the Seven Mile Recreation area, 8 km (5.6 miles) from the put-in. The first half-dozen or so kilometres offer a number of exciting, though not terribly challenging Class II features. But the majority of this run is an easy float to the take-out, 20 km (12.4 miles) from where you put-in. It will take about an hour to get to the Seven Mile Recreation Area, and about three to get to the Forestry Trunk Road Bridge.

Put-in: Forestry Trunk Road Bridge (Map 28/D4)

Take-out: Highway 54 Bridge (Map 29/D2)

There are few noteworthy features on this Grade I/II section of the river, but beginner paddlers might want to give this 37 km (23 mile/6–8 hour) section of the Clearwater a pass. Why? Deadwood. This section of the river has a number of dangerous sweepers and logjams. Some of these logjams block the entire river, and paddlers will have to portage around.

Cline River Area (Maps 25, 26, 32, 33)

Highway 11 crosses the Cline just before the river flows into Abraham Lake, and that's it for road access. Paddlers looking to experience some challenging paddling through remote wilderness terrain had better be prepared to put a bit of work into getting to the put-in.

Put-in: Above the Coral Creek Canyon (Map 33/B7)

Take-out: Highway 11 Bridge (Map 33/C7)

Coral Creek Canyon is the most popular section of the Cline, if only because it is the easiest accessible run on the river. You will have to hike up about 3 km (1.8 miles) to the top of the run, and then paddle down through a very narrow, steep-walled canyon leading to the Cline River and the take-out at the bridge on Highway 11. Sweepers and other debris often block the route, so it is imperative that the whole creek is scouted before attempting this Grade IV route. The Coral Creek Trail provides access up the creek to the start. Most people take at least three hours to paddle this section, which attests to the difficulty of the route.

Put-in: Pinto Lake Canyon ((Map 25/F1)

Take-out: Highway 11 Bridge (Map 33/C7)

This entire Cline is seldom paddled because of the 10 km (6.2 mile) carry up and over Sunset Pass to Pinto Lake. If the hike does not discourage you, then be prepared for a 30 km (2–3 day) Grade III/IV paddle, with nearly continuous rapids. Near the end at the Highway 11 bridge, the Coral Creek Canyon (see above) provides the biggest challenge and is rated Grade IV/V. The canyon can be portaged around.

Crowsnest River (Maps 4, 5)

Flowing east from Crowsnest Lake, this medium size river has some good, scenic paddling routes before the river reaches the Oldman River:

Put-in: Frank Lake (Map 5/A6)

Take-out: Hillcrest Mine Road (Map 5/A6)

This short, 1.5 km (1 mile) section of the Crowsnest is a delightfully challenging Grade III/IV paddle. The route offers continuous rapids with two very difficult stretches (Class III/IV and Class IV/V) created by uninviting boulder fields.

Put-in: Hillcrest Mine Road (Map 5/A6)

Take-out: Lundbreck Falls (Map 5/C6)

Below the Hillcrest Mine Road, the Crowsnest loses some of its excitement. This section is a 21 km (13 mile/4–5 hour) Grade II route. The paddle ends at the Lundbreck Falls Campground, or rather, just upstream of the campground, as the campground itself is below the falls, and you really don't want to paddle over the falls. In the upper reaches, some sweepers and logjams challenge paddlers whereas the middle section provides entertaining Class I/II rapids around the bends in the river. Towards the take-out, the river slows considerably, and is an easy paddle to the take-out.

Put-in: Lundbreck Falls (Map 5/C6)

Take-out: Highway 3 bridge (Map 5/C6)

If you are a beginner paddler looking to cut your teeth on something fairly easy (but with some rapids), try this short, 4 km (2.4 mile/1.5 hour) Grade II paddle. Beginning below the falls, the river runs through a bedrock area for a few kilometres. The rock creates some nice Class II ledges and rapids that will provide the paddler some excitement.

Elbow River (Maps 11, 16)

Highways 66 and 22 follow the Elbow River for part of its length. About 35 km (22 miles) of the river is paddleable, and is a mixture of flat water, rapids and some drops. The put-in and take-out area depends on how far you want to paddle. Simply pick your parking spots next to the highways or try one of these known routes:

Put-in: Cobble Flats Recreation Area (Map 11/B1)

Take-out: Beaver Flats Recreation Area (Map 16/B7)

The start of this run begins on a braided section of the river, which is not too challenging. However, the river soon enters a 1.5 km long boulder garden creating many mid-stream obstacles and plenty of pools and rapids. After the boulder garden, the river slows making it an easy paddle to the take-out. This section of the Elbow is 5 km (3 miles/1–1.5 hours) and is a Grade I/II run, with a Class II boulder garden.

Put-in: Beaver Flats Recreation Area (Map 16/B7)

Take-out: Paddy's Flat Recreation Area (Map 16/D7)

This 9 km (5.5 mile/3 hour) section of the Elbow is Grade II+ in low water and Grade III+ in high water. The run leads through a series of narrow bedrock canyons with plenty of nice ledges as well as the 5 m (16 foot) high Elbow Falls.

Put-in: Paddy's Flat Recreation Area (Map 16/D7)

Take-out: Town of Bragg Creek (Map 16/E6)

This section of the Elbow River is a 17 km (10.6 mile) Grade II run, with a few easy rapids. The worst (or best, depending on your skill level and interest in running rapids) of them are rated a Class II+ and come just before the take-out, at the bridge in Bragg Creek. It will take most paddlers 3–4 hours to do this section.

Highwood River (Maps 11-13)

Highwood River is a mid-size river that flows through Kananaskis Country and into the Bow River north of High River. Most whitewater enthusiasts will find this river a bit boring but there are a couple sections worth checking out in a canoe:

Put-in: Eyrie Gap Picnic Site (Map 11/E7)

Take-out: Highwood Recreation Area (Map 11/F7)

This section is a 7 km (4.3 mile/2 hour) Grade II paddle. Most of the run is fairly easy with the exception of a boulder garden near the confluence of Cataract Creek and a Class II rapid near the take-out.

Put-in: Highwood Recreation Area (Map 11/F7)

Take-out: Green Ford Recreation Area (Map 11/G6)

The Highwood provides plenty of challenging waters between Highwood Recreation Area and the Green Ford Recreation Area. This 12 km (7.5 mile/3–4 hours) Grade II/ III paddle begins with some Class II rapids before entering a series of chutes with rock ledge drops. Double Trouble is one of the highlights of the trip, with two back-to-back drops of a total of 3m (6 feet). Highwood Falls is a rip-roaring Class III/IV falls, falling 3 m (6 feet) in one heart-pounding drop.

Put-in: Green Ford Recreation Area (Map 11/G6)

Take-out: Ings Creek (Map 12/A5)

This section of the Highwood is best left to the expert kayaker. It features several Class III/IV drops and ledges through narrow chutes with boiling water, holes and rapids throughout. The 17 km (3-4 hour) paddle is Grade II+ in low water and Grade III+ in high water. The take-out is reached from Highway 541 by heading down the road embankment and through a gully.

Put-in: Ings Creek (Map 12/A5)

Take-out: Highway 22 bridge (Map 12/C5)

This 12 km (7.4 mile/2 hour) Grade II paddle starts in a narrow, steep valley with many sharp corners and rock ledges, resulting in some good rapids and standing waves. The river bottom soon widens resulting in more flat water than rapids.

Put-in: Town of High River (Map 12/G4)

Take-out: Highway 547 (Map 13/A2)

An easy 23 km (14.3 mile/3.5–5 hours) Grade I paddle, this section of the Highwater begins from a road bridge near the railroad bridge in High River. From there, the easy canoe route takes you through open prairie farmland along a meandering river full of waterfowl, especially in May and June when the birds make the river their nesting grounds. The take-out is at the bridge on Highway 547.

Hummingbird Creek (Map 27/B2)

Take the Onion Lake Road off the Forestry Trunk Road to the put-in located downstream of the gorge and waterfalls on Hummingbird Creek. A short hike down a steep gully from the road brings you to the start. From there, it is a short (3 km/1.8 mile) 1–2 hour Grade II paddle in high water and Grade III paddle in low water. The first half of the paddle brings you through a steep-walled canyon of the creek with several short drops before breaking out onto the Ram River and the take-out, which is located at the end of a short trail on the Onion Lake Road approximately 3.5 km (2.3 miles) from the junction with the Forestry Trunk Road. It is possible to continue downstream on the Ram River-Upper South Ram Canyon Route.

Kananaskis River (Map 15)

The Kananaskis River drains the Kananaskis Lakes into the Bow River at the Bow Valley Provincial Park. The best paddling is downstream of Barrier Lake on the Lower Kananaskis. This section is dam controlled, and flow rate can vary greatly. Occasionally during low water, the dam will be turned off for a few hours. During these times, the only way to travel the river is to walk up and down the streambed.

Put-in: Barrier Lake Dam (Map 15/G4)

Take-out: Canoe Meadows (Map 15/G4)

Despite being only 4 km (2.4 miles/1 hour) long, this section of the Kananaskis is very popular. On a busy weekend there can be up to 100 paddlers playing in the standing waves, running the short rapids, and otherwise having a good time. Because of this, a number of new standing waves were built by constricting the river with boulders, to alleviate the bottlenecks at some of the more popular rapids. Most people put at the Widowmaker parking lot (which is just down from the dam). Widowmaker is the first, and most difficult rapid on the river. Other features include Good Humour (a rodeo hole for pulling endos) and the Green Tongue of Death (a great surfing wave). The route is rate Grade II, with some Class II/III+ rapids.

Put-in: Canoe Meadows (Map 15/G4)

Take-out: Highway 1 bridge (Map 15/G3)

This 6 km (3.6 mile/1.5 hour) easy Grade I paddle is ideal for canoeists looking for a scenic paddle. The river has few tough spots, except for the occasional logjam or sweeper. The views of the Bow Valley are truly spectacular.

Livingstone River (Maps 7, 8)
Livingstone River is a small river that flows into the Oldman River. Most of its length can be paddled in higher water.

Put-in: Livingstone Falls Recreation Area (Map 7/G5)

Take-out: White Creek (8/A7)

From just north of the Livingstone Falls Recreation Area, this is a Grade II paddle extending 17 km (10.6 miles/3–4 hours) to White Creek. While not graded high, it is still a highly technical paddle due to many obstacles, continuous rapids, tight corners and low water volume. It is a good run for intermediate kayakers and advanced canoeists. The Class III Livingston Falls can be avoided, but the take-out is difficult to find along an unmarked trail.

Put-in: White Creek (Map 8/A7)

Take-out: Oldman River junction (Map 8/A7)

The Livingstone and the Oldman converge a few kilometres south of the Forestry Trunk Road bridge over the Oldman. In this technical 8 km (5 mile/2 hour) section, paddlers will cut through a Grade II canyon with many rapids, ledges and tight bends. Watch for sweepers. Both the put-in and take-out are hard to find since they are both are reached by short, unmarked trails.

Mistaya River (Map 25)
The Mistaya River is a small river flowing in a northwestern direction into the North Saskatchewan River near Saskatchewan River Crossing in Banff National Park. The Icefield Parkway parallels the river, offering good access.

Put-in: 8 km south of Mistaya River Canyon (Map 25/G5)

Take-out: Mistaya River Canyon (Map 25/G4)

Watch for a short trail off the highway, 8 km (5 miles) north of the Mistaya River Canyon Parking Area. This will take you to the start of an 8.2 km (5.1 mile) Grade II/III paddle to the top of the canyon (don't try paddling the canyon itself!). This section of river has a lot of obstacles, which can make for a fun, or annoying run, depending on whether you like obstacles.

Put-in: Mistaya River Canyon (Map 25/G4)

Take-out: Highway 93 Bridge (Map 25/G3)

Don't try and put-in at the top of the Mistaya Canyon; it just won't be any fun. Instead, walk downstream along the canyon wall to a spot where you can easily access the river. From here, paddle 3.5 km (2.2 miles/2–2.5 hours) to the Highway 93 Bridge. This section is a tight and technical Grade III route through the lower section of the canyon. There are lots of obstacles to avoid, and plenty of rapids.

Nigel Creek (Map 32/C7)
This small, fast flowing creek offers a short, 2.5 km (1.6 mile/1–2 hour) paddle near its confluence with the North Saskatchewan River. The paddle begins from the Highway 93 Bridge and ends anywhere you can access the North Saskatchewan River along Highway 93. Along the way, there are a multitude of challenges including many drops, obstacles and boulder gardens. The first part of the paddle is toughest but as you near the river, the creek flows out into a plain and slows.

North Saskatchewan River (Maps 24-25, 32-33)
The North Saskatchewan River is one of the largest rivers in Alberta. Most of its length can be paddled with minimal difficulty as it lacks the canyon and treacherous sections of other foothill rivers. However, there are some faster sections in the mountains.

Put-in: Nigel Creek (Map 32/C7)

Take-out: Rampart Creek (Map 25/E2)

When running this section of the North Saskatchewan, make sure you portage around the 10 m high (33 feet) falls (in the canyon). Also, watch out for sweepers around tight corners. The river is mostly a Grade II paddle through an open valley with lots of braiding, but there is a 3 km long (1.8 miles) canyon, with some nice rapids and standing waves. And the falls. Don't forget the falls. Below the canyon, the river again becomes braided

and flows over a gravel bottom. There is a 1 km stretch where the river channel narrows, offering some standing waves and rapids. To reduce the length of the paddle, you can put-in or take-out at a number of locations along Highway 93.

Put-in: Rampart Creek (Map 25/E2)

Take-out: Highway 93 Bridge (Map 25/G3)

The scenery is spectacular along all the upper North Saskatchewan, and, while the water is very chilly, this is a mostly easy 16 km (9.8 mile) paddle through an open valley. Mostly easy, but there is a 1.5 km long (1 mile) canyon with two Class IV/V drops, and a number of Class III standing waves.

Put-in: Highway 93 Bridge (Map 25/G3)

Take-out: Highway 11 near the Cavalcade Campsite (Map 26/A2)

As the river flows out of the mountains, the difficult parts become fewer and fewer. This section is a steady, 27 km (16.8 mile/4–6 hour) Grade I/II paddle. The river at this location is braided and flows over a gravel bottom with few obstacles.

Put-in: Forestry Trunk Road (Map 34/A4)

Take-out: Trout Creek Road (Map 34/E3)

Below Abraham Lake, the North Saksatchewan cuts cross country for a ways before the Forestry Trunk Road crosses it. While this section is just as paddleable as the rest, most people pick the river up again at the Forestry Trunk Road bridge. From here to the Trout Creek Road Bridge is 28 km a (17.4 mile/4–6 hour) Grade II paddle through an open valley. The paddle is generally easy except for a few rapids. The river does pick up volume towards the end of the run with the last third of the run having some nice rapids and standing water around the bends.

Put-in: Trout Creek Road (Map 34/E3)

Take-out: Horburg (Map 35/D4)

This 40 km (28.4 mile/5–8 hour) section of the North Saskatchewan can be paddled by most people in a long day. It is a Grade II paddle with some standing waves around the corners, as well as some ledges and boulders.

Put-in: Horburg (Map 35/D4)

Take-out: Rocky Mountain House (Map 36/A4)

By far the most popular canoe route on the entire river, this section is a Grade I/II run, with six notable sections of Class II+ rapids. The river flows through the transition zone between the foothills and the parkland forests. About 5 km (3 miles) along the paddle, you will come across the Devil's Elbow Rapids, which has standing water up to 2 m (6 ft) high with small rollers and waves. Below Devil's Elbow, there are several rapids including the Old Stoney, Fisher's Rapids, Grier Rapids and Brierley's Rapids.

Oldman River (Maps 5, 6, 7)
The Oldman River is one of the major rivers of Alberta's foothills. Towards the upper reaches, the river offers some challenging paddling routes highlighted by several small falls and numerous ledges, obstacles and rapids.

Put-in: Hidden Creek (Map 7/G7)

Take-out: Oldman River North Recreation Area (Map 7/G7)

This section of the Oldman is a Grade II/III in high water extending some 7 km (4.3 miles/1.5 hours). The run is highlighted by a series of Class II/III rapids as well as boulder gardens making the run highly technical.

Put-in: Oldman River Recreation Area (Map 7/G7)

Take-out: Forestry Trunk Road (Map 5/A1)

The upper portion of this technical 14km (8.7 mile/3–4 hour) Grade II/III paddle (the section north of Dutch Creek), has numerous Class II/III rapids created by rock outcrops, boulders and ledges in a narrow canyon. Below the canyon, the run offers continuous rapids as the river flows over an open gravel bed.

Put-in: Forestry Trunk Road (Map 5/A1)

Take-out: Camp Creek (Map 5/A1)

This run begins at the cattleguard on Secondary Highway 517 to the east of the junction with Highway 940. The paddle is 8 km (5 miles/2–3 hours) to

Camp Creek and is considered Grade II+/III. The run is almost continuous rapids and ledges with the Class IV/V Oldman Falls in the middle inviting either a portage or a challenging drop. The take-out can only be reached by driving through private property so permission from the landowner is a must.

Put-in: Camp Creek (Map 5/A1)

Take-out: Highway 22 Bridge (Map 5/D2)

The put-in for this 18 km (11 mile/2–3 hour) run, near the confluence of Camp Creek, can only be reached by driving through private property so permission from the landowner is a must. The run offers continuous Grade II rapids created by bends in the river as well as numerous ledges and rock outcrops.

Put-in: Just east of Highway 22 (Map 5/D2)

Take-out: 2.5 km east of Highway 22 (Map 5/E2)

The put-in for this section of the Oldman River, known as the Maycroft Rapids, is reached by driving to the east on a gravel road starting 400 m north of the Highway 22 Bridge near the junction with Secondary Highway 517. Park at the grassy picnic area near the river, pack your kayak down to the river and hang on. It is a short, 2 km (1.2 mile/1 hour) Grade III+ paddle in low water and Grade IV+ paddle in high water, highlighted by a series of Class III/V ledges and drops culminating with the Class V Waldron Falls. The paddle is best left for the expert kayaker or for commercial rafters.

Boulder Run (Map 6/A3)
Just east of the Oldman Reservoir is a whitewater slalom course that was constructed in the early 1990s. It has numerous large boulders and small back eddies making the short run a technical challenge.

Panther River (Map 21/B2)
The put-in for this run is reached by travelling about 9.5 km up the Panther River Road and finding a spot to park next to the river. From there, the Grade II route leads 8.5 km (5.3 miles/1–2.5 hours) to the Forestry Trunk Road Bridge over the Red Deer River. In high water, the many rocks and boulders are covered, creating some challenging standing waves and small holes. In lower water, the exposed rocks offer some technical challenge while the many bends in the river provide some rapids. Towards the confluence, the river valley opens up and it is an easy paddle to the bridge.

Ram River: North Ram (Map 34/B6–35/B5)
The put-in to this 31 km (19.3 mile/5–6 hour) Grade II paddle is found at the North Ram Recreation Area, 300 m (1000ft) south of the junction between the Forestry Trunk Road and the North Fork Road. The take-out is found at the bridge on the North Fork Road near where the Ram River flows into the North Saskatchewan River. While the route is rated Grade II, know that once you get past the confluence with the South Ram River, there are a number of Class V or higher features that will need to be portaged by most paddlers. Every year, canoeists abandon their canoes at Sulfur Canyon (see South Ram, below) and hike out, because they underestimated the difficulty of the run. (The canyon can be portaged.) If you want to avoid the lower Ram, there is a very, very rough 4wd road to the confluence. Most vehicles (even 4wd vehicles) won't be able to drive it.

Ram River: South Ram (Map 27/D2–35/B5)
Remote. Dangerous. Beautiful. These are just a few of the adjectives that describe the South Ram. Road access into this area is almost non-existent as the river cuts across a mostly untouched wilderness from Ram Falls on the Forestry Trunk Road to the North Fork Road Bridge. All paddlers must be self-sufficient. Getting down to the river below Ram Falls can be a bit of work, but is not impossible. The Grade III/IV paddle leads some 54 km (33.5 miles/2–4 days), and while there are long sections of easy paddling, there are also several canyons, numerous waterfalls and lots of ledges, rapids and boulder gardens. There are two major waterfalls—Tapestry Falls and Table Rock Falls—getting down these falls is similar to getting down Ram Falls—steep scree slopes. Think twice before attempting to run the falls, which are rated Class V/VI, and successfully running them are beyond the abilities of most mere mortals. Also of note is Sulfur Canyon, downstream of the confluence with the North Ram, where the river is funneled through a narrow canyon. The lower section of the canyon is Class V+/VI series of falls, rapids and chutes. After all this excitement, the last section of the river is an easy float. To shorten the float, there is a difficult to find take-out (Map 35/A6) on a road that heads west a few kilometres north of the Prairie Creek Recreation Area. The pipeline leads from the end of that road to the river. In wet weather, this area is unpassable.

Ram River: Upper South Ram Canyon (Map 27/B2)
This paddle begins where the Hummingbird Creek paddle ends (approximately 3.5 km/2.2 miles along the Onion Lake Road). From there, this Grade II paddle extends 8 km (5 miles/1–2 hours) to the take-out near the Ram River Bridge on the Forestry Trunk Road (reached by a short road leading upstream from the bridge). The paddle begins on a gravel bar before entering a short, exciting canyon and soon breaks out into a wider section of the river with few rapids. Don't miss the take-out, as the 30 m high (100 ft) Ram Falls are downstream.

Red Deer River (Maps 20-22, 27-30, 37-38)
The Red Deer River offers some challenging paddling in the foothills between Bighorn Creek and Coalcamp Creek. The main access route into the area is the Forestry Trunk Road.

Put-in: Bighorn Creek (Map 27/G7)

Take-out: Forestry Trunk Road (Map 21/C1)

The Ya-Ha Tinda Road will take you to an informal campsite on the banks of Bighorn Creek. Paddlers will have to walk just about 1 km from the campsite to the put-in on the Red Deer River. From here, it is a 26 km (16.2 mile/6–8 hour) Grade II paddle through an open valley. The first 5 km (3 miles) of the paddle is heavily braided, with lots of shallow channels and the occasional sweeper, logjam and boulder garden. Below this, the river stays in a single channel and picks up speed offering a series of ledges and small rapids.

Put-in: Forestry Trunk Road (Map 21/C1)

Take-out: Deer Creek Recreation Area (Map 21/F1)

This 12.5 km (7.8 mile/2–4 hour) of the river is rated Grade II/III. The main feature of this section is Gooseberry Ledge, a Class III drop. There is a series of small rapids leading to the ledge as the river flows over a gravel bed with a few large boulders. Below the ledge, the river becomes more difficult, and there is a series of Class III drops and rapids.

Put-in: Deer Creek Recreation Area (Map 21/F1)

Take-out: Cache Hill (Map 21/G1)

Finding the take-out at Cache Hill will probably be the most difficult part of this 11.5 km (7.1 mile/1.5–2 hour) Grade II paddle through a wide valley. There are some large surfing waves that develop during high water and some large rapids towards the take-out in both low and high water.

Put-in: Cache Hill (Map 21/G1)

Take-out: Williams Creek (Map 22/A1)

This is an easy 8 km (5 mile/1–3 hour) Grade I paddle in low water and a Grade II paddle in high water. The route takes you through a wide valley where the river flows over a continuous gravel bed with few boulders and obstacles. There are a several rapids, a few narrow channels and some sweeping corners that add challenge to the paddle.

Put-in: Williams Creek (Map 22/A1)

Take-out: Coalcamp Creek (Map 22/B1)

More challenging than the previous stretch of river, this 9 km (5.6 mile/1–2.5 hour) Grade II/III route leads through an open valley with some challenging rapids and drops. Double Ledge, towards the middle of the run, and the Coalcamp Ledge, near the Coalcamp Creek take-out, are a couple of classic drops to lookout for.

Put-in: A-Soo-Wuh-Um (Map 37/G7)

Take-out: Highway 11 bridge (Map 38/D6)

From A-Soo-Wuh-Um to the Highway 11 bridge east of Red Deer, it should take a very long day to canoe this easy section of the Red Deer. There is one set of rapids (at high water only) along this section, but you will need to watch out for the water treatment plant intake as you pass through the city of Red Deer. As you might expect, there are a number of alternative put-ins and take-outs en route.

Sheep River (Maps 11-12)
The Sheep River begins in Kananaskis Country and flows eastward into the Bow River. It is a small volume river that offers some fun runs:

Put-in: End of Secondary Highway 546 (Map 11/B4)

Take-out: Indian Oils Picnic Site (Map 11/D3)

This 14 km (8.7 mile/4–5 hour) run is best left to expert kayakers. This section is rated Grade III/IV. The put-in is reached by walking the old road upstream from the end of Secondary Highway 546. From there, you soon enter a constricted canyon with three major waterfalls, numerous ledges and plenty of rapids. Portaging the waterfalls is certainly an option! If you want to reduce the run to 9 km (5.6 miles/2–3 hours) then put-in at the Bluerock Recreation Area. The most challenging part of the run is below this recreation area, where you will find three major falls, including the Sheep River Falls, which is the first, and easiest, rated a mere Class IV.

Put-in: Indian Oils Picnic Site (Map 11/D3)

Take-out: Sandy McNabb Recreation Area (Map 11/F3)

This section of the Sheep is much easier than the higher reaches, and is a fairly easy Grade II paddle through a scenic canyon. However, there are many boulders, ledges and tight bends, which create some challenging Class II/II+ rapids. The paddle extends 11 km (6.8 miles/2–3 hours) from the Indian Oils Picnic Site off Secondary Highway 546 to the picnic grounds at Sandy McNabb Recreation Area.

Put-in: Sandy McNabb Recreation Area (Map 11/F3)

Take-out: Turner Valley (Map 12/B2)

As the Sheep River leaves the mountains, it gets easier and easier. This section is a 27 km (16.8 mile/4 hour) Grade I/II paddle. The first few kilometres of the run begin in an open valley and then the river enters a 5 km long (3 mile) canyon with many sharp corners, small ledges and the odd boulder garden that create some Class II rapids. Below the canyon, the river broadens and slows as it flows through an open valley. There is the occasional riffle or rapid, but nothing too challenging.

Siffleur River (Map 26/D3)
The Siffleur River is a challenging, remote wilderness paddle, which can only be reached by a strenuous 7 km (4.3 mile) portage along the Siffleur Falls Trail. If the hike does not discourage you then the challenging 6 km

(3.7 mile/4–5 hour) Grade IV/V paddle might. The run takes you through a series of canyons with very challenging whitewater sections, particularly in the canyon below the lower falls. Portions of these canyons must be portaged depending on your skill level. After reaching the confluence with the North Saskatchewan River, a short paddle brings you to the take-out at the south end of Abraham Lake.

Waterton River (Map 3)
Waterton River flows northeast from Waterton National Park and offers two paddling routes, one north of the Waterton Reservoir and one south of the reservoir:

Put-in: Highway 6 Bridge (Map 3/A6)

Take-out: Waterton Reservoir (Map 3/C3)

This 29km (18 mile/4–6 hour) run begins in Waterton National Park and continues through the grasslands of Southwestern Alberta. The run is Grade I/II, which begins with an easy paddle through the first third of the route. Eventually, the river gradient increases and you will find numerous Class II rapids and some obstacles.

Put-in: Waterton Reservoir (Map 3/C2)

Take-out: Highway 810 Bridge (Map 3/E1)

The first section of this 30 km (18.6 mile/5–6 hour) route is the most difficult. There is a strong Class III current below the reservoir spillway, which can be avoided by launching farther downstream. Next is a pair of short canyons with some Class II rapids. Once you pass the canyons, the route is an easy paddle.

Willow Creek (Maps 8/F4-9/A4)
Willow Creek is best paddled in April and May during spring run-off (later in the year, there may not be enough water). Most paddlers start at bridge near Kuntz Creek and run the creek to Highway 527 near the Willow Creek Provincial Park. The run is 27 km (16.8 miles/5–6 hours) and is rated as a Grade II/III. It has three small canyons along the route with Class II/III rapids created by small ledges, tight corners and boulder gardens.

Mussio Ventures' Staff

Parks

(Provincial Parks, Recreation Areas & National Parks)

Provincial parks and recreation areas are great ways to discover the beauty and splendor of Southwestern Alberta. In fact, many of the most spectacular areas in Alberta are to be found in Provincial Parks. These sites range from roadside camping facilities to remote backcountry parks with no roads, no facilities and, if you're lucky, a few developed trails.

Most camping areas are open from May to October but some of the parks and recreation areas also have limited camping during the winter months. Picnic tables, pit toilets, fire pits, pump water, and firewood are found at most recreation areas, while parks often offer a few more amenities including running water and on occasion showers. Camping fees vary, based on services provided; prices currently range from $7/night to $23/night, with the maximum allowed stay at any one park is 16 consecutive nights. Since many of the provincial park campgrounds are very busy in the summer, a reservation system is in place for a fee. We have included the numbers to these parks.

Alberta's protected areas are divided into a number of different categories. Some of these categories have a high emphasis on recreational opportunities, while others focus on environmental protection. Some do a little of both.

Ecological Reserves are designated to protect some of the provinces rarest landscapes, plants and animals. The emphasis is on environmental protection, and they are not intended for public use.

Natural Areas are a cross between Ecological Reserves and Wildland parks. Some are very fragile, with little recreational use. Others are more accessible and used for hiking, skiing, berry picking and wildlife watching. There is no camping at these areas, and only a few are written up here. The public is welcome to visit, as long as they respect the sensitive areas these sites protect.

Provincial Parks protect provincially significant natural, historical and cultural features. A balance is struck between recreation and conservation, with an emphasis on both. Some parks are more recreation oriented, with hundreds of campsites, RV hookups, playgrounds, stores and showers, trails, and boating. Others are more conservation oriented, with fewer facilities.

Recreation Areas are usually small areas that emphasize recreation. Camping, picnicking, hiking, mountain biking, fishing, canoeing, power boating, water skiing, wildlife viewing, horseback riding and cross-country skiing are all examples of activities carried out in recreation areas. There are both **Provincial Recreation Areas** and **Forest Provincial Recreation Areas**, and while there are differences between the two, they are not significant enough to note. In fact, the Alberta Community Development Website (www.cd.goc.ab.ca/enjoying_alberta/parks/index.asp)lists them all as Provincial Recreation Areas. We simply call them Recreation Areas.

Wilderness Areas border the national park and protect some dramatic mountain landscapes. There is no road access into these large areas, and, while backpacking and backcountry camping is permitted, fishing and hunting is not.

Wildland Parks are large, undeveloped areas with few facilities. Hiking, horseback riding and backcountry camping are permitted.

Backroad Mapbooks

www.backroadmapbooks.com

Provincial Parks and Recreation Areas

Allison Recreation Area (Map 4/E4)
Located 9 km (5.6 miles) north of Crowsnest, this recreation area has ten picnic tables and a picnic shelter. The main activities at the recreation area are hiking in the summer as well as cross-country skiing in the winter. There are a total of 17.5 km (10.9 miles) of trails, as well as a warm-up shelter. There is a fish hatchery adjacent to the picnic area, which you may wish to visit.

Aspen Beach Provincial Park (Map 37/F3)
On the shores of Gull Lake, Aspen Beach was established in 1932, making it Alberta's oldest provincial park. It has big sand beaches and warm shallow water, making a popular destination in summer for paddling, sunbathing and swimming. It is a big park, with 586 campsites, spread out across two separate areas. Brewers Campground has un-serviced sites, while the Lakeview Campground has a mix of serviced and un-serviced sites. You will also find hiking/biking/cross-country ski trails, a boat launch, a playground and showers. The park is open year-round, and snowmobilers can use the boat parking lot as a staging area to access the lake only. The park may be closed for several weeks in spring due to soft roads and washouts that require drying and repair. Campsite reservations can be made by calling 1-877-277-3645.

Atlas Road Recreation Area (Map 4/E4)
Located 11 km (6.8 miles) northwest of Crowsnest, this recreation area is adjacent to 18.7 km (11.6 miles) of snowmobile trails. A 35 unit parking lot and pit toilets are the only other facilities found at the recreation area.

Aylmer Recreation Area (Map 34/A4)
Aylmer Recreation Area is used as a staging area for the Aylmer hiking/equestrian trails (30 km/18.6 miles of trails) as well as a boat launch facility for paddlers on the North Saskatchewan River. From the recreation area, it is about a 12 hour paddle leading to Rocky Mountain House. Fishing for trout and rocky mountain whitefish is also popular. In total, there are seven primitive campsites, which can be used for a fee. The recreation area is located 14 km (8.7 miles) south of Nordegg on the Forest Trunk Road.

Beauvais Lake Provincial Park (Map 2/D1)
This provincial park provides you with a chance to camp in the foothills of the Rockies. There are a total of 85 campsites for vehicles, and another ten walk-in sites within the main camping area (Beauvais Campground). There are also 21 sites in the group camping area. In the winter, the park has 17 designated campsites, which are used by cross-country skiers, snowmobilers and ice fishermen. There are also two day-use areas: one at Beaver Creek, and one on the north side of the lake. Beauvais Lake provides a boat launch (ramp and hand launch), wind surfing, fishing (brown trout and rainbow trout), swimming and paddling. The park also has a well-developed trail system, which offers 15 km (9.3 miles) of hiking/biking trails in the summer or cross-country skiing/snowshoeing in the winter. Part of the trail network is a self-guided interpretative walk.

Beaver Creek Recreation Area (Map 5/G1)
Located 40 km (24.9 miles) north of Pincher Creek, there are 87 camping units at this year-round recreation area. In addition to camping, visitors can hike, canoe, fish or swim. There are rainbow and cutthroat trout in the creek. At the recreation site are three picnic tables, pit toilets, firepits and firewood. In the winter, snowmobilers use the area.

Beaver Mines Lake Recreation Area (Map 2/B2) 🏕 🍽 ⛵ 🏊 🎣 🚶 🚵 🐎 ⛷ 🎣

Open from May through October, the recreation area has 97 camping spots and a day-use area with eight picnic tables. The recreation area is located on the shores Beaver Mines Lake, which is found 30 km (18.6 miles) west of Pincher Creek. The lake provides boating, paddling and fishing (rainbow trout and bull trout) while the area is popular with horseback riders.

Beaverdam Recreation Area (Map 34/B3) 🏕 🍽 ⛵ 🚶 🚵

🎣

Located 5 km (3.1 miles) east of Nordegg off of Highway 11, this recreation site is open from May to September and can be used for a fee. There are ten sites together with 31 overflow camping spots located near the walk-in tenting area. In addition, there is a day-use area with two picnic tables, one picnic shelter as well as firepits and firewood. Hiking, canoeing and fishing (brown trout and brook trout) are the primary attractions.

Beehive Natural Area (Map 7/D5) 🚶 📍

The Beehive Natural Area is one of the largest Natural Areas in the province, protecting mountains, valleys and the alluvial plains of the Oldman River. Like all natural areas, there are no developed facilities for recreation. Unlike most, however, there are a number of popular hiking and backpacking trails. The Great Divide Trail passes through Beehive as it makes its way north.

Big Hill Springs Provincial Park (Map 17/A1) 🍽 🚶 🚵 📍

This provincial park is located 7 km (4.3 miles) east of Cochrane off Secondary Highway 567 between the parkland and foothills area. The principal attraction is a series of small waterfalls, which flow year-round over a neat rock formation covered by vegetation. A day-use area, set on the banks of the Big Hill Creek, provides four picnic tables with firepits and water pumps set under a poplar and spruce stand.

Bigelow Reservoir Recreation Area (Map 31/F5) 🍽

The Bigelow Reservoir is located 35 km (21.7 miles) northwest of Trochu on Secondary Highway 587. The small site is for day-use only and provides tables and pit toilets.

Bighorn Wildland Recreation Area (Maps 20-21, 25-28, 32-33) 🅰 🚶 🚵 🐎 ⛷ 🏊 🎣

This recreation area covers 2,463 sq km of rugged alpine terrain and is Alberta's first wildland recreation area, having been established in April 1986. The Bighorn contains breathtaking mountainous backcountry terrain and very few facilities or services, so it is best left to the experienced outdoors person to explore. In total, the Bighorn has about 700 km (435 miles) of trails. These trails, which are popular with hikers, horseback riders and cross-country skiers, are a combination of the old pack trails established in the early 1900s as well as a number of mineral exploration roads and trails. The trail system is not maintained but does offer designated campsites at the Foley Lake (Map 26/E2), Pinto Lake (Map 25/E1) and Waterfalls Creek (Map 25/G1) as well as several informal sites. The stream fishing for trout is considered the best in the province where as some of the high elevation sub-alpine lakes have been stocked with the unique golden trout. Hunting for trophy bighorn sheep, mountain goat and grizzly bear is internationally recognized. Motorized vehicles are prohibited within the recreation area. The main access points are provided along Highway 11, the Forestry Trunk Road (Secondary Hwy 734) and Red Deer River Roads.

Blackstone Recreation Area (Map 33/E1) 🏕 🍽 ⛵ 🚶 🚵

🐎 🚵 🏊 🎣

Located 30 km (18.6 miles) north and Nordegg on the Chungo Road, this recreation site is located next to the Blackstone River. There are a total of ten campsites with pit toilets, firepits and firewood but no water offered as well as a small day-use area. The river offers canoeing, kayaking and fishing (rainbow trout and rocky mountain whitefish). Snowmobilers use the recreation area in the winter, while in the summer hiking and equestrian use is popular.

Bluerock Wildland (Map 11/C3) 🅰 🍽 🚶 🚵 📍

Bluerock Wildland Park protects the Sheep River Valley between Elbow-Sheep Wildland and the eastern boundary of Kananaskis Country. It is a natural wildlife corridor for elk, moose, bighorn sheep and grizzly bear, just to name a few. There is fishing in Ware Creek, day-use facilities at Volcano Ridge and backcountry camping for six groups at Three Point Backcountry campsite.

Bob Creek Wildland (Map 5/A1-8/B5) 🚶 📍

Centred around the Whaleback Ridge, a fairly well known hiking destination that is considered to be Alberta's last remaining area of montane wilderness, this park preserves a special landscape. The park also provides habitat for many large animals, and is one of Alberta's most important elk ranges. Birds are also a common sight here. Access to the park is often through private lands; please respect the landowners.

Bow Valley Provincial Park (Map 15/F3) 🏕 ⛵ 🏊 🎣 🚶

🚵 🐎 🎣 📞

This popular provincial park is located 28 km (17.4 miles) east of Canmore along the Trans-Canada Highway. There are two full facility campgrounds, the Bow Valley Campground and the Willow Rock Campground, as well as smaller sites at Lac des Arcs, Twin Sisters, Bow River, Grouse and Hall, offering a total of 400 campsites in the park. Many of these sites are within earshot of the busy Trans-Canada highway (the closest is the Bow Valley Campground), which can make for a unsettled night, especially for tenters. In addition to the campgrounds, there are 11 different day-use areas that help you enjoy the recreation pursuits in the valley. Hiking and biking trails are available in the summer, as is fishing at a number of rivers and lakes within the valley. To reserve a space at the Willow Rock or Bow Valley Campgrounds, phone (403) 673-2163.

Symbols Used in Reference Section

🏕	Campsite /Trailer Park
🅰	Road Access Recreation Site
🅰	Trail or Boat Access Recreation Site
🍽	Day-use, Picnic Site
🏖	Beach
⛵	Boat Launch
🚶	Hiking Trail
🚵	Mountain Biking Trail
🐎	Horseback Riding
⛷	Cross Country Skiing
🛷	Snowmobiling
🎿	Downhill Skiing
🏂	Snowshoeing
🧗	Mountaineering /Rock Climbing
🛶	Paddling (Canoe /Kayak)
🏍	Motorbiking /ATV
🏊	Swimming
🏠	Cabin /Hut /Resort
📖	Interpretive Brochure
🎣	Fishing
📍	Viewpoint
🎯	Hunting
♿	Wheel Chair Accessible
📞	Reservations
$	Enhanced Wilderness Campsite

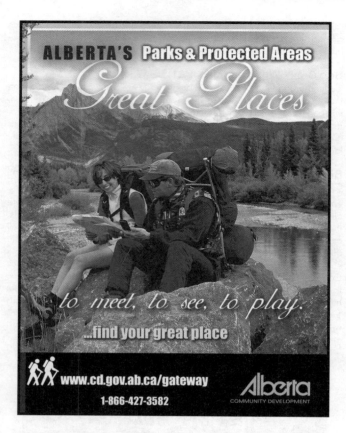

Bow Valley Wildland Park (Map 15/C6-F3)

Bow Valley Wildland Park is located at the north end of Kananaskis Country, and is an amalgamation of Wind Valley and Yamnuska Natural Areas, as well as several smaller areas. The park is designed to expand wildlife habitat and protect wildlife corridors between this area and Banff. In addition to several trails, the rock walls of the Yamnuska are a popular rock climbing destination.

Bragg Creek Provincial Park (Map 16/E6)

Southwest of Bragg Creek on Highway 758, the Bragg Creek Provincial Park has 84 day-use picnic areas. The highlight of the area is the Elbow Falls, a spectacular falls on the Elbow River.

Brown-Lowery Provincial Park (Map 11/G1)

Located 41 km (25.5 miles) south of Calgary off Highway 762, this year-round provincial park provides a day-use area for visitors as well as 11 km (7 miles) of hiking trails. The provincial park was donated by an oil company in 1962 and has been set aside for preservation because of its rich foothill flora and fauna. The trail network offers an excellent opportunity to explore a preserved foothill ecosystem. There are no facilities in the park other than the hiking trails.

Burnt Timber Recreation Area (Map 21/E3)

This recreation area, which is located 65 km (40.4 miles) southwest of Sandra on the Forestry Trunk Road, has two campgrounds that can be used for a fee. On the north side of Burnt Creek are 22 vehicle campsites whereas on the south side of Burnt Creek are eight walk-in sites. The main activities at the recreation area are hiking and creek fishing.

Canmore Nordic Centre Provincial Park (Map 15/A3)

In the winter, the Canmore Nordic Centre has 70 km (43.5 miles) of cross-country ski trails including 2.5 km (1.6 miles) of lit trails. The cross-country ski trails turn to mountain biking, hiking and roller-blading trails during the summer.

Carbondale Recreation Area (Map 2/A1)

Located between Carbondale and West Castle Rivers about 25 km (15.5 miles) southwest of Crowsnest, this is a winter recreation area with 40 km (24.8 miles) of snowmobiling trails. There is a 35 unit parking lot with pit toilets at the trailhead off Secondary Highway 774.

Cartier Creek Recreation Area (Map 22/A1)

For a fee, you can use one of 19 campsites at this relatively remote recreation area on the Red Deer River. The recreation area is located about 22 km (13 miles) southwest of Sundre and is open from May through September. Kayaking, fishing and rafting on the Red Deer River are the main attractions to the recreation area.

Castle Falls Recreation Area (Map 2/A1)

This recreation area is found southwest of Pincher Creek. There are 46 camping sites here, which see a lot of use from anglers coming to fish in Castle River. The site is also used by canoeists/kayakers, and, of course, folks just looking to get away for a while.

Castle River Recreation Area (Map 5/F7)

Located 8 km (4.8 miles) west of Pincher Creek on Highway 510, this recreation area has 20 campsites, which can be used for a fee. The recreation area is open year-round and has fire pits, firewood and pump water. Nearby Castle River provides canoeing, kayaking and fishing (cutthroat, rainbow trout and rocky mountain whitefish).

Castle River Bridge Recreation Area (Map 2/A1)

Open from May to October, this recreation area is located next to Castle River about 23 km (14.3 miles) southwest of Crowsnest on Highway 774. For a fee, you can use one of the 30 campsites complete with pit toilets, firepits, pump water and firewood. There is also a day-use area with a picnic shelter and two picnic tables. Kayaking, canoeing and fishing (rainbow, cutthroat and bull trout) on the Castle River as well as hiking are the main recreation pursuits.

Chain Lake Provincial Park (Map 8/C2)

Chain Lake is a man-made lake, found in a grassy rangeland with a few groves of conifer trees surrounding the lake. The provincial park has 120 drive-in campsites on the east side of the reservoir, as well as 35 group camping sites. The camping sites are open from May to October as well as during winter when there are 12 sites open. There are two boat launches together with drinking water, a sani-station, picnic area and group shelters. A series of interpretive trails lead from the camping area to the waterfront and along the dam. Fishing and wildlife viewing are also common activities.

Chambers Creek Recreation Area (Map 35/C3)

Next to Chambers Creek off Highway 11, some 30 km west of Rocky Mountain House, this year-round recreation area has 26 campsites as well as a group camping area. Creek fishing for brown trout, brook trout, pike and mountain whitefish is popular, or you can explore the 86 km (53.4 miles) of unmaintained snowmobiling trails, which suit hikers and ATVs in the summer. Reservations for the group camp can be made by calling (403) 721-3975.

Chinook Lake Recreation Area (Map 4/E4)

Next to Chinook Lake, there are a total of 74 campsites as well as a day-use area with six picnic tables and a shelter. The campsite is open from May through October and offers swimming, paddling and fishing on the lake. In the winter, cross-country skiing opportunities exist.

Cow Lake Natural Area (Map 35/G6)

Located off Highway 752 to the east of Strachan, this former recreation area has 55 campsites complete with a boat launch, pump water and beach. There are boat rentals, beach volleyball nets, horseshoe pits and showers available. It is open from May to October with most of the recreation pursuits occurring on the lake.

Crescent Falls Recreation Area (Map 33/E4)

Located next to beautiful Crescent Falls on the Bighorn River, this recreation area has 26 camping sites, in addition to a picnic area with six tables. In the area, there are hiking/equestrian trails as well as river fishing for bull trout, cutthroat and rocky mountain whitefish. The recreation site is open from May through September. Please note that the access road from Highway 11 to the falls is very steep and narrows in places.

Crimson Lake Provincial Park (Map 35/G3)

Located northwest of Rocky Mountain House off Highway 756, this popular provincial park is situated where the foothills of the western Rockies meet the northern boreal forest and the eastern aspen parkland. There is an abundance of wildlife such as waterfowl, moose and deer as well as year-round recreational pursuits. The Crimson Lake campsite offers 162 campsites and offers full facilities including a boat launch, sani-station, showers and water. An alternative campsite can be found to the southeast at Twin Lakes where there are 46 campsites as well as a day-use area with eight picnic tables. Picnickers will also find a day-use area with 32 picnic tables and a picnic shelter at Crimson Lake. There is a well developed hiking/biking trail circling Crimson Lake that links with Twin Lakes. It is also possible to camp in the winter, while enjoying the 10 km (6.2 miles) of groomed cross-country skiing trails. There are also non-groomed trails, ice fishing and skating. To reserve a campsite, phone (403) 845-2330.

Cutoff Creek Staging Area (Map 27/G4)

This day-use site is used as a staging area for hikers and horseback riders heading into the Upper Clearwater River Land Use Zone. Motorized vehicles are prohibited.

Deer Creek Recreation Area (Map 21/F1)

This recreation area is a group use only site. It is located next the Red Deer River and Red Creek which both offer fishing (bull trout and brown trout) as well as canoeing and rafting. It is opened from May through September.

Dickson Dam (Gleniffer Lake) Recreation Area (Map 30/C2)

This recreation area is actually divided between five separate camping areas on Gleniffer Lake and two day-use sites on the Red Deer River below the Dickson Dam. There are a total of 83 camping spots for RVs and tenters in addition to a group camping area. Both the Gleniffer Lake and the Dickson Trout Ponds provide swimming, paddling and fishing. There are four boat launches on the lake and one launch on the Red Deer River, which is used by kayakers, fishermen and canoeists.

Don Getty Wildland Park (Maps 7, 8, 11, 15, 16)

This Wildland area takes the award for most confusing layout of a protected area. It is divided into no less than seven separate parcels of land stretching from points north of Kananaskis, to areas on the edge of K-Country, to areas farther south. Access into these areas is mostly by trails. Many of the features in these Wildland parcels are spectacular by nature. They include Alberta's deepest known caves, mountain vistas and one of the province's finest trout fishing streams (Cataract Creek).

Dry Haven Creek Recreation Area (Map 33/G3)

On Highway 11 about 14 km (8.7 miles) west of Nordegg, this recreation area is a popular overnight stop for travellers accessing the Banff/Jasper Parkway. There are 14 campsites as well as six tables and a picnic shelter at the day-use area. Visitors can try their luck fishing for brook trout and bull trout or hike the trails found nearby.

Dutch Creek Recreation Area (Map 5/A1)

Found next to the Forestry Trunk Road (Secondary Hwy 940), this site offers 43 campsites in addition to a day-use area with four picnic tables and two shelters. Hiking and creek fishing for cutthroat are the main recreation pursuits.

Elbow-Sheep Wildland Provincial Park (Maps 10-11, 15)

Sandwiched between the Forestry Trunk Road (Hwy 40) and Kananaskis Country, the Elbow-Sheep Wildland Park is accessible only by foot, mountain bike, or horse. For the few who make the effort to get here, this area contains vast Lodgepole pine and spruce forests set in the foothills of the Rockies.

Elk Creek Fishpond Recreation Area (Map 27/F2)

This day-use recreation area is located just off the Forestry Trunk Road, next to a small fishing pond. The pond is stocked with rainbow and there are three picnic tables for visitors to enjoy.

Elk Creek Recreation Area (Map 27/G2)

Open from May to October, this recreation site is located next to Elk Creek, which provides fishing for brown trout and bull trout. There are total of 13 campsites that can be used for a fee as well as five day-use sites available. The site is about 65 km (40.4 miles) southwest of Rocky Mountain House.

Evan-Thomas Recreation Area (Map 15/D6)

This day-use only area is located in the heart of the Kananaskis Valley. There is no camping here, but there are a couple private sites nearby, as well as hotels in Kananaskis Village. Fishing and picnicking are the most common pursuits here. Hiking is also popular.

Fallen Timber Recreation Area (Map 22/C2)

Located 25 km (15.5 miles) northwest of Cremona, this recreation site has 20 campsites. It is used by canoeists and anglers on Fallen Timber Creek, as well as ATV and snowmobile riders.

Fallen Timber South Recreation Area (Map 21/G4)

There is a total of 179 km (111.2 miles) of off-road ATV trails in the area. These trails are opened for snowmobiling during the winter. Falling Timber Creek provides fishing for trout and whitefish as well as swimming and paddling. The actual recreation site offers 63 campsites complete with a day-use area and is open from May 1 to October 15.

Fish Creek Provincial Park (Map 17/F6)

Established in 1975, the park is now one of the largest urban parks in North America. Within the park boundaries you will find the historic Bow Valley Ranch House, a great blue heron colony and archaeological sites. There are 11 day-use areas with 299 picnic sites that are open year-round. Sikome Lake provides a recreation swimming area and fishing is offered in the Bow River, Sikome Lake or Fish Creek. You can hike/bike or horse back ride on the 80 km (49.7 miles) of red shale and paved trails that wind through the park, including the interpretative Walk the Stream Changes Trail along Fish Creek. In the winter, there are 20 km (12.4 miles) of ungroomed cross-country ski trails, as well as snowshoeing, tobogganing and ice-skating.

Fish Lake Recreation Area (Map 33/G3)

Also called Shunda Lake, Fish Lake is located 8 km (4.8 miles) west of Nordegg on Highway 11. The recreation area, which has 92 camping units, which can be used for a fee from May through to the end of October. There is also a day-use area with nine picnic tables. Fish Lake, which has electric motor only restriction, is ideal for fishing rainbow trout or paddling. There is a series of trails nearby which are used by cross-country skiing during the winter and hikers and mountain bikers in the summer.

Ghost Airstrip Recreation Area (Map 21/G6)

Located 50 km (31 miles) northwest of Cochrane on Forestry Trunk Road (Highway 40), this group camping area has a total of 40 campsites. Nearby Waiparious Creek provides fishing while a number of trails provide for summer and winter enjoyment. The main camping area is open from May through to the end of October.

Ghost Reservoir Recreation Area (Map 16/D1)

Found next to Ghost Lake off the Bow Valley Highway (Highway 1A), this recreation area has 25 drive-in campsites and seven walk-in sites. Most of the vehicle sites have electrical hook-ups. There is also a day-use area with five picnic tables and two boat launches on the lake. Ghost Reservoir is a popular multi-purpose recreation lake offering fishing for lake trout and walleye, canoeing, kayaking, water skiing and swimming. For campsite reservations, call (403) 851-0766.

Ghost River Wilderness Area (Map 21/B6)

Bordering on Banff National Park, this wilderness area is far removed from any roads. The only access in is via a trail up the Ghost River and trails leading from Lake Minnewanka.

Ghost River Wildland Park (Map 21/B6)

Located 30 km (18 miles) north of Canmore along ever rougher roads (the last 10 km into the park is hike-in access only), or from Lake Minnewanka, this large Wildland is located beside Banff National Park. It protects the rugged mountain terrain that forms the headwaters of the Ghost River and boasts of peaks to 3,353m (10,900ft).

Goldeye Lake Recreation Area (Map 33/G3)

Set on the shores of Goldeye Lake, this recreation area has a total of 44 campsites and a day-use area with three picnic tables. A series of hiking/ cross-country skiing trails provide land based activities while fishing and paddling on Goldeye Lake are possible.

Greenford Recreation Area (Map 11/G6)

There are 13 camping units at this site, located just down the road from Kananaskis Country (indeed, it is often considered a K-Country Campsite). The fishing is good in the Highwood River, and anglers are among the most common users of this site.

Harlech Recreation Area (Map 34/C2)

Located 13 km (8.1 miles) east of Nardegg off Highway 11, this recreation area is open year-round. There are total of 17 campsites and good access to Shunda Creek, which provides fishing for brook trout and brown trout. In the winter, snowmobilers use the area.

Horburg Recreation Area (Map 35/C4)

Horburg is an ideal location to launch a boat on the North Saskatchewan River. From the recreation site, it is about a four hour paddle to Rocky Mountain House. Other uses of the river include jet boating and fishing for trout and whitefish. The recreation site is open from May to September and has seven tenting sites.

Hummingbird Recreation Area (Map 27/B2)

This day-use recreation area is used as a staging area for trips into Bighorn Wildland Recreation Area. It is popular with both horseback riders and hikers and can be used as a launching point for paddlers.

Indian Graves Recreation Area (Map 8/A2)

On the southeast tip of Kananaskis Country, there are 40 RV and tenting sites at this recreation area. The area is popular with horseback riders as there are extensive equestrian trails, horse -holding facilities and the facility operator even offers guided trail rides. Other attractions include fishing for rocky mountain whitefish on Johnson's and Willow Creek as well as hunting in the fall. For campsite reservations call (403) 601-3051.

Island Lake Recreation Area (Map 4/D5)

Located near the BC/Alberta border on the Crowsnest Highway (Hwy 3), this year-round recreation area has 41 tenting and RV sites. Island Lake is a popular recreation lake for swimming, paddling and trout fishing, while snowmobilers use the lake in winter.

Jackfish Lake Recreation Area (Map 34/G2)

Located east of Nordegg on the David Thompson Highway (Hwy 11), this year-round recreation site provides ATV, hiking and equestrian trails in the summer and snowmobiling and ice fishing during the winter. Not surprisingly, Jackfish Lake has northern pike. It also holds perch. There is a boat launch (speed limit of 12 kph), floating dock, pit toilets, picnic tables a picnic shelter but no water at the recreation site. There are also five camping sites, which can be used for a fee.

James River Bridge Recreation Area (Map 29/E5)

Located 16 km (9.9 miles) north of Sundre off Highway 587, this recreation area is situated on the shores of the James River, a multi-use recreation river providing swimming, paddling and fishing. Within the recreation area are 8 campsites, which can be accessed by RVs.

James-Wilson Recreation Area (Map 28/E6)

Found on the Forestry Trunk Road (Secondary Hwy 734), this recreation area has 32 campsites that can be used for a fee. The campsite is open from May through September and offers hiking trails as well as ATV/snowmobiling routes in the area. There is also a day-use area with picnic tables and a picnic shelter. James River and Wilson Creek provide fishing for bull trout, brown trout and rocky mountain whitefish.

Jarvis Bay Provincial Park (Map 37/E5)

This provincial park is found on the shores of Sylvan Lake and is open year-round for camping. There are a total of 200 campsites with full facilities (showers, sani-station, water, and public phones) and a hand launch for canoeists. Canoeing, fishing, hiking and cross-country skiing are the main recreation pursuits. For campsite reservations, call (403) 887-5522.

Kananaskis Country (Maps 7-8, 10-11, 15-16)

Kananaskis Country is the name for the vast, 4,250 square km area of Alberta southwest of Calgary between the Stoney Indian Reserve and Banff National Park. The area provides a popular alternative to the expensive national parks with easily as many year round outdoor activities. The region has spectacular scenery ranging from rolling foothills to rugged high alpine areas. This is not one area, but rather a conglomeration of parks, recreation areas and wildland areas. What is and is not a part of Kananaskis Country varies depending on whom you talk to. The various parks in K Country are described alphabetically in this section, while the major recreation areas or access points are described below:

Elbow Valley Recreation Area (Maps 11/A1-16/E6)

Found only 30 minutes from Calgary, this area offers a total of 13 different campgrounds ranging from full service RV sites with hook-ups (McLean Creek) to several hike-in destinations (Romulus Backcountry, Big Elbow Backcountry, Three Point Backcountry and Wildhorse Backcountry). As well, the many rivers and streams in the valley offer decent fishing for brown trout, cutthroat trout, rainbow trout and rocky mountain whitefish. The McLean Creek Off-Highway Vehicle Trails are quite popular year round. Other trail systems offer hiking and equestrian trails in the summer and snowmobiling and cross-country skiing trails in the winter. Whitewater kayaking is also possible in the summer. The area is accessed by the Elbow Falls Trail (Hwy 66) south of Cochrane.

Big Elbow Provincial Recreation Area (Map 11/B2) is best known for its walk-in fishing along the Elbow River. In addition to a good trail system, there is backcountry camping available for about six groups at the Big Elbow Backcountry campsite.

Cobble Flats Recreation Area (Map 16/C7) is a day-use only site located on Highway 66 southwest of Bragg Creek. You can stop for a picnic, or go fishing in the Elbow River.

Elbow Falls Recreation Area (Map 16/C7) is comprised of a 55 site campground at Beaver Flats as well as the Elbow Falls day-use area. The main highlight of the area is Elbow Falls.

Elbow River Recreation Area (Map 16/D7) is a day-use recreation area located 16 km (10 miles) southwest of Bragg Creek on Highway 66. Tourists looking for a place to stop for lunch mostly use it, but it also sees a fair bit of usage by anglers fishing in the Elbow River.

Fisher Creek Recreation Area (Map 11/F1) offers camping space for 30 groups. The recreation area is located 27 km (16.8 miles) southwest of Bragg Creek and is a fair ways off the beaten trail. There is a better chance of finding a camping spot here on a busy weekend than at some of the other recreation areas in the region.

Gooseberry Recreation Area (Map 16/E6) is located 10 km (6.2 miles) southwest of Bragg Creek on highway 66. The site has space for 83 camping units.

Ing's Mine Recreation Area (Map 16/B6) is a day-use site was best known as the starting point for the trail to the Ice Cave. Unfortunately, access to the caves has been blocked, and few people come here anymore.

Little Elbow Recreation Area (Map 11/A1) offers 94 sites in the main camping area, as well as another 46 sites in an equestrian area. This is a popular staging area for horseback and backpacking trips in the area.

McLean Creek Recreation Area (Map 16/D7) is the primary camping lot for ATVers and snowmobilers taking trips into the McLean Creek OHV Zone. There is space for 170 groups. Some sites have power, but most don't. This is a huge site located in a Lodgepole pine forest, with access to miles upon miles of trails. There is also a pair of day-use areas in the area.

Mesa Butte Equestrian Recreation Area (Map 11/F1) offers space for 15 groups. While you don't have to have a horse to camp here, it is mostly used as an equestrian staging area.

North Fork Recreation Area (Map 11/F1) is located 33 km southwest of Bragg Creek on Secondary Highway 549. There is space for 24 groups, as well as a day-use area that is used as a staging area for horseback trips. Fishing in Threepoint Creek is a relatively popular pursuit.

Ware Creek Recreation Area (Map 11/E2) is a day-use area used as a staging area for equestrians, as well as backpackers and bikepackers.

West Bragg Creek Recreation Area (Map 16/D6) is a day-use area that marks the trailhead for the West Bragg Creek Cross-Country Ski trails. In the summer, hikers and mountain bikers use these trails.

Wildhorse Campsite (Map 11/C1) is a backcountry campsite that is accessible by trail only. The site is found at the junction of four trails (Wildhorse, Volcano Ridge, Hog's Back, and a alternate route off the Hog's Back.). Permits are needed to camp here.

Highwood Valley/Cataract Area (Maps 7/E2-11/D7)

Located 45 km (28 miles) west of Longview along the Highwood Trail (Hwy 541) is the Highwood River Valley. Cataract Creek continues south from the river to meet up with the Forestry Trunk Road (Secondary Hwy 940) and the foothills. This area of K country is home to eight different campgrounds with a total of 240 vehicle sites and six walk-in sites. There are full facilities at some of the campgrounds which can all be used for a fee. In addition, there are several day-use areas to help explore the many hiking trails, equestrian trails and other recreation facilities in the area. Highway 40, between Peter Lougheed Park and the Highwater Trail is closed from December to June 15.

Cat Creek Recreation Area (Map 11/C7) is a small day-use only site. There are picnic tables for 35 groups, plus parking for people using the trail system.

Cataract Creek Recreation Area (Map 7/F1) is a large 102 site campsite located about 12 km (7.5 miles) south of the Highwood Junction. Fishing in Cataract Creek is a popular pastime for visitors, as is hiking in the nearby Don Getty Wildland.

Etherington Creek Recreation Area (Map 7/D1) is located 7 km (4.3 miles) south of the Highwood Junction. This recreation site has 61 sites for campers, a separate group camp, and a separate area for equestrian users.

Eyrie Gap Recreation Area (Map 11/F7) is a day-use site commonly used by anglers to access the Highwood River.

Fitzsimmons Creek Recreation Area (Map 11/F7) is a day-use area located alongside the Forestry Trunk Road (Hwy 40), near the confluence of Fitzsimmons Creek with the Highwood River. Picnicking, fishing and hiking are the most common pursuits in the area.

Highwood River Recreation Area (Map 11/F7) is not to be confused with the half-dozen or so other Highwoods along Highway 40 (Highwood Junction, Highwood Meadows, Highwood Pass, etc.). This recreation area is located east of the Highwood Junction and offers a group campsite. The picnic area sees a lot of use from anglers.

Highwood Junction Recreation Area (Map 11/D7) is a day-use recreation area that has been developed as a rest stop. Highwood House is located here and is a welcome outpost of civilization after a fairly long drive, especially when heading north along the Forestry Trunk Road. There are indoor washrooms, a concession and pay phones.

Indian Graves Recreation Area (Map 8/A2) offers 40 RV and tenting sites that attract a lot of horseback riders due to the extensive equestrian trails in the area and horse-holding facilities on-site. (The facility operator even offers guided trail rides.) The recreation area, open from May to mid October is quite primitive in nature. Fishing for rocky mountain whitefish on Johnson's and Willow Creek is another attraction to the recreation area, as is hunting in the fall. For reservations call (403) 601-3051.

Lantern Creek Recreation Area (Map 11/B6) is a day-use site used primarily as an equestrian staging area. Hiking is also popular in the area.

Lineham Recreation Area (Map 11/C6) is a day-use site that is used as a staging area for short day hikes.

Mist Creek Recreation Area (Map 11/B6) is a day-use area that is used as a staging area for hikers and horseback riders.

Picklejar Recreation Area (Map 11/B6) is a day-use site that is used as a staging area for hikers and horseback riders heading up to Picklejar Lakes. Many of these folks are anglers.

Sentinel Recreation Area (Map 11/F7) is a day-use site that sees some use from day-hikers, as well as anglers fishing in the Highwood River.

Strawberry Equestrian Recreation Area (Map 11/D7) is used mostly by horseback riders. There is space for 18 groups, with horses.

Trout Pond Recreation Area (Map 11/B6) is a day-use area located along Highway 40, near Odlum Creek. It is mostly used as a rest area by travelers.

Wolf Creek Campsite (Map 11/F4) is a backcountry campsite that is accessible by trail only. There is space for a handful of groups, who can hike, bike or ride to the site along the Wolf Creek Trail or Junction Mountain Trail.

The Kananaskis Valley (Map 15/E6)

The Kananaskis Valley, through which the Kananaskis River flows, is found south of the Bow Valley Provincial Park on the Kananaskis Trail (Highway 40). Within the valley are extensive recreation facilities, including a number of private campgrounds. There is camping at the Mt. Kidd RV Campground (229 sites with 88 electrical hook-ups), Eau Claire Campground (51 sites with no electrical hook-ups) and the Sundance Lodge (23 vehicle sites). In addition, there are two group sites (Canoe Meadows and Stoney Creek), which provide an additional 65 units. Within the valley there are numerous day-use areas with picnic facilities and picnic shelters to help you enjoy the trail systems, fishing, swimming and paddling opportunities available.

Sibbald Creek Trail Area (Map 16/B4)

This year-round recreation area is found south of the Trans-Canada Highway on the Sibbald Creek Trail (Secondary Hwy 68). It has a number of different campgrounds as well as day-use sites, which can be used for a fee. The recreation area is a popular retreat for both summer and winter recreationists. In the summer, there are a number of trails including the Jumpingpound Demonstration Forest Interpretative Drive and Centre. In addition, several nearby creeks and lakes provide fishing for brook trout, cutthroat trout, rainbow trout and bull trout. In the winter, ice fishing, snowshoeing and snowmobiling are the main attractions.

Dawson Equestrian Recreation Area (Map 16/C4) is used as a staging area for trips along the Tom Snow or Coxhill Ridge or Eagle Hill trails. There is space for 17 groups plus their horses.

Sibbald Lake Recreation Area (Map 16/B4) is the main campground in the area with room for 134 vehicles.

Sibbald Meadows Pond Recreation Area (Map 16/B4) is a day-use area located on the Sibbald Creek Trail. It sees some use from anglers and day-hikers, but mostly it is used as a rest stop for travelers.

Lusk Creek Recreation Area (Map 15/G4) is a day-use only site located near Barrier Lake on the Sibbald Trail. The picnic area is on Lusk Creek, which can offer pretty good fishing.

Pine Grove Recreation Area (Map 16/C4) is made up of two large group use campgrounds with space for groups with up to 40 camping units.

Kootenay Plains Nature Area (Map 26/C2)
Kootenay Plains is an ecological reserve set aside to preserve the unique grasslands and vegetation of the area. Use of motorized vehicles on the Plains is strictly prohibited. A 5 km (3.1 miles) trail leads from the highway to a scenic viewpoint overlooking Siffleur Falls. Two O'Clock Creek Campground has 20 campsites together with a day-use area containing 4 picnic tables and 2 picnic shelters, while the Cavalcade Campground is for group camping only. Both campgrounds are located in open grassland without shade. Fishing is offered in Abraham Lake.

Livingstone Falls Recreation Area (Map 7/G5)
Located 60 km (37.3 miles) north of Crowsnest on the Forestry Trunk Road (Secondary Hwy 940), this recreation sites is open from May through to the mid-October. There are a total of 22 campsites and a day-use area within the recreation area. Fishing for cutthroat on Livingstone River is the most popular pursuit here, although there are a number of trails in the area, too.

Lundbreck Falls Recreation Area (Map 5/C6)
There are a total of 45 RV sites and eight walk-in sites within this recreation area, which is located along the Crowsnest Highway (Hwy 3). The site is open from April 15 to October 15 and also offers a day-use area with 3 picnic tables and a picnic shelter. The highlight of the area is a short hike to the 12 m high (36 ft) falls that plunges into a scenic canyon on the Crowsnest River.

Lynx Creek Recreation Area (Map 1/G1) ⬛🏕🏊🚶🚣 🛶🐟

Located 20 km (12.4 miles) south of Crowsnest, this recreation area is found next to Lynx Creek, a small creek providing fishing for cutthroat trout and rainbow. There are 28 camping sites and a day-use area with five picnic tables. In addition to paddling or fishing on the Carbondale River, there are a number of trails in the area.

Maycroft Recreation Area (Map 5/D2) ⬛🛶🐟♿

There are 12 campgrounds within this scenic recreation area, which is located on Secondary Highway 517 just west of Maycroft. The Oldman River provides canoeing, kayaking, a cartop boat launch and fishing.

Mitchell Lake Recreation Area (Map 35/G7) ⛺🚣🏊🐟

This recreation area is located southeast of Strachen off Strubble Road. There are five walk-in camping spots next to the lake, a floating dock and a cartop boat launch. The lake, which has electric motor only restriction, offers fishing for trout and canoeing opportunities.

North Ghost Recreation Area (Map 21/G6) ⬛🚶🚵🚣🛶 🐎🐟

One of the largest recreation areas in the province, you will find 179 RV accessible camping spots as well as a group camping area. Fishing for cutthroat, brook trout and rocky mountain whitefish is provided in Waiparous Creek and in nearby Margaret Lake. The is also a good trail network in the area that are enjoyed year-round.

North Ram River Recreation Area (Map 34/A6) ⬛🏕🏊🚶 🚵🐎🚣🐎🐟

Located next to the North Ram River off the Forestry Trunk Road (Secondary Hwy 734), there are a total of 19 camping sites and a day-use area with nine picnic tables. The North Ram River provides fishing for cutthroat trout, with a catch and release, single barbless hook restriction.

Oldman Dam Recreation Area (Map 5/G6)

⬛🏕🚣🏊🚣🐟

Camping is the name of the game at this recreation area. In fact, there are a total of 173 campsites spread over several sites. The largest is the Chinook RV Park, which offers 30 sites with electrical hook-ups. The three other main campgrounds are Cottonwood, Island View and Windy Point. Group camping is found at the Three Rivers, while a secluded one vehicle spot is found at South Cove. The large recreation area also boasts six day-use areas which have picnic tables and in many cases, shelters. The reservoir and the rivers nearby (Castle River, Crowsnest River and Old Man River) provide swimming, paddling and fishing.

Oldman River Recreation Area (Map 6/F3) ⬛🏊🚣🐟

Located on the Crowsnest Highway (3) just west of Fort McLeod, this recreation area has a picnic area with 40 tables together with a 40 unit camping area for RVs and tenters. The main summer recreation pursuits at the recreation area are paddling and fishing on the Oldman River. In the winter, snowmobiling is popular within the area.

Oldman River North Recreation Area (Map 7/G7) ⬛🚶🚵 🐎🚣🏊🐎🐟

Found north of Crowsnest and west of the Forestry Trunk Road, this ten unit site is a popular destination for anglers. There is also a very affordable group campground here (flat fee of $60/night), making it popular with school groups. There are hiking, horse and snowmobile trails in the surrounding area.

Paine Lake Recreation Area (Map 3/D6) ⬛🚣🚣🏊🐟

Found south of Mountain View off Highway 5, Paine Lake is a popular recreational lake offering good fishing, paddling and other water sports. The recreation area has a total of 30 campsites, which can be used by RVs and tenters, two boat launches and a small day-use area.

Peppers Lake Recreation Area (Map 27/E2) ⬛🚣🚶🐎🚵 🏊🐎🐟♿

The foothills open up west of Peppers Lake, offering a wonderful view of the front range of the Rocky Mountains. In addition to a hiking trail around the lake, there is an equestrian staging area 2 km (1.2 miles) to the east of the lake. But the real reason people come to Peppers Lake is to fish for brook trout. There is a launch for electric motor boats only at the east end of the lake but no drinking water. Water is found at the Elk Creek Recreation Area, 5 km (3.1 miles) to the east.

Peter Lougheed Provincial Park (Maps 10/E4-15/C7) ⬛ ⛺🏕🚣🚣🏊🚶🚵🐎🚣🐎♿📞

Peter Lougheed Provincial Park was established in 1978 and is Alberta's only provincial park in the Rocky Mountains. The park preserves vast areas of alpine and sub-alpine and contains the Highwood Pass, the highest drivable pass in Canada. Within the park are many of the big game species (mountain goats, big horn sheep, wolves, elk, moose and deer) typical of the Rocky Mountains. The park also provides a wide range of recreation pursuits including hiking, mountain biking, cross-country skiing, fishing and paddling. It has a total of seven main campgrounds (Boulton, William Watson, Canyon, Elkwood, Interlakes, Lower Lake and Mount Sarrail) with 516 camping units. Only Boulton Creek Campground takes reservations. Mount Sarrail Campground is the most rustic with 44 walk-in sites for tenters, while the campground on the Lower Lakes is arguably the most beautiful. The park is open year-round and is accessed by the Kananaskis Trail (Highway 40) or the Smith-Dorrien Spray Trail (Secondary Hwy 742). For campsite reservations, call (403) 673-2163.

Phyllis Lake Recreation Area (Map 29/A2)

⬛🚣🚣🐎🏊🐟

Open year round, Phyllis Lake Recreation Area provides swimming, canoeing and good fishing for rainbow trout. There are eight campsites, a cartop boat launch and pit toilets. Snowmobilers use the area in the winter.

Police Outpost Provincial Park (Map 3/F7) ⬛🚣🚣🏊🚶 🚵🐎🚣🐟

Alberta's southern most provincial park is situated where the foothills parkland and grasslands meet. The rolling hills are filled with wildflowers during the early summer while Outpost Lake offers some decent trout fishing in the spring and fall. There area total of 46 campsites for RVs and tenters, a boat launch as well as the picnic area with 10 tables located at the south end of the lake. Hikers will find 7 km (4.3 miles) of self-guided interpretive trails circling the southern shores of the lake. In the winter, cross-country skiing, ice fishing and snow shoeing is offered.

Prairie Creek Recreation Area (Map 35/C7) ⬛🚶🐎🐎🚵 🚣🐎🐟

Located on Secondary Road 752 about 41 km (25.5 miles) southwest of Rocky Mountain House, this recreation area has a 50 vehicle unit campground and a group area. There is also a day-use area with five picnic tables and a picnic shelter. Visitors can try their luck fishing or walk the interpretative trails. In the winter, cross-country skiing and snowmobiling are popular.

Racehorse Creek Recreation Area (Map 4/G1) 🏕 🎏 🚶 🏍 🏞 🎣

Located 25 km (15.5 miles) north of Crowsnest on the Forestry Trunk Road (Secondary Hwy 940), this recreation area has 38 campgrounds. There is also a day-use area with a pair of picnic tables. Racehorse Creek provides fishing for trout and whitefish while the area hosts several hiking trails.

Ram Falls Recreation Area (Map 27/D2) 🏕 🎏 🚣 🚶 🏍 🐎 🛶 🎿 🎣

Located next to popular Ram Falls, this recreation area has 54 campsites as well as a large day-use area with 20 picnic tables and a picnic shelter. Fishing, a series of hiking/horse trails and access to a difficult but scenic paddle down the Ram River are offered. In the winter, snowmobilers use the area. The recreation area is reached by the Forestry Trunk Road about 64 km (39.8 miles) south of Nordegg.

Raven Recreation Area (Map 29/G2) 🏕 🎏 🚣 🚶 🎣

This recreation area offers 16 camping units for RVs and tenters that are open from May 1 to October 15 as well as a year-round day-use area. The main attraction to the recreation site is paddling and fishing on the Raven River.

Red Deer River Recreation Area (Map 21/C1) 🏕 🎏 🚣 🚶 🏍 🐎 🎣 📞

Set on the shores of the Red Deer River, there are a total of 64 campsites as well as a day-use area with a picnic shelter and picnic tables. The river provides rafting, canoeing and fishing, while a number of hiking and equestrian trails are found nearby. The recreation area is accessed by the Forestry Trunk Road about 55 km (34.2 miles) south of Sundre. Campsite reservations can be made by calling (403) 335-3467.

Red Lodge Provincial Park (Map 30/B4) 🏕 🚣 🏊 🎣 📞

Located 14 km (8.7 miles) west of Bowden along Secondary Highway 587, this park has 117 campsites for RVs and tenters. Full facilities are offered including: water, public phone, beach, pay showers, and sani-station. The park is on the shores of the Little Red Deer River and is open from May to mid October. There is fishing (brown trout and northern pike), swimming, hiking and paddling at the park. Campsite reservations can be made by phoning (403) 224-2547.

Saunders Recreation Area (Map 34/E3) ⛺ 🎏 🚣 🚶 🎣

Located on the shores of the North Saskatchewan River, this recreation site provides a boat launch for paddlers and anglers. From the recreation area, it is an eight hour canoe trip to Rocky Mountain House. The recreation area has seven walk-in campsites as well as a day-use area with two picnic tables.

Seven Mile Recreation Area (Map 28/C3) 🏕 🎏 🚣 🚶 🐎 🏍 🛶 🎣 🚻

This campground is located on Seven Mile Flats, a well known elk habitat alongside the Clearwater River. The recreation area has 36 campsites as well as a day-use area with 2 picnic tables and a picnic shelter. The Clearwater River provides canoeing, rafting and fishing.

Sheep River Provincial Park (Map 11/C3) 🏕 ⛺ 🎏 🚣 🚶 🏍 🐎 🎿 🎣 🚻

Once part of the expansive Kananaskis Country, the area around the Sheep River has been converted to parkland to help protect the Bighorn Sheep common to the area. Two different drive-in camping areas are found off the Sheep River Trail, Sandy McNabb and Bluerock, as well as five backcountry camping areas. There are also nine different day-use areas scattered along the road. All the day-use sites have picnic tables and pit toilets. The various creeks and rivers within the valley provide paddling and fishing opportunities, while a number of hiking, cross-country skiing and equestrian trails are found within the valley. The Highway is closed beyond the Sandy McNabb Recreation Area in the winter.

Shunda Viewpoint Recreation Area (Map 34/E3) 🏕 🏍 🚻 📞

Located near the old Shunda Ranger Station, this group use campsite is popular with off-road vehicle enthusiasts. The ranger station is now the site of the forest protection crew and fire fighting operations. The viewpoint offers a panoramic view of the Brazeau Range in the North Saskatchewan River Valley. Campsite reservations can be made by calling (403) 721-3975.

Siffleur Falls Recreation Area (Map 26/C2) 🚶 🏍 🎿 🎣

This staging area provides parking for hikers accessing the Siffleur Wilderness Area or the Kootenay Plains Ecological Reserve. There is also fishing in the North Saskatchewan River, which is located a short distance from the parking area. Please note, that the Siffleur River is closed to fishing. There is no camping or developed facilities in the recreation area.

Siffleur Wilderness Area (Map 26/C4) ⛰ 🚣 🚶 🎿 🥾 🚻

This 255 square kilometre wilderness area contains picturesque valleys, high peaks and alpine meadows. It offers backpacking, climbing and camping in the summer as well as snowshoeing and alpine cross-country skiing in the winter. There are no vehicles or pack animals allowed in the wilderness area, which is best accessed by following the Siffleur River Valley via the Siffleur Trail or Siffleur Falls Trail. No fishing is allowed in the Siffleur River.

Snow Creek Recreation Area (Map 33/F3) 🏕 🚶 🏍 🐎 🎣 📞 🚻

Found next to Highway 11 about 17 km (10.5 miles) west of Nordegg, this group campsite is open year-round. It is used as a staging ground to the local attractions such as the Crescent Falls, Big Horn Dam, Goldeye Lake and Fish Lake. Hiking, biking, equestrian and ATV trails are located nearby. In the winter, the area is used by cross-country skiers. Campsite reservations can be made by calling (403) 721-3975.

South Fork Recreation Area (Map 35/F7) 🏕 🚶 🏍 🐎 🎣 📞

Located next to Vetch Creek, which provides fishing for trout, this group campsite is open from May–September but the recreation trails popular with horseback riders and snowmobilers are in use throughout the winter. Campsite reservations can be made by calling (403) 845-7009.

South Ghost Recreation Area (Map 22/A7) 🎏 🏍 🛶

Located 43 km (26.7 miles) northwest of Cochrane on Highway 40, this recreation area is open year-round and has several picnic tables but no campground. It is used as a staging ground for snowmobilers in the winter and ATV riders in the summer.

Spray Valley Provincial Park (Maps 10/E1-15/B7) 🏕 ⛰ 🎏 🚣 🚶 🏍 🐎 🎿 🛶 🎣

Bordering on Banff National Park, the hub of this area is found 18 km (11.2 miles) south of Canmore on a good gravel road called the Smith-Dorrien Spray Trail (Secondary Hwy 742). Spray Lake contains two drive-in campgrounds (Spray Lake West and Buller Mountain) containing a total of 62 camping spots, which are best used by tenters or campers but not RVs. Within the park there are also six different day-use areas with picnic tables but no other facilities as well as several backcountry campsites. At the various creeks, ponds and lakes, various recreation activities such as power boating, paddling and fishing are popular. The trail systems are enjoyed year-round.

Strachan Recreation Area (Map 35/E6) 🏕 🎏 🛶 🎣

Located just west of Strachan on Secondary Road 752, this recreation area has a campground with 27 campsites together with a day-use area with eight picnic tables and one picnic shelter. Prairie Creek, which flows past the recreation area, provides fishing for brook trout and rainbow trout. In the winter, snowmobilers use the area.

Strubble Lake Recreation Area (Map 35/G7) 🚣 🚣 🎿 🎣

To the southeast of Strachan off Strubble Road, this recreation area is open year-round. It is a popular all-season fishing lake surrounded by privately owned land. The lake contains stocked rainbow trout as well as a float dock. There is a 12 km/h (7.5mph) powerboat limitation on the lake. In the winter, the area is popular with cross-country skiers with Terratima Lodge providing accommodation. No other facilities are at the recreation area except pit toilets.

Swan Lake Recreation Area (Map 28/E1)

This recreation area has 16 RV accessible campsites together with a floating boat dock, boat launch, picnic shelter and a 16 table picnic area. Fishing is the main attraction to the recreation area since some big fish come out of Swan Lake each year. Please note that there is a powerboat restriction on the lake (maximum 12 km/h).

Sylvan Lake Provincial Park (Map 37/E6)

This popular provincial park is somehow shoehorned between the town of Sylvan Lake and Sylvan Lake itself. It is basically a 1.6 km (1 mile) long beach providing waterfront access to the thousands of people who flock here in the summer. It is a day-use only park, and while there is fishing in Sylvan Lake, there is no boat launch here. There are a couple of marinas on the north side of the lake.

Syncline Recreation Area (Map 2/A1)

Located 28 km (17.4 miles) southwest of Crowsnest, this in the winter, Syncline is used as a cross-country staging area. Campsite reservations can be made by calling (403) 627-5554.

Tay River Recreation Area (Map 28/F2)

There are 34 campsites (for RVs and tenters) at this recreation area, which is located off Secondary Road 591 southwest of Caroline. The day-use area is open year-round while camping is open from May 1 to October 15. Fishing, paddling and swimming on the Tay River are the main attractions to the recreation area.

Thompson Creek Recreation Area (Map 26/A3)

Located just outside the gates of Banff National Park on Highway 11, this recreation site has 55 camping units that can by used for a fee. There is also a day-use area with two picnic shelters and six picnic tables. Thompson Creek provides fishing for brook trout.

Upper Shunda Creek Recreation Area (Map 34/A2)

Situated close to intersections of several historic aboriginal trails, Upper Shunda Recreation Area is on a terrace overlooking Shunda Creek. There are spectacular views of the surrounding mountains from this site, which hosts 21 campsites and a day-use area with four picnic tables. Shunda Creek provides fishing for trout, while nearby Coliseum Mountain offers a series of trails at the foot of the mountain. Snowmobiling and cross-country skiing are popular winter activities.

Waiparous Creek Recreation Area (Map 21/G7)

Next to Waiparous Creek on the Forestry Trunk Road (Highway 40) is a multi-use recreation area. There are a total of 57 campsites, a group camping area and a three table day-use area. The campground is open from May to mid October, whereas the group camping area is open year-round. The main attraction to the recreation area is hiking in the summer and snowmobiling in the winter. Waiparous Creek provides reasonably good trout fishing, while the nearby **Waiparous Valley Viewpoint** offers a scenic viewpoint overlooking the Waiparous Creek Valley.

Wapiabi Recreation Area (Map 33/D1)

Wapiabi Recreation Area is located northwest of Nordegg and protects Wapiabi Creek and its valley from Wapiabi Gap east to the Blackstone River. This is an important wildlife corridor that offers no public facilities.

Waterton Reservoir Recreation Area (Map 3/C2)

Located on Secondary Road 505, this recreation area has 25 campsites ideal for RVs and tenters. The campground is open from May to September whereas the day-use area is open year-round. Fishing, paddling and swim-

ming on the reservoir are the main attractions to the recreation area. There is a boat launch available at the recreation site.

White Goat Wilderness Area (Maps 25-26, 32-33)

This 445 square km wilderness area contains hanging glaciers, tarns, alpine meadows, waterfalls and beautiful mountain lakes. The area offers backpacking, climbing and camping in the summer as well as alpine cross-country skiing and snowshoeing during the winter. No vehicles or pack animals are allowed within the wilderness area, which is also closed to hunting and fishing. To access the southeastern portion of the wilderness area, take the Cline River Trail (Map 26/B1) from the David Thompson Highway (Hwy 11) were it meets the Cline River west of Abraham Lake. If you want to access the southwestern portion of the wilderness area, follow Norman Creek on the Sunset Pass Trail (Map 25/E1) from the Icefield Parkway (Hwy 93) in Banff National Park. To reach the more rugged northern portion of the wilderness area requires a hike up Nigel Creek Trail (Map 32/B7) from Highway 93.

Wildhourse Recreation Area (Map 21/C1)

Located next to Wildhorse Creek, as it flows into the Red Deer River, this group recreation area is open from May–September. The area has hiking and equestrian trails as well as snowmobile trails in the winter. Campsite reservations can be made by calling (403) 335-3467.

Willow Creek Provincial Park (Map 9/A4)

This provincial park, located southwest of Stavely off Secondary Road 527, is set in the rolling grasslands broken by tree-lined creeks. It is known to contain over 200 species of plants typical of the prairies as well as Douglas-fir and Lodgepole Pine trees. There is a 40 site camping area as well as a day-use area with 3 picnic shelters and 10 picnic tables set along the edge of the Porcupine Hills. Willow Creek provides swimming and fishing and there is an interpretive hike within the park. For campsite reservations, call (403) 549-2162.

Wyndham-Carseland Provincial Park (Map 18/F7)

Situated on Highway 24, this provincial park is very popular with Calgarians. It is possible to paddle down the Bow River from Calgary and stop over at the park. The river also offers good fishing, while Johnson's Island provides a bird sanctuary for bird watchers. The park has a main camping area, Wyndham, which contains a total of 196 sites, 19 of which are walk-in sites and 177 are RV/camper sites. There are also three group areas, three day-use areas and two boat launches. In the winter, you will find 2.4 km (1.5 miles) of non-groomed cross-country trails as well as 56 designated camping sites.

National Parks

The Canadian Rocky Mountain National Parks contain some of the most dramatic scenery in the world, let alone the country. There are three national parks touched on in this book. Banff National Park is Canada's first National Park, and is the flagship park in the entire National Park system. Gracing the southeastern most corner of these maps, Jasper is the largest of the Rocky Mountain parks. (For more information on Jasper and points north, check out our Central Alberta mapbook.) Waterton is not as well known as the other two points, but it is easily as spectacular.

This section looks at the parks with an eye toward camping. For information on other pursuits in the parks (hiking, fishing, etc.), please turn to the appropriate section.

Banff National Park (Maps 10, 14-15, 19-21, 24-26, 30)

This world famous park hardly needs an introduction. Covering a vast area of the Canadian Rocky Mountains, the park is known for its spectacular vistas and friendly and abundant wildlife. The park offers easy access to all extremes of outdoor adventure. Whether you are looking for an enjoyable car camping experience or looking to explore some remote and rugged trails, Banff National Park has many wilderness camping options to choose from. With 2,468 vehicle accessible campsites across 13 separate campgrounds, you would think finding a campsite in Banff would be easy. Think again. In the summer, campgrounds are often full. And because campgrounds in Banff National Park are on a first come, first serve basis, there are no guarantees of success. For a good chance at obtaining a vehicle access campsite, drop by before checkout time (11 am). In addition to the park permit, there is a daily fee for vehicle camping, which ranges from $13/night to $30/night. For those looking for a campfire, there is a $3 fire permit charge.

Frontcountry Campgrounds

Castle Mountain Campground (Map 14/C1) is located 34 km (21.1 miles) from Banff on the Bow Valley Parkway and is open from June 20 to September 2. There are 44 sites situated in a beautifully wooded area. Some of the facilities that are close by are a small store, gas bar and restaurant.

Johnston's Canyon Campground (Map 14/D1) is found across from Johnston's Canyon, 25 km (15.5 miles) from Banff. It is opened from May 30 to September 22. This picturesque campground of 140 sites has a flowing creek as well as two waterfalls up nearby Johnston Canyon. Since it also offers showers, it is the most popular campground on the scenic Bow Valley Parkway. Group camping is available by reservation.

Lake Louise Campground (Map 19/G5) is one of the most popular campgrounds in Banff because of its proximity to Lake Louise. Campers who aren't in a soundproofed RV might want to think twice about staying here. (While the site is close to Lake Louise, the highway is closer and the railway closer still.) It is open year-round and has 189 RV sites with electric hook-up and 216 non-serviced sites. The campground is 1 km from Lake Louise Village and 4 km (2.4 miles) from the famous lake.

Mosquito Creek Campground (Map 19/E1) offers a superb view of Mount Hector from many of the sites in this campground. Found 24 km (14.9 miles) north of Lake Louise, this rustic campground has 32 sites with pit toilets. This campground is open year-round.

Protection Mountain Campground (Map 20/A5) is 48 km (29.8 miles) from Banff and is opened from June 20 to September 2. The area, with lots of wildlife, is great for hiking. This campground has 89 sites and flush toilets.

Rampart Creek Campground (Map 25/E2) is found on the Icefield Parkway 88 km (54.7 miles) north of Lake Louise, on the way to the Columbia Icefield, this is the most remote of the vehicle-accessible campgrounds in Banff. It is a small campground—with 50 sites and pit toilets, but no showers—and is open from June 20 to September 2.

Tunnel Mountain Campgrounds (Map 14/G2) are made up of three campgrounds that contain almost half of the campsites in the park. No wonder, as the campgrounds are within easy walking distance of downtown Banff. The area offers a spectacular view of the valley, hoodoos,

and the Banff Springs Golf Course. Services, such as food, laundry and a waterslide are close by. There are 322 full service sites in the Trailer Court, 189 power only sites in Village II, plus 622 non-serviced sites in Village I (4 km/2.4 miles from Banff). Showers are available at all three areas. Tunnel Mountain Village II is open year-round with only group camping available in the summer (reservations are required).

Two Jack Main Campground (Map 15/A1) is slightly less busy than the Tunnel Mountain Campsite (but usually full in the summer). Two Jack Main is 12 km (7.5 miles) from Banff and opened from May 16 to September 2. This campground is situated on the Minnewanka Lake Drive in a wild and beautiful wooded area. There are 381 secluded campsites with flush toilets and picnic shelters. There is a lot of wildlife in the area, so proper food storage is a must. Group camping is available by reservation.

Two Jack Lakeside Campground (Map 15/A1) is across the road from the main campground. This is a small (well, for Banff, with only 80-sites) campground with showers facilities.

Waterfowl Lake Campground (Map 26/A5) is 57 km (35.4 miles) north of Lake Louise on the Icefield Parkway. The pretty area is found where the bubbling Mistaya River enters Waterfowl Lake. Trails also lead to Cirque and Chephren Lakes. Open from June 13 to September 22, this campground has 116 sites with flush toilets.

Backcountry Campsites

There are more than 54 different backcountry campsites in Banff. An informative Backcountry Visitors' Guide lists all of the backcountry campsites available. Currently, fees are $8/night, plus a reservation fee for the busier backcountry campsites. There is a grazing fee ($1/night) and a horse permit ($3/night) required for horseback riders. Facilities often include pit toilets, picnic tables and bear-proof storage. Some of the more popular sites include:

Baker Creek Campsite (Map 20/A5) is located in an open meadow on the Baker Creek Trail. When the flowers are in bloom, it is a gorgeous place to be.

Baker Lake Campsite (Map 20/A4) has ten sites and can be accessed by a number of trails, including the Baker Creek Trail (20.5 km/12.7 miles) and the Skoki Trail (12 km/7.5 miles. Open fires are not permitted at this campsite, but camp stoves are allowed.

Hidden Lake Campsite (Map 19/G4) is found near Boulder Pass at the Hidden Lake Trail junction. Ten sites are available with pit toilets, picnic tables, and bear-proof storage. Pack a camp stove because open fires are not permitted.

Merlin Meadows Campsite (Map 20/A3) offers an excellent view of Mount Richardson. It is a ten site backcountry campsite.

Red Deer Lakes Campsite (Map 20/A3) is found near Red Deer Lakes through a number of trail options. This backcountry campsite also has ten places to pitch a tent.

Wildflower Creek Campsite (Map 20/A5) is a smaller five site campsite.

Jasper National Park (Map 32)

Jasper Park is the largest national park in the Canadian Rockies, but only the southeastern most corner of the park is captured within this book. Most of the recreation takes place further north (which is in our Central Alberta Backroad Mapbook) but there is one vehicle accessible campground and several backcountry campsites to enjoy. In addition to the park permit, there is a daily fee for camping.

With only 33 camping units at this remote campground, the **Columbia Icefield Campground** (Map 32/A7) is the second smallest vehicle accessed campground in Jasper. The campground is located near the dramatic Columbia Icefield, one of the most spectacular bits of scenery anywhere. Because of its high elevation, it can get cool at night. The campground is open from mid-May until snowfall.

Most of the backcountry campsites found in this corner of Jasper are accessed on the South Boundary Trail. These include, **Boulder Creek** (Map 32/B6), **Four Points** (Map 32/B6), **Cline** (Map 32/C5), **Wolverine South** (Map 32/C4), **Arete** (Map 32/E2), **Isaac Creek** (Map 32/F1), **Brazeau**

Meadows (Map 32/D4) and **Brazeau Meadows Horse** (Map 32/D4). In addition, the Brazeau Loop Trail offers backcountry sites at **Jonas Cutoff** (Map 32/A4), **John John** (Map 32/B4) and **Brazeau Lake** (Map 32/C4). These rustic campsites offer a place to pitch a tent, pit toilets and bear-proof storage.

Waterton Lakes National Park (Maps 2, 3) 🅿️ ⛺ 🚏 🛬 🛶 🧍 🚴 🏊 ⚓ ⛴️

Known as the park where the mountains meet the prairies, this spectacular area joins with Montana's Glacier National Park to the south. The scenery is truly amazing. The lakes are a deep blue colour, there are summer wildflowers and snow capped mountain peaks, which rise up to 3,250m (10,500ft) above the prairies. There is an abundance of wildlife including elk, mule deer, bighorn sheep, grizzly and black bears.

Accessed by Highway 5 and 6, Waterton is open year round and offers over 190 km (118 miles) of trails. Activities enjoyed at the park include: fishing, hiking/biking, horseback riding, golf and wilderness camping in the summer; and winter camping, cross-country skiing and snowshoeing in the winter.

In addition to six hotels, motels and resorts in Waterton Townsite, there are three vehicle accessed campgrounds run by Parks Canada within the park:

Townsite Campground (Map 2/G7) is the largest of the campgrounds, with 95 full-service sites and 143 un-serviced sites. The campground is found on the shores of Waterton Lake, inside the Waterton townsite. The site is open and frequently buffeted by winds that blow up the lake. It's not a pretty campground, and privacy is at a minimum, but the location can't be beat. The campground is open mid-May to mid-September. No open fires allowed.

Crandell Campground (Map 3/G6) is located along the Red Rock Parkway in the Blakiston Valley. There are 129 semi-serviced sites. Crandell Lake is a short hike from the campground.

Belly River Campground (Map 3/C7) is located on the Chief Mountain Highway on the way to the Montana border. This self-registration campsite has 24 un-serviced sites along the Belly River.

In addition to the frontcountry campsites, there are nine backcountry campsites scattered throughout the park. These rustic sites offer little more than a place to pitch a tent, pit toilets and bear-proof storage and are found at Alderson Lake, Bertha Lake, Bertha Bay, Boundary Bay, Crandell Lake, Goat Lake, Lone Lake, Snowshoe and Twin Lakes.

Backcountry Huts

If your interest lies in exploring some remote regions, the Alpine Club of Canada maintains several backcountry huts in the Canadian Rockies. These backcountry huts are huts range from rustic shelters to cozy log cabins. They serve as a base for hikers, climbers and backcountry skiers to explore remote mountainous areas. Call (403) 678-3200 or visit www.alpineclubofcanada.ca for more information on location and cost.

Abbot Pass Hut (Map 19/E6) is a stone structure that can hold up to 24 people. Mountaineers exploring Victoria Glacier and Mount Lefroy enjoy it.

Balfour Hut (Map 19/B2) is located to help travelers explore the famous Wapta Traverse (Wapta Icefield). Up to 18 people can use the hut. Access is difficult, and only folks who are well experienced in glacier travel should attempt to use the hut, which is set below Mount Balfour.

Bow Hut (Map 19/B1) is the largest hut on the Wapta Icefield, with space for 30. It is used as a base for mountaineering, glacier travel and backcountry skiing. It is found above Bow Lake.

Castle Mountain Hut (Map 20/A7) can be accessed by rock climbers on Castle Mountain. This rustic cabin holds six people.

Neil Colgan Hut (Map 19/F7) is the highest habitable structure in North America (higher than the Abbott Pass Hut by a mere 33 m (100 ft). Found in the Valley of the Ten Peaks south of Lake Louise, it holds up to 18 climbers.

Peter & Catharine Whyte (Peyto) Hut (Map 19/A1) is the northern most hut on the Wapta Icefield and is found above Peyto Lake. It holds up to 18 people who are well experienced in glacier travel.

Scott Duncan Hut (Map 19/B2) holds 12 people who are well experienced in glacier travel. It is found at the base of Mount Daly and is the southernmost hut on the Wapta Icefield.

Banff National Park is also home to several backcountry lodges for those looking to pamper themselves while exploring the wild. These include the **Sundance Lodge** (Map 14/F3), which is located at the base of the Sundance Range next to Brewster Creek. The lodge holds up to 20 people and makes a fine ski-in destination near 10 km from Healy Creek. Call (403) 762-4551 or visit www.xcskisundance.com for more information. The **Shadow Lake Lodge** (Map 14/B2) is a popular destination for visitors to the Redearth Creek area. It is found 14 km from the trailhead and provides access to several other trails in the area. Call (403) 762-0116 for more information. The **Num-Ti-Jah Lodge** (Map 19/C1) is situated on the shores of majestic Bow Lake and can be accessed by vehicle. It is often used by explorers working their way up to Bow Summit and the Bow Hut. Call (403) 522-2167 or visit www.num-ti-jah.com for more information.

Trails

(Hiking, biking, ATV, horseback and more)

Southwestern Alberta is blessed with some of the greatest destinations in the world for hikers, as well as bikers, horseback riders and ATVers. There are hundreds of trails that have been built to lead explorers to destinations: trails to waterfalls and trails to mountain peaks. There are trails through remote valleys, over alpine passes and alongside raging rivers. Trails through spectacular gorges, and alongside dramatic cliffs. Trails to...well, you get the picture. These trails range from well-defined, easy family-style hikes that will take a few hours to wilderness treks following unmarked routes that will take a few weeks.

Some of these trails are only open to hikers, some only to bikers. Others are open to all users. We have included icons beside the names of each trail and on the maps to show what user groups can use the trail. To help you select the trail which best suites your abilities, we have included elevation gain, return distance and special features whenever possible. Please note that all distances and times are for round trip hikes unless otherwise noted.

References to the level of difficulty use the following guidelines:

Easy is a gentle grade excellent for family excursions;

Moderate is a fairly strenuous trail with climbing involved. These trails will challenge most trail users and should not be underestimated;

Difficult is for experienced users as the trails are often rough and or unmarked.

A word of caution: higher elevation trails (over 1,000m/3,250 ft) may have a limited season due to late season snow. These trails are best travelled from July until October. Also, if you are travelling on unmarked trails, we recommend that you have mountaineering knowledge and are equipped with a topographic map and compass.

Below we have included information on over 300 trails and routes. These have been divided into the following regions:

Area North (includes Nordegg and Rocky Mountain House)

Area South (includes the Crowsnest Pass)

Kananaskis Country (includes Canmore area trails)

Banff National Park

Waterton National Park

Area North

There are two main roads in the north half of this mapbook that provide good access to this remote area. The Forestry Trunk Road runs relatively north and south and offers access to a great variety of activities and trails to explore. Running east and west, the David Thompson Highway (Highway 11) is an outdoor recreationists dream highway. It passes through the Bighorn Wildland and into Banff National Park providing access to an unparalleled variety of rugged wilderness treks and gentle, well-developed trails.

Allenby–Ram Falls Trail (Map 27/D1–E1) 👟🐎🏕️
The trail begins along a well-defined cart track at the Ram Falls Recreation Area. The initial 1.5 km (0.9 mile) stage of the trail allows for good views of the narrow and rugged Ram Canyon. For those more adventurous types, follow the old ranger patrol route for some 15 km (9.3 miles). This later route does require creek crossings.

Allstones Creek Trail (Map 33/D6) 👟🐎🏕️
The sharp walls of the gorge provide the backdrop for the hiker as the trail leads upstream. There are numerous stream crossings, making the footing quite tricky. This 5.5 km (3.4 mile) trail gains 80 m (260 ft) in elevation. At the end of the trail there is a 6 m (20 ft) high waterfall begging to be photographed. The trail can be accessed through the campsites on the east side of Highway 11.

Allstones Lake Trail (Map 33/D6) 👟🏕️
This trail can be accessed on the east side of Highway 11 at Allstones Creek or along a gravel road south of the causeway across the creek. The trail is 12 km (7.4 miles) long and requires a full day if the hiker stops to admire the spectacular view during the steady 560 m (1820 ft) gain in elevation. Campsites around the shores of the crystal clear lake give an opportunity for rest before the descent.

Aura Creek Trails (Maps 21/G6-22/A7) 👟🚲🏇
There are two routes leading to Aura Creek. The first route begins 9 km (5.6 miles) north of the Waiparous Creek Bridge on a grassy road. This 7.5 km (4.7 mile) easy day hike could be biked as well. You follow the road and cross Cow Lake Creek before ascending through a dry forest to a cutline that runs in a northeasterly direction. The second route begins at the Ghost Ranger Station. The trail runs along the road through four gates before crossing Waiparous Creek. The trail continues through a coniferous forest and crosses the creek one more time before reaching the aforementioned cutline. Here the two routes converge, to head down a dirt road and onto a sandy trail.

Aylmer Trail (Map 34/A4-E3) 👟🐎
Hikers also enjoy this popular equestrian trail. It begins from the Forestry Trunk Road at the Aylmer Recreation Area. The moderate day hike leads 19 km (11.8 miles) one-way along the North Saskatchewan River to the David Thompson Highway. There is minimal elevation gain of 55 m (179 ft). A less developed route leads west along the North Saskatchewan, eventually meeting a series of undeveloped trails near Abraham Lake.

Baseline Lookout Trail (Map 28/A1) 👟🚲🏇🏕️
At the lookout gate off Forestry Trunk Road, a 4 km (2.5 mile) hike climbs through dense fir and alder forests. It is an easy 410 m (1333 ft) ascent to the lookout, which sports panoramic views of the area.

Beaverdam & East Bush Falls Trails (Map 34/A3) 👟🐎🏕️
The **Beaverdam Trail** is a loop trail that starts along the Canadian Northern Railway in Nordegg. The gentle trail (elevation gain 40m/130 ft) and the orchids that are abundant at Beaverdam make this a popular 13.8 km (8.6 mile) hike. Leading south is the East Bush Falls Loop Trail. The 6 km (3.7 mile) trail gains 90 m (293 ft) in elevation and cuts across a couple of creeks as it makes its way to some pretty waterfalls. There are a number of old roads in the area that can make finding the falls rather tricky.

Bighorn River Trails (Map 33/A5–E4) 🔺👟🏕️
The Crescent Falls Recreation Area provides access to several excellent trails. The **Bighorn Canyon/Crescent Falls Trail** is an easy 3 km (1.8 mile) one-way hike through the Bighorn Canyon to some gorgeous falls. The **Bighorn Meadows Trail** leads to a sub-alpine meadow. You gain 270 m (878 ft) over the moderate 18 km (11.2 mile) route. There are a couple of creek crossings along the way. The **Bighorn River Trail** is a 23 km (14.3 mile) route that should take seven hours to hike. It leads through a mountain forest and terrace meadows, with scattered campsites along the way. The true highlight of this trail is the scenic alpine lakes, which require some bushwhacking through steep terrain. In all you will gain 1,130 m (3,673 ft). If this is not enough, you can continue on to the Littlehorn Creek Valley along a seldom-used trail.

Bighorn–Blackstone Trail (Map 33/A1–D4) 🔺👟🐎
This is a 47 km (29.2 mile) trail that begins from the Crescent Falls Road. Because of the flat terrain, it is great for horseback riding. It leads through forested land and valleys with a few creek crossings. Camping sites can be found along the way.

Black Canyon Creek Trail (Map 33/G3) 👟🚲🏕️
An 18.5 km (11.5 mile) hike or bike takes you through meadows and forests and up steep slopes. Two viewpoints along the way provide views of the

North Saskatchewan River Valley and the Black Canyon Creek. The trailhead is located at the Fish Lake Recreation Area.

Black Rock Mountain Trail (Map 21/E7)

This trail leads 5.5 km (3.4 mile) one-way to the old lookout on Black Rock Mountain. Expect a strenuous hike as you gain 890 m (2,893 ft) over the steep route. Be careful as you walk this rough trail and keep your eyes on the horizon for the tremendous view of Devil's Head Mountain, which stands to the west.

Blackstone Gap Trail (Maps 33/B1-32/G1)

Accessed along the Blackstone River, 21 km (13 miles) west of the Blackstone Recreation Area, this is a moderate trail of about 13 km (8 miles). It runs up the gap, through open meadow, to reach three small lakes. The elevation gain is a mere 220 m (715 ft). It is possible to continue your hike to Opabin Creek by way of a side trail at Mons Creek Campsite.

Blue Hill Lookout Trail (Map 21/D1)

Off the Forestry Trunk Road, this easy trail follows a steep, forested old road to the scenic lookout. It is an 8 km (5 mile), half-day hike or bike that gains about 580 m (1,885 ft).

Brazeau Gap Trail (Map 34/B4–E3)

Accessed at the Saunders Recreation Area on the North Saskatchewan River, this is a 13 km (8 mile) moderate trail. It will take the better part of a day to reach the gap as some bushwhacking (through prickly raspberry and gooseberry bushes) may be required. Hiking along the river's edge helps avoid the bushes.

Brazeau Lookout Trail (Map 34/A3)

This is a 23 km (14.3 mile) hike or bike from Nordegg that will take at least a day. With a graveyard and two abandoned coalmines along the way, you are provided with a little history. The climb to the lookout it tough, and confusing in spots, but the views near the top are very rewarding.

Bridge Creek Trail (Map 26/C1)

Accessed on the north bank of Bridge Creek (Off Highway 11), this is a moderate 6 km (3.7 mile) hike. Bushwhacking, and many stream crossing are necessary when hiking this trail. However, you will be rewarded with a very pretty waterfall.

Canary Creek Trail (Maps 27/B2-26/G2)

A difficult, 20 km (12.5 mile) multi-use route begins at the Hummingbird Creek Recreation Area off Onion Lake Road. To start, you must ford Onion Creek. From here the route leads through meadows and climbs into the Ram Range. It ends at a junction, where you may continue to either Ram River or along Hummingbird Creek. Mid-June to mid-October is the best travelling time for the trail.

Cline Canyon & Coral Ridge Trails (Maps 25/C1-33/C7)

The trail to Cline Canyon is an easy 7.7 km (4.8 mile) loop along well-maintained trails that leads down Cline River and loop north to Coral Creek. There is an elevation gain of 155 m (504 ft). A side trail leads up to Coral Ridge where numerous fossils can be found. It is a difficult (13.5 km/8.4 mile) side route that requires some bushwhacking as you gain 1,025 m (3,330 ft) in elevation.

Cline Fire Lookout (Maps 26/D2-33/D7)

The 19 km (11.8 mile) journey to the lookout is a three or four day excursion best undertaken in the fall when the bush is less lush. After crossing both the North Saskatchewan and Siffleur River footbridges, you need to bushwhack north (through dense Wolf Willows) to the ridge. At the 10 km mark you will encounter the turquoise coloured waters of Abraham Lake. Skirt the lake to eventually meet the old road leading to the scenic lookout. The lookout is manned from May until September.

Coliseum Mountain Trail (Map 34/A2)

Found off the Upper Shunda Road, this is a 17 km (10.6 mile) popular multi-use trail offering panoramic view of the surrounding area.

Coral Creek Trail (Maps 32/G4-33/C7)

The Coral Creek Trail heads northwest form the Cline Canyon/Whitegoat Trail across a pass to Job Valley, where it is possible to access Job Lake. This difficult 42 km (26 mile) trail takes two or three days one-way and gains 600 m (1,950 ft). The best time for this trail is late summer to mid-fall, when the water is lower for the numerous creek crossings. To avoid a lot of the creek crossings, you can access the trail from the cutline that runs alongside Whitegoat Creek to a pass north of Mount Stelfox.

Crimson Lake Provincial Park Trail (Map 35/G3)

There are about 20 km (12 miles) of trails available to explore at Crimson Lake Provincial Park. The most popular is the Amerada Trail, which is a 10 km (6.2 mile) loop around the lake. Another popular option is the multi-use trail connecting with Twin Lakes to the south.

Devil's Gap Trail (Maps 21/E7-15/D1)

This trail runs 7 km (4.3 miles) to the Devil's Gap, which marks the Banff National Park boundary. You can stretch this trail into a multi-day trek, depending on how far or long you want to hike. The trail eventually joins the Lake Minnewanka Trail, which runs another 29.5 km/18.3 miles past Ghost Lake to the Minnewanka parking lot. There is camping at Ghost Lakes, in Banff.

Dormer Mountain Circuit Trail (Maps 20/G3-21/A2)

This is a 44 km (27.3 mile) hiking/horseback trail that will take a couple of days to travel. Due to the many tricky river crossings, it is best travelled in late summer and autumn. The elevation gain is 835 m (2,714 ft) but the views are fabulous. The trailhead is located at the Mountain Aire Lodge off the Forestry Trunk Road.

Eagle Mountain Trail (Map 34/C3)

Accessed from the Old Alberta Forestry Woodlot on Highway 11, this is a 15 km (9.3 mile) multi-use route. It begins in forested land but soon breaks out to a rocky slope offering great views of the Brazeau Range along the way to the summit. You may have to scramble for part of the way. In the winter, snowmobiles frequent the area.

Esker Trails (Maps 27/C1-34/C7; 27/D2-F4)

A moderate, 14 km (8.7 mile) hike begins off the Forestry Trunk Road at Lynx Creek. It gains 260 m (845 ft) in elevation as it runs north through an open valley with views of the Front Ranges. The trail can be hard to follow in places. A second trail can be accessed further south at the Elk Creek Bridge. This 16 km (10 mile) option passes Peppers Creek and the Clearwater River.

Fish Lake Loop (Map 33/G3)

A 5 km (3 mile) stroll along the shoreline of Shunda Lake can be accessed from the Fish Lake Recreation Area. At the 2 km (1.2 mile) junction, a 4.5 km (2.8 mile) side trail leads to Goldeye Lake.

Forbidden Creek Loop Trail (Maps 27/D6-28/B3)

A long 78 km (48.5 mile) backcountry route takes you through the beautiful alpine of the Bighorn Wildland Recreation Area. From the end of the Cutoff

Creek Road, a trail takes you over to the Clearwater River. Continue south to the Forbidden Creek Trail. Eventually, you will loop back along the Clearwater River Trail. Due to the river crossings, the four-day hike is best left until late summer or early fall.

Gap Lake Trail (Map 34/C4–D6) 🚶 🐟
Most visitors only follow this hiking trail from the North Ram Road to the lake to sample the good fishing. This section is an easy 4 km (2.5 mile) jaunt that requires one creek crossing along the way. It is possible to continue 2 km (1.2 mile) on to the Brazeau Gap, but the terrain is difficult and your views are limited.

Ghost River Trail (Map 21/A6–D7) 🚶 🏕
The Ghost River Trail follows the Ghost River for 25 km (15.5 miles) to the base of Mount Oliver, near the Banff park boundary. There are several river crossings and it is likely you will need to bushwhack near the headwaters of the river, so the hike is best left for August or September. It will take two or three days to do this scenic route unless you try sampling one of the side trails including the **Spectral Creek Circuit**, which is a 15.5 km (9.3 mile) loop that is best done over two days. Take note that the circuit requires considerable bushwhacking and several creek crossings on the way to Spectral Lakes, Spectral Pass or Aylmer Pass. Further along the Ghost is the **Spirit Creek Trail**, which leads through the flat and dry upper valley.

Ghost Recreation Area (Maps 21/G4–22/A7) 🛶 🛥
This popular snowmobiling area, found within the Rocky Mountains Forest Reserve, is accessed off the Forestry Trunk Road. There are 183 km (114 miles) of trails, cutlines and roads that ATVers use in the summer. The trails can be accessed from the north at the Fallen Timber South Recreation Area, the Ghost Airstrip and from the South Ghost Recreation Areas.

Goldeye Lake Trail (Map 33/G3) 🚶 🚲 🛷 🐟
This is an easy 5 km (3 mile) walk around Goldeye Lake, which is at the centre of a series of interconnecting trails. An alternate, starting point is found at the Dry Haven Recreation Area, along a 2 km (1.2 mile) trail. A 4.5 km (2.8 mile) trail connects this lake with nearby Shunda (fish) Lake.

Hoodoo Creek Trail (Map 33/C7) 🚶 🏕
This 5 km (3 mile) trail begins off Highway 11 at Hoodoo Creek. It gains 400 m (1,300 ft) in elevation, providing you with spectacular views of some Hoodoos. The trail leads into a ravine and up to a shallow cave.

Hummingbird Creek Trail (Maps 26/F2–27/A2) 🚶 🚲 🐎 🏕
Onion Creek Road is the starting point for this 28 km (17.4 mile) trail along the creek to Hummingbird Pass. After reaching the pass, you can continue to the headwaters of the North Ram River via the Hummingbird Pass Trail. A great view of the surrounding area can be seen off a high column above Hummingbird Creek.

Hummingbird Pass Trail (Map 26/F2) ⛺ 🚶 🏕
Farley Lake, which is found about 32 km/20 miles from the nearest road access, provides camping and a starting point to this 14 km (8.7 mile) trail that gains 365 m (1,186 ft) in elevation. The trail is very scenic as it runs through beautiful meadows, past a waterfall and provides inspiring views from the pass itself. The difficult trail, which can be muddy, requires you to cross the North Ram River.

Icefall Trail (Map 26/D3) 🚶 🏕
This trail begins across the highway from the Siffleur Falls Staging Area, at a gate about 200 m (650 ft) up an old road. This 7 km (4.3 mile) trail offers an easy scramble to an icefall, climbing 205 m (666 ft) along the route.

Indian Springs and Enviros Lake Trail (Map 21/E7) 🚶 🚲 🏕
This is a relatively easy 12 km (7.4 miles) loop that passes through meadows and pine trees. The highlights are Enviros Lake, with its lime green and turquoise waters, and the presence of Devil's Head and Black Rock Mountain in the distance.

James Pass Trail (Map 28/B7) 🚶 🚲 🏕
This moderate 11 km (6.8 miles) trail will take you along the James River to James Pass and Eagle Lake. The trailhead is located north of the Mountain Aire Lodge on the Forestry Trunk Road.

Johnson Canyon Trail (Map 21/D7) 🚶 🏕
Beginning from the Ghost River Road, this trail leads to two waterfalls, and natural pools. The 11 km (6.8 mile) trail gains 350 m (1,138 ft) as it follows the ridge above Johnston Creek.

Joyce River Trail (Maps 33/G5–34/A5) 🚶 🏕
This is an easy but long 28 km (17.4 mile) hike that leads to a pass between Joyce River and Kidd Creek. The views are limited from the summit, but further exploration up nearby knolls will provide better viewpoints. It is possible to continue on down Kidd Creek, 15 km (9.3 miles) further to Bighorn Dam. The trailhead is located on the Forestry Trunk Road, 4 km (2.5 mile) north of the North Ram Recreation Area.

Kiska Creek Lookout (Maps 33/G6–34/A6) 🚶 🚲 🛷 🏕
Branching from the North Ram Ridge Trail, this 13 km (8 mile) trail follows an old road that has seen its bridges burned. It is a moderate route that takes you to the site of a former fire lookout, where views are quite spectacular. Be sure to keep your eyes open for mountain sheep, which are quite numerous in the region.

Kootenay Plains Trail (Map 26/D2) 🚶 🚲 🐎 🏕
This is a 27 km (16.8 mile) moderate bike and horseback ride along an old road that will take you crashing through forested uplands and then down to the grasslands of the Kootenay Plains. Access to this trail is off the east side of the North Saskatchewan is from the Siffleur Falls Staging Area. The route can be confusing as there are several side roads and trails, including a popular side trail to Survey Hill. On the west side of the river, the **Figure Eight Trail** is a 3 km (1.8 mile) trail that takes you through meadows up to a rocky viewpoint.

Lake of the Falls Trail (Map 26/A1) ⛺ 🚶 🐟 🏕
Access to this trail is off of Pinto Lake Trail west of Entry Creek. Scenic views of a waterfall, a serene lake and a thick canopy of conifers, make this a worthwhile three-day trip. The distance from the trailhead off Highway 11 (33 km/20.6 miles return) and the elevation gain (765 m/2,486 ft) make this a challenging trail. A trail continues south of Lake of the Falls through a shallow gorge and up the summit overlooking the lake.

Landslide Lake Trail (Map 26/B1) ⛺ 🚶 🐟 🏕
Famous for cutthroat trout, this is a popular fishing destination despite the difficult journey to get there. From Highway 11 just south of the Cline River Bridge, it is a 34 km (21 mile/) return trail that gains 640 m (2080 ft) in elevation. Allow the better part of two days to hike in. An alternate but more difficult trail begins from the south at Wildhorse Creek. This scenic 11 km (6.8 mile) return trail is shorter but steeper, climbing 1,140 m (3705 ft).

Lesueur Creek Trail (Map 21/G7) 🚶 🚲 🛷 🏕
The Lesueur Creek Trail is an unmarked trail that leads through a series of beaver ponds to Meadow Creek. This 8 km (5 mile) trail gains 95 m (309 ft) and takes half a day to complete. There are a number of creek crossings, so the hike is best left until late summer. The trail starts at the end of an exploration road off Ghost River Road.

Limestone Lookout Trail (Map 28/B5) 🚶 🏕
This trail follows the south ridge of Limestone Mountain to the summit. There, the hiker can enjoy an incredible view from the Clearwater River area out to the prairies. This moderate 6 km (3.7 mile) return hike takes half a day and gains 150 m (488 ft) in elevation.

Littlehorn Pass Meadows Trail (Map 33/A6) 🚶 🏕
Accessed at the Waste Transfer Site on Highway 11, this is a 27 km (16.8 mile) hiking trail. The route passes the Whitegoat Falls on Whitegoat Creek and later, the Littlehorn Falls on Littlehorn Creek. There are a couple stream crossings before climbing through meadows to the alpine pass.

McDonald Creek Trail (Map 32/D6–G7)
This is a long 72 km (45 mile) journey, which takes between four to six days from the Whitegoat Trailhead. Although very challenging, it is well worth your effort as you enjoy spectacular alpine meadows, clear blue lakes and several mountain views including the Columbia Icefields to the southwest. We recommend attempting it in late summer when the fords are more easily crossed and there is less bush to impede travel (bikers take note). The trail also links up with the Coral Creek Trail, Cataract Creek Trail and the South Boundary Trail in Jasper.

Mockingbird Lookout Trail (Map 21/F6)
This steep 3.2 km (2 mile), half-day hike can be reached from Waiparous Valley Road. The climb to the lookout is a steady uphill journey through dense Lodgepole pine with an abundance of berry bushes (raspberries, black currents and strawberries). At the summit look southwest to the immense Devil's Head or Calgary to the southeast.

Nordegg Mines Ridgewalk (Map 34/A3)
Although this trail can be followed from the town of Nordegg, it is better accessed off the Forestry Trunk Road south of town. This moderate, 8 km (5 mile) trail follows a series of roads, past three abandoned coal mines, to a ridge full of great viewpoints of the North Saskatchewan River Valley and Brazeau Range. The trail, which follows part of the Brazeau Lookout Trail, gains 340 m (1,105 ft) in elevation.

North Cripple Creek Trail (Map 32/A7)
An 11 km (6.8 miles) trail, begins off the Forestry Trunk Road between the North and South Ram Rivers. It gains 440 m (1,430 ft) in elevation, while running through meadows and valleys to reach a narrow but scenic pass. Give yourself about four hours to hike this route.

North Headwaters Trail (Maps 26/F1–33/E7)
A 26 km (16.2 mile) hike begins at the Bighorn Dam parking lot off Highway 11 and takes you into the Rockies timberland. There are several game trails that stray away from the main trail, making it hard to find your way along. Allow a couple of days to hike the trail.

North Ram River Trail (Maps 26/E2–34/A7)
This 19 km (11.8 miles) trek takes the hiker on a journey along the North Ram River (and beyond as a myriad of trails link to this trail system). You can locate the trail at an outfitting camp, which is 7.5 km (4.7 miles) west of the North Ram River Recreation Area. The muddy Farley Lake, which offers camping, is a popular destination.

Onion Lake Trail (Maps 26/G1-27/B2)
A 33 km (20.5 mile) multi-use trail leads along an old road next to the cascading creek and through the Ram Range to Onion Lake. Mid-June to mid-October is the best time to travel the trail. It is possible to continue on to the North Ram River or the Canary Creek Trails.

Peppers Lake Trail (Map 27/E2)
This 16 km (10 mile) trail runs west, then south from Peppers Lake to connect up with the Esker Trail. This trail can also be accessed from the end of a side road off the Forestry Trunk Road.

Pinto Lake Trail (Maps 25/E1-26/C1)
This is a long 32.5 km (20.2 mile) hike that leads from Highway 11 to Pinto Lake. There are waterfalls, river crossings, camping spots and viewpoints as well as muddy spots to keep the hiker busy. At the lake, a 7 km (4.3 mile) loop takes you around the lake, while trails continue south to an alternate trailhead on the Icefields Parkway via Sunset Pass. The trail also connects with the Whitegoat Trail as well as a difficult route up Waterfalls Creek.

Ram Lookout Trail (Map 34/E5)
From the North Fork Road (watch for a gated road), this trail climbs a stiff 700 m (2,300 ft) in 8 km (5 miles). On a clear day, there are great views of the Front Ranges to the west and the open prairie to the east.

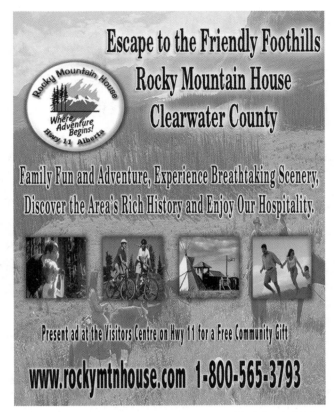

Ranger Creek Trails (Map 27/A4–B3)
The main trail leads from an outfitters camp south of Hummingbird Recreation Area to a small mountain lake, set in a colourful meadow. This difficult 26 km (16.2 mile) trail gains 515 m (1,674 ft) in elevation and takes two days to hike. Expect wet and boggy terrain, especially after a rainfall. It is possible to combine this trail with the **Lost Guide Canyon Trail** at a left turn after 15.5 km (9.3 miles). The hiker will reach Lost Guide Lake after following this route along a creek for 6 km (3.7 miles). Yet another option is to follow the 11 km (6.8 miles) trail to Clearwater River. This area is ideal for exploring during the summer through to mid-fall.

Ranger Station Walk (Map 34/A2)
The trailhead for this easy 7 km (4.3 mile) trail is found at the Coliseum Trail parking lot. It is an easy walk to Shunda Creek and it's beaver dams. Some bushwhacking may be required.

Rocky Mountain House Historic Site (Map 35/A5)
A 5 km (3 mile) trail links Rocky Mountain House with the Historic Park to the west. On site, there are three short, easy interpretive trails (only one open to bikes, called, oddly enough, the Bike Trail) through the site and along the river.

Saskatchewan River Trail (Maps 25/G3-26/C2)
This is a long, moderate 48 km (29.8 mile) trail from the Siffleur Falls Staging Area to the Saskatchewan River Crossing. It provides fine views, with minimal elevation gain but requires crossing Spreading Creek is required about halfway. Many simply follow the old road to Loudon Creek for a 14.5 km (9 mile) journey that passes a ravine. Allow for a full day and be prepared for some bushwhacking.

Shunda/Baldy Mountain Lookout Trail (Maps 33/G2-34/A2)
This trail is best accessed from the Upper Shunda Creek Recreation Area. The 6.5 km (4 mile) trail is rough and rocky, and has limited views along the way. Is it worth it? Yes. Once at the lookout, you are provided with panoramic views of Nordegg and the surrounding Front Ranges. Hikers will need about three hours to complete the moderate hike.

Siffleur Falls Trail (Map 26/C2)

This is probably the most popular trail in the area. So much so that the trailhead for the dozen or so trails that start at the suspension bridge over the North Saskatchewan is called the Siffleur Falls Staging Area. The easy, 12 km (7.4 miles) hiking and biking trail offers views of the Siffleur River Canyon as it makes its way to a viewpoint overlooking the titular falls.

Siffleur River Trail (Map 26/C2–D4)

A challenging 30 km (18.6 mile) route connects with the Dolomite Pass Trail and the Clearwater Valley Trail. It pushes through forest and dangerously crosses rivers while offering a scenic traverse of the Siffleur Wilderness Area. Bushwhacking routes to Escarpment Lakes and Porcupine Lake are accessible off the main trail. These trails are best done later in the year, when the river crossings are easier.

Skeleton Creek Trail (Map 27/E6–G7)

This 27 km (16.8 mile) route follows an old exploration road north from the Ya-Ha Tinda Ranch to the Forty Mile Patrol Cabin on the Clearwater River. It is a difficult route that climbs 450 m (1,463 ft) along the way. Several side routes, including Bighorn Pastures and Scalp Creek, are worth exploring.

Snake Hill Trails (Map 29/E7)

Located in the northwest corner of Sundre, Snake Hill has a series of trails that are used by cross-country skiers in winter, and hikers and bikers in summer. Most of the 3 km (1.8 miles) of trails are easy.

South Ghost River Trail (Map 15/C1–G1)

This trail is accessed off the Ghost River Road, 700 m (2,275 ft) past Lesueur Creek. The trail runs along what should be the South Ghost River to South Ghost Pass. However, once spring run-off is over, there is no actual river, only a few stretches of water every now and then. It is a strenuous climb to the pass, but views of the meadows and trees below make the climb worthwhile. It is possible to bushwhack to Carrot Creek or Cougar Canyon.

South Ram River Trail (Map 27/B2)

This 54 km (33.5 mile) trail gains 345 m (1,121 ft) in elevation, and will take hikers at least two days to hike. From Hummingbird Recreation Area, the trail skirts South Ram River and has a few challenging river crossings that are best attempted in the fall. The scenic trail does offer numerous campsites for the weary traveller.

Stelfox Loop (Map 33/B7)

This difficult 22 km (13.7 mile) hike incorporates sections of the Whitegoat Creek and the Coral Creek Trails, joined by a connecting trail just north of Mount Stelfox. If you do not want to walk an extra 10 km (6 miles) or so down Highway 11, you will need two vehicles. There are several creek crossings and a 560 m (1,820 ft) climb to Whitegoat Pass, which offers a view of the Coral Creek Valley below.

Two O'clock Ridge Trail (Map 26/C2)

The name Two O'clock is named after a common phenomenon that occurs in mountain streams from late spring to early summer. Melt water from the mountains is at its highest level around two o'clock in the afternoon, making creek crossings dangerous during that time. This trail offers a difficult 18 km (11.2 mile) hike from the recreation area to an alpine area with a beautiful view. It takes a full day to complete this trail that gains 1,150 m (3,738 ft) in elevation.

Upper Cascade Fire Road (Map 20/F1)

The 11 km (6.8 miles) road to Scotch Camp, is closed to cyclists but offers an enjoyable route for horseback riders and hikers. Scotch Camp is a beautiful meadow area. Travellers can continue on the Upper Cascade Fire Road and the Red Deer River Trail in Banff National Park.

Viewpoint Trail (Map 33/C7)

This 4 km (2.5 mile) loop trail is a refreshing hike that takes you to Abraham Lake with minimal elevation gain along the way (15m/49 ft). The trail is accessed at the David Thompson Resort.

Vision Quest Trail (Map 33/C7)

Found off Highway 11 at the Cline Solid Waste Transfer Site, this 5 km (3 mile) hike climbs steadily (765m/2,486 ft) along an unmarked trail through pine trees to an open slope where the route is obvious. You pass through an old native Vision Quest Site to a panoramic ridge overlooking Abraham Lake.

Waiparous Creek Trails (Map 21/G6)

From the Waiparous Valley Road, this picturesque 13.5 km (8.4 miles) one-way trail leads to a dramatic gorge on the creek. It is a popular off-roading area, and other users (hikers, bikers and equestrian users) should be careful. The trail to the gorge climbs 305 m (991 ft) but most visitors sample one of the many other options in the area. These include the trails south past Devil's Head Meadows to the Johnson Canyon Trail, the route up to Black Rock Viewpoint or the trail to Margaret Lake. The trail to the lake is a popular 17 km (10.6 mile) return trip that offers spectacular views of the Ghost River Wilderness Area.

Waskasoo Park (Map 38/A6)

This park is spread out along the banks of the Red Deer River in the city of Red Deer. There are over 80 km (50 miles) of multi-use trails that stretch throughout the park. Horseback riding is allowed in the Heritage Ranch area.

Whitegoat Trail (Maps 25/E1-33/C7)

This trail stretches over 32.3 km (20 miles) from Highway 11 to Pinto Lake along the north side of Cline River and requires at least two days to hike one-way. The challenging trail crosses Coral, Boulder, McDonald, and Cataract Creeks, and is best left to more experienced hikers. There is an elevation gain of 415 m (1,349 ft) along the way.

Whitegoat Creek & Falls Trail (Map 33/B7)

From the Cline Solid Waste Transfer site, an easy 2.5 km (1.6 mile) hiking trail climbs 45 m (146 ft) to the gorgeous Whitegoat Falls. Beyond the falls the trail becomes poorly defined and troublesome creek crossings make it more difficult to continue along the creek to Crescent Falls. Your rewards are found in the variety of vegetation and the views of the North Saskatchewan River Valley. The best season for this 19.5 km (12.1 mile) trail is late spring to early fall.

Whitegoat Lakes Loop Trail (Map 33/C7)

This 9 km (5.6 mile) loop is an easy hike for seeing some of the local points of interest. The trail starts at the David Thompson Resort and heads south to Abraham Lake. It then follows the shore of the lake to Little Indian Falls and continues along a creek to the Whitegoat Lakes and back to the resort. It is possible to connect to Whitegoat Falls Trail, shortly after Little Indian Falls.

Whiterabbit Creek Trail (Map 26/C2–G4)

This is a moderate 42 km (26 mile) return trail, perfect for the backpacker prepared for a two or three day excursion. It provides a large variety of terrain linking Kootenay Plains to the North Ram River. This section of the trail gains 610 m (1,983 ft). Another option is to head to Ram River. Choosing this trail requires three or four days to complete the 54 km (33.6 mile) trail, which gains 760m (2,479 ft). Travel on wet, boggy ground and bushwhacking is required, therefore appropriate footwear is recommended.

The Trans Canada Trail

There was a huge push to see this trail completed by the Year 2000. It was not, and, while interest from the general public has waned, the project is still underway, spearheaded in Alberta by the Alberta Trailnet Society. There has been about 1,000 km (625 miles) of the TCT routed through the province, with about the same again left to route. The trail across the province actually splits at Calgary, one arm running north to the Northwest Territories, one arm continuing west to the BC border. Much of this section remains undeveloped, but there are a couple large sections that have been finished, especially around Calgary, Red Deer and Canmore. Although hiking the Southwest Alberta TCT route is a bit of a pipe dream right now (at least, not without a lot of road walking), there are some nice sections, mostly incorporating pre-existing trails.

Area South

Highway 3 bisects the southern portion of our mapbook, running west from Pincher Creek through the Crowsnest Pass. This is a hotspot for outdoor recreation, tinged with a historical flavour. Many of the trails follow old roads and lead to ghost towns or abandoned mine sites. Chances are, if there is an old road people are walking or riding it. Unfortunately, the Lost Creek Fire in 2003 has affected many of these trails. Also included in this area is the popular Castle River Valley to the south and a host of trails off the Forestry Trunk Road, which once again forms the backbone of recreation in the south.

Adanac Ridge Trail (Maps 4/G7-5/A7)

Adanac Ridge runs east between Lynx and Byron Creeks and is home to the Adanac Mine Site. The trail gains 213 m (692 ft) in elevation over 7 km (4.3 miles). A picturesque view of the foothills and open prairie are offered over this half-day hike. The Lost Creek Fire affected the area in 2003.

Allison-Atlas Area (Map 4/E4-D4)

The cross-country ski trails set at the foot of Mount Tecumseh offer hikers and mountain bikers 31 km (19.3 miles) of trails to explore. A popular hike in the area is the **Chinook Lake Loop Trail**. This easy 3 km (1.8 mile) walk follows old roads from the Chinook Lake Recreation Area through the remains of the old McLaren Lumber Company. This is a gorgeous area in the Crowsnest Pass that hooks up with many more kilometres of old roads and trails, including the Atlas Snowmobile Trails to the north. From April 1–November 30 off-road vehicles and horseback use is permitted in the area.

Beauvais Lake Trails (Map 2/D1)

There are 15 km (9.3 miles) of trails in Beauvais Lake Provincial Park. These are easy strolling trails along the lakeshore, past old homestead sites and through the woods. In winter, the trails are used for cross-country skiing. Most of the trails are short (around a kilometre/0.6 mile), with the 5 km (3 mile) long Homestead Trail being the longest.

Beaver Creek Trail (Maps 7/G4–8/A4)

This trail is accessed near Livingstone Falls Recreation Area and takes you to Westrup Creek near Chimney Rock Road. Experienced mountain bikers as well as hikers and horseback riders will appreciate the challenge and the beauty that this 12.5 km (7.8 mile) one-way trail has to offer. You pass by Beaver Creek, which is dry in the summer, and the lower part of Mount Livingstone. Keep your eyes open for wild berries in late summer.

Beaverdam Creek & Ridge Trails (Maps 5/B1–8/C7)

Both of these trails begin at the end of the A7 Ranch Road. The **Beaverdam Creek Trail** is better left for the winter season as it gets too wet and boggy in the summer to enjoy it. Allow five hours to hike the trail, which runs through meadows and valleys and along a mountain ridge. The **Beaverdam Creek Ridge Trail** should take four hours as you gain 300 m (975 ft). Along the way, there are many interesting springs as well as Bob Creek to cross. Try to avoid crossing the creek when the water level is high.

Beehive Mountain Trail (Map 7/E5)

This difficult trail follows an old road 7 km (4.3 miles) one-way to the flanks of Beehive Mountain, gaining 700 m (2275 ft). From here, it is possible to continue along a historical route through Windy Pass and into BC.

Bruin Creek Trail (Maps 7/G6–8/A6)

The first thing you have to do on this route is ford the Oldman River, which serves notice that this is not going to be an easy route. The route gains a ridge above Bruin Creek, which can be followed to Chaffen Ridge. Give yourself about four hours to do this 13 km (8 mile) return hike, which climbs 655 m (2,129 ft).

Burmis Mine Ridge Trail (Map 5/B6)

This hike can be accessed off Secondary Highway 507 at the Hiawatha Campground. The trail starts and concludes at the dirt road to the west, not at the indicated trail sign. Incredible views and the mining history of the area are the highlights of this 7 km (4.3 mile) easy trail, which gains 245 m (796 ft). It should be noted that there is a small fee to park at the campground.

Byron Hill Trail (Map 5/A7)

This is a difficult hike, due in no small part to the 580 m (1,885 ft) gain in elevation. It is 11 km (6.8 miles) long and should take about half a day. The trail runs past an old mine site, through woodlands, across streams and finally up to the hilltop. The view is excellent from here, but beware of strong winds. The trailhead is located along the Hillcrest East Access Road (Off Highway 3).

Cabin Ridge Route (Map 7/F6)

An old road is used by hikers, bikers, equestrians and ATVers to access the scenic Cabin Ridge. The trailhead is found 13.6 km (8.5 miles) down the Oldman River Road. Return the way you came, or via Honeymoon Creek. You will gain 550 m (1,800 ft) climbing to the ridge.

Cache Creek Trail (Map 7/E6)

Cache Creek is located inside the southern boundary of the Beehive Natural Area. The difficult route is tough to find at times, but the effort is worth it as you wind up at a beautiful lake and sub-alpine meadows. The trail is 19 km (11.8 miles) return, climbing 320 m (1050 ft). Give yourself a full day to hike this route.

Camp Creek Trails (Maps 5/A1-8/A7)

Both The Lower and Upper Camp Creek offer five hour hikes, gaining about 250 m (813 ft). The trails lead through forests and lush vegetation to the meadows of the Camp Creek Valley.

Carbondale Hill Lookout Trail (Map 2/A1)

A moderate 9 km (5.6 mile) trail takes you to a fire lookout, offering spectacular views along the way. ATVers and bikers will find several other options in the area (the Carbondale Snowmobile Trails offer 40 km/24 miles of trails) to explore.

Castle River Road Trails (Map 2/B4)

This large 1,700 square km area offers an excellent selection of easily accessed multi-use trails. Many of the trails in the area have off-highway vehicle restrictions. Call (403) 562-3210 for more information. Depending on how far you are willing to drive up the South Castle Road affects how far each of the trails in this popular recreational area will be. Even the road itself is a popular route. The distance traveled ranges from 24–53 km (15-33 miles). Other than a few hills, there is little elevation gained. Along your path you will observe some beautiful views of the Rocky Mountains. The route is best travelled from June to October when the ground is dry. Several side routes can be explored, including:

Avion Ridge Route (Map 2/D5) is a difficult hiking route that continues from the end of the Castle River Road/Trail. The ridge route heads south to the Castle River Divide, climbing 275 m (894 ft) in 1.2 km (0.7 miles). The ridge forms the boundary for Waterton Lakes National Park and offers phenomenal views of the surrounding area.

Font Creek/Sage Mountain Trail (Map 2/C5) is a difficult 8 km (5 mile) route that takes you up to Sage Mountain where you have a fabulous view of the Castle Valley. The trail runs along an overgrown logging road and requires a few creek crossings as you gain 215 m (699 ft) in elevation.

Grizzly Creek Trail (Map 2/A3) climbs 13.5 km (8.4 mile) climbs to the Ruby and Grizzly Lakes. The terrain is difficult and you must ford the Castle River, making biking difficult.

Jutland Brook Route (Map 2/B4) is more of a bushwhack that follows Jutland Brook up the shank of Jutland Mountain. It connects up with the Scarpe Creek Trail (see below) and trails in the Sage Creek drainage, in BC.

Lys Lake Trail (Map 2/B4) is almost rather difficult to locate among the many game trails that lead from the Castle River near the ford. This has been done on purpose to keep folks away from the good fishing lake. Needless to say, it hasn't worked, but you will want a map and a compass. The trail, when found, is easy to follow, and gains 625 m (2,050 ft) to the beautiful lake over 7 km (4.5 miles) one-way.

Scarpe Creek Trail (Map 2/B4) is another difficult trail behind Jutland Mountain. It is easy to connect to the Jutland Brook Trail (see above) as well as the Sage Creek drainage in BC. A common destination is South Scarpe Lake, 5 km (3 miles) from the trailhead.

Whistler Mountain Lookout (Map 2/B2) is accessed by a 5 km (3 mile) hike that starts from the South Castle River Road, 5.5 km (3.4 miles) past Beaver Mines Lake. The hiking is moderate but route finding skills will be needed to pick your way up the ridge and the lookout. Be forewarned that this site is very windy. You can access Table Mountain from here.

Coat Creek Trail (Map 7/G5) 🚶 🚵 🐎 🎿 🛶

The trailhead is found 2.5 km (1.5 miles) south of Livingstone Falls along the Forestry Trunk Road. It follows an old road, then trail, along the north bank of Coat Creek. The moderate 6 km (3.7 mile) one-way trail gains 426 m (1,400 ft) before meeting a snowmobile route to Savanna Creek, which can be followed. The more adventurous can bushwhack their way up to Cabin Ridge.

Crowsnest Lake Trail (Map 4/D5) 🚶 🛶

There is a 7 km (4.3 mile) hiking circuit around the picturesque lake. About half way, you will come across a cave with pictographs (historic Indian rock paintings). The trailhead is located at the Crowsnest Lake Information Centre, off Highway 3.

Crowsnest Mountain Trail (Map 4/E3) 🚶 🛶

Access to this trail is found 10.5 km (6.5 miles) up the Allison Creek Road (Off Highway 3). This is a challenging, 12 km (7.4 mile) hiking trail leading to the summit of Crowsnest Mountain. With loose terrain, steep slopes and high winds, the route can be quite strenuous, so give yourself at least five hours to hike. The elevation gain is 1,110 m (3,608 ft). The excellent views along your climb will compensate for the struggle.

Daisy Creek Trail (Map 4/G1-3) 🚵 🛶

This 22.5 km (14 mile) trail is found along Daisy Creek (off the Forestry Trunk Road or the Coseka Resources Road). The route is used mostly by ATVers and mountain bikers since it is not an exciting hiking route. The trail follows an old road that takes you up and down through open alpine and should be snow free by mid-June.

Deadman's Pass Trail (Map 4/D4) 🚶 🚵 🎿 🛶

Found at Chinook Lake, this easy 15 km (9.3 mile) route takes you past some lakes and through forests full of beautiful vegetation. If hiking, allow 3-4 hours one-way. You gain 120 m (390 ft) in elevation.

Drum Creek Trail (Maps 4/G6–5/A6) 🚶 🛶

Park your vehicle on Lyons Creek Road (off Highway 3) and walk to the trailhead found on 230th Street and 7th Avenue at the Hillcrest Mines. The trail is a 9 km (5.6 mile), moderate hike and gains 396 m (1,287 ft) in elevation. The trail is well groomed, making your climb to the great views easier. This area was affected by the Lost Creek Fire in 2003.

Fort MacLeod Wilderness Park (Map 6/G3) 🚶 🚵 🐎

There are about 3 km (1.8 miles) of trails in the Fort MacLeod River Valley Wilderness Park to explore. The trails follow the Oldman River Valley.

Frank Slide Trails (Map 5/A5) 🚶 🛶

This historical site is accessed off the Crowsnest Highway at the Frank Slide Interpretive Centre. In and around the area are a number of trails to explore. The **Frank Slide Trail** is a moderate, one-hour return hike through one of the world's largest rockslides. This trail connects with several other trails. It is a short 1.2 km (0.7 mile) return walk past Frank to an abandoned mine site worth exploring. The **Livingstone Ridge Trail**, which begins on an old gravel road past the Interpretive Centre, follows the gas cutline to the base of the rocky Livingstone Ridge. Climbing the ridge to the rock cairn provides a magnificent view of Turtle Mountain and the prairie below. This 12.5 km (7.8 mile) day hike gains 670 m (2,178 ft). Another option is the **Skirting the Slide Trail**. This easy 8 km (5 mile) return hike takes you out to the West Canadian Collieries Bellevue mining operation and back. En route you notice the road is littered with coal slack, subsidence pits and other signs of the industry in the area. At the end there is a ridge where one can overlook the town of Bellevue.

Gardiner Creek Trail (Map 1/G2) 🚵 🐎 🚵 🛶

Accessed 2.5 km (1.6 miles) down the Carbondale River Road, a difficult trail begins. It is 24 km (14.9 miles) long and is best suited for horseback riding, biking and ATVs. This trail is for the adventurous types who like winding and climbing through varied terrain. The trail can be quite busy on the weekends, especially with ATVs.

Goat Creek Loop (Map 4/F7) 🚵 🐎 🚵 🛶

Hikers will probably want to skip this 32 km (19.9 mile) route that combines a bunch of old roads in the Goat Creek/Lost Creek drainage into a loop. Mountain bikers will find this an easy, if unremarkable ride. Other roads in the area run up the north and south forks of Goat Creek. This area was affected by the Lost Creek fire in 2003.

Grassy Mountain Trails (Map 4/G6–5/A6) 🚶 🚵 🚵 🛶

The main route up Grassy Mountain is a moderate 12 km (7.4 miles) trail that begins off the Blairmore Creek Road at the 9 km (5.6 mile) junction. The trail gains 490 m (1593 ft) in elevation and offers fabulous views of Waterton National Park and Kananaskis Country. The route leads down an old road where you can view an old open pit-mining site or take a side trip to the left, which takes you along the **Fault Trail**. This easy 5 km (3 mile) side trip accesses a viewpoint of the Turtle Mountain Fault, which splits Grassy Mountain. Also in the area is the moderate **Greenhill Ridge Trail**. This 8 km (5 mile) trail passes the historic Greenhill Mine, a designated historic site.

Gravenstafel Brook/Haig Mountain Trail (Map 1/G3) 🚶 🚵 🎿 🛶

From the parking lot at Castle Mountain Ski Area, an easy 7 km (4.3 mile) old road heads up Gravenstafel Creek to the tiny Haig Lake, at the base of Haig Mountain. The trail splits; keep right. The left trail leads to the top of Haig Mountain along a difficult route.

Hastings Ridge Trails (Maps 4/G6-5/A7) 🚶 🚵 🛶

These interconnected trails range from 5 km (3 mile) to 20 km (12.5 miles) or more, depending on which route you take. The trails can be hiked or biked, beginning on the Adanac Road. They climb to a summit along Hastings Ridge, providing views of the Flathead and Clark Ranges. From here, you may explore the old Adanac Mine or continue climbing to the main trail at the north end of Hastings Ridge. The Lost Creek Fire affected this area in 2003.

Hidden Creek Trail (Map 7/F7) 🚶 🚵 🐎 🚵

The Hidden Creek Trail begins with a ford of the Oldman River. The moderate 24 km (14.9 mile) trail then leads up the creek to the base of Tornado Mountain. It is possible to make your way up to Tornado Pass and follow the Great Divide Trail climbs up the mountain, but a map and compass are needed.

Isolation Creek Trail (Map 7/G4) 🚶 🚵 🛶

An old road crosses Livingstone River and heads west along Isolation Creek. This moderate 30 km (18.6 mile) trail climbs 853 m (2800 ft) as it heads up the side of Isola Peak.

Lille Trail (Map 5/A4) 🚶 🚲 🏍 ⛺

This easy trail follows Gold Creek north past the remains of the old Number One Mine. There is a bridge out over the Creek, which means most hikers will get their feet wet in the shallow creek. The trail is a 12.6 km (7.8 miles) return trip, and gains a mere 50 m (160 ft), but you can string together a few other old roads to make it a 23 km (15.6 mile) trip. You will pass through the remains of Lille, a once-thriving town, built in 1901. Lille has been designated an historic site and must be left undisturbed.

Little Whaleback Ridge Trail (Map 8/B7) 🚶 ⛺

This trail climbs the Little Whaleback Ridge, before descending east to the Bob Creek Valley. This is a scenic trip, alternating between forests and subalpine meadow with lush vegetation throughout the route.

Livingstone Fire Lookout Trail (Map 8/A7) 🚶 🏍 🏍 ⛺

It is 10 km (6.2 miles) up to the Livingstone Fire Lookout along an old road found just north of the Dutch Creek Recreation Area. There is no bridge across the Oldman River, and fording the river is not recommended until later in the year. From the new lookout, it is possible to continue another 3.5 km (2.2 miles) one-way to the site of the old lookout, and from there descend south on a poorly marked hiking only trail down to the river, then back to where you started.

MacDonald Creek/North Kootenay Pass Trail (Map 1/F1) 🚶 🏍 🏍

This trail varies in length from 15.2 km-36 km (9.5-22.5 miles), depending upon where you begin your trek along the Carbondale River Road. Most vehicles can only drive about 5.2 km (3.2 mile) past the Lynx Creek Recreation Area. This trail is best suited for skilled mountain bikers looking for some difficult terrain. Biking up to the pass takes you along the North Kootenay Pass Trail.

McGillivray Creek Trail (Map 4/F4) 🚶 🏍 ⛺

This 14 km (8.7 mile) trail is best suited for mountain bikers looking for a pleasant half-day ride. The trail, which climbs 520 m (1,690 ft), can get boggy and there are many creek crossings so expect to get your feet wet. There are fine views of Ma Butte and the volcanic rock along the way. A short side trail leads to the base of the Seven Sisters.

Middle Kootenay Pass Trail (Maps 1/G5-2/A4) 🚶 🏍 🐎 🏕 🏍 ⛺

This long, difficult 46.5 km (28.9 mile) route is best travelled by experienced riders (on bike or ATV). It has two access points: one in BC, from the Commerce Forest Service Road and the other from Alberta at the West Castle Ski Area. Expect to encounter your share of steep hills and a need for plenty of bushwhacking. Along your trek keep your eyes peeled for waterfalls and bears, which frequent the sub-alpine forests.

Mill Creek Trail (Map 2/C2-4) 🚶 🏍 🐎 🏕 🏍

Part of the Castle Management Area, this long (32 km/19.9 mile return) old road leads to the end of the Mill Creek Valley, and the base of Victoria Ridge.

Nez Perce Trail (Map 4/G4) 🚶 ⛺

Also known as the Old Miner's Trail, a 4.5 km (2.8 mile) return trail leads to the old McGillivray Mine. It can be accessed from Highway 3 at the Coleman Information Centre. It is a nice little walk, where many local residents stroll after dark. The trail that continues up Nez Perce Creek takes you to a small waterfall and becomes less distinct the further you travel. Another option is to climb the stairs to the top of the ravine above the waterfall. At the top, turn left, and head into a meadow, climb the fence and follow the indistinct route that leads to Saskatoon Mountain. The trail climbs 400 m (1300 ft) in 5 km (3 miles).

North Fork Pass Trail (Maps 4/D1–7/D7) 🚶 🏍 🐎 🏍 ⛺

An old road runs up the north fork of Dutch Creek to North Fork Pass on the BC/Alberta boundary. This trail hooks up with Hidden Creek by following the Great Divide Trail over Tornado Mountain. The trip to the pass and back again is 16 km (10 miles), gaining 300 m (975 ft).

North Lost Creek Trail (Maps 1/E1-4/E7) 🚶 🏍 🏍 ⛺

Locals claim that this scenic valley is the prettiest in the Rockies, high praise, especially in an area with such superlative scenery. Check it out for yourself. The moderate biking route is 22-35 km (13.6-21.7 miles) in length depending on where you begin on Lost Creek Road. There are several steep climbs, a waterfall and two lakes at the top, which can be reached by hiking northeast. The spectacular area was affected by the Lost Creek fire in 2003.

Oldman River Headwater Trails (Map 7/D5) 🚶 🏍 🐎 🏍 🏍 🐟 ⛺

The trailhead to this series of multi-use trails is located at the end of the Oldman River Road. The Headwaters Trail is a moderate 14 km (8.7 mile) return route. Give yourself about three hours as you follow the trail up the river to Memory Lake. The Great Divide Trail, which takes you to the Galtea Miracle Mine, can be accessed from the lake.

Oyster Creek Trail (Map 7/D2-4) 🚶 🏍 🏍 🏍

This trail is part of a mess of trails in the Oldman Headwater area. It leads 26 km (16.2 miles) one-way to Cataract Creek. In the summer, it is a hiking, biking and ATV route, while in the winter the route becomes a snowmobiling trail. The route sticks to the valley bottom, and isn't very visually interesting.

Pincher Creek Trail (Map 2/D3) 🚶 🏍 🐎 ⛺

The Pincher Creek Trail is most often used to access Victoria Ridge. To do so will net you 1,615 m (5,250 ft) of elevation over 6 km (3.6 miles). From Victoria Ridge, it is possible to continue south to the Castle River drainage or Waterton Park. You will probably want a shuttle if you try either of these options.

Playle Creek Trail (Map 8/D7) 🚶 🏍 🏍

This easy 13 km (8 mile) trail follows a cart track, which in turn follows Playle Creek east from Highway 22. Elevation gain is 350 m (1,150 ft) as you pass through open grasslands.

Police Outpost Provincial Park (Map 3/F7) 🚶 🏍 🏕

Tucked up against the Alberta/Montana border, there are 7 km (4.3 miles) of easy interpretive trails in this park.

Ptolemy Pass Trail (Map 4/D6) 🚶 🏍 🐎 🏍 🏕 ⛺

It is 6.5 km (4 miles) from the trailhead, on Chinook Coal Road, to the pass, gaining 210 m (690 ft). Past the pass, the trail (like so many trails in the area, it is actually an old mining road) continues into BC, but the route down is through a dense forest with limited views.

Racehorse Pass (Map 4/D3) 🚶 🏍 🐎 🏍

An old road runs up from the Atlas Forestry Road through Racehorse Pass, connecting to trails, then roads, in the Alexander Creek drainage in BC. It is possible to turn this into a 39 km (24 mile) loop, returning via Deadman's Pass.

Racehorse Roundabout Trail (Map 4/G2) 🚶 🏍 🏍 🏕 ⛺

From Racehorse Creek Recreation Area, this trail heads upstream along the creek and loops back along the Racehorse Creek Road and Forestry Trunk Road. Some highlights of this 24 km (14.9 mile) trail, which gains 265 m (861 ft), include pine and poplar forests and open meadows. The best time to hike or bike this trail would be early summer through fall. Snowmobilers also use this trail system.

Rainy Ridge Lake (Map 2/A3) 🚶

While the usual visitors to this lake are anglers, looking to fish one of Alberta's few golden trout lakes, hikers should not overlook this beautiful lake set beneath Rainy Ridge. There is a good trail to the lake, and a lot of trails (mostly old roads) that lead away from the lake. Picking the right route will be much more difficult that the actual hike. If you find the right route, you should cover 4 km (2.4 miles) as you climb 365 m (1,200 ft) to the lake. If you do not find the right route, you could be hiking for hours. The West Castle Road is in poor repair past the ski area, and you may have to hike or bike to the trailhead.

Ridge Creek Trail (Maps 7/G5–8/A5)

Nature, mountain ridges, and meadows are just a few of the attractions to be discovered on this easy hike. The 16 km (10 mile) trail may be accessed south of Livingstone Falls Recreation Area. The beginning and end of the route is found at the fence, near the bridge at Livingstone River. It should take four hours to complete the trail, which gains 120 m (390 ft).

Rumrunners Run–Phillipp's Pass Trail (Map 4/C4)

This 10.5 km (6.5 mile) trail was named for its use during the days of Prohibition. It is best to leave a shuttle vehicle at the CPR tracks in Sentinel, where the hike ends. The trail starts at the Crowsnest Provincial Park and climbs to the top of the Phillipp's Pass. From the pass, you can hike 3.5 km (2.2 miles) to the transmitter tower on the top of Crowsnest Ridge. Below the ridge are Island, Crowsnest and Emerald Lakes.

Shale Creek Trail (Map 7/G6)

This is a difficult hiking, biking and ATV route found off Oldman River Road. It is a 9 km (5.6 mile) trip in which you gain 490 m (1,593 ft) in elevation, as you climb to Cabin Ridge. Excellent viewpoints are found once up on the ridge.

Slacker Creek (Map 7/E5)

Do not let the name fool you. You have got to work a bit to complete this 17 km (10.6 mile) trail, especially if you are on foot, as you climb 615 m (2,000 ft) along the way. (The name comes from a group of World War One draft dodgers who hid in the area.) The route follows old roads as it works its way up the creek. It is fairly easy to work your way to Savanna Creek, and follow the old roads down to the Forestry Trunk Road, a popular option with snowmobilers in the winter.

South Drywood Creek Trail (Map 2/D4)

A hiking, biking and ATV trail leading up the creek to Bovin Lake, can be accessed off the Front Range Road on the South Drywood Road. It is a difficult, 10.5 km (6.5 mile) route along a rough and rocky trail. Bovin Lake is an amazing blue colour, which stands out against the red and green hills of the Drywood Range. Camping is available at the lake, and you can continue up to a ridge overlooking the lake and then descend to the Castle River Road.

Southfork (Barnaby) Lakes Trail (Map 2/A2)

From the trailhead on West Castle Road, 10 km (6.2 miles) past the South Castle Bridge, this moderate 12 km (7.4 mile) trail climbs 1,415 m (4,600 ft) to Southfork Lakes. The lake is popular with anglers as it is one of the few lakes in Alberta that contain golden trout.

South Lost Creek Trail (Map 1/G1)

This biking trail can be found on Lost Creek Road, but varies in length from 17 km-30 km (10.6 miles-18.6 miles) return, depending upon your origin. Expect some moderate climbs as you follow the creek. At the conclusion of the trail, park your bike and walk down to the creek and look to the west, where you will see the spectacular limestone walls of Center Mountain. The Lost Creek Fire affected this area in 2003.

Spionkop Creek Trail (Map 2/D4)

This moderate 17.5 km (11 mile) return route takes you through a canyon along a dry and rocky route, with a few creek fords. The best time to travel this trail is mid-June to mid-October. Please also note that the access road is closed to all motor vehicles.

Star Creek Falls–Three Cabin Trail (Map 4/E5)

It is best to have a shuttle waiting for you at the Travel Information Centre in Sentinel, where this hike ends. If you do not, you will have to hike the (admittedly easy) 9.5 km (5.9 mile) trail twice. The Star Creek Falls Trailhead is just outside of Coleman, and the trail follows an old mining road past a series of canyons and waterfalls on the creek. There are good views of the Flathead Range. At the far end of your journey, you will see three old log cabins, which are remnants of mining in the area. From the Star Creek Falls parking lot, you can also visit the Lower Star Creek Falls along an easy 1.5 km (0.9 mile) trail.

Sugarloaf Fire Lookout (Map 7/F7)

The trail to Sugarloaf Fire Lookout climbs steeply from the Dutch Creek Road, gaining 990 m (3,250 ft) in 8 km (5 miles). Keep left when the trail splits. This is the highest lookout in the region, and the highest active lookout in Canada. As you might guess, this lookout offers great views of the surrounding area. In addition to the great views, the lookout features a large rock mosaic, created by a former denizen of the lookout.

Syncline Creek Trail (Map 1/G2)

This easy 10 km (6.2 mile) trail follows Syncline Creek up the valley between St. Eloi Mountain and the Castle Mountain Ski Area.

Syncline Cross-Country Trails (Map 2/A1)

This cross-country ski area offers 13.5 km (8.4 miles) of trails that can be enjoyed by all levels of bikers and hikers in the summer. Allow a couple hours to explore the trails, which lead past ponds, raspberry bushes and cliffs.

Table Mountain Trail (Map 2/B2)

This trail passes through an aspen forest, then a larch forest before finally breaking out in the alpine. The trailhead is located at the Beaver Mines Lake Campground, and you will climb 1,477 m (4,800 ft) in 4 km (2.4 miles) one-way to the top.

Tornado Pass Trail (Map 7/D7)

This hike starts from a washout, some 25 km (15.5 miles) up the Dutch Creek Road. Some vehicles can make it past the washout to the end of the road, 6 km (3.6 miles) beyond. From the end of the road, the trail leads up to Tornado Pass, gaining 370 m (7070 ft) along the way.

Trail to the Promised Land (Map 4/B3)

This amazing, 16 km (10 mile) return hike and bike is one of the best in the Crowsnest Pass area. Explore some of the numerous caves as you gain 1,000 m (3,250 ft), including 760 m (2,470 ft) in the final 1.8 km (1.1 mile). There are enough attractions in the area, including karst formations, frost pockets and huge subsidence holes to keep you exploring for several days. The trail follows the **Trail of the Seven Bridges** to the top of the second major climb, where the two split. Take the right-had fork to get to the Promised Land. Hikers without proper spelunking gear should keep away from the caves; many feature dangerous drop-offs that can be deadly to the unprepared. The left hand fork takes you to high alpine meadows and to the tiny, emerald green Ptolemy Lake. Please note that most of the bridges have vanished, although occasionally someone will drop a log over a creek.

Turtle Mountain Trail (Map 5/A6) 🚶 🚴 ⛺
This is a popular 7.8 km (4.8 mile) trail taking you to the top of the north peak. Two vehicles are recommended for this trail, one at the corner of 230 St. and 7 Ave. in Hillcrest and the other at the abandoned motel on Highway 3 between Frank and Blairmore. From the motel, follow your nose to the sulphur spring and continue up to the peak. The final stretch of trail overlooks Frank Slide, which disfigured the turtle profile of the mountain. The backside of Turtle Mountain burned in the Lost Creek fire in 2003.

Two Mine Trail (Map 5/A6) 🚶
This is a 9.8 km (6 mile) trail that starts on the Leitch Collieries Trail. For this hike it is recommended to utilize a second vehicle at the trailhead at the west end of 28th Ave in Bellevue. This hike is enjoyable because it will allow you to explore some old mining ruins. Be careful as you make your way up the ridge, as the mining sites can be dangerous.

Wedge Mountain Trail (Map 4/F4) 🚶 ⛺
This 8.5 km (5.3 mile) hike can be accessed off Highway 3, west of Coleman at the Crowsnest Pass sign. The trail starts at the Iron Ridge Trailhead (across the highway from the sign) and gains 762 m (2,477 ft). Stunning vistas and volcanic rock formations are major features of this trail, which can be covered in snow until early summer.

Whaleback Ridge Trails (Maps 5/B1–8/C7) 🚶 🚴 ⛺
Accessed through the Waldron Ranch on the A7 Ranch Road, picking the right trail can be difficult. The north ridge trail is a moderate 15 km (9.3 mile) route that climbs 325 m (1,000 ft) as it follows the Whaleback Ridge. There are some great panoramic views from the ridge, and a good chance to see deer and elk. The south ridge trail climbs a bit more since it features more up and down sections. You will have to pass through some cattle gates; leave them as you find them.

White Creek Trail (Map 8/A7) 🚶 🚴 🐎 🛶 🐟
The access point for this multi-use trail is situated on Forestry Trunk Road, close to Livingstone River Canyon. The 27 km (16.8 mile) return trip requires many creek crossings as you follow the good fishing stream. It will take a full day, or two part days to hike this trail.

Window Mountain Lake Trail (Map 4/E3) 🚶 🐟
Window Mountain Lake is a perfect spot to fish or picnic. The 4 km (2.5 mile) trail does continue around the lake, bringing you back to your starting point. The steep trail climbs 215 m (699 ft) and should be left until early summer, as it can be snowy (or at least muddy) earlier in the year.

Yarrow Canyon Trail (Map 2/D5) ⛺ 🚶 🚴 🐎 ⛺
The beautiful Yarrow Canyon is accessed on a gated road off of Spreadeagle Road. The 20.5 km (12.7 mile) moderate route climbs 550 m (1,788 ft) and is used by hikers, bikers and horseback riders. The route takes you past a noisy gas compressor station to an alpine waterfall where camping is possible.

York Creek Trails (Map 4/F6) 🚶 🚴 🛶 ⛺
Accessed 6.2 km (3.8 miles) up the York Creek Road, a series of trails begin. The **Ironstone Lookout Trail** is a moderate 14 km (8.7 mile) trail that requires a creek crossing and a little bushwhacking. It leads up the Willoughby Ridge to the fire lookout with panoramic views. The 580 m (1885 ft) climb is not too steep, but it is long and tiring. The **Coulthard Mountain Meadows Trail** is a difficult 11.5 km (7.1 mile) return hike that climbs steadily up an old road through forest lined with salmonberries and raspberries. The trail ends in a large meadow, where you can pick your way up to a saddle on the northeast ridge or bushwhack up to the mountain tarn. The **North York Creek Trail** offers stunning mountain views, caves, and the plane wreckage of the RCAF Dakota. At 14 km (8.7 mile) in total, this difficult hike should last a full day. The elevation gain is 795 m (2,584 ft), more if you climb up Andy Good Peak to a pretty little cirque. The area, which links up with the Lynx Creek Trails, is popular with snowmobilers in the winter.

Kananaskis and Canmore
Kananaskis Country is the name given to a pastiche of parks, wildland areas, recreation areas, ecological reserves and multiple use areas on the eastern slopes of the Canadian Rockies southeast of Banff. This vast 4,000 square kilometre area includes Peter Lougheed and the newly found Sheep River Provincial Parks and has longed served as the outdoor playground for locals looking for an escape from the overcrowded national parks. The area provides endless, year-round opportunities for every type of traveller. There are off-highway vehicle areas, cross-country ski systems, hiking, biking and horseback trails as well as unmarked routes leading to spectacular vistas. The area has a history of resource extraction activity, and many of the trails follow old exploration and logging roads, seismic lines and animal paths. Although they usually provide easy travel, the routes can be somewhat confusing and hard to follow as they interweave with other old roads and trails. The most popular routes are signed, but many are not.

9999 & Curley Sand Trails (Map 11/F1) 🚶 🐎 ⛺
The **9999 Trail** is a 7 km (4.3 mile) trail that takes the hiker or the horseback rider from grassy grazing lands around Threepoint Creek to the meadows of Ware Creek Valley. There is an elevation gain of 90 m (293 ft) from north to south. Also beginning at the Mesa Butte Recreation Area but offering multiple access points is the **Curley Sand Trail**, a short 4 km (2.5 mile) walk. The well-marked trail joins up with 9999 Trail, but not before crossing Threepoint Creek a couple times. You must also be careful as you near the North Fork Recreation Area as the route crosses the highway. The trail offers fine ridge views.

Aster Lake Trail (Map 10/D4) 🚶 ⛺
From the Upper Lakes Parking Lot, this 11 km (6.8 mile) day hike takes you past Hidden Lake as it makes its way up and down through forests, meadows and across creeks. Spectacular views can be seen along the way. A shorter option would be to turn around at the Waka Nambe Viewpoint.

Baldy Pass Trail (Map 15/G5) 🚶 🚴 ⛺
There are a couple ways to reach the pass. From the south, at the Baldy Pass Parking Lot off Highway 40, is a moderate hike or difficult bike ride. This 10 km (6.2 mile) trail climbs 490 m (1,593 ft) through trees up to the pass. Since the view is limited, you may want to continue on to Mount Baldy for better viewpoints. From the north, at the Lusk Creek Picnic Area off Highway 68, is an 11.5 km (7.1 mile) hike. It leads through forest and along the Old Mill Road to reach the pass.

Baril Creek Trail (Map 7/C1–D1) 🚶 🚴 🐎 ⛺
Beginning in a gravel pit off the Forestry Trunk Road, this is a 26 km (16.2 mile) biking or hiking trail. It is fun and easy and provides access to great scenery. It links up with the Great Divide and Fording Pass Trails. Dry weather from July to mid-October is the best time to hike and bike the trail. The Baril Loop Trail, a difficult 4 km (2.5 mile) hiking and biking trail, can be accessed from the Baril Creek Trail or Etherington Creek Trail. The west part of the loop is a rough, uncompacted road and results in some tough cycling. However, the trail is well marked and tends to ease up on the east part.

Bear Creek Trail (Map 7/C1) 🚶 ⛺
A hike, which gains 564 m (1,833 ft) in elevation, can be accessed at the Miller Creek Road junction with Pekisko Creek Road (Highway 540). There is several creek crossing as well as hills along the way. To extend your journey, continue onto the ridge of Mount Burke.

Bear Pond Trail (Map 7/G2) 🚶 🐟
A popular angler route, this trail takes you by Bear Pond, Johnston Creek, the Iron Lakes and Iron Creek. The lakes are stocked with grayling, making them popular fishing spots. The country is beautiful along this 3.5 km (2.2 mile) one-way hike, which is accessed off the Johnson Creek Trail (Hwy 532).

Big Elbow Trail (Maps 10/G1-11/B1) ⛺ 🚶 🚴 🐎 ⛺
This moderate 26.5 km (16.5 mile) one-way route gains 350 m (1,138 ft) as it follows an old fire road along the Elbow River. Most people who travel this trail, do so as part of the popular Elbow Loop or to explore the surrounding peaks. There is backcountry camping along the route, as well as some great mountain views. **Banded Peak** can be reached by a difficult 5 km (3 mile) route that takes you 1,015 m (3,300 ft) up to the mountain summit.

The route to **Mount Cornwall** is a full-day journey that gains some 1,340 m (4,355 ft). The 12 km (7.4 miles) trek veers off the main trail near South Glasgow creek. The trek has no steep slopes and provides some glorious scenery including a long ridge of orange shale.

Black Prince Cirque Trail (Map 10/D2)
Beginning at the Black Prince Picnic Area, this is a moderate hike of 4.5 km (2.8 miles). The trail leads to both Warspite Lake and the Black Prince Lakes, passing Warspite River along the way. Be warned that it is quite a climb (591 m/1,921 ft gain) to view the Black Prince Lakes.

Bluerock Trails (Map 11/C3)
Accessed at the Bluerock Recreation Area are a series of trails. The **Bluerock Creek Trail** is a moderate but short 2 km (1.2 miles) trail. The trail provides beautiful vegetation and great viewpoints. Those looking for more of a challenge will find the **Blue Rock Trail** fills this bill. It is a difficult 24 km (14.9 mile) hiking and biking trail that gains 750 m (2,438 ft) through the beautiful foothill country. Follow the road up Bluerock Creek to the footbridge. Here, the trail climbs up Bluerock Mountain for a great view, before the steep descent. It is possible to follow Gorge Creek to the Indian Oils Trails. This trail is easier but still climbs over a dry ridge.

Boulton Creek Trail (Map 10/F3)
An easy 3 km (1.8 mile) walk through the forest and valley. The trailhead is accessed at Boulton Bridge Picnic Area. As you walk the trail, you will hear, if not see, the rushing water of Boulton Creek.

Bow Valley Trails (Map 15/F2)
The Bow Valley Provincial Park offers a series of easy trails. The **Bow River Trail** is a short 2.5 km (1.6 mile) wheelchair accessible trail that follows the shoreline of the Bow River from the campground. There are fishing opportunities and a possible side trip option to the sand forest. The **Bow Valley Bike Path** links the visitor centre with the campground via a 4.4 km (2.7 mile) one-way trail. The trail follows undulating terrain through forest and meadows. The **Many Springs Trail** is an easy 2 km (1.2 mile) route that follows an access road from the Many Springs Parking Lot through meadows to a series of warm springs. It is only open from mid-May to mid-October but it is possible to find flowers here while the rest of the valley is still shaking off winter. **Middle Lake Interpretive Trail** provides an easy 2.5 km (1.6 mile) walk around the lake. The trail begins at the Middle Lake Parking Lot and is a good stroll for families as there is plenty of wildlife, including several species of ducks. **Moraine Trail** also begins as the Bow Valley Campground. The 3 km (1.8 mile) trail climbs some rubble to offer fabulous views all around.

Bryant Creek Trail (Maps 14/G6-15/A7)
Accessed from the Mount Shark parking area (off Spray Lakes West Road), this is one of the most popular trails in the Canadian Rockies. It is a 22.5 km (14 mile), moderate trail that gradually climbs 520 m (1,690 ft) to meet up

with the Allenby Pass Trail. Most travellers continue on to Mount Assiniboine Park in BC (see below).

Buller Pass Trail (Map 15/B7)
This moderate, 10 km (6 mile) hike begins at the Buller Mountain Picnic Area. It gains 670 m (2,178 ft) in elevation, making the trail quite a steep climb. Fit hikers might want to attempt this in one long day, others may choose to make it an overnight trip. Either way, you get to see a small waterfall and a fabulous view of Ribbon Lake. The scenic **Guinn's Pass Trail** can be accessed off this trail, 1 km (0.6 mile) west of Ribbon Lake.

Burstall Pass Trails (Map 10/B1)
This 13 km (8 mile) trail begins at the Mud Lake Parking Lot. It leads past glaciers and across streams to the pass. The trail offers lots of opportunity for further exploration. You can descend to the Upper Spray Valley, access Burstall and Hogarth Lakes or explore the **French Creek Trail**, which provides access to three beautiful waterfalls. The 7 km (4.3 mile) trail ends at the base of the French Glacier, where further exploration needs an ice axe and ropes.

Canadian Mount Everest Expedition Trail (Map 10/F3)
The name of this trail makes it sounds like it should be a difficult trail. It is not. In fact, it is a moderate loop, covering 2.2 km (1.4 mile) as it passes through primarily spruce forest as well as fields of green and pink coloured wintergreens. The trail, which begins off the Kananaskis Lakes Trail at the White Spruce Parking Lot, finishes with spectacular views over the Kananaskis Lakes. The trail was re-named in 1984 after the successful Canadian expedition to Everest's peak.

Canmore Nordic Centre Trails (Map 15/A3)
This area offers 65 km (40 miles) of looping trails, good for all levels of cyclists, hikers or cross-country skiers. The trails vary from wide paths to tricky single-tracks. There are trail maps at most major intersections along the trail. Access is off the Smith-Dorrien Spray Lakes Trail or from Canmore at 8th Street and 8th Avenue. The Canmore access requires climbing a 4 km (2.5 mile), steep trail to the nordic centre. Another option is the **Georgetown Trail**. This is an easy 8.5 km (5.3 mile) hike to an old coal-mining town.

Carnarvon Lake Trail (Map 11/C7)
From the Cat Creek Picnic Area, this 17 km (10.6 mile) scenic multi-use trail climbs an old road to the foothills of the High Rock Range. To reach the lake, which offers good cutthroat trout fishing, a scramble off the main road is necessary. A ford of the Highwood River limits access to the trail until after spring run-off (late June). The **Strawberry Hill Trail**, found in between Fitzsimmons and Carnarvon Creeks, can be accessed from the 6 km (3.7 mile) mark of the main trail.

Cat Creek Trails (Map 11/C7)
From the Cat Creek Picnic Area, **Cat Creek Waterfalls Trail** is a popular 4 km (2.5 mile) return trail that leads to the falls. Many people combine this trail with a side trip to the Cat Creek Hills. There is no one route up to the hills, but, unlike many other interweaving trails, it does not matter which route you take. As long as you keep heading up, you will eventually get to the top, where you will find good views west over the Elk Range.

Cataract Creek Falls Trail (Map 7/E1)
This trail is accessed from the Cataract Creek Recreation Area (on the east side of the Forestry Trunk Road). Follow the road over Cataract Creek to the upper falls. This 10 km (6.2 mile) trail does have some difficult sections, including the initial crossing of the Highwood River. An easier trip is to hike this trip in reverse, from the campground, which eliminates the crossing of the Highwood River.

Cataract Loop Trail (Map 7/D2)
The Cataract Loop Trail begins on a no vehicle road leading west up the Cataract Creek Valley. The road climbs through cutblocks and is quite rough until it passes Lost Creek. It is best to wait until it is dry to tackle this 29 km (18 mile) loop that gains 430 m (1,398 ft) in elevation. Allow 4.5 hours to bike it. The trail up Cataract Creek accesses many other multi-use trails in the area including the Cummings and Lost Creek Trails heading south and the Rye

Ridge Trail heading north. The ridge trail is narrow and rooty and requires some bike pushing, before the fabulous ridge and the descent. Return along Etherington Creek Road to get back to the Forestry Trunk Road.

Chester Lake Trail (Map 10/C1) 🚶 🐟 🎿 👣
This is a 5 km (3 mile) hiking trail accessed from the Chester Lake Parking Lot. It takes you to a beautiful mountain lake, by climbing through forests and meadows. Three Lakes Valley and Rummel Lake can also be accessed if you wish to continue past the lake. Alternatively, an 8 km (5 mile) trail leads northeast to The Fortress. Some scrambling up rocky terrain will bring you to the summit, where you can enjoy the views.

Cougar Creek Trail (Map 15/C3) 🚶
The moderate trail along Cougar Creek can be used for a half hour stroll or a two-day hike. Numerous creek crossings are required on this 11 km (6.8 miles) trail, which gains 640 m (2,080 ft) to Cougar/Carrot Column. Fortunately, the main creek bed usually dries up after the creek forks. However, this makes it difficult for the backpacker to obtain water. Access is found on Benchlands Trail, off the Bow Valley Trail (Hwy 1A) just before Cougar Creek crossing. The best season for this hike is mid summer to early fall.

Cox Hill Ridge Trail (Map 16/A5) 🚶 🚴 👣
Accessed off the Siddbald Creek Trail (Hwy 68) at the Dawson Trailhead, this 20 km (12.5 mile) hiking and biking trail follows the Tom Snow Trail before crossing Jumpingpound Creek and becoming Coxhill Ridge Trail. It starts to steeply climb up the hill to the breathtaking view at the top. Jumpingpound Ridge Trail leads you back down to the starting point.

Death Valley Trail (Map 11/F2) 🚶 🎿 👣
Not to be confused with its more famous namesake in the US, this easy trail is accessed from the Sandy McNabb Cross-Country Trails. The route is 12.5 km (7.8 miles) long in which you gain 222 m (722 ft) in elevation. Hikers should wait until the area is dry to enjoy the meadows and woodlands along the way. There are several side trails to be explored.

Eagle Hill Trail (Map 16/A4) 🚶 🚴 👣
Accessed at the Sibbald Lake Recreation Area, this moderate 8 km (5 mile) biking and hiking trail climbs 330 m (1,073 ft). It follows a rough road and trail that cuts through a poplar forest, past several clearings to a lookout overlooking the Stony Indian Reserve in the Bow Valley. A sweat lodge offers a relaxing end to this rough route, which should take about 2.5 hours to hike. The **Deer Ridge Trail** is a moderate 7 km (4.3 mile) trail that branches west off the Eagle Hill Trail. It climbs to a ridge overlooking Sibbald Creek.

Elbow Pass Trail (Map 10/G3) 🔺 🚶 🚴 🐎 🐟 👣
Accessed off Highway 40 at the Elbow Pass Trailhead, a difficult 9 km (5.6 mile) trail begins. The trail gains 305 m (991 ft) in elevation and takes about seven hours on foot. If biking, some pushing may be required as there are some steep rises. Elbow Lake is beautiful and great for trout fishing, while Tombstone Backcountry Campground provides a good base for other side trips including continuing to Elbow River via the Big Elbow Trail. Further south, the **Piper Creek Trail** is a 4 km (2.5 mile) hike into a beautiful valley that strays away from the main trail near Edworthy Falls. It requires a crossing of the Elbow River and Piper Creek. Some may wish to continue 560 m (1,820 ft) up to the passes beyond.

Elbow Valley Trail (Map 16/C7) 🚶 🚴 🐎 👣
A 10 km one-way trail joins the Elbow Falls and Elbow River Recreation Areas. The forested trail climbs 365 m (1,186 ft) as it winds up and down next to the highway. Canyon Creek must be forded along the way. Branching from the main trail are a couple loop trails. The **Sulfur Springs Trail** is a 4.5 km (2.8 mile) trail that takes you past the smelly springs, to a great viewpoint. The **Riverview Trail**, which begins at Paddy's Flat and concludes at Elbow Valley Trail and Sulfur Springs Trail junction, is a 4.5 km (2.8 mile) hike that gains 105 m (.

Elk Pass Trail (Map 10/F4) 🔺 🚶 🚴 👣
The Elk Pass Trail is part of the Trans Canada Trail that heads over Elk Pass to Elk Lakes Provincial Park in BC. It is easy travelling on an old road until Fox Creek where the trail forks. The upper section is easier but less interesting. Once on the pass the trail improves. The meadow in Elk Lakes Park offers

good camping and a base for some excellent hiking trails. The difficult, 19 km (11.8 mile) trail begins at the Elk Lakes trailhead, off the Kananaskis Lakes Trail.

Etherington Creek Trail (Map 7/D1) 🚶 👣
This hiking trail is accessed at the Etherington Creek Recreation Area. The trail requires you to wade across the creek, near the bathing pools at the campground. It is possible to continue your trip up to Hell's Ridge off the main trail for some great views.

Evan-Thomas Bike Path (Map 15/F7) 🚶 🚴
This paved path stretches 10 km (6.2 miles) one-way from Kananaskis Village to Wedge Pond. It passes Ribbon Creek, the golf course, and Mount Kidd RV Park. As the name implies, most people bike this trail, although it can be walked as well.

Evan-Thomas Creek Trail (Map 15/F7) 🚶 🚴 🐎
A 15 km (9.3 mile) trail that gains 760 m (2,470 ft) in elevation begins at the Evan-Thomas Creek Parking Lot. You can also access it from the Little Elbow Trail to the south. It can be used for hiking, but is better left for biking or horseback riding as it is not very scenic. The trail involves a few steep climbs through an open forest that does offer a nice view of the Northern Opals. There are side trails or routes to explore from the main trail.

Exshaw Pass Trail (Map 15/E3) 🚶 👣
A moderate, but long 13 km (8 mile) hike is accessed at the Exshaw Creek Bridge off the Bow Valley Trail (Hwy 1A). There are a few stream crossings and over 900 m (2,925 ft) in elevation to gain before reaching the marvelous viewpoints at the pass. It is possible to return via Exshaw Ridge to the east but this alternative is more difficult.

Fitzsimmons Creek Trail (Map 7/C1-11/C7) 🚶 🚴
This 22 km (13.7 mile) hiking and biking route follows a series of old roads. The trailhead is located at the Fitzsimmons Creek Recreation Area. You have to wade Highwood River before heading into the forest. Mountain views are found throughout the trip. A popular loop includes following the **Baril Creek Trail** down to the Forestry Trunk Road.

Flat (Trap) Creek Trail (Map 11/F6) 🚶 🚴 🐎 👣
This multi-use trail can be accessed from the Flat (Trap) Creek Bridge (on Secondary Highway 541). It is a moderate, 38 km (23.7 mile) route through meadows and grassy hills with good views of the surrounding area. The elevation gain is 435 m (1,414 ft). Options such as the 9.5 km (5.9 mile) **Grass Pass Trail**, the 3 km (1.8 mile) **Sullivan Pass Trail** and the 7.5 km (5.3 mile) **Head Creek Trail** are all accessible from the main trail, which is best hiked from June through October.

Ford Creek Trail (Map 11/A1-16/A6) 🚶 🚴 🐎 👣
The Ford Creek Trail is an 18 km (11.2 miles) one-way trail that is usually used to access the trails in the Jumpingpound Valley. The popular multi-use trail climbs 590 m (1,918 ft) along the Nihahi Ridge.

Ford Knoll Trail (Map 11/A1) 🚶 👣
This 4 km (2.5 mile) hiking trail begins from the Forgetmenot Pond Picnic Area. It gains 235 m (764 ft) in elevation and is quite strenuous. Your reward comes at the top, with great views of the surrounding mountains and the river valley.

Fording River Pass Trail (Map 7/B1) 🔺 🚶 🚴 👣
A difficult 35 km (21.7 mile) one-way trail can be accessed off the Baril Creek Trail (in Alberta) or the Elk River Road (in BC). This is a long trip that follows logging roads, old exploration roads and the Great Divide Trail. A shuttle would be nice, but it is actually quicker to bike back. Hikers can also turn around at the Fording River Pass. This is a dry weather trip, which takes you through some rough, steep sections. There is backcountry camping, and side routes to explore.

Fortress Lake and Ridge Trail (Map 15/D7) 🚶 👣
Accessed at the Fortress Mountain Ski Area, this difficult 5 km (3 mile) hiking trail leads to a pretty blue lake. It is difficult trail, gaining 270 m (878 ft) in elevation as it climbs through forest and along the Fortress Ridge, until

and provides great views of mountains and waterfalls. From the end of the upper lake you can continue on to see some pictographs.

Grotto Canyon Trail (Map 15/D3) 🚶 📷 ⛺
With rock climbing opportunities, excellent scenery and Indian Pictographs, this is a popular hike. It is a 6 km (3.7 mile) trail that gains 670 m (2,178 ft) in elevation from the Grotto Mountain Picnic Area. If you cross the creek after the first canyon, be careful of rising water levels, as you may get stuck behind the canyon. Many choose to stop at the canyon, an easy 2 km (1.2 mile) walk that passing by a waterfall en route.

Grotto Mountain Trail (Map 15/C3) 🚶 📷 ⛺
From the Indian Flats Road (off the Bow Valley Trail) at the parking lot of the Alpine Club, is a 10 km hiking trail. The trail should be left to equipped rock climbers, as you must scramble 50 m (163 ft) up a cliff (after climbing a daunting 1,365 m/4,436 ft in elevation). After, as you travel along the ridge, you will be provided with views of the country below.

Ha Ling Peak Trail (Map 15/B4) 🚶 ⛺
This short 1.6 km (1 mile) grind to the summit can be located off of the Smith-Dorrien Spray Trail at the Goat Creek Parking Lot. During your climb, do not be surprised to see several other hikers attempting the route, as it is very popular. At the summit you will appreciate the bird's eye view of Canmore and the Bow Valley. Keep to the most beaten path as the trail is poorly defined, and fairly braided.

Hailstone Butte Fire Lookout Trail (Map 7/G3)
🚶 🚴 🐴 🏍 ⛺
Many people access Hailstone Butte from the closest point of access on Secondary Highway 532, 3.8 km (2.4 miles) east of the Forestry Trunk Road. The route up is faint, if any (simple head uphill). This 2.4 km (1.5 mile) route is the shortest access. An alternate route is a 9.3 km (5.8 mile) trip, accessed from a side road off the Forestry Trunk Road, 100 m (325 ft) northwest of the 532 Junction. This route climbs more (500 m/1,625 ft, as opposed to 335 m/1,100 ft), but has a definite trail (road, even) that can be followed by all trail users to the lookout.

Heart Creek Trails (Map 15/C3) ⛺ 🚶 ⛺
This 4 km (2.5 mile) interpretive hike takes you through a lush canyon to a rock step and hidden waterfall. The trailhead is located off the off Lac Des Arcs Interchange on the Trans-Canada Highway and requires several creek crossings along the way. The steep **Heart Mountain Horseshoe Trail** veers off from the main trail. Also in the area is the 10 km trail to the Quaite Valley Backcountry Campsite.

Indian Graves Ridge Trail (Map 8/A2) 🚶 ⛺
Beginning at the Indian Graves Recreation Area, this is a 6 km (3.7 mile) hike. The trail cuts up (200 m/650 ft) through forest to the open slopes above. A well site can be reached 2 km (1.2 miles) further on.

Indian Oils Trail (Map 11/C3) 🚶 ⛺
A half-day trail off Sheep River Trail, the Indian Oils Trail covers 7.5 km (4.7 miles), with a moderate elevation gain of 395 m (1,295 ft). It crosses several small creeks, while meandering through a mix of meadow, aspen and pine forest. There are several scenic viewpoints as you trek between Gorge Creek and the Sheep River.

Iron Springs Trail (Map 16/C6) 🚶 🚴 🚴
This moderate 8 km (5 mile) trail can be accessed from the north (Bragg Creek Road) and the south (Elbow Falls Trail). This trail follows several logging roads/ ski trails where one encounters a mill site and can see Moose Mountain to the west. The ultimate destination of this hike, Iron Pond, is located in the valley bottom with flowery meadows and grazing cows. Allow a few hours to enjoy the hike. In the winter, this is groomed as part of the Bragg Creek Trails.

Jewell Pass Trail (Map 15/F4) 🚶 🚴 ⛺
From the Heart Creek Trailhead, this 10.5 km (6.5 mile) one-way bike or hike gains 280 m (910 ft) in elevation. Follow the rolling trail to the Quaite Valley Trail. Here, you climb to Jewell Pass where the trail joins Stoney Trail.

descending to the lake. Keeping left at the junction is the less strenuous way to reach the lake from the ridge.

Fullerton Loop Trail (Map 16/C6) 🚶 ⛺
A 7 km (4.3 mile), moderate early season hiking trail begins at the Allan Bill Pond Picnic Area. Following along Elbow River, the trail climbs 213 m (692 ft) to the ridge for a view of Moose Mountain. There are a few creek crossings.

Galatea Creek Trail (Map 15/D7) ⛺ 🚶 ⛺
From the Galatea Parking Lot, a 6.5 km (4 mile) hiking trail climbs 460 m (1,495 ft) to Lillian Lake. You can continue another 1.5 km (0.9 miles) and 155 m (504 ft) to the picturesque Upper Galatea Lake. This is a difficult day hike that is rewarded with waterfalls, canyon views and mountain lakes. The scenic **Guinn's Pass Trail** can also be accessed from the main trail. This 3 km (1.8 mile) trail climbs 260 m (845 ft) to the Ribbon Creek/Buller Pass Trail allowing hikers to create a two-day round trip hike, rather than the usual out-and-back variety. The two trailheads are about 4 km (2.4 miles) apart on the Smith-Dorrien Spray Lakes Road.

Gorge Creek Trail (Map 11/C3) ⛺ 🚶 🚴 🐴 ⛺
The Gorge Creek Trail makes its way along the boundary between the Bluerock Wildland and McLean Creek Off-Highway Vehicle Area. As it is mostly in the former, off-highway vehicles are not allowed. It is 14.5 km (9 miles) from the Gorge Creek Picnic Area to the Threepoint Trail/Volcano Creek Trail junction. There is 400 m (1,300 ft) of elevation gained along the route.

Grass Pass Trail (Map 11/E7) 🚶 🚴 ⛺
This trail begins at the Sentinel Picnic Area. It is a 9.5 km (5.9 mile) route, leading through lush vegetation to the Flat Creek Valley. A worthy side trip leads to the Bull Creek Hills, a ridge offering gorgeous meadows and excellent views of Mount Head, and Holy Cross Mountain. Although you only climb 365 m (1,186 ft) over 2.5 km (1.6 miles) to the ridge, you should allow more time to explore the area. The hiking season lasts from April through to November.

Grassi Lakes Trail (Map 15/C3) 🚶 🐟 ⛺
This moderate walking trail is 4 km (2.5 miles) long and gains 300 m (975 ft) in height. The trailhead is located at the Spray Residences parking lot, off of the Smith-Dorrien Spray Trail. The trail takes you to two gorgeous blue lakes,

The lower part of the trail offers fine views of a falls, Barrier Lake and Mount Baldy.

Johnson Creek Trail (Map 8/A3)

A trail running through meadows and along the creek begins at the Indian Graves Recreation Area. The trail gains 710 m (2,308 ft) in elevation.

Jumpingpound Demonstration Forest (Map 16/A3)

An easy interpretive 10 km (6.2 miles) long trail weaves through the Jumpingpound Demonstration Forest.

Jumpingpound Ridge Trail (Map 16/A4-A6)

Following a sandstone ridge, this 22 km (13.7 mile) trail is quite popular with mountain bikers and hikers alike. It can be readily accessed at the Dawson Equestrian Parking Lot of Highway 68. At the top of your trek you reach 2,180 m (7,085 ft) where you are immersed in alpine flowers and experience views of Fisher Range and Compression Ridge. Along your trek, do not miss the summit of Jumpingpound Mountain with its panoramic views.

Junction Creek Trail (Map 11/C4)

Accessed at the Junction Creek Picnic Area, this 11 km (6.8 miles) trail passes by Junction Creek and leads to a meadow above the Sheep River. A less formal route heads east up to the lake.

Junction Mountain Lookout Trail (Map 11/E5)

This 16 km (10 mile) long trail system is open to hikers and mountain bikers. It starts at the Indian Oils Parking Lot and offers several side trails to explore. The hike's primary destination is Junction Lookout, which stands just below Junction Mountain and offers views to Calgary (on a clear day) as well as Bluerock Mountain to the northwest. This trail is essentially one continuous dirt road, with several dips and valleys over many creeks and rocky stretches.

Jura Creek Trail (Map 15/E3)

Following along the creek and up through the Fairholme Range, this 8 km (5 mile) hike gains 670 m (2,178 ft) in elevation. There are a few creek crossings along the way, but the hiker is rewarded with views of many rock formations. The trailhead is located off the Bow Valley Trail (Hwy 1A) at Exshaw.

Kananaskis Canyon Trail (Map 10/E3)

Found at the Canyon Campground is a short 1 km (0.6 mile) loop trail that follows the Kananaskis River into an impressive canyon. Hundreds of years ago it was used by the Kootenay Indians from BC on their annual quest for buffalo meat. The easy trail does require a lot of steps to climb.

Kananaskis Lakes Trail (Map 10/E3)

This paved, multi-use trail is frequented by families, usually out biking. The moderate 24 km (14.9 mile) return route should take most groups about four hours. It starts at the Visitor Centre and follows the rolling asphalt through Lodgepole Pine forests with glimpses of the surrounding peaks. The trail also offers good cross-country skiing in the winter. There are three individually named sections offering different access points and views. The Lodgepole section stretches 4.8 km (2.9 miles) from the Visitor Centre to Elkwood Campground. The Wheeler section continues 4.6 km (2.9 mile) to Boulton Creek. Finally, the Lakeside section, which is the most scenic section, continues another 5 km (3 miles) to the Sarail Campground.

King Creek Trail (Map 10/F2)

The marked trail found at the King Creek Picnic area is a short (1.5 km/.9 mile) walk through a scenic gorge . Be careful, as the trail is popular with Grizzly Bears, too. This easy hike is best undertaken in late afternoon when the western sun illuminates the Opal Range. For more adventuresome types, bushwhack up the creek for about 12 km (7.4 miles) to a remarkable view of Elpoca Mountain.

Lawson Lake & North Kananaskis Pass (Map 10/C2)

This trail begins at the North Interlakes Picnic Area and climbs 550 m (1,788 ft) over 19 km (11.8 miles) to the North Kananaskis Pass. At the beautiful Lawson Lake, Mount Maude and Haig Glacier make for a spectacular

backdrop. Further along, and a little off the main trail is Turbine Canyon Campsite, for those seeking an overnight excursion.

Link Trail (Map 11/E2)

This trail can be accessed at several points. One of which is off the Gorge Creek Trail at Volcano Ridge Recreation Area. This 10.5 km (6.5 mile) trail connects trails in the east Sheep region to those by the Front Ranges region in the west. You gain 375 m (1,219 ft) as you hike through pine forest and meadows.

Little Elbow Trail (Maps 10/F1-11/A1)

This easy 23 km (14.3 mile) one-way trail follows a fire road up the Little Elbow River until reaching the Mount Romulus Campsite where it rises steeply to the pass. There are many side trips and alternate routes that can be taken along the way. This half of the Elbow Loop gains 400 m (1,300 ft). A popular option is to join the Elbow Pass Trail, which will take you to the Elbow Pass Picnic Area (off Highway 40). It is a 6 km (3.7 mile) hike or bike up to the pass and then down to the lake.

Little Highwood Pass Trail (Map 10/G3)

This tough jaunt of 3.5 km (2.2 miles) goes to a pass to join with the Pocaterra Cirque and the West fork of Pocaterra Creek. There is an elevation gain of 396 m (1,287 ft) and a loss of 640 m (2,080 ft). Access can be reached at the Little Highwood Pass Picnic Area.

Lookout Trail (Map 10/F4)

The Kananaskis Lookout can be reached from two directions. If on a mountain bike we recommend starting the trail from the Kananaskis Trail (Highway 40) at the Pocaterra Hut Parking Lot. From here it is 4 km (2.5 miles). If hiking, try starting your 6.5 km (4 mile) journey from the Kananaskis Lakes Trail at the Boulton Creek Campsite. If originating from the campsite, do not be surprised to find yourself on the Whiskey Jack Trail as it does continue on to the Lookout. At the summit take your time to enjoy the 360 degree view, which takes in the Kananaskis Lakes, Elk Lakes and Mount Fox.

Loomis Creek Trail (Map 11/B6)

Loomis Creek can be accessed at the Lineham Creek Picnic Area off of Kananaskis Trail (Highway 40). The multi-use trail is 13 km (8 mile) return and follows a logging road along the Loomis Creek Valley. Hikers will take about six hours to finish the trail, gaining 240 m (780 ft) in elevation. At the midpoint of the trail, hikers can bushwhack to Loomis Lake, a tucked away jewel, or continue south to Bishop Ridge. You climb 425 m (1,381 ft) to access the ridge. The trail should be left until July, as you will have to cross the creek a number of times.

Lost Creek Trail (Map 7/D3)

This trail can be accessed from the old road running up Cataract Creek. This trail is mainly used to join to other trails. It completes the Cataract Creek Loop (see above), and the Cummins Creek Trail (see above) to Oyster Creek Trail (see Area South).

Lower Kananaskis Lake (Map 10/E3)

An easy 3.3 km (2 mile) one-way walk around the eastern shore of Lower Kananaskis Lake, this trail begins at the Canyon Picnic Area. Low water levels in early summer reveal unattractive mud flats. There are terrific views of the Spray Range from along the trail.

Lusk Pass Trail (Maps 15/G4-16/A5)

This trail connects Jumpingpound Valley with the Kananaskis Valley. The trail gains 350 m (1,138 ft) over 7 km (4.3 miles) one-way as you climb through a thick pine forest with occasional views. Access can be found at Lusk Creek Picnic Area on Highway 40.

Lyautey Trail (Map 10/D4)

Providing access to the Forks Campsite and the Three Isle Lake and Upper Lake Trails, this 2 km (1.2 mile), one-way hike curves around the base of Mount Lyautey.

McLean Creek OHV Zone (Maps 11 & 16)

Nearly 200 square kilometres have been set aside for multiple users in the McLean Creek area. While hikers, mountain bikers and horseback riders

are allowed in this area, it is truly a domain ruled by 4X4s, ATVs and motor-bikes. There are hundreds of kilometres of formal and informal trails winding through this area, ranging from easy cruising to mud bogging. There are two staging areas, one at McLean Creek Recreation Area (Map 16/D7), one at the Fisher Creek Recreation Area (Map 11/E1). Some of the major trails to explore include the Elbow Valley Trail, Fish Creek Trail, Fisher Trail, McLean Trail, Quirk Trail and Silvester Trail.

McPhail Creek Trails (Map 11/B7) 🏕 🥾 🚴 🐟 🧗

The McPhail Creek Trail is a 10 km (6.2 mile) day hike, which can be easily accessed at the Cat Creek Picnic Area. The trail is known for the large groups of elk, which graze the hills around the creek. The initial crossing of the High-wood River is tricky, and should be left until later in the season. From a rustic creek side campsite near the end of the trail, you can access several exciting options. Lake of Horns is a gorgeous alpine lake that requires climbing another 200 vertical metres (650 ft) in 1.5 km (0.9 miles) up a headwall. The Weary Creek Gap Trail climbs 4 km (2.5 mile) to a pass between Mount Muir and Mount McPhail. The pass, which marks the southern end of the Elk Range and the northern end of the High Rock Range, was known as the Elk Trail Pass to the Stoney Indians because of the graceful animal that frequents the area. Another option is to climb the Strachan Ridge Trail. This 7 km (4.3 mile) trail begins at the 6 km (3.7 mile) mark of the McPhail Creek Trail. There are a few steep hills along the trail, which takes you to the open ridge northeast of Mount Strachan.

Missinglink Trail (Map 11/E2) 🥾 🧗

This moderate, 8 km (5 mile) trail can be accessed at the Missinglink Trail-head or from the Link Creek Trail. This hike is mostly boring with the only highlight being a view of Missinglink Mountain.

Mist Creek Trail (Map 11/A3) 🥾 🚴 🐎 🧗

This 12 km (7.4 miles) trip gains 555 m (1,804 ft) as it climbs to Rickert Pass, and the Sheep Trail junction. It begins at the Mist Creek Picnic Area on High-

way 40. For the most part it is an easy route with some route finding required through pine and spruce forests. At the 8.8 km (5.5 mile) mark you will ascend to Rickert's Pass, which offers a tremendous view up Misty Basin to Storm Mountain. Hardcore hikers may wish to try the Mist Ridge Route. This difficult 23 km (14.3 mile) route climbs 745 ft (2,445 ft) and can be walked in a long, hard day. The route is usually travelled in a counterclockwise direction, taking the right-hand branch when the trail splits after about 1 km (0.6 miles). Follow this up onto the ridge, which features gorgeous mountain views, before descending into Rickert's Pass for the long walk home along the Mist Creek Trail.

Mist Mountain Route (Map11/A4) 🥾 🧗

Random bits of flagging tape are all that mark this rough route up Mist Moun-tain. If you can find the trail, it begins in a boggy forest before heading nearly straight up. While the views are nice once you get above trees, the route is steep climbing 1,330 m (4,323 ft). There is a small warm spring (32°C/83°F) located on the east side of the mountain. It should take about six hours to scramble to the top and back, longer if you try to find the springs.

Moose Mountain Lookout Trails (Map 16/B5) 🥾 🚴 🧗

From the Moose Mountain Road, hikers and mountain bikers will find a popular series of trails. The Moose Mountain Fire Lookout Road climbs 470 m (1,528 ft). The 7 km (4.3 mile) trail takes you along the spectacular ridge of Moose Mountain. Moosepackers Trail is a 22 km (13.7 mile) jaunt with some 500 m (1,625 ft) gained in elevation. It has several locations for good views as it meanders through the forest. Incidentally, Moose Mountain is a huge domed limestone structure, thereby making it a natural reservoir for gas. There are active sour gas wells in the area. Watch for signs.

Mount Allan Trails (Map15/D5) 🥾 🧗

The summit of Mount Allan can be climbed starting from 2 different loca-tions. From the north, an 11 km (6.8 miles) journey begins at the Trans-Canada Highway near the Alpine Resort Haven. This is a long, difficult hike whereby it is essential to start early and utilize vehicles at either end. But it is one of the most delightful ridge walks in the Rockies. The second hike also 11 km (6.8 miles), begins from the Kananaskis Trail (Highway 40) at the Ribbon Creek Parking Lot. Like the first, it also is a long day requiring you to start early and bring plenty of water. This long outing is well worth your effort when you discover a row of 25 m (81 ft) high conglomerate pinnacles that are simply breathtaking.

Mount Assiniboine Trail (Maps 14/D3-15/A7) 🏕 🥾 🚴 🧗

This long 62 km (38.5 mile) trail loops from Alberta to BC and back into Alberta again. It can be done as one long multi-day hike, or it can be done in a couple shorter hikes, starting at either end. There are two points from which a hiker can start; the Sunshine Village Parking Lot (near Banff) or from the south, at the Mount Shark Trailhead. There are many features to see and several campgrounds along the route for those looking to camp. The highlights include Mount Assiniboine, one of BC's highest peaks, at 3,618 m (11,759 ft), Lake Magog, as well as the Valley of the Rocks, which was created by one of the world's largest landslides. Once in the Mount Assini-boine Area, there are numerous trails to explore. These are described in our Kootenay edition of the Backroad Mapbook Series. Grizzly Bear sightings are common in the area.

Mount Indefatigable Trail (Map 10/E3) 🥾 🧗

A spectacular ridge leads up to a breathtaking viewpoint below Mount Indefatigable. It is a moderate climb of 503 m (1,635 ft) over 5 km (5 miles) return that should take two hours to hike from the North Interlakes Picnic Area. If possible, the hike should be done in early June, when snow cover has receded, revealing the yellow wildflowers that grow abundantly here. For the more adventurous and experienced backcountry traveller, it is possible to continue up the ridge to the peak (add two hours and another 2.5 km/1.5 miles return) or to some glacier lakes (add 45 minutes). The trail can also be accessed from the Gypsum Quarry Trail to the north.

Mount Kidd Lookout Trail (Map 15/E6) 🥾 🧗

From Kananaskis Village and the Nakiska Ski Area (see below), the Ter-race Trail heads south to the Kovach Trail junction. Continue on the Kovach Trail for about 1.5 km (0.9 miles) to a faint trail, which may or may not be marked. This trail climbs up onto a ridge, which can easily be followed to the site of the former lookout. The lookout was situated on a grassy slope, and it is not uncommon to see sheep, elk and grizzly bear in the area.

Mount McNabb Trail (Map 11/F4) 🥾 🛗

This 6 km (3.7 mile) hike is a relatively easy meadow walk. It has both north and south access points. The northern point is from the Sandy McNabb Recreation Area along the Price Camp Trail, while the southern access is the Green Mountain Trail. At various points this trail nears and finally reaches the banks of North Coal Creek. Towards its conclusion there is a three-way junction with the Phone Line and Green Mountain Trails, where one can explore additional tributaries.

Mount Shark Trails (Map 15/A7) 🥾 🚴 🐴 ⛷ 🐟 🛗

Accessed off the Smith-Dorrien Spray Trail at Mount Shark Trailhead, there are 20 km (12.5 miles) of ski trails that can be enjoyed by hikers, bikers and horseback riders. The moderate trails range in length from 2-15 km (1.2–9.4 miles) and give access to several other trails in the area. The **Commonwealth Lake Trail** is found 2 km (1.2 miles) south of the Mount Shark Road off an old road. The 2 km (1.2 mile) trail to the pretty little green lake gains 183 m (595 ft). Those that wish to go further could loop around Commonwealth Lake, a steep trail which gains 290 m (943 ft) over 6 km (3.7 miles), or continue south to the Smuts Pass. **Karst Spring Trail** is a 7.5 km (5.3 mile) return walk to the north shore of Watridge Lake. Karst Springs is one of the largest springs in North America. **Marushka (Shark) Lake Trail** is a 4.5 km (2.8 mile) hike out to Shark Lake. It follows Marushka Creek until it reaches the sparkling green lake, with Mount Smuts in the background. The **Watridge Lake Trail** is a 6 km (3.7 mile) trail, which takes you down a short steep incline to the lake, known for its cutthroat trout fishing. The trail is best hiked from late spring to early fall when the White Bog Orchids are out. It follows old logging roads, and portaging a canoe is possible. **White Man Pass Trail** is a six hour 17 km (10.6 mile) trail that climbs 425 m (1,381 ft) to White Man Pass. It is a quiet backcountry trail, full of history and mystique, and you will likely find yourself surrounded by the ghosts of the past. The best season for the trail is mid-summer to early fall.

Nakiska (Marmot Basin) Ski Area (Map 15/E6) 🥾 🚴 🛗

A popular summer route in the Nakiska Ski Area is the **Aspen Loop**. This easy trail follows the **Terrace Trail** from the west end of the parking lot to the **Kovach Trail**. Turn on this trail, which brings you to the Aspen Trail proper. The loop takes you into the splendor of a flowery meadow, before connecting back up with the Kovach Trail. Another popular option is the 10.5 km (6.5 mile) **Hummingbird Plume Lookout Trail**. The lookout is actually an old shack, dating back to 1941 when there actually was a view. The view is now blocked by tall timbers, but a short trip from the meadows, up a 130 m (423 ft) slope, will provide views of the Kananaskis Valley and Fisher Range. To return, follow the powerline road past Troll Falls. To the north a combination of old roads and trails provide access to **Marmot Basin**. By following the **Skogan Pass Trail** (see below), there are about 7.5 km (5.3 miles) of trails that lead to an area between Mount Allan and Lower Collembola Ridge.

North Fork Trail (Map 11/E1) 🥾

This 5 km (3 mile) trail connects Threepoint Creek Trail with the Ware Creek Recreation Area.

Nihahi Ridge Trail (Map 11/A1) 🥾 🚴 🐴 🛗

This is a 5 km (3 mile) hike, which climbs quite steeply (390 m/1,268 ft) up a rocky ridge, providing great views of the Front Range. Summer through fall is the best time to hike the trail.

Northover Ridge Trail (Map 10/C4) 🥾 🐟 🛗

Once at Three Isle Lake, this 11 km (6.8 miles) trail leads over the ridge to Aster Lake. The route can be windy and the rocky terrain makes the walk a bit dangerous, if care is not taken. From the ridge, a fabulous view of the Great Divide is available. On your return from the lake, you gain 620 m (2,015 ft). With this in mind, some hikers may choose to begin this trail at Aster Lake.

Odlum Creek Trail (Map 11/B6) 🥾 🚴 🐴 🛗

This 9 km (5.6 mile) trail provides access to Odlum Pond and Ridge as well as Bishop Ridge and the Loomis Creek Trail to the south. There are a few creek crossings and some falls along the scenic route. The trailhead is located at the Lantern Creek Picnic Area.

Old Baldy Trail (Map 15/F7) 🥾 🛗

The Old Baldy Trail gains 860 m (2795 ft) in elevation as it climbs 8 km (5 mile) return to a fabulous viewpoint. It is accessed at the Evan-Thomas Creek Parking Lot. There is an optional return down the west flank or via the left hand fork. For those looking for more of a challenge, you can continue up to the summit of Mount McDougall.

Ole Buck Trail (Map 16/B4) 🥾 🛗

A moderate, 2.5 km (1.6 mile) trail takes you up the mountain to an excellent view of Sibbald Lake and Moose Mountain. The vegetation can make the hike quite colorful during the spring and fall.

Old Goat Glacier Route (Map 15/B5) 🥾 🛗

Topo maps do not show a glacier here, and if global warming keeps on its current trend, perhaps it won't be in a few years. For now, this glacier remains hidden from view behind a rock headwall. People interested in bushwhacking up an open slope to the hanging valley where the glacier resides, can start at the stream cascading down the headwall to the road.

Opal Ridge Trail (Map 10/E1) 🥾 🛗

Accessed off the Kananaskis Trail (Hwy 40) at the Fortress Junction, a 3 km (1.8 mile) hike begins. The trail takes you through meadows as you catch views of the Kananaskis Lakes and Opal Range. An optional return follows the Grizzly Creek Trail south.

Palliser Pass Trail (Maps 10/A1-15/A7) ⛺ 🥾 🛗

Beginning at the Mount Shark Trailhead, this 21 km (13 mile) one-way route follows the unspoiled Upper Spray Valley and passes Leman Lake before climbing to the pass. There are camping areas along the way to help you enjoy this 2-3 day wilderness trip. The Burstall Pass Trail can be used as a shortcut to the Palliser Pass.

Pasque Mountain Route (Map 7/E3) 🥾 🛗

Accessed off the Forestry Trunk Road, 7.5 km (5.3 miles) south of the Cataract Creek Bridge, this difficult 14 km (8.7 mile) hiking trail begins. On your way to the summit, expect some tough walking and scrambles. To create a loop, you may choose to head down the east and then north ridges.

Phone Line Trail (Map 11/E4) 🥾

A 7 km (4.3 mile) hike along old logging roads, runs between the Sentinel Ranger Station and the Bighorn Ranger Station. It gains 180 m (585 ft) in elevation. The trailhead is accessed from the south, along the Junction Mountain Trail and from the north, along the Green Mountain Trail.

Picklejar Creek & Lakes Trails (Map 11/B5) 🥾 🐟 🛗

Accessed of the Kananaskis Trail (Hwy 40) at the Picklejar Creek Picnic Area, this 5 km (3 mile) difficult hike begins. The route leads between Picklejar and the unmarked Cliff Creeks. There is a connecting trail to Picklejar Lakes as well as another access trail from Lantern Creek Picnic Area. It is about 4 km (2.5 mile) to reach the first lake, where the fishing is good. In fact, the name for this area comes from an old saying that the fish were so plentiful here, you could catch them in a...well, you get the picture.

Plateau Mountain Trail (Map 7/F2) 🥾 🚴 🏍 🛗

This 10 km (6.2 mile) moderate trail takes you to a fabulous viewpoint of the Canadian Rockies. Be careful of strong winds once at the summit. The trailhead is located off the Forestry Trunk Road at the Wilkinson Summit. It is possible to continue 3 km (1.8 miles) to an Ice Cave by heading northeast along a ridge cutting into Salter Creek.

Pocaterra Trail (Map 10/F3) 🥾 🚴 🛗

This 10 km (6.2 mile) one-way trail begins at the Pocaterra Hut Parking Lot. It leads through open meadows and forested land, providing views of Mount Wintour and the Opal Range. Enroue 290 m (943 ft) in elevation is gained as you hike or bike the trail. The Lookout, Whiskey Jack and Rolly Road Trails all join the Pocaterra Trail.

Porcupine Creek Trails (Map 15/G6) 🥾

Accessed off the Kananaskis Trail (Hwy 40) at the Porcupine Creek Bridge, the main trail is a 7 km (4.3 mile) hike. The terrain is mostly easy as you travel alongside Porcupine Creek. Further exploration is possible on the surrounding peaks and trails. It is possible to hike up either fork of Porcupine Creek.

Powderface Trails (Map 16/A5–A7)

Access is found at the Powderface Parking Lot on Highway 66. It is 7 km (4.3 miles) to Powderface Pass along a hiking and biking route that travels the full length of Powderface Creek before heading up to the pass. Once there, views of Nihahi Ridge can be seen. If biking, be prepared to do some pushing. To continue, travel north, 2.5 km (1.6 miles) to Powderface Ridge. This route will gain another 130 m (423 ft) in elevation but provides views of Fisher Range and Belmore Browne Peak. Powderface Ridge can also be reached from the end of Highway 66. This route climbs 640 m (2080 ft) over 7 km (4.3 miles).

Prairie Creek Trails (Map 16/A7)

An 8 km (5 mile) multi-use trail will take you along varied terrain and past some beaver ponds. The muddy trail climbs 180 m (585 ft) from the Powderface Parking Lot. The **Prairie Link Trail** is a 3 km (1.8 mile) trail connecting to the Powderface Creek. It is found 5 km (3 miles) along the main trail. The **Prairie Mountain Trail** is a popular but tough 5 km (3 mile) trail climbing 715 m (2324 ft) in elevation. The view from the summit is superb. This is a good early season hike.

Prairie View Trail (Map 15/G4)

This trail leads to a plateau overlooking Barrier Lake and Jewell Pass. The 13 km (8 mile) trail climbs 420 m (1,365 ft) from east end of the lake. Many also visit the active Barrier Lake Fire Lookout, which sits about 1 km (0.6 miles) from the main trail.

Ptarmigan Cirque Trail (Map 10/G4)

While the climb through a steadily thinning forest is pretty stiff (210m/683 ft in about 2 km/1.2 miles), the alpine scenery is nothing short of breathtaking. The route is 6 km (3.7 miles) return and offers an interpretive brochure that points out all the interesting sites to see along the way. The trail starts in the Highwood Pass, at the 2,300 m (7,475 ft) mark, where snow remains until early summer. You will rarely find alpine scenery so accessible, making this a very popular trail in the summer. Fall is a great time to hike this trail, as the larches turn a lovely golden colour. If you wish to avoid the crowds, the

nearby **Arethusa Cirque Route** is located just 1 km (0.6 miles) to the south. The 1.5 km (0.9 mile) trail up has been flagged from a point just south of the creek to the treeline. From here you can wander the cirque, or hike up to the top of Little Arethusa.

Quirk Creek Trail (Map 11/C1-16/C7)

This 20 km (12.5 mile) return, multi-use trail begins at the Cobble Flats Picnic Area. From here, you ford the river and follow the fairly level road up Quirk Creek. Hikers will find the route uninspiring. Bikers should return on the Wildhorse Trail, where a smooth trail offers a more enjoyable downhill ride. Add another 4.5 km (2.8 miles) and a whole lot more elevation by climbing the scenic **Quirk Ridge Trail**.

Raspberry Ridge Lookout Trail (Map 7/D2)

This moderate 4.5 km (2.8 mile) trail gains 650 m (2,112 ft) as it follows a zigzagging fire road to an active fire lookout. Alpine flowers and numerous raspberries and Saskatoon berries can be found along the way. Over time, hikers have created a shortcut, cutting off the switchbacks. This trail goes straight up to the ridge, making it more difficult on the ascent, but it does shorten the descent time by about an hour (if your knees are up to it). Access is found off the Forestry Trunk Road at Cataract Creek Road.

Rawson Lake Trail (Map 10/E4)

Gorgeous views and fishing this mountain lake are the main attractions of this trail. The 8 km (5 mile) hike is accessed along the Upper (Kananaskis) Lake Trail. It climbs 320 m (1,040 ft) to a meadow near the southeast end of the lake. Mid-summer to early fall is the best time of year for this trail.

Ribbon Creek Trails (Map 15/D6)

From the Ribbon Creek parking lot, a 20 km (12.5 mile) trail leads up the spectacular valley. You pass waterfalls, canyons and cliffs on route to the campsite at Ribbon Falls. From here a difficult scramble is necessary to reach the lakes. The route climbs 595 m (1,934 ft), including 255 m (829 ft) after the falls. A short option is the **Ribbon Creek Loop**. This moderate 6 km (3.7 mile) offers the tranquility of Ribbon Creek. Others stop at Ribbon Falls, which is an 11 km (6.8 mile) trail that gains 311 m (1,011 ft).

Rummel Lake Trail (Map 15/C7)

Rugged beauty awaits those who hike this 5 km (3 mile) trail, which gains 350 m (1,138 ft). The access point lies along the old logging road across the highway from the Mount Shark Road. Hikers may wish to continue toward Rummel Pass (3 km/1.8 miles from the lake) and Lost Lake (2 km/1.2 miles from the pass). Mid-summer to early fall is the best time of year for this trail.

Running Rain Lake Trail (Map 11/A5)

Never mind that this rough, difficult to find route is mostly an access route for anglers. The fact is that this is a pretty 2.7 km (1.7 mile) hike to a pretty lake. There are some muddy sections, and a trio of river crossings, but the hike is not too difficult, gaining 153 m (497 ft) to the lake.

Rye Ridge Trail (Map 7/C2)

This moderate 31.5 km (19.6 mile) trail offers travellers gorgeous mountain vistas in a rugged backroad setting. It takes seven hours to complete by cycling; longer on foot or by horse. It is also possible to connect to **Raspberry Pass Trail** (a 6 km/3.7 mile connection between Etherington Creek and Cataract Creek), Lost Creek Trail, Great Divide Trail, and the **Baril Connector** (a 4 km/2.5 mile old road connecting Etherington Creek and Baril Creek). The trail starts on the Cataract Creek Loop and follows old roads north to Etherington Creek Trail, where it returns to the Forestry Trunk Road and the start.

Salter Creek Trail (Map 7/G2)

A 14 km (8.7 mile) hike and bike begins at the Cataract Creek Recreation Area. The route runs from Plateau Mountain to Mount Burke and ends in a pass between Salter and Pekisko Creeks. Views of Sentinel Peak and Pass can be seen from here. It is a rocky terrain at first, but turns smooth as you travel through open meadows. To continue, follow the **Willow Creek Trail** for 12 km (7.4 miles). Salter Meadows can also be accessed off the main trail. An alternate access to Salter Pass is via Pekisko Creek. This trail begins off Highway 22, on Miller Creek Road. It is 14 km (8.7 mile) long and gains 400 m (1300 ft) in elevation.

Sandy McNabb Cross-Country Trails (Map 11/D2) 🚶 🚴 🐎 ⛷️

37 km (23 miles) of ski trails can be found in the rolling foothills at the Sandy McNabb Recreation Area. Most of the trails are easy, but there are a few tougher sections. In the summer, these are popular multi-use trails. The 5 km (3 mile) **Price Camp Trail**, an alternate start to the Sheep Trail, is accessed here. It leads through forest and meadow and requires a significant river crossing.

Sentinel Pass & Peak Trail (Map 7/G3) 🚶 🚴 🐎 ⛷️ 🏕️

The 7 km (4.3 mile) trail leads to the pass with an impressive view of Plateau Mountain. The peak is another 1.2 km (0.7 mile). The trailhead is the same as the Hailstone Butte Lookout (near the junction of Forestry Trunk Road & Highway 532). When the rough access road switches back (just shy of the 6 km/3.6 mile mark), leave the road and follow a valley heading north, along a cow trail to the pass. You will cover 8.6 km (5.3 miles) to the pass, gaining 280 m (920 ft) in elevation.

Sheep Trail (Map 11/B4) 🚶 🚴 🐎 🏕️

Most often accessed at the Junction Creek Picnic Area, this 22 km (13.7 mile) trail begins. It provides views of the Gibraltar Mountain and the Front Ranges as well as beautiful meadows along the way. The trail can also be accessed at the Sandy McNabb Recreation Area. There are many side trips to keep you busy, including the 4 km (2.5 mile) Green Mountain Trail, a tricky, twisting 6 km (3.7 mile) trail to Burns Lake and a 50 km (31 mile) trip on the Big/Little Elbow Trails.

Sibbald Lake Trails (Map 16/B4) 🚶 🏕️

Two easy trails begin at the Sibbald Lake Recreation Area. Beginning on the middle fork, a 5 km (3 mile) hiking trail leads along a forestry exhibit trail to a great viewpoint, featuring the Sibbald Flats below. Beginning on the left fork, a 1 km (0.6 mile) trail loops through trees and meadows to a ridge viewpoint. When returning, the Moose Pond can be accessed off the main trail.

Skogan Pass Trail (Map 15/D4-E5) ⛰️ 🚶 🚴 🏕️

This 19 km (11.8 mile) trail can be accessed from either the Nakiska Ski Area or the Pigeon Mountain Ski Area (off the Trans-Canada Highway). Whether biking or hiking, you will travel through the Nakiska Ski Area to the powerlines. The route would be nicer if it was not under the powerlines for most of its length, especially on the north side of the pass. The views from the pass include the Three Sisters and the Canmore Corridor. From the north access point, the **Pigeon Mountain Trail** is a 5 km (3 mile) side trip that gains 550 m (1,788 ft) in elevation. The summit provides a splendid viewpoint.

Smith-Dorrien Mountain Trails (Map 10/D1) 🚶 🚴 ⛷️

This area has 32 km (19.9 miles) of trails, ranging from smooth roads, to rough, steep trails. It offers something for all levels of cyclists, hikers or cross-country skiers. The area is fun to explore, while admiring the rugged Spray Mountains. Branching from this system is the **James Walker Creek Trail**. It is an easy 4 km (2.5 mile) trail to a mountain lake. From there, you can continue 2 km (1.2 miles) into the scenic Upper Valley.

South Kananaskis Pass–North Kananaskis Pass (Map 10/C3) ⛰️ 🚶 🏕️

This 10.5 km (6.5 mile) trek can be started either from the South Pass via Three Island Lake Trail (13 km/8 miles from trailhead) or from the North Pass via the Lawson Lake Trail (19 km/11.8 miles from trailhead). The hike is a strenuous trip, and hikers should bring plenty of water and expect tremendous height gains. Near Beatty Creek look for the miniature valley of rocks, which is comprised of trees, boulders, sink holes and blue tarns.

Sparrowhawk Creek Trail (Map 15/C6) 🚶 🏕️

A trail leads to Read's Ridge, and further on, Mount Sparrowhawk from the Sparrowhawk Picnic Area. The ridge is a fabulous viewpoint and provides access to Read's Tower, after a good climb, gaining 270 m (878 ft) in 1 km (0.6 miles). The harder option, to Mount Sparrowhawk is 5 km (3 miles) and gains over 1,430 m (4,648 ft) in height. The Sparrowhawk Tarns can also be reached from the trailhead. It is a 5 km (3 mile) hike to reach several small lakes.

Stoney Trail (Map 15/F4) 🚶 🐎

A long 20.5 km (12.7 mile) one-way trail follows the powerline west of Barrier Lake. This popular equestrian route can be accessed at Stoney Parking Lot, Barrier Dam or the Grouse Group Campsite.

Terrace Trail (Map 15/E6) 🚶 🚴 ⛷️

This trail takes you from the Galatea Trailhead across the river and then follows its west bank, north to the Ribbon Creek Trailhead. It is better to bike or ski the 11.5 km (7.1 mile) return trail.

Three Isle Lake Trail (Map 10/D3) ⛰️ 🚶 🚣 🏕️

This is one of the most popular trails in the Kananaskis Lakes area. From the Upper Parking Lot, a 13 km (8 mile) trail skirts Mount Indefatigable, crosses the Palliser Rockslide and winds it way through a sub-alpine forest to the mountain lakes. The trail gains 580 m (1,885 ft). For overnight hikers, there is a backcountry campground along the way. From here, a 3 km (1.8 mile) trail leads past the north side of Three Isle Lakes to South Kananaskis Pass. The height gain is 125 m (406 ft) to the pass. Beatty Lake is a further 2 km (1.2 miles) away, in BC.

Three Sisters Trails (Map 15/B4) 🚶 🚴 🏕️

Providing a spectacular backdrop to the city of Canmore, the Three Sisters have long enticed hikers. Many of the trails follow old roads that provide remnants of logging activities from years ago. The **Three Sisters Creek Trail** ends at a waterfall. Many turn around here, but it is possible to scramble down and across the creek, then up again on the other side. The road soon peters out into a trail, which leads to the ruins of two old cabins. A strenuous climb leads to a viewpoint of the Three Sisters, and an even more strenuous climb will take you to Three Sisters Pass. It is possible to hike out via the **Three Sisters Pass Trail**, and down to the Smith-Dorrien Spray Lakes Road. Most hikers travel this trail from the Spray Lakes side since you only climb 595 m (1,934 ft) over 3 km (1.8 miles) to the viewpoint. The **Middle Sister Trail** follows Stewart Creek for an 8 km (5 mile) one-way trek. The old road up Stewart Creek seems easy enough, but as you get a glimpse of the Middle Sister, you will realize you are in for a struggle later on. The 1,400 m (4,550 ft) scramble to the summit is strenuous, but not technical. Viewpoints along the way will provide glimpses of Little Sister and the Bow Valley.

Threepoint Mountain Trail (Map 11/B2) ⛰️ 🚶 🚴 🐎 🏕️

This rough multi-use trail takes you from the Big Elbow Trail to the Volcano Creek Trail. After fording the river, you push your way up the ridge to cross the divide and then descend to the campsite at Volcano Creek. It is a 10 km trail one-way, and gains 460 m (1,495 ft) in elevation. A 7 km (4.3 mile) side trip to Upper Threepoint Creek is possible.

Timber Creek Trail (Maps 7/G3-8/A3) 🚶 🚴 🐎 🏕️

This difficult hiking and biking route is 18 km (11.2 miles) one-way. The east trailhead is located on Johnson Creek Trail before the Indian Graves Recreation Area. It begins on a road that runs gently through the valley. Then it climbs steeply, up a rocky track to a pass within the Livingston Range. Creek crossings and muddy sections along the way may slow you down.

Tom Snow Trail (Map 16/C5) 🚶 🚴 🐎 ⛷️

This is a 30 km (18.6 mile) multi-use trail that has several access points. This route is the main connector between the Sibbald Creek Valley (at the Spruce Woods Picnic Area) and the Elbow River Valley (at the West Bragg Picnic Area). The Bragg Creek end climbs 155 m (504 ft) making it the easier access route. This low elevation, easy trail offers an earlier season than most of the trails in the area. It follows old roads through meadows, grasslands and mixed forests.

Twin Summit Odyssey Trail (Map 7/G3) 🚶 🚴 ⛷️ 🏕️

While hikers will not have much difficulty with this trail, mountain bikers might find the rolling 2wd and 4wd roads difficult. An alpine meadow, rocky canyons and two summits provide the scenery along this 38.5 km (24 mile) trail. It takes up to six hours for the cyclist to complete the loop that takes you up Plateau Mountain Road, east to Hailstone Butte Lookout and then down to the Forestry Trunk Road and back to the start. The best time of year to attempt this trail is early July through mid-October.

Tyrwhitt Loop Trail (Map 10/G5) 🚶 👣
This difficult 12 km (7.4 miles) trail is perfect for the adventurous nature lover. Some of the highlights of this trail include a valley brightly covered with wild flowers, a high column, two ridge walks, and a viewpoint on an arch. The trail gains 900 m (2,925 ft) in elevation and can take up to eight hours to complete. The best time of year for trying this trail is mid-July through mid-October. Access is found on Highway 40 at Highwood Pass.

Upper Canyon Creek Trail (Map 16/A6) 🚶 👣
To explore Upper Canyon Creek, begin off the Powderface Trail at Canyon Creek. It is also possible to get to this trail via a 5.5 km (3.4 mile) trail from Prairie Creek to Canyon Creek. This trail gains 150 m (488 ft).

Upper Kananaskis Lake Trails (Map 10/E4) 🚶 🚴
It is possible to circle Upper Kananaskis Lake via a moderate 16 km (10 mile) trail, which can be broken into three sections. All three sections have their own charm and perspective of this man-made lake surrounded by majestic peaks. The East Shore Trail is the most popular section. This 3.6 km (2.2 mile) section can be mountain biked and is accessed from the Upper Lake Parking Lot and follows a wide trail over the dam. The West and South Shore section is 8 km (5 miles) long while the North Shore section is 4.7 km (2.9 miles). The loop can also be accessed from the North Interlakes Picnic Area or White Spruce Parking Lot.

Upper Wilkinson Creek Trail (Map 7/D3) 🚶 🚴 🏍 🛷 👣
A difficult route to locate and follow will take you to the meadows of Upper Wilkinson Creek. This 5 km (3 mile) route is found just west of Plateau Mountain Road and gains 190 m (618 ft). The best season to travel this trail is early summer to early fall.

Volcano Ridge Trail (Map 11/C2) ⛺ 🚶 🚴 👣
This trail is a good one to incorporate with others to form a loop. One of which is a 13 km (8 mile) loop that incorporates Gorge Creek, Link Creek

and Gorge Link Trails. This loop is accessed via Gorge Creek Truck Trail. Another loop is Volcano Ridge/ Threepoint Creek Loop. This is a difficult 41.5 km (25.8 mile) trail that requires about seven hours to complete by bike. This trail starts on the Volcano Ridge Trail at the Gorge Creek access and continues over the ridge and along the road to Threepoint Creek Trail. Follow this smooth trail to the bumpy, exposed tree roots of the North Fork Trail. This trail will eventually lead back to Gorge Creek Road. The best time of year for this trail is mid-July to mid-October, when the snow is gone. The **Volcano Creek Trail** is an easy 4 km (2.5 mile) extension the follows the north side of Volcano Creek to the Threepoint Mountain and Gorge Creek Trail junction. This trail climbs 120 m (390 ft) while offering fine views of Bluerock Mountain and access to surrounding peaks.

Ware Creek Trails (Map 11/F2) 🚶
The access point for these trails is located at the Ware Creek Parking Lot and can be reached along Gorge Creek Truck Trail. The **Ware Creek Trail** begins left of the fence and concludes at the field where the trail sign is located. Filled with the simplicity of nature, this route is 2.8 km (1.7 mile) long, gaining only 20 m (65 ft). The trail joins the well-marked 5 km (3 miles) North Fork Trail as well as Volcano Ridge Trail. The **Ware Creek North Bank Trail** is found along the No Motorized Vehicles road off the Gorge Creek Truck Trail. The 2 km (1.2 mile) route crosses the creek before meeting the 9999 Trail. The best season for these trails is June to early fall.

Wasootch Ridge Trail (Map 15/G6) 🚶 📷 👣
The Wasootch Ridge Trail can be reached at Wasootch Creek Picnic Area. Less seasoned hikers can follow the trail until a meadow is reached just beyond the ridge above Wasootch Creek. More experienced hikers may wish to continue toward the summit. The trail is 16 km (10 mile) round trip gaining 890 m (2,893 ft). It is possible to access the Baldy Pass Trail via a 3 km (1.8 mile) connector to Porcupine Creek (going over Fisher Range). The trail starts at the end of Wasootch Ridge and ends at the four-way junction, where the hiker may choose to go straight, to Baldy Pass Parking Lot or right, to Baldy Pass. Also in the area is the Wasootch Slabs, a popular rock climbing area. Mid-summer to early fall is the best time of year for these trails.

West Wind Loop (Map 15/C5) 🚶 🚴
This is a confusing 13 km (8 mile) route that follows assorted trails, old mining roads and railway tracks. You will visit an old mine site (now being made into a golf course) as you pass Three Sisters Creek, Stewart Creek and later Deadman Flats. The route gains 380 m and offers access to the Wind Valley and Three Sisters Trails.

Whiskey Jack Trail (Map 10/F4) 🚶 🚴
This rough trail has some steep segments as it climbs 5 km (3 mile), one-way from the Boulton Creek Parking Lot. The trail connects with the Lookout and Pocaterra Trails.

Whiskey Lake Loop Trail (Map 11/C4) 🚶 🚴 🐎 🚶
This loop is accessed from the end of the Sheep River Trail. From there, the trail follows the Sheep Trail and loops around Whisky Lake. It is possible to link up with the Bluerock Equestrian Recreation Area before heading back to the trailhead. This 3.5 km (2.2 mile) hike is best done in the late spring through mid-fall.

Wildhorse Trail (Map 11/B1) 🚶 🚴 👣
This popular mountain biking trail is found at the Little Elbow Recreation Area. The 16 km (10 mile) one-way trail climbs 355 m (1,165 FT) around Forgetmenot Mountain. A nice loop is formed with the Quirk Creek Trail (see above).

Willow Creek Trails (Maps 7/G1–8/A2) 🚶 🚴 👣
The **Willow Creek Trail** is 12 km (7.4 miles) long and provides access to a few trails including the **Corral Creek Trail**. This easy 5 km (3 mile) trail follows Corral Creek exploration road through some small pine forest to the steep eastern slopes of Sentinel Peak, gaining 290 m (943 ft). There the hiker has the option to go bushwhacking on the many foothills. The **Mount Burke Trail** is an 8 km (5 mile) unmarked trail to the summit. It is better suited for the experienced hiker since the trail is difficult to locate and it climbs 850 m (2,790 ft) in elevation. It begins at Salt Creek and finishes at the weather

beaten Cameron Lookout, now abandoned. Highlights include the wild landscape of yellow scree slopes and extraordinary cliff bands.

Wind Valley Trails (Map 15/C4-D5) 👤 🏕
A series of trails can be found west of the Pigeon Mountain Ski Area. The **Upper Wind Trail** is a short 1.3 km (0.8 mile) trail gaining 35m (114 ft). This route offers a stunning view of the Windtower and Wind Ridge. The **South Wind Hoodoos Trail** is a short but strenuous 3 km (1.8 mile) hike that takes you to The Obelisk, one of the world's highest hoodoos. The **Wind Pond Trail** is a moderate trail that climbs 825 m (2,681 ft) over 10 km (6 miles) to the pond found near Mount Allan. The **Wind Ridge Trail** leads 7.5 km (4.7 miles) from the West Wind Loop (see above). Your climb of 760 m (2,470 ft) offers incredible views of the Windtower. Beware of Grizzly Bears in this area.

Windtower Trail (Map 15/B5) 👤 🏕
Unlike the Wind Valley Trails which happen in the shadow of the Windtower and which are accessible from the north, this trip starts from the Smith-Dorrien Spray Lakes Road. Why? Silly question, if you have ever seen the Windtower, you would know that three sides of it are sheer cliff, and the peak is only approachable from the west. The trail passes through Wind Pass (itself a fine destination), then climbs steeply up along a scree/shale slope. This 2 km (1.2 mile) grunt up to the top features some good views out over the Spray Valley. As you come to the top, the mountain falls away from you on three sides, dropping nearly 750 m (2,438 ft) straight down. Needless to say, this is not a hike for those scared of heights.

Windy Peak Hills Trail (Map 7/G3) 👤 🏕
This hike, with its beautiful views of rolling hills, may be accessed at the Hump off Secondary Highway 532. Depending on the trail you choose, the hike can take up to a full day, as it is approximately 9 km (5.6 miles), gaining 685 m (2,226 ft). The best hiking season is mid-summer to early fall.

Windy Point Trails (Map 11/F3) 👤 ⛷ 🏕
This is a popular hike leading through some beautiful country. It begins just west of the Sandy McNabb Recreation Area, but be warned that the trail becomes difficult to follow (look carefully for the signs and red markers). The 15 km (9.3 mile) trail starts on the Sheep Trail before heading north and looping back. There are some steep sections as the trail leads to a ridge with panoramic views of the surrounding area. The best season is mid-July to mid-October.

Wolf Creek Trail (Map 11/F4) 👤 🚵 🐎 ⛷ 🏕
Access to this 11 km (6.8 miles) trail is at the Sandy McNabb Recreation Area. It leads through forest and meadow as it travels up Wolf Creek. The highlight of the route is a black gorge you come across. Other connecting trails, such as the Phone Line, Mount McNabb and Price Camp Trails, can be added on to make a loop back.

Yamnuska Ridge and CMC Valley Trail (Map 15/F3) 👤 🐎 🏕
A very popular trail is found at the end of Quarry Road off of the Bow Valley Trail (Hwy 1A). The trail climbs an old gated road and horse trail to the ridge with spectacular views. You climb 435 m (1,414 ft) over 7 km (4.3 miles) return. For the more ambitious, it is possible to continue an additional 7 km (4.3 miles) to a viewpoint of the CMC Valley and the impressive Ephel Duath Cliff. This trail drops 150 m (488 ft) to the valley bottom where the trail deteriorates before climbing back up to the vantage point.

Zephyr Creek Trail (Maps 7/F1-11/E7) 👤 🏕
Be prepared to get wet on this one. From the Sentinel Picnic Area, a difficult 9 km (5.6 mile) route leads you to some ancient Indian Pictographs. You must first wade the Highwood River to an old road, which will eventually lead you to the Zephyr Creek Valley. Continue to the Painted Creek Valley where several creek crossings will take you to the pictographs (found where the two ridges meet). More pictographs are found higher up the ridge. Other routes include continuing up Zephyr Creek to Bear Pass 15 km (9.3 miles) gaining 670 m (2,178 ft), or following the unique undulating north ridge of Mount Burke (19 km/11.8 miles gaining 1,010 m/3,283 ft).

Banff National Park
The spectacular alpine scenery, abundant wildlife and over 1,600 km (1,000 miles) of trails attract visitors year round. The usual hiking season ranges from mid-May to mid-October, with high elevation trails sporting snow later into the year. The trails in this park see a lot of activity, especially those around the towns of Banff and Lake Louise. Remember, there is a daily fee and a backcountry camping permit required when in the park. Please ensure you have registered before heading out on the trails.

Alexandra River Trail (Map 25/B2-D1) 👤 🐎 🚵 🏕
Beginning at the Icefields Parkway, this old fire road runs along the North Saskatchewan River for a few kilometres, before heading west to parallel the Alexandra River. The 11.7 km (7.3 mile) trail takes you through spectacular terrain and scenic views. While the old fire road continues on to the junction of the Alexandra and Castleguard Rivers, there are numerous stream crossings. Most people stop at the difficult Terrace Creek crossing.

Allenby Pass Trail (Map 14/F2-G6) 👤 🐎 🚵 🏕
This long trail will take hikers three or four days to complete. It can be accessed from Sunshine Road, along the Brewster Creek Fire Road. It is a moderate 27 km (16.8 mile) trail that climbs steeply to the Allenby Pass. Along the way you catch views of the Sundance Range. An option to continue to the Bryant Creek Trail is possible.

Arnica & Twin Lakes Trail (Map 14/A1) ⛺ 👤 ⛷ 🎣 🏕
Found at the Vista Lake Viewpoint on Highway 93, 2 km (1.2 miles) east of the BC border, the **Arnica Lake Trail** is a popular 5 km (3 mile) hike. The trail actually drops down to Vista Lake before climbing 580 m (1,885 ft) through the woods to Arnica Lake. The lake provides good fishing for cutthroat trout. Most choose to explore the scenic routes up (800 m/2,600 ft) Storm Mountain or onto the Twin Lakes. The trail to Twin Lakes climbs 675 m (2,215 ft) over 16.8 km (10.4 miles) return. The trail does continue through Gibbon Pass to Redearth Creek and Shadow Lake. The best time of year for this hike is mid-June through September.

Aylmer Pass Trail (Maps 15/C1-21/A7) ⛺ 👤 🏕
A popular overnight trip, this trail begins at Lake Minnewanka before ascending towards Mount Aylmer. Along the way, many visitors take the side trail to the scenic lookout. The 27 km (16.8 mile) hike to the pass is difficult, and should be left to those hikers who are fit. It is possible to link up with the Ghost River Trail outside of the park. Reservations are required for camping in the park.

Badger Pass Trail (Map 20/C6) ⛺ 👤 🏕
Accessed off the Johnston Creek Trail, this difficult, 21 km (13 mile) hike takes you through remote, high alpine terrain. In fact, it is one of the highest trail access passes in Banff Park. The trail connects with the Cascade River Trail and is best hiked from August through to September. Give yourself the better part of a day to complete this hike.

Baker Lake Trail (Maps 21/G4-20/A4) 👤 ⛷ 🎣
The shortest route into this good fishing lake is from Boulder Pass off the Skoki Valley Trail (see below). The moderate trail is only 4.5 km (2.8 miles) long but it is hilly and the route is often muddy as it follows the north shore of Ptarmigan Lake. The longer, more difficult route in follows the Baker Creek Trail. The trail between Redoubt Creek and Baker Lake is quite rough.

Boom Lake Trail (Maps 14/A1-19/G7) 👤 ⛷ 🎣
Anglers looking for a relatively easy hike-in lake may wish to pick this 5 km (3 mile) trail. However, the trail starts off with a tough climb before descending to the lake. It is possible to continue along more difficult routes leading to O'Brien, Taylor and Moraine Lakes.

Boundary Lake Trail (Map 32/A7) 👤 🏕
The trailhead for this short, 1.5 km (0.9 mile) scramble is found on Icefields Parkway (Hwy 93) at Sunwapta Pass. Most visitors also follow the side trail at the lake to view Boundary Glacier.

Bourgeau Lake Trail (Map 14/D2) 👤 🎣 🏕
Accessed off the Trans-Canada Highway, this is an 8 km (5 mile) trail that is home to a lot of wildlife. It should take a couple of hours as you ascend

through the Douglas-fir forest to a fairly high elevation. At the 7.5 km (4.7 mile) mark, there is a side trail to Harvey Pass. This is a 3 km (1.8 mile) trail that will take you around Bourgeau Lake and up to the pass.

Bow Glacier Falls & Hut Trail (Map 19/B1) 🚶 📷 ⛺ 🏕
Num-ti-jah Lodge on the Icefields Parkway is the access point for this 4.5 km (2.8 mile) hike. You first skirt along the Bow Lake shoreline before climbing steeply to the edge of a canyon, where the trail leads to the base of some beautiful falls. It is a moderate hike in which you gain 170 m (553 ft). Mountaineers use this trail to gain access to the Bow Hut. The difficult route up climbs 440 m (1,430 ft). On the descent, it is possible to visit the source of Bow Glacier Falls.

Bow River Loop (Map 19/G5) 🚶 🚴 ⛷ 🚶
Found at the end of Sentinel Road in Lake Louise, this is an excellent trail for the hiker or biker who is interested in nature. The 7.2 km (4.5 mile) trail follows both banks of the Bow River and would take about 1.5 hours to walk.

Bow Summit Lookout Trail (Maps 19/B1-26/B7) 🚶 🏕
Accessed from the Bow Summit Parking Area, this is an easy trail to an old fire lookout. The 3 km (1.8 mile) trail only climbs 32 m (105 ft) to the summit. From here, the Timberline Trail begins its loop through a sub-alpine meadow.

Brazeau Lake Trail (Map 32/B7-C3) ⛺ 🚶 🐎 🐟 🏕
Beginning 7.5 km (5.3 miles) south of the Banff-Jasper Park Border, this 32.5 km (20 mile) trail takes you all the way to Brazeau Lake in Jasper National Park. (Most of the hike is in Jasper.) It leads through the scenic Nigel Pass, and along the Brazeau River. There are several campgrounds along the way.

Brazeau Loop Trail (Map 32/B7-A4) ⛺ 🚶 🐎 🐟 🏕
Taking the Brazeau Lake Trail a little further, this 78.5 km (48.8 mile) loop trail offers a great week long excursion for the ambitious hiker. Through forested land and over avalanche slopes, the trail provides access to the best of the Canadian Rockies. The terrain can become tricky at times, so take extra care and be prepared. Several campgrounds are located along the way. The scenic **Jonas Pass Trail** can be accessed at the 14 km (8.7 mile) point. This adjoining trail is 19 km (11.8 miles) long one-way, including a 13 km (8 mile) section above the treeline. It leads past towering peaks, through wildflower meadows and through prime mountain caribou habitat.

C Level Cirque Trail (Map 14/G1) 🚶 🏕
This 4 km (2.5 mile) one-way hike is one of the more attractive walks in the Banff Townsite region. Look for it off of Lake Minnewanka Road at the Upper Bankhead Picnic Area. It takes you part way up the Cascade Mountain as it leads to a glacier-carved bowl. Within half an hour of your hike you will encounter two old buildings, which are the remains of an anthracite coal operation. As well, expect some uphill climbing through forest before it finally opens up to views of the Three Sisters and the Bow Valley.

Carrot Creek Trail (Map 15/B2) ⛺ 🚶 🏕
A 23 km (14.3 mile) one-way trail begins off the Trans-Canada Highway, 2 km (1.2 miles) from the east entrance of Banff Park. A little bushwhacking,

many creek crossings and some steep climbing (550m/1,788 ft gain) will get you to the Carrot Creek Summit, found 10.5 km (6.5 miles) along the route. Here, there are views of Lake Minnewanka below. The trail eventually meets up with the Lake Minnewanka Trail. Camping is available along the route.

Cascade Amphitheatre Trail (Map 14/G1) 🚶 🏕
A popular 15 km (9.3 mile) hike begins at the Mount Norquay Ski Area. The trail gains 610 m (1,983 ft) through scenic country to view the glacier-carved cove. A crossing of Forty Mile Creek and some steep switchbacks make the trip a bit strenuous. It should take about five hours to hike.

Cascade Fire Road (Maps 15/A1-20/C1) ⛺ 🚶 🚴 🐎 ⛷ 🐟 🏕
After the collapse of two bridges in the summer of 1984, the Cascade Fire Road was converted to a multi-use trail. This 75 km (46.6 mile) road runs from the Sawback Range to the Bare Mountains, passing the Palliser Range along the way. Wildlife such as bear, elk and sheep can be seen along the route. Creek and river crossings are necessary, including the Panther River. The trail can be broken down into two sections: the **Lower Cascade Fire Road**, which leads north from the Lake Minnewanka Road at the Upper Bankhead Picnic Area to Stoney Creek and the **Upper Cascade Fire Road**, which continues to the Red Deer River Valley. The Lower Cascade Fire Road is 15.2 km (9.4 miles) long, gaining 256 m (832 ft) of elevation and losing 70 m (228 ft). Because of its high Grizzly Bear population, this section has been designated as a biking path in order to minimize furry encounters of the unfriendly kind. The Upper Cascade Fire Road is 55.5 km (34.5 miles) long, gaining 830 m (2,698 ft) and losing 850 m (2,763 ft). It takes three days to hike this section one-way. The northern access is found at the Ya-Ha Tinda Ranch (look for the spur road south of the locked gate before the ranch building).

Castle Mountain Lookout Trail (Map 20/B7) 🚶 📷 🏕
This 4 km (2.5 mile) trek up the side of Castle Mountain leads to the old Mount Eisenhower Fire Lookout. You can find the trailhead 5 km (3 miles) west of Castle Junction on the Bow Valley Parkway (Hwy 1A). Although short, the trail is quite steep, gaining 520 m (1,690 ft) in elevation. The trail leads from the forest to meadows full of wildflowers (in season) and an exposed cliff, which offers great views of the Bow Valley. Experienced rock climbers can continue from the scenic lookout and onto Goat Ledge.

Castleguard Meadows Route (Map 25/A1) ⛺ 🚶 📷 🏕
The Castleguard Meadows Trail follows the Alexandra River Trail to the Castleguard River. From here, the trail becomes a route as it makes its way to the spectacular alpine meadows. The meadows are some of the most impressive in Banff, and because of the long, difficult access, few people visit them. It is a 35 km (21.7 mile) trip that should take two or three days. Experienced glacier travellers can continue onto the Saskatchewan Glacier. Check at the Lake Louise Visitor Centre for conditions.

Chephren Lake Trail (Map 26/A6) 🚶 🐟
This 7 km (4.3 mile) trail is accessed at the Waterfowl Lake Campground. It leads to a glacier-fed lake after climbing 90 m (293 ft). At the 2 km (1.2 mile) junction, it is possible to head left to arrive at Cirque Lake. The best hiking time is mid-June through October.

Citadel Pass Trail (Map 14/D4) ⛺ 🚶 ⛷ 🏕
Accessed from the Sunshine Village Ski Area, this is a 9.5 km (5.9 mile) hike that gains 615 m (1,999 ft) in elevation. The trail climbs through alpine meadows and then descends to a lake and campground below. It is possible to continue to Lake Magog in Mount Assiniboine Park through the Golden Valley. Allow two days to hike that 28 km (17.4 mile) trail.

Clearwater Valley Trail (Map 26/C6-G7) ⛺ 🚶 🚴 🐎 🐟 🏕
This long, difficult trek leads 58 km (three or four days) from the Siffleur River to the Clearwater River Valley. Hiking this trail takes you through some of the most remote regions in Banff National Park. You will pass Upper Devon Lake (good fishing) as well as a warden's cabin. One good location to camp is the east end of Trident Lake. Watch for the elk that often congregate here. There are several joining trails including the Divide Creek Trail and the Clearwater River Trail, which continues east into the Bighorn Wildland.

Consolation Lakes Trail (Map 19/G7)
This is a short, easy 5 km (3 mile) hike, which begins at Moraine Lake. The trail climbs past a rockslide to a beautiful open meadow with wildflowers in season. At Lower Consolation Lake enjoy the view of Bident Mountain and Mount Quadra before continuing on over a narrow ridge and discovering Upper Consolation Lake. When Grizzly Bears are active in the area, hikers need to hike in groups of six or more. There is a sign-up sheet at the trailhead.

Cotton Grass Pass Trail (Map 20/A3)
The Cotton Grass Pass Trail is 5.8 km (3.6 mile) long, and can be started from either direction. It takes you between Baker Lake and Red Deer Lakes. This trail is quite appealing as most of it is above tree line, offering splendid views of the cliffs of Fossil Mountain and Pipestone Mountain.

Crowfoot Pass Trail (Map 19/C2)
If you are an adventurous hiker or skier, you are going to love this trail, or rather, route. Finding the unmarked trail is tough. From the Icefields Parkway, 1.3 km (0.8 miles) south of the Crowfoot Glacier Viewpoint, make your way down to Bow River, which you must cross. You then climb steeply for 7 km (4.3 miles) to the pass, with magnificent views. It is possible to continue on to the Mount Balfour viewpoint.

Divide Creek Trail (Maps 20/C1-27/B6)
This difficult multi-use trail begins off the Red Deer River Trail. It runs through meadows and forests and requires some creek crossing as you climb 625 m (2,031 ft) to the Divide Summit. From here, enjoy the great views of the surrounding mountains before descending to Peters Creek and Clearwater River. Wildlife may be encountered along the 26 km (16.2 mile) one-way route. Most hikers choose to follow the Clearwater River Trail back into Banff Park (the ford of the Clearwater River is best left until August at the earliest). From the Clearwater River/Peters Creek end, the trail gains 900 m (2,925 ft) in elevation.

Dolomite Pass & Creek Trail (Maps 19/C1-26/D6)
The Dolomite Pass Trail is a 9 km (5.6 mile) one-way multi-use trail that is accessed at the Crowfoot Glacier Viewpoint. The climb to the pass is rather steep (650 m/2,112 ft gain), but if you travel it in the summer, you will be surrounded by colorful meadows with great views and access to Lake Helen (12 km/7.5 miles return). From the pass, the Dolomite Creek Trail continues to Isabella Lake passing some waterfalls along the way. It is a difficult, 10 hour hike that gains 550 m (1,788 ft). There is also a 7 km (4.3 mile) option from the pass heading down past Katherine Lake to Dolomite Peak, but this route is seldom used and you may have to bushwhack. These trails are best left to the fit hiker to do from mid-July through October.

Dormer Pass & River Trails (Map 20/G6)
Accessed from the Cascade Fire Road at the 15 km (9.3 mile) mark, the trail up Dormer Pass 13 km (8 mile) and requires a few stream crossings. From the pass it is a steep descent to the river, which also needs to be crossed. The trail has many scenic viewpoints and side trails to Stoney Pass, Dormer Mountain and Panther River.

Edith & Cory Pass Trails (Map 14/E1)
Accessed from the Fireside Picnic Area, off the Bow Valley Parkway is a pair of strenuous 13 km (8 mile) hikes. The Edith Pass Trail gains 520 m (1,690 ft) in elevation and offers glimpses of Mount Norquay and Mount Edith along the way. The Cory Pass Trail will take about 6 hours to climb the 900 m (2,925 ft) up through a beautiful alpine forest. The rocky ascent is steep, but the scenic reward makes it worth it. It is possible to link the trails or continue north from Edith Pass to the Forty Mile Creek Trail. The later option is a 12.8 km (8 mile) one-way hike to Mount Norquay.

Eiffel Lake Trail (Map 19/E7)
While this trail is no longer maintained or promoted, Eiffel Lake is still a popular destination with those in the know. Alpine flowers bloom in profusion near the lake, and Eiffel Lake is set in the heart of the stark Desolation Valley. The trip is 10 km (6.2 miles) return from the trailhead at Moraine Lake, although many people make their way past the lake (there is no trail here) to connect up with the Wenkchemna Pass Trail, 10 km (6.2 miles) one-way. You will gain 400 m (1,300 ft) to the lake, taking you through forests and meadows. Climbing to the pass takes you up another 350 m (1,138 ft) through fabulous rock formations and past the foot of the Ten Peaks. This trail is best hiked after July.

Elk Lake & Pass Trail (Maps 14/F1-20/G7)
Accessed from the Mount Norquay Ski Area, this multi-use trail begins. It is a 14 km (8.7 mile) one-way trip to the lake that gains 610 m (1,983 ft) in elevation. It is 12.8 km (8 miles) one-way to Elk Pass proper. There are many small lakes and scenic viewpoints along the way. Before reaching the lake, you will find a campsite a popular trail linking to the beautiful Cascade Valley. Allow five hours to hike to the lake.

Elkhorn Summit Trail (Map 20/E2)
This 13 km (8 mile) hike leads to a series of meadows, found between the Red Deer and Panther Rivers.

Fatigue Creek Trail (Map 14/F4)
Accessed from the Allenby Pass Trail, this is a 13 km (8 mile) trail that crosses the creek many times on your way to Fatigue Pass. You gain 780 m (2,535 ft) in elevation, making it a grueling route. However, once you are above the treeline the views are great. The trail can be used as a link to Citadel Pass.

Flint's Park Trail (Map 20/E5)
This 8 km (4.6 mile) connecting trail follows the Cascade River from the Cascade Fire Road to the Forty Mile Creek Trail. The campsite at Flint's Park is a popular equestrian destination, and makes a good hub for exploring the area.

Great Divide Trail
This is an extensive trail system, running along the BC/Alberta border. It combines many different trails, stringing them together into one 500 km + (300 mile +) route. The hiking trail weaves in and out of the two provinces; some sections are covered in the Southwestern Alberta mapbook, some are not. Keep in mind that there are many side trails to wander making topographic maps essential. Also recommended is a copy of *The Great Divide Trail*, by Dustin Lynx. These following sections are some of the more popular routes in Southwestern Alberta:

Kananaskis Country (Maps 7/D7-11/D7) marks the southern terminus of the Great Divide. From the North Fork Trail, south of Tornado Mountain, it is possible to follow a route through the Beehive Nature Area and the series of trails west of the Forestry Trunk Road. Eventually you will link up with the Fitzsimmons Creek Trail, which leads to Highway 40. This section is best done over a two or three-day stretch.

The Meadow Section (Map 14/G7–A1) runs 88 km (55 miles) from the southern end of Banff Park through the Upper Shunda River Valley, Mount Assiniboine Area and the Sunshine-Egypt Lake complex. It ends on the Banff-Windermere Highway (Hwy 93). Be careful when travelling the section between Currie Creek and Marvel Pass, as avalanche debris makes the route difficult. Egypt Lake Campsite provides the weary hiker with an overnight resting spot. For fishermen, the lake is good for trout fishing. The best time to hike the trail is early June through September, when the vegetation will be most colourful.

The Glacier Section (Maps 19, 24) offers the hiker some gorgeous waterfalls, glaciers and wild rivers. The whole section runs 92 km (57 miles) from Field, BC to the Saskatchewan River Crossing. A missing section of trail in BC (from Kiwetinok Pass to Amiskwi River) makes this an awkward route to complete. However, the final stretch of the trail from Howse Pass (Map 25/G6) to the Saskatchewan River Crossing (Map 26/G3) is relatively easy to follow.

The Caribou Section (Maps 25/E3-32/A3) is the longest section, running 164 km (102 miles) from Norman Creek, off the Icefields Parkway (Hwy 93), to Maligne Lake Road, near Jasper. The trail is in good condition, except through Cataract Pass, where a route leads through the scenic alpine to Nigel Pass. Gorgeous meadow passes and wildlife are encountered throughout the trip. Caribou are found especially on Amber Mountain and Jonas Pass. Between Nigel Pass and Sunset Pass, lay the steepest grades of the entire Great Divide Trail, climbing to a maximum elevation of 2,515 m (8,174 ft).

Forty Mile Creek Trail (Maps 14/F1-20/E6)

This trail follows the Cascaded Amphitheatre Trail for less than a kilometre before splitting off to follow Forty Mile Creek. From the junction to Flint's Park—the end of the Forty Mile Creek Trail—is 27.8 km (17.2 miles) one-way. It should take backpackers at least three days to hike out and back. The trail can get muddy, so try to hold out for dry weather. Highlights include the excellent view of Sawback Lake once you reach Forty Mile Summit. Sawback Lake and Rainbow Lake are accessed off the trail, just north of the summit. It is very easy to create a multi-day loop trail with the many connecting trails. Popular options include following the Badger Pass Trail to the Johnston Creek Trail or the Flint's Park Trail to the Cascade Fire Road.

Gibbon Pass Trail (Map 14/A1)

A 6 km (3.7 mile) hiking trail begins from the Shadow Lake Campsite. It gains 470 m (1,528 ft) in elevation on its way to the pass, before dropping down to the Twin Lakes.

Glacier Lake Trail (Map 25/E4)

Accessed from the Icefields Parkway, it will take the better part of a day to hike this 20 km (12.5 mile) trail. It is a climb 685 m (2,226 ft) up through open forest to Glacier Lake where there are great views of the surrounding mountains. To continue past Glacier Lake, you must bushwhack your way along Glacier River. A campsite by the lake provides a base for further explorations or anglers.

Goat Creek Trail (Maps 14/G2-15/A3)

Follow the Spray River Fire Road south to the disused dirt road that follows Goat Creek east towards Spray Lakes Reservoir. The east end of the route is rougher and requires creek crossings. The moderate 9 km (5.6 mile) multi-use trail is accessed from the Banff Springs Hotel or at the Bow River Bridge in town. For the biker looking for a challenging loop, combine the Goat Creek Trail with the Rundle Riverside Trail and the golf course road to complete a 48 km (29.8 mile) loop.

Great Divide Trail (Maps 14, 19, 24, 25, 32)

See insert in this section.

Headwaters (Indianhead Creek) Trail (Maps 26/G4-27/A6)

This 13 km (8 mile) one-way hike starts from the Clearwater Valley Trail (at the 27.4 km/17 mile mark) and leads to the Indianhead Creek headwaters. It begins by paralleling the Clearwater River before climbing steeply to a saddle. From here on, the open trail provides nearly continuous views of nearby summits as it makes its way to the old Headwaters Patrol Cabin (outside of Banff) via the Indianhead Creek Drainage.

Healy Pass Trail (Map 14/C3)

From the Bourgeau Parking Lot, two different routes provide access to the pass. The most scenic involves hiking up to Sunshine Village, while the more direct route follows the old road up Healy Creek. No matter what route you take, you will find beautiful meadows, ponds, wildflowers and streams. In the winter, frozen waterfalls provide you with some ice climbing opportunities. Egypt Lake can be accessed from the main trail, which is 20 km (12.5 mile) long and gains 215 m (699 ft). Another popular side trail is the easy 2.5 km (1.6 mile) Redearth Pass Trail. From the scenic pass, it is possible to continue toward East Verdant Creek, which will eventually take you down to Highway 93 in BC. June through September is the best hiking time.

Hector Lake Trail (Map 19/D3)

Accessed from the Icefields Parkway, this 2 km (1.2 mile) hike requires fording the Bow River, which is not safe until late in the season when water levels are low. The trail runs along the Bow River for a while, and is often used by fishermen to access to some great fishing spots. There is camping by Hector Lake as well as a 5 km (3 mile) trail leading to Lake Margaret, where you will find an excellent view of Mount Hector.

Helen Creek Trail (Map 19/D1)

This 5 km (3 mile) trail begins off the Icefields Parkway, south of Crowfoot Glacier Viewpoint. The trail, which gains 490 m (1,593 ft) in elevation, is an alternate route to Lake Helen.

Howse Pass Trail (Map 25/F5)

The trailhead for this 54 km (33.6 mile) multi-day trip is located by the Mistaya River Bridge at the Mistaya Canyon Pullout off the Icefields Parkway. The trail provides access to the Freshfield Range Glacier Area, a popular rock climbing area. This trail runs by Howse River and requires a bit of bush-whacking to avoid those icy stream crossings. Early June through September is the best time to hike the trail.

Johnson Lake Trails (Map 15/A1)

The 11.7 km (7.3 mile) network of trails in and around Johnson Lake are a series of ski trails that follow old roads around the lake. These trails can be hiked in the summer. In fact, they are some of the first trails in Banff to be relatively snow free in spring. The busiest of the trails is an easy 8 km (5 mile) circuit of the lake. Also in the area is a 700-year-old Douglas-fir, one of the oldest known fir trees in Alberta, and the old Anthracite Mine site, found below some Hoodoos.

Johnston Canyon & Creek Trails (Maps 14/D1-20/B6)

The **Johnston Canyon Trail** is a popular 3 km (1.8 mile) trail that leads to an impressive limestone canyon that is home to a series of waterfalls. The trailhead is accessed off the Bow Valley Parkway at the Hillsdale Meadows Parking Area. This was probably one of the most expensive trails to build in the park, as there are hundreds of feet of catwalks, and a tunnel that bringing hikers through the heart of the canyon. Past the upper falls, the **Johnstone Creek Trail** continues to the Ink Pots and beyond. This two or three day 38.5 km (24 mile) hike weaves it's way through a valley bottom and is best undertaken from mid-July to September. It has several points of interest including Pulsatilla Pass, Badger Pass and Mystic Pass. For those who plan to camp, there is a campsite at Luellen Lake (16.1 km/10 mile) and another on a small scenic knoll (20 km/12.5 miles).

Lake Agnes Circuit (Map 19/F5)

Climbing the trail to Lake Agnes with the Big Beehive and Plain of Six Glaciers creates a truly sublime circuit. As an added bonus, you will pass both of the backcountry teahouses on this 14.5 km (9 mile) circuit. The trails to Lake Agnes and the Plain of the Six Glaciers are both extremely popular, but the trail linking the two together, over the Big Beehive, is not quite as popular, so you might have a few kilometres of solitude. Might. The trail to Lake Agnes will take about 4 hours as you climb 438 m (1,424 ft over 8 km (5 miles) return. Alternatively, try the **Highland Trail**, which starts at Mirror Lake off of the Lake Agnes Trail. This trail takes the hiker or horseback rider through trees to open slopes, revealing the whole length of Lake Louise. This demanding 14 km (8.7 mile) return trail does not see the crowds other trails do.

Lake Louise Shoreline Trails (Map 19/F5)

A 3 km (1.8 mile) walk or ski around the lake provides great views of Mount Victoria towering above. At the far end of the lake is rock climbing opportunities (Wicked Gravity and Exquisite Corpse are two popular routes). The **Fairview Lookout Trail** is a short 2 km (1.2 mile) trail that provides you with an excellent view of Lake Louise. Accessed from the Boathouse in Lake Louise, the trail is rather steep. An alternate route back is the South Lakeshore Trail.

Lake Louise Ski Hill (Map 19/G4)

The lower slopes of the Lake Louise Ski Hill have been designated Grizzly habitat, and are closed to hikers. However, the gondola remains in operation over the summer and fall, taking hikers to mid-mountain. From here, it is possible to hike across as well as up the mountain along ski runs and trails. The views across the valley to Lake Louise, the lake, are phenomenal, and get better as you climb. To get to the summit of the mountain from the gondola station, give yourself at least two hours up, and make sure you fill up with water before heading out. Because this is active Grizzly Bear habitat, it is recommended that you hike in groups of six or more.

Lake Minnewanka Trail (Maps 15/A1-21/E7) 🏕 🚶 🚲 🐎 ⛷ 📷

This trail runs along the north shore of the large, beautiful Lake Minnewanka and past the three Ghost Lakes to the Devil's Gap, which marks the park boundary. The first Ghost Lake is dried up and the second is marshy, but the third is a beautiful blue. You will find signs directing you to other trails, including the Devil's Gap Trail. There is camping at the second Ghost Lake.

Lakes and Larches Hike (Map 14/B2) 🚶 🏕 🚶 🐟 📷

Ease of access and post card perfect scenery make this series of trails attractive to the hiker. This route strings together a series of trails to create a point-to-point hike, so you will need a shuttle. While it is possible to do this 40.3 km (25 mile) one-way route in two days, don't rush. Spend three or four days exploring this gorgeous area. From the Sunshine Road, this route follows the Healy Pass Trail to Egypt Lake. Here, branch trails take you to Pharaoh Lake and Black Rock Lake to the North, and Scarab and Mummy Lake (3.5 km/2.2 miles) to the south. Through hikers should follow the Whistling Pass Trail to Shadow Lake (although you can take the Pharoah Creek Trail to the Shadow Lake Lodge, a great place to overnight if you have the funds). From here, a trail runs through Gibbon Pass to Twin Lakes, and the Arnica Lake Trail. If you left your vehicle at the Vista Lake Trailhead, go left. If you left it at the Copper Lake Trailhead, go right.

Larch Valley Trail (Map 19/F7) 🚶 📷

This trail is spectacular in the fall when the larch trees turn a bright golden yellow. It is 9.5 km (5.9 miles) return to the valley, gaining 500 m (1,625 ft) along the way. Once at the valley, the hiker has the option to go north to Sentinel Pass, which requires another three hours to climb 720 m (2,340 ft). Once there, the views are magnificent. Going through Sentinel Pass, the fit hiker can descend 500 m (1,625 ft) to Paradise Valley to the west or go east to Lake Annette. Eventually, both options will lead back to Moraine Lake Road.

Lost Lake Trails (Map 19/E4) 🚶

Off the Trans-Canada Highway, 9 km (5.6 miles) west of the Lake Louise overpass there are a couple of routes that will get you to Lost Lake. The rougher Bath Creek Route is 2 km (1.2 mile) long, starting across the CPR tracks near the creek. The Hillside Route is 1 km (0.6 mile) long and is the steeper of the two routes. It begins at the trail sign. Both trails will take you to this green lake, surrounded by a heavy canopy of trees and mountains.

Louise Creek Trail (Map 19/G6) 🚶 🐟

This trail is the quickest way from the village to Lake Louise Ski Hill. The trailhead for this 3 km (1.8 mile) trail starts at the campground on the southwest side of the Bow River Bridge and takes the hiker or fisherman through heavy forest as it follows along Louise Creek. The elevation gain is 200 m (650 ft).

Marvel Pass & Owl Lake Trail (Map 14/G7) 🏕 🚶 🐟 📷

Marvel Pass is 9.3 km (5.8 miles) from the Bryant Creek Trail Junction, which in turn is 11.7 km (7.3 miles) from the Mount Shark Parking Area. Head west on Bryant Creek Trail, until you come to the Owl Lake Trail junction (it is 4 km/2.5 miles to the pretty lake). Follow the trail past Owl Lake and on to Marvel Pass. This trip could easily be done in a day. However, many people connect this trail with Marvel Lake via a rough, ill-defined route south from Marvel Pass to connect with the Wonder Pass Trail, which passes by Marvel Lake. This 46.5 km (28.9 mile) loop is best left for experienced route finders carrying topo maps. Be forewarned that the area at the south end of Marvel Lake is boggy and there may or may not be some log bridges over the creek. Expect to get your feet wet.

Molar Pass Trail (Map 19/D1) 🏕 🚶 🐎 📷

The Molar Pass Trail is a 10 km (6.2 mile) hike. One can expect miles of rolling alpine meadows below looming glaciers. After the first 1.5 km (0.9 mile) the trail parallels Mosquito Creek until it splits at 6.5 km (4 miles) and begins to climb uphill to Molar Pass (at 2,377 m/7,725 ft). The rocky towers of Molar Mountain, which indeed looks like the titular tooth, can be seen to the south. You can also continue on to North Molar Pass but be prepared for a stiff climb (up to 760 m/2,470 ft) and the possibility of seeing grizzly bears. Snow can also be a problem until late July.

Moraine Lake Trail (Map 19/G6-7) 🚶 🚲

This 8.5 km (5.9 mile) one-way trail begins on the banks of the Bow River in the village of Lake Louise. For those riding mountain bikes there is a longer version (30 km/18.6 miles), which loops around and follows Paradise Creek up the Giant Steps past Lake Annette. For most, the shorter version is a terrific journey that climbs up the side of Mount Temple and leads to the beautiful Moraine Lake. The trail essentially parallels Moraine Lake Road, and in July and August the forest floor is a high mountain flower garden. A popular viewpoint at the north end of Moraine Lake is accessed by the **Rockpile Trail**. This short interpretive trail leads 1 km (0.6 miles) through a jumble of boulders to a viewpoint overlooking the lake and the Ten Peaks. At sunrise and sunset, the viewpoint is usually teeming with photographers.

Mosquito Creek Trail (Map 19/E1) 🏕 🚶 🐎 🐟 📷

The trail up Mosquito Creek starts at a fairly high elevation, and just gets higher. You climb quickly to the alpine around North Molar Pass before dropping down to the first of the Fish Lakes. There is camping and good cutthroat trout fishing at the lakes. Plan for an overnight trip, as the 15 km (9.3 mile) one-way trail is difficult to hike in a day.

Mount Coleman Route (Map 25/D1) 🚶 📷 📷

Getting to the summit of Mount Coleman is tough, but well worth the effort. Beginning at the 1 km (0.6 mile) mark of the Sunset Pass Trail off the Icefields Parkway, you ascend some 1,180 m (3,835 ft) over 4.8 km (3 miles) to reach the summit. This trail is not for the inexperienced as parts of this route qualify as scrambling, and can be dangerous. Carry an ice axe. But once at the 3,135 m (10,189 ft) peak, the view offers a magnificent panorama of Banff National Park. Look northwest where Mount Columbia lies; the highest point in Alberta at 3,747 m (12,178 ft).

Mount Rundle Trail (Maps 14/G2-15/A2) 👣 📷 🏕

While this trek offers great views of the Spray Valley and Banff Townsite, the ascent is a steady, arduous 10.6 km (6.5 mile) return climb up the south-west slope of the mountain. The trailhead is near the first green at the Banff Springs Golf Course, along the Spray River Loop. At the 5.3 km (3.3 mile) mark the main trail ends, but for experienced rock climbers the peak lies a grueling 1,120 m (3,640 ft) above. Be careful; many inexperienced climbers have lost their lives here.

Mystic Lake & Pass Trail (Map 20/D7-E7) 🚻 🏕 👣 🐎 🐟 🏕

This 14.5 km (9 mile) one-way trail links lower Johnston Creek with Forty Mile Creek. The trail starts at the 15.2 km (9.5 miles) mark of the Forty Mile Creek Trail (at the Mystic Junction Campground and warden cabin), and will take you the better part of the day to hike as it gains some 550 m (1,788 ft) in elevation. It is quite a scenic trek with stark limestone walls and scatterings of larch, which are a striking gold colour in the fall. The difficult trail has numerous creek crossings and tiresome climbs, but the scenery, especially at Mystic Pass itself, is well worth the effort. Many choose to stop at Mystic Lake to try their luck fishing. This alternative is a 19.5 km (12.1 mile) trek from Mount Norquay.

Nigel Creek Trail (Map 32/B7) 👣 🏕

A 16 km (10 mile) hike leads from the Icefields Parkway up to Nigel Pass. It gains 370 m (1,203 ft) in elevation as it runs through open meadows with great views of Mount Athabasca to the south. Late June through September is the best time to hike the trail, which should take about six hours.

North Fork Pass Trail (Map 20/D4) 👣 🏕

This 12 km (7.4 miles) trail starts at the 30 km (18.6 miles) mark of the Lower Cascade Fire Road, making it a 42 km (26 mile) one-way hike. It gains 540 m (1,770 ft) in 12 km (7.4 miles). The hike begins alongside the Panther River, before crossing over to reach a narrow valley. From here the climb starts to the pass. Excellent views of the surrounding mountain ranges are provided once up on top. The **North Cascade River Route** is a rough 9.6 km (6 mile) route that continues down to Flint's Park Campsite. You can hike out via Forty Mile Creek, or the Flint's Park Trail back to the Cascade Fire Road. Be wary of Grizzly Bears in the area.

Panorama Ridge Route (Maps 14/A1-19/G7) 🏕 👣 🐟 🏕

This difficult, 23 km (14.3 mile) route extends from the Boom Creek Picnic Site (off Highway 93) through to Moraine Lake south of Lake Louise. The first 2.3 km (1.4 miles) follows the trail to Boom Lake. But after the climb up to the first ridge the route becomes rough, indistinct and even boggy. You will need a lot of patience and a good topographic map as you search for the occasional 70-year-old blaze to assure you that you are on the right route. Overall, you gain 650 m (2,112 ft) in elevation. There is camping at Taylor Lake.

Panther River Trail (Maps 20/E3-21/A2) 🚻 👣 🐎 🐟

A 15 km (9.3 mile) trail follows along the north side of Panther River. It connects the Cascade Fire Road with the Dormer Mountain Trail, and continues on into the Bighorn Wildland Area. It should take most people about six hours to hike this trail.

Paradise Valley Trail (Map 19/F6) 🏕 👣 ⛷ 🏕

This trail leads 18 km (11.2 miles) along the shores of Lake Annette, past the falls of the Giant Steps and to the foot of the Horseshoe Glacier. The route, enjoyed by hikers and backcountry skier, gains 390 m (1,268 ft) elevation gain.

Parker Ridge Trail (Map 32/B7) 👣 🏕

This is a 5 km (3 mile) hike that takes you to a fine viewpoint of the Saskatchewan Glacier. The ridge is over 2,000 m (6,500 ft) above sea level, so be prepared for some cold temperatures. The trailhead is found off the Icefields Parkway, 4.5 km (2.8 miles) north of the Nigel Creek Parking Area.

Peyto Lake Trails (Map 26/B7) 👣 🐟 🏕

Off the Icefields Parkway at the Mistaya Mountain Viewpoint, there are two trails that drop to Peyto Lake. The shortest is 1.5 km (0.9 miles), while the longer trail is 2.5 km (1.6 mile). A 5 km (3 mile) route continues south to Caldron Lake.

Pharaoh Creek Trail (Map 14/B2) 🚻 🏕 👣 🐎 🐟

This 9 km (5.6 mile) trail along the Pharaoh Creek is mainly used as an access trail to and from Egypt Lake. It gains 260 m (845 ft) in elevation. A side trail takes you to Pharaoh Lake. The trail is accessed from the Egypt Lake Campground via the Healy Pass Trail.

Pipestone River Trail (Map 19/F1-F5) 🚻 👣 🚲 🐎 🏕

The Pipestone River Trail follows the Pipestone River for 36 km (22.4 miles) to the Pipestone Pass. The first 7 km (4.3 miles) are open to bikers, while the rest of the trail is open to hikers and equestrians. Most hikers avoid the trail, which is rough (from all the horse traffic), and uninspiring. A shorter, prettier route to the pass is via the Mosquito Creek Trail through North Molar Pass. The view from the pass is inspiring, allowing views of the Siffleur Valley all the way to the Kootenay Plains. Other branch trails include the Little Pipestove Creek Trail, a difficult trail providing access to Red Deer Lakes and Drummond Glacier, as well as a trail up Molar Creek.

Plain of Six Glaciers Trail (Map 19/E5) 👣 🏕

This is one of the most scenic trails in an area famous for scenic trails. The route offers the visitor great views of towering mountains, majestic glaciers (yes, there really are six of them), mountain goats, and, just to be different, a teahouse at the end of the trail. Past the teahouse you can continue 1.5 km (0.9 miles) to view Abbot Pass and the Death Trap. It should take about three hours to hike this popular 10.8 km (6.7 mile) return trail, gaining 335 m (1,089 ft).

Red Deer River Trail (Map 20/A3-F1) 🏕 👣 🐎 🐟

This long, but moderately graded trail begins at the Ya-Ha Tinda Ranch. Allow at least two days to complete the trail one-way. It gains 345 m (1,121 ft). An alternate is to start from the south end, and travel the 14.5 km (9 miles) from the Lake Louise Ski Area to Red Deer Lakes before camping.

Redoubt Lake Trail (Map 20/A5) 👣 🐟 🏕

This trail is best accessed from the Baker Creek Trail. The 5.5 km (3.4 mile) hike has some steep sections on route to the meadows around the lake. Mountain goats, deer and elk frequent the area.

Rock Isle Lake Trail (Map 14/C3) 👣 ⛷ 🏕

From the Sunshine Village Ski Area, a moderate 5 km (3 mile) hike leads south to Rock Isle Lake, gaining 90 m (293 ft). This lake is one of three small picturesque alpine lakes clustered together. It is possible to extend the hike to Citadel Pass by following a side trail just before reaching Rock Isle Lake. Mid-June to September is the best time for this hike.

Rockbound Lake Trails (Map 20/B7) 👣 🐟 🏕

This five hour, 15 km (9.3 mile) trail climbs 730 m (2,373 ft) past Tower Lake to the rich, deep blue waters of Rockbound Lake. Fishermen can try their luck for cutthroat and rainbow trout. Along the way, the trail passes rocky alpine meadows and sparkling mountain streams. There are a few other trails that are accessed from this one. Silverton Falls, a 90 m (293 ft) high waterfall found at the base of Castle Mountain, is found at the end of a 1 km (0.6 mile) trail. It branches right shortly after starting on the main trail, which starts at the Castle Mountain Warden Cabin. Another route leads to Castle Mountain from the southeast shore of Rockbound Lake. This difficult four hour trail gains 870 m (2,828 ft) and loses 230 m (748 ft) as it climbs Castle Mountain and the north end of Helena Ridge.

Ross Lake Trail (Map 19/E5) 👣 🚲 🐎 ⛷ 🐟 🏕

The Ross Lake Trail is accessed from the cross-country trail system at the back of the Chateau Lake Louise. Ross Lake is actually located in Yoho National Park in BC. It offers visitors a quiet getaway to a pretty lake, which offers good fishing. This 15 km (9.3 mile) return trail takes 3.5 hrs to complete and gains 120 m (390 ft) in elevation. You follow an old road that narrows to a trail. Along the route to Ross Lake is **Minewakun Lake Trail**, a 4.5 km (2.8 mile) trail that starts at the intersection of Minewakun Creek and the Ross Lake Trail. The beautiful colours of this lake will make this detour worthwhile. However one must be extremely careful when scaling steep rocky slopes, especially when wet.

Rundle Riverside Trail (Map 15/A2) 🚶 🚵 🐎 🎣
This 8 km (5 mile) trail starts at the Banff Springs Golf Course road and follows the river to the park boundary. From here it is possible to continue along the well developed Banff Trail to the Canmore Nordic Trails. The Banff side of the trail is quite rooty and crosses rocky avalanche paths. Early summer to early fall is the best season for this trail.

Saddleback Trail (Map 19/F5) 🚶 🏕️
A strenuous, 7 km (4.3 mile) hike takes you from the Giant Steps Trail to a fabulous viewpoint. The trail gains 580 m (1,885 ft) in elevation to the Saddleback summit. However, you can continue another 400 m (1,300 ft) up Fairview Mountain for better views. An alternate access begins 2.5 km (1.6 miles) up the Moraine Lake Road.

Sarbach Lookout Trail (Map 25/G4) 🚶 🏕️
This 10.5 km (6.5 mile) hike begins from the Mistaya Canyon Parking Area. The trail starts by descending into Mistaya Canyon, a spectacular pot-marked gorge. Those that venture on will follow a windy trail up Mount Sarbach to the site of this former lookout, gaining 580 m (1,885 ft) in elevation. Many will be disappointed by the views from the lookout site, which are mostly blocked by the surrounding forest. But old trails, cut by the occupants of the lookout, will take you to much better viewpoints of the valley below. To the north lies the junction of three rivers: Howse, Mistaya and North Saskatchewan.

Saskatchewan Glacier Trail (Map 32/B7) 🚶 📷 🏕️
From the Icefields Parkway to the toe of the Saskatchewan Glacier requires hiking a 12 km (7.4 mile) return trail. The trail, which gains 155 m (504 ft), is not marked, making it hard to follow. To actually reach the ice is treacherous, and proper equipment is required.

Sawback Circuit (Maps 14/G1-20/B6) ⛰️ 🚶 🏕️
This is a multi-day trip, running 73 km (45.4 miles) through the Sawback Range. The route is filled with beautiful lakes, creeks, valleys and mountain passes. It is not one trail, but a combination of trails that starts along the Johnston Creek Trail. You loop through the mountain range by cutting over Badger Pass to the Forty Mile Creek Trail. Head south and cut back to Johnston Creek via Mystic Pass.

Sentinel Pass Trail (Map 19/G7) 🚶 🏕️
Sentinel Pass is the highest trail accessed pass in the Canadian Rockies. The 12 km (7.4 miles) hike offers unbelievable views of Moraine Lake and Ten Peaks along the way. In all you climb 790 m (2,568 ft) from the lake to the pass. To complete your journey, you may return the same way or continue to north Paradise Valley.

Shadow Lake Trail (Map 14/C1) 🎣 ⛰️ 🚶 🚵 🐟 🏕️
Accessed from the Trans-Canada Highway at the Redearth Creek Trailhead, this 22 km (13.7 mile) trail is enjoyed by hikers and bikers. The popular trail takes you to the lake where you can continue (on foot) to Ball Pass, Gibbon Pass, Ball Glacier Ice Cave, Haiduk Lake or Egypt Lake. While it is possible to bike in and out in a day, this is one of the most glorious areas in Banff. Spend a few days exploring.

Skoki Valley Trail (Maps 19/G3-20/A3) 🚶 📷 🐟 🏕️
The Skoki Valley area is one of the foremost hiking destinations in Canada. Period. Although day trips are possible it is simply too beautiful of an area not to spend more time in. If you are looking to explore in style, there is no better option that to hike up and over Boulder Pass (at 8.6 km/5.3 miles) to Skoki Valley Lodge (at 14.4 km/8.9 miles), which you can use as your base camp. If you are roughing it, there are backcountry campsites at Hidden Lake, Red Deer Lake, Merlin Meadows and Baker Lake. From the Fish Creek Parking Lot, you gain 450 m (1,463 ft) in elevation to the pass. Easy destinations from the valley are Hidden Lake (less than 1 km), Baker Lake (see above), Merlin Lake and ridge (3 km/1.8 miles to the lake) and Skoki Mountain (climbs an additional 220 m/720 ft).

Smith Lake Trail (Map 14/B1) 🚶 🐟 🏕️
For fishermen and hikers, a 5 km (3 mile) trail heads uphill to Smith Lake. It is accessed off the Trans-Canada Highway at the Altrude Picnic Area. It begins along the same path taken for Twin Lakes, then heads left up a steep

incline. Once at the lake, you can continue up a ridge overlooking the lake, 122 m (397 ft) higher.

Spray River Fire Road (Maps 14/G2-15/A7) ⛰️ 🚶 🚵 📷 🐎
From the Banff Springs Hotel, this old fire road runs to the Spray Lakes Reservoir, outside the park's eastern boundary. Most hikers will not want to bother with the valley bottom hike that covers 51.5 km (32 miles). Mountain bikers, however, will love it. It is easy, and strong bikers can bike it in a day, return. There are ever a number of backcountry campsites, to turn this into a great overnight trip.

Spray River Loop (Map 14/G2) 🚶 🚵 🐎 📷 🏕️
This 12.5 km (7.8 mile) multi-use trail runs from the Banff Springs Hotel alongside the Spray River on the Spray River Fire Road (see above), before looping back to the golf course. Along the fire road, you are provided with great views. The Goat Creek Trail can also be accessed along this route.

Stoney Squaw Trail (Map 14/G1) 🚶 🚵 🏕️
A biking and hiking trip for all ages begins at the Mount Norquay Ski Area. It is a 5 km (3 mile) round trip, with an elevation gain of 150 m (488 ft). The trail leads along the Stoney Squaw Ridge, to a lookout point. From here, panoramic views of the Bow River Valley, the Cascade Mountain Ridge, Lake Minnewanka and Mount Rundle are seen. June through September is the ideal time to explore this route.

Sulphur Mountain Trails (Map 14/G2) 🚶 🚵 📷 🏕️
This is one of Banff's most popular peaks, due in no small part to the fact that there are splendid views of Banff Townsite and the Bow Valley, and people can ride the gondola to the top. Some hikers and bikers will eschew this mechanized method of getting to the top. Instead, they can take a 12 km (7.4 miles) trail to the top and back from the Upper Hot Springs Parking Lot. It should take about five hours for hikers prepared to climb the 670 m (2,178 ft). A restaurant and cafeteria are located at the top. Other options are to continue over the mountain to Sundance Canyon or follow the short boardwalk trail leading to Sanson Peak.

Sundance Canyon Trail (Map 14/F2) 🚶 🚵 🐎 🏕️
Found close to the Banff Townsite, this popular 2.5 km (1.6 mile) trail starts at the Sundance Picnic Area off of Cave Avenue. Be warned that this trail is quite busy and you will likely share the path with cyclists, rollerbladers, strollers and horseback riders. The impressive rocky canyon and the view of Bow Valley are your rewards for climbing the many stairs along the route. The 3 km (1.8 mile) **Marsh Loop** can be accessed from the Sundance Trail. On this loop, you can enjoy the many species of birds as you travel past beaver dams and lodges along the Bow River.

Sunset Pass Trails (Map 25/E1) ⛰️ 🚶 🐟 🏕️
This 13.7 km (8.5 mile) trail climbs up to Sunset Pass through an extensive meadow system at the base of Mount Coleman. The first few kilometres climb steeply from the Icefields Parkway for about 3 km (1.8 miles), then levels out a bit as it passes into the Norman Meadows and Norman Lake. Sunset Pass is 4 km (2.4 miles) beyond. The **Sunset Lookout Trail** branches

west for a 6 km (3.6 mile) return jaunt. The old fire lookout is set on the lip of an impressive limestone cliff and provides amazing views over the North Saskatchewan River. From the pass, the trail continues on to Pinto Lake, losing 415 m (1,349 ft) in 5 km (3 miles). At Pinto Lake, there are a number of trail options, including a 7 km (4.3 mile) trail around the lake, and a 65 km (40.4 mile) multi-day backpack along the Pinto Lake Trail to the trailhead on Highway 11.

Taylor Lake Trail (Maps 19/G7-20/A7) ▲ 🚶 🐎 🏕

The trailhead to this 16 km (10 mile) trail is located at the Taylor Creek Picnic Area, off the Trans-Canada Highway. Taylor Lake is a glacier-fed lake surrounded by Mount Bell and the Panorama Ridge. There are many options to explore for this trail. From the lake, you can continue another 2 km (1.2 miles) to O'Brien Lake or 2 km (1.2 miles) to the Panorama Ridge. Optional accesses to Taylor Lake can be found at the Boom Creek Picnic Site and at Moraine Lake.

Tramline Trail (Map 19/F5) 🚶 🚴 🎿

This 4.5 km (2.8 mile) trail follows an old railway from the Station Restaurant on Sentinel Road in Lake Louise. The route climbs steadily to gain 200 m (650 ft). The Louise Creek Trails can be added on to make a 7 km (4.3 mile) loop.

Tunnel Mountain Lookout Trail (Map 14/G2) 🚶 🚴 🐎 🏕

To reach a viewpoint overlooking Bow Valley and the Banff Townsite, follow this 5 km (3 mile) hiking trail. It begins in Banff, by the Banff Centre for the Performing Arts. The trail climbs steadily gaining over 250 m (813 ft).

Tunnel Mountain-Hoodoo Loop Trail (Map 14/G1) 🚶 🚴 🐎 🏕 📷

Accessed from the Bow Falls Viewpoint, on Tunnel Mountain Road, this popular 12 km (7.4 miles) multi-use trail runs along the pretty river through forest and meadows. It eventually leads to the Hoodoos Viewpoint. The **Hoodoos Interpretive Trail** can be accessed at the 2.7 km (1.7 mile) T-junction.

Tyrell Creek Trail (Map 20/D1) 🚶

The Tyrell Creek Trail starts at the 6.4 km (4 mile) mark of the Upper Cascade Fire Road (heading southwest from Ya-Ha Tinda Ranch). This difficult 11.3 km (7 mile) route travels from Red Deer River up Tyrell Creek. It takes up to 3.5 hours one-way and gains 585 m (1901 ft) in elevation.

Upper Hot Springs Trail (Map 14/G2) 🚶

For those looking to hike to the relaxing hot springs, a 2 km (1.2 mile) trail is available. It begins at the signed trailhead behind the Banff Springs Hotel.

Warden Lake Trail (Map 25/G3) 🚶

This hike begins at the Saskatchewan River Crossing Warden's Station and concludes at beautiful Warden Lake. The trail is 4 km (2.5 mile) return and gains 30 m (98 ft). Mid-summer to early fall is the best time to hike this trail.

Whistling Pass Loop (Map 14/B3) ▲ 🚶 🏕

This 27 km/16.8 mile wilderness circuit can be accessed by any one of three trails but the Shadow Lake Trail is the least strenuous. The loop, which climbs 820 m (2,665 ft) to a height of 2,280 m (7,410 ft), is dotted with alpine lakes and offers great views of the surrounding peaks, including the towering Pharaoh Peaks. There are four campsites along the loop, which can be used as base camps to explore the many side trails that exist (including a short trail to Scarab and Mummy Lakes).

Wonder Pass Trail (Map 14/G7) ▲ 🚶 🐎 🏕

This wonderful trail begins at the McBride Campground Junction, 14 km (8.7 miles) along the Bryant Creek Trail. The 8.9 km (5.5 mile) trail runs past Marvel Lake and up to pass along the Great Divide. The pass is very scenic, with great views over both the southern corner of Banff and Mount Assiniboine Provincial Park, in BC. Most visitors continue down to Lake Magog.

Waterton Lake National Park

Accessed by Highways 5 and 6, this national park is open year-round. There is over 255 km (191 miles) of trails, many of which connect to extensive trail systems in Glacier National Park in Montana and the Akamina-Kishenina Provincial Park in BC. The area boasts spectacular scenery including summer wildflowers, deep blue lakes and snow capped mountain peaks. As with all National Parks, there is a daily fee to use the park, as well as frontcountry and backcountry camping fees.

Avion Ridge (Map 2/D5) 🚶 🏕

This unmarked ridge walk can be accessed from either Castle River or from the Red Rock Canyon Trailhead. Follow the Snowshoe Trail to the Snowshoe Picnic Site and head northwest toward the Castle River Divide and the National Park boundary. From here, there is no formal trail as you climb up Avion Ridge, although there is the occasional game trail to follow. Avion Ridge is an amazingly beautiful place in good weather, with open views and bright red argillite rock. In foul weather, it can be a dangerous place to be. Follow the ridge until Newman Peak. From here, you can make your way down to Goat Lake, and back to the trailhead. This 25 km (15.5 mile) route can be done in one long day, but it is best to plan for two.

Bear's Hump Trail (Map 2/G7) 🚶 🏕

This is a short (2.5 km/1.5 mile), moderate hike to a marvelous viewpoint above the Waterton Park Townsite. It begins from the information centre and climbs steeply, gaining 215 m (700 ft) to the hump. Below, you will see the splendor of the Canadian Rockies.

Belly River Trail (Map 3/C7) 🚶 🚴 🐟

At the Belly River Campground off Highway 6, this easy 2.5 km (1.6 mile) trail begins. It follows an access road next to the river.

Bertha Lake Trail (Map 2/G7) ▲ 🚶 🐎 🏕

This popular hike can be accessed from the Waterton Park Townsite (off Evergreen Ave). The 7 km (4.3 mile) trail is steep as it gains 460 m (1,495 ft) in elevation. Along the way you pass Lower Bertha Falls and catch glimpses of Upper Waterton Lake. This hike could be made into an overnight trip.

Blakiston Creek Trail (Map 2/E6) 🚶 🎿 🏕

Accessed from the Red Rock Canyon Parking Area, this 11 km (6.8 miles) trail begins. It leads past Blakiston Falls (at the 2 km/1.2 mile mark) and gradually ascends up the valley to reach views of Mount Bauerman and Anderson Peak. Trails to the South Kootenay Pass and the Twin Lakes can be accessed once at the head of the creek.

Boundary Trail (Map 2/F7-G7) 🚶 🏕

Much of this hike happens outside of the scope of this mapbook (and in the USA). From Summit Lake on the Carthew Summit Trail, a trail heads south (losing most of the elevation gained climbing up to Summit Lake) to West Boundary Creek, which runs parallel to the Alberta/Montana Border on the Montana side. The Boundary Trail hooks up with the Waterton Shoreline Trail (below). Hike back to town along the lake, for a 24 km (15 mile) total trek. You could also hike south to Goat Haunt and catch the boat back to Waterton, but this route would be longer than just hiking to Waterton. This route is not as spectacular as the Carthew Summit Trail.

Cameron Lake Trail (Map 2/E7) 🚶 🎿 🐟

This pleasant 1.5 km (0.9 mile) walk can be easily located by following the Akamina Parkway to Cameron Lake. It is ideal for families looking for a spot to picnic, as there are several fine gravel beaches for relaxing. It is also quite easy to continue to the Canada/US border at the south end of the lake. However, the authorities do not recommend it, as Grizzly Bears graze this area. Also in the area is a short (1 km) trail to Akamina Lake. The small, pretty lake is a popular destination that can be circumnavigated if you are willing to wade through Akamina Creek twice to do so.

Carthew Summit Trail (Map 2/F7) 🚶 🐎 🎿 🐟 🏕

The 20 km (12.5 mile) hike climbs 650 m (2,112 ft) before dropping 800 m (2,625 ft) to the Waterton Park Townsite. This long day hike or overnight trip leads past lakes, glaciers, meadows and along a mountain pass. The meadows are abundant with wildflowers in the summer, and there are great views of the surrounding mountains. The trailhead is located at the Cameron

Lake Parking Lot, off the Akamina Parkway. From the townsite side, many people choose Alderson Lake as a destination. This hike involves a long, steady climb, gaining 580 m/1,885 ft in 7 km (4.3 miles). The grade is steady through a thick forest with limited viewpoints. However, the lake is a rewarding destination.

Crandell Lake Trail (Map 2/D4) 🚶 🚵

There are two access points to this short walking trail. The easiest access is from the Akamina Parkway, 7 km (4.3 miles) west of Waterton. This trail is 2.4 km (1.5 miles) return, gaining 100 m (325 ft). From Crandell Campground on the Red Rock Parkway, the trail is 4 km (2.4 miles) return, gaining 150 m (492 ft). Both routes are popular and lead to this pretty lake below Mount Crandell and Ruby Ridge. The Cameron Creek Trail can also be accessed from this trail.

Crandell Mountain Circuit (Map 2/D4) 🚵 🚶

This relatively easy cycling trip is a popular route for families. The 23 km (14.3 mile) circuit loops the Waterton Parkway (Highway 5), Red Rock Parkway, Crandell Lake Trail and the Akimina Parkway (19 km/11.8 miles of the route are on pavement). The Crandell Campground is the most popular starting point. Along the route, you will encounter high plains grasslands, mountain climbs and the picturesque Crandell Lake. Please be careful, as the roads are often quite narrow and somewhat dangerous.

Crypt Lake Trail (Maps 2/G7-3/A7) 🚶 🏕

This hike is fabled in song and story as the nicest day-hike in Waterton, perhaps all the Rocky Mountain Parks. It is certainly one of the most interesting. To get to the trailhead, most people catch a boat from the Waterton townsite (it is possible to hike in via the Wishbone trail, but few people do, especially now that all the campsites along the trail are closed). Once at the trailhead, the 8.6 km (5.3 miles) one-way trail climbs 680 m (2,210 ft) to Crypt Lake. Along the way you will travel through some spectacular scenery, pass a waterfall that falls up (if its windy enough), traverse a cliff face (chains are provided), and squeeze through a cave. You have to do it all before the boat returns, or else you are stuck overnight. If you have time on your way down, swing past Hellroaring Falls, which is found off the main trail.

Goat Lake Trail (Map 2/E5) 🚶 🐟 🏕

This is a 7 km (4.3 mile), one-way hike that gains 515 m (1,674 ft) in elevation, almost all of that in the last 2 km (1.2 mile) slog up to the hanging valley that the lake is set in. To begin, the trail follows the relatively flat Snowshoe Trail where you get a great view of Anderson Peak. As you continue, the views get more impressive.

Kishinena Creek Trail (Map 2/A7-E7) 🚵 🚶 🏕

This long 53.5 km (33.2 mile) trek is a designated bicycle trail, although hikers are also welcome. Due to its length, it is recommended to have a shuttle at the other end (although the drive around will take at least a day). Starting from the Akamina Parkway, you follow the Akamina and Kishinena Creek drainages over to the Flathead Road in BC. Be prepared for a wilderness excursion with several fallen trees to hop. One point of interest is an old iron pipe, where water seeps out carrying minerals to the surface for the abundant deer and elk in the area. For those interested in a shorter trip, Akamina Pass is only 3.2 km (2 miles) return after gaining 125 m (406 ft). The main trail also provides access Wall Lake, Forum Lake and the Akamina Ridge, all of which are easier to get to from the Alberta side of the border. The best hiking and biking season is mid summer to early fall.

Lineham Lakes Routes (Map 2/E7) 🚶 🐟 🏕

The easiest way to get to the Lineham Lakes is via a difficult hike past Rowe Lakes. Even so, the route down to the lakes is sketchy, steep, and unmarked. A second route to the lake, up Lineham Creek, is much more difficult, and comes to an end on a 100 m (325 ft) cliff above the lakes. (Most people only follow this route as far as Lineham Falls.) Those who do make it to the lakes will find some of the prettiest, most secluded lakes in Waterton.

Park Line Trail (Maps 2/G5-3/A5) 🚶 🚵

This 13 km (8 mile) rough road gives access to the Oil Basin Warden Cabin. Access is found off the Chief Mountain Highway (Highway 6) at the Buffalo Paddock Road. It can be hiked or biked, and gains 280 m (910 ft) in elevation.

Red Rock Canyon Trail (Map 2/F6) 🚶 🏕

This short (less than a kilometre) trail is quite possibly the most popular trail in Waterton, as it makes its way around the red and green walled canyon. There is almost no elevation gain.

Rowe Lakes Trail (Map 2/E7) ⛺ 🚶 🐟 🏕

This is a very difficult, 13 km (8 mile) return hike that takes 5.5 hours to complete and gains 560 m (1,820 ft) in elevation. The trail leads uphill along a wide rocky hillside to the lakes and is best hiked from mid-July through mid-October.

Snowshoe Trail (Map 2/E5) ⛺ 🚶 🚵 🐴 🐟 🏕

This 11.5 km (7.1 mile) one-way hiking and biking route begins at the Red Rock Canyon Parking Area. It ascends along Bauerman Creek to reach the Twin Lakes area. The lakes are one of the most popular overnight backcountry destinations and your space at the campsite needs to be booked in advance. There is a 2 km (1.2 miles) option north to tiny Lost Lake at the Snowshoe Warden Cabin. Also, at the 4.3 km (2.7 mile) mark, a trail to Goat Lake is accessed. This is prime Grizzly bear habitat.

Tamarack Trail (Map 2/E7-F6) ⛺ 🚶 🐟 🏕

Considered one of the best backpacking routes in the Southwestern Rockies, this strenuous, 31.6 km (19.6 mile) hike is accessed off the Akamina Parkway at the Rowe Lakes Trailhead. It leads through valleys, crosses ridges and passes several lakes as it makes its way along the northwest boundary of the park to the Red Rock Canyon Trailhead. It is best to arrange to have a shuttle waiting here. The Red Rock Trailhead is slightly lower, but the route can be hiked either direction.

Townsite Trails (Map 2/G7) 🚶

There are a number of short, easy walking trails in and near the Waterton Park Townsite including the 3.2 km (2 mile) **Townsite Loop Trail**, the 4 km (2.4 mile) **Emerald Bay Loop**, the 1 km (0.6 mile) **Linnet Lake Loop**, and the 2 km (1.2 mile) **Prince of Wales Loop**.

Vimy Peak Trail (Map 3/A7) 🚶 🐴 🏕

From the Chief Mountain Highway (Highway 6) at the locked access gate, this 11 km (6.8 miles), 5 hour one-way hike gains 820 m (1,690 ft), mostly in the last 5.2 km (3.2 miles). The last stretch is steep and strenuous, with limited visibility. The trail follow a gravel road for the first 2 km (1.2 miles), then becomes a grassy and overgrown route. The trail does not actually get to the peak, but ends in a basin below. From here it is a moderate scramble up to the top. Enjoy the outstanding view of the Watertown Valley and the Crypt Cirque to the south from the peak. A rather long (35 km/21.7 mile) return walk along Vimy Ridge is also possible.

Wishbone Trail (Map 3/A7) 🚶 🚵 🐟 🏕

The Wishbone Trail follows the Vimy Peak Trail to the 6 km (3.7 mile) mark. Rather than climbing, this route is flat and runs through meadows near the Middle and Upper Waterton Lakes shorelines, taking you to the former Wishbone campground. Keeping right past the campground leads to the narrow channel (the bosporus) that joins the two lakes, a distance of 11 km (6.8 miles). Keeping left takes you to the Crypt Lake Landing (3.2 km/1.9 miles past the Wishbone), and on to Crypt Lake itself (see description above). Both the Crypt Landing and the Wishbone Campsites have been closed due to poor camping practices. Mountain bikers can follow this trail as far as the Wishbone.

Waterton Lakeshore Trail (Map 2/G7) ⛺ 🚶 🐴 🐟 🏕

The Waterton Lakeshore Trail begins at the end of Evergreen Avenue in the Waterton Park Townsite and takes you to the Goat Haunt boat dock near the Goat Haunt Ranger Station in Montana. Once in Glacier National Park, there are a number of other trails that can be hiked. There is also a tour boat, called the International, available at the south end of the lake for the return trip to the townsite. One-way, the trail takes 4-5 hours and it is 13 km (8 miles) long. Overall you climb 100 m (328 ft).

Wildlife Viewing

Spotting animals has always been a popular pastime, but in the last decade or so, the more specific pursuit of bird watching has become extremely popular as well. Avid birdwatchers are always looking to add a new species to their list of birds spotted.

Some of the sites below cater mostly to birders, while other sites are noteworthy for a high density of large ungulates like deer and bighorn sheep.

Is this an exhaustive list? No. Birds and other animals can be seen almost anywhere, even in the heart of downtown Calgary there are dozens of species of birds. These are areas that have been set aside because of their unique characteristics. Sometimes it is because of the unique species (Outpost), and sometimes it is because of the density of birds and animals in an area (Gaetz Lake). For more information on bird watching and wildlife watching in the area, contact a local naturalist club, like the Calgary Field Naturalist's Society or the Red Deer River Naturalists.

Beehive Natural Area (Map 7/D5)
There is more than 800 hectares of old growth forests still standing in the Beehive Natural Area. This provides habitat for mammals like martens and fishers, and birds like woodpeckers and wood warblers. Other possible sightings include grizzly and black bears, elk, moose, and bighorn sheep. Access to this area is on foot or by skiing.

Big Sagebrush (Map 2/D4)
This unique area has 35 species of plants that are rare in Alberta, 10 of which are rare in Canada, including the delicate, creamy white Mariposa lily. Birds in the area include blue grouse, Clark's nutcracker, Townsend's solitaire and varied thrush. Mammals include ground squirrels, mule deer, pika, moose, elk, bighorn sheep and grizzly and black bears. Road access is rough and may be impassible during winter.

Bow Valley/Yamnuska Mountain (Map 15/F3)
Hiking trails at the base of Yamnuska Ridge lead hikers through a mixed forest, meadow, and wetland environment. Flower spotters will be delighted at all the orchids, while birdwatchers will tune into the songbirds. Folks who like watching larger animals should head higher up the mountain, where they stand a good chance of spotting a bighorn sheep or mountain goat. Finally, those with herpetological tendencies can explore the wetlands, where they will find long-toed salamanders, tiger salamanders, boreal toads, wood frogs and spotted frogs.

Burnstick Lake (Map 29/B3)
Extensive areas of bulrushes and water lilies make this a scenic spot for canoeing. Common loons, grebes and ducks nest here, while aquatic mammals such as beaver, muskrat and mink are common. Much of the shoreline is mixed forest, where hikers can observe mule deer, moose, ruffed grouse and spruce grouse. Birdwatchers might want to swing by nearby Birch Lake, where northern orioles and great blue herons nest.

Crimson Lake (Map 35/G3)
Hiking trails wind through black spruce bogs, tamarack swamps, open sedge and shrub fens and boreal forest. The flora is diverse, as is the fauna, and the park supports populations of sandhill cranes, boreal owls, northern pygmy-owls, greater yellowlegs, western tanagers and solitary sandpipers. Mammals include northern bog lemmings and water and pygmy shrews.

Crowsnest Lake and River (Map 4/D5)
Crowsnest Lake is a small, deep lake-one of the deepest in Alberta-found near the top of Crowsnest Pass. As the lowest pass through the Rockies in the region, the pass provides habitat for birds normally found further west, such as the house finch and the red-naped sapsucker. Numerous ducks, geese and swans can often be seen on the lake, as can loons and grebes. Look for long-toed salamanders, spotted frogs and boreal toads along wetland areas. Bighorn sheep frequently graze nearby.

East Porcupine Proposed Natural Area (Map 5/F1)
Watch for mountain chickadees, crossbills, and snowshoe hares at the higher elevations of this proposed Natural Area. Coniferous forests are home to red-breasted nuthatches and spruce grouse, and the patches of open prairie are home to red-tailed hawks, ground squirrels, elk and mule deer.

Fish Creek Provincial Park (Map 17/F6)
This urban park is an island of natural habitat located along the southern edge of Calgary. A visitor centre offers year-round events and interpretive displays.

Gaetz Lake (Map 38/A6)
Despite being located inside the Red Deer city limits, this is prime wildlife habitat, and an important stopover point on the migration route. Yellow-headed and red-winged blackbirds are prominent in the willows and cattails around the lake, while the surrounding mixed woodland and old growth forest provide habitat for woodpeckers, chickadees, nuthatches, sparrows and olive-sided flycatchers. There are viewing blinds along the shores of the lake, where all manner of waterfowl nest. Mammals include muskrats, beavers, coyotes, red foxes, and deer. The Kerry Wood Nature Centre offers nature walks, exhibits, an excellent selection of books, and a bulletin board featuring recent wildlife sightings.

Inglewood Bird Sanctuary (Map 17/F4)
A short network of trails passes by the floodplain ponds and along the Bow River through grassland, shrubs and riverbank cottonwoods. Naturalists have recorded 216 bird species and 271 plant species here. Prominent birds include bald eagles, Swainson's hawks, nesting great horned owls, ring-necked pheasants, gray partridges and a range of warbler species. The backwaters and old channels of the Bow River provide nesting sites for many ducks and Canada geese. This is the best place in the province for seeing the colourful wood duck. Mallards, common goldeneyes and common mergansers live here year-round, along with muskrats and beavers. The sanctuary, only a few kilometres from the city centre, is also home to white-tailed and mule deer, coyotes, foxes and long-tailed weasels.

McKinnon Flats (Map 18/C7)
McKinnon Flats provide a varied habitat of willow margins, tall cottonwoods and brushy slopes for an impressive spectrum of songbirds, as well as larger birds, like herons, pelicans, Canada geese and ducks. Higher up the river valley, you can see birds of prey riding the currents, hunting for smaller birds and mammals. Mule deer and coyote are the most common larger mammals.

Outpost Wetlands Natural Area (Map 3/F7)
This 65 hectare site, adjacent to Police Outpost Provincial Park, contains a system of unimproved trails, which provide access to hikers and cross-country skiers in winter. It is a great place for birdwatchers, and is home to some species not normally found in Alberta, including sandhill cranes, cinnamon teals, American goldfinches and the vesper sparrow.

Peter Lougheed Provincial Park (Maps 10/F2-F4)
A natural mineral lick at King Creek attracts bighorn sheep, deer, elk and moose, making this a great place for watching larger ungulates. Another good spot is Pocaterra Fen, where you will also see a variety of birds. Pikas can also be seen at close range along the Rock Glacier Interpretive Trail near Highwood Pass.

Ram Falls Recreation Area (Map 27/D2)
Bighorn sheep can be seen on the slopes of the Ram Range throughout the year; near Ram Falls, where the river plunges 20 m (66 feet) over a ridge of sandstone. The Ram River Canyon offers a dramatic view of eroded shale and sandstone, and golden eagles may be seen soaring on the canyon air currents. In the fall, bald eagles, merlins and American kestrels wing south along the eastern slopes of the Rocky Mountains. Red squirrels are abundant in the pine and spruce forests, and black bears may be seen from mid spring to late fall.

Sheep River Wildlife Sanctuary (Map 11/D3)
A large band of bighorn sheep lives year-round in this sanctuary, with its abundant grasslands and convenient escape routes along the river canyon

walls. The sanctuary is an excellent place to watch sheep feeding, interacting and on occasion, being stalked by coyotes. During the fall, mature rams can often be closely observed from the comfort of your vehicle. This is also one of the best areas in the province for observing migrating birds of prey, which follow the foothill ridges in spring and fall. Golden eagles are especially prominent. Cougars have occasionally been observed in the area, but more likely are small mammals, like Columbian ground squirrels. The sanctuary is closed to vehicles December 1 to May 15 to protect the winter sheep range.

Siffluer Wilderness Area (Map 26)
The Siffluer Wilderness is a large wilderness area located just east of Banff. There is no road access into the area; instead, you will have to explore this area on foot. If you stay in the valleys, expect to see ungulates such as moose, elk and deer. You may also see predators, such as grizzly bear, cougars, wolves and wolverines. If you venture higher into the alpine, watch for mountain goats, woodland caribou, golden-mantled ground squirrels, bighorn sheep, hoary marmots and pikas. Hikers should be experienced and well prepared for wilderness travel before setting out on any of the several access trails. The routes are challenging and remote, and many of the animals encountered here have little fear of humans.

Slack Slough (Map 38/A7)
This extensive bulrush marsh is an exceptional area for viewing waterfowl-including ducks and marsh birds. There is a raised viewing platform on the north side of the slough.

Waterton Lakes National Park (Maps 2, 3)
Waterton is known as the place where the prairie meets the mountains. This helps explain the density and variety of wildlife found here. Cameron Lake is one of the best places to see grizzly bears anywhere in Alberta. They forage along the avalanche slopes on the far side of the lake, so bring binoculars. There is a bison paddock near the entrance of the park, and a wide variety of birds can be found in both the low wetland areas in the valley bottom, and at some of the higher lakes. Twenty-two of Alberta's 26 orchid species occur here; the greatest concentration of species in the province.

White Goat Wilderness Area (Maps 25, 26, 32, 33)
Large mammals inhabit the valleys and the lower slopes of this Wilderness Area. Watch for moose, elk, white-tailed and mule deer, black bears, and coyotes. Less common, and therefore more exciting to spot are grizzly bears, cougars, wolves and wolverines. In alpine areas, watch for mountain goats, woodland caribou, golden-mantled ground squirrels, bighorn sheep, hoary marmots and pikas, as well as white-tailed ptarmigans, gray-crowned rosy finches, water pipits and horned larks. Hikers should be experienced and well

prepared for wilderness travel before setting out on any of the several access trails. The routes are challenging and remote, and many of the animals encountered here have little fear of humans.

Wyndham-Carseland Provincial Park (Map 18/F7)
This area provides excellent habitat for nesting songbirds. To the west, at the Carseland Dam, you can observe a number of fish-eating birds, including belted kingfishers, great blue herons and American white pelicans. Birds of prey are also seen along the slopes of the valley.

Winter Recreation
(Cross-country Skiing, Snowshoeing and Snowmobiling)

One of the greatest times to explore Southwestern Alberta is during the winter. The crisp, cool, clean air and the lack of other human activity (not to mention lack of mosquitoes) will allow you to experience the peace and solitude local residents have known for years. While Banff still attracts a lot of visitors, even in winter, other mountain parks (like Waterton or Peter Lougheed Provincial) are nearly deserted.

Snow can hit the mountains as early as October. By late November, keen winter recreationists will be able to explore many of the higher elevation (above 1,500 m/4,875 feet) areas as well as a few of the lower elevation areas. The winter season usually lasts into March in the valleys and even as late as June in the mountains.

Cross-country Skiing & Snowshoeing

Listed below are many of the popular cross-country skiing areas found in Southwestern Alberta. We have also noted those areas that can be used by snowshoers. If snowshoeing in a ski area, please stay off the ski tracks.

Allison/Chinook Cross-Country Area (Map 4/E4)

There are 31 km (19.3 miles) of groomed trails set at the foot of Mount Tecumseh in this gorgeous area of the Crowsnest Pass. The Crowsnest Pass Cross-Country Ski Association, who charge a small fee to use the trails, maintains the trails from December 1 to March 31. Skiers or snowshoers will also find many more kilometres of ungroomed trails explore further north towards Chinook Lake. Snowmobiles are not permitted in the ski area except for a 6 km (3.6 mile) multi-use trail on the western edge of the ski area.

Aspen Beach Provincial Park (Map 37/F3)

On the shores of Gull Lake, Aspen Beach was established in 1932, making it Alberta's oldest Provincial Park. The park is open year-round, and has 4 km of ungroomed trails for cross-country skiing or snowshoeing.

Banff National Park (Maps 10, 14, 15, 19, 20, 21, 25-27, 32)

Banff is a winter wonderland. Not only does the park sport three downhill ski areas (Norquay, Sunshine and Lake Louise), but also there are many, many kilometres of groomed and ungroomed cross-country trails. Add to that an almost endless opportunity for backcountry ski touring and snowshoeing, and you have a great place to go in the winter.

Baker Creek Trail (Map 20/A6) is a track set trail that follows Baker Creek for 6 km (3.6 miles) and then a powerline for another 3.5 km (2.2 miles). It climbs 185 m (600 ft), and is a slightly more challenging trails for beginners.

Banff Golf Course (Map 14/G2) is not groomed, and is often short of snow, but it is an easy place for beginners to get the feel for a pair of cross-country skis.

Boom Lake Trail (Map 14/A1) is a 5 km (3 mile) one-way trail that is not groomed, but is usually well tracked. The trail climbs 170m (560 ft) to the lake.

Bow River Loop (Map 19/G6) begins from the Station Restaurant or from the Samson Mall in Lake Louise. This is an easy groomed and track set loop that covers 6.9 km (4.3 miles). There are a few ups and downs, but the trail is mostly level as it follows the edge of the river. It does connect with the Campground Loop.

Brewster Creek Trail (Map 14/G2–F3) follows the same route as the Healy Creek Trail (see below), but branches off onto the Brewer Creek Fire Road. Backcountry skiers/snowshoers can follow a network of trails beyond the Sundance Lodge, but most people turn around (or stay) here. If you turn around at the lodge, you will cover 22 km (13.7 miles) by the time you get back to the parking lot. The trail is groomed and track set to this point, too, which is another reason why most people stop at the lodge.

Campground Loop (Map 19/G6) is actually a pair of short, easy loops known as the inner and outer loop. If you were to ski them both, you

would cover 4.5 km (2.8 miles) by the time you finished. The trails connect with the Bow River Loop and are track set and groomed with a skating lane.

Carrot Creek Trail (Map 15/B1) is an easy, ungroomed trail that runs up and down Carrot Creek. Route finding can be difficult, especially if no one has broken trail. Most people make it a 5 km (3 mile) return trip as you only gain about 100 m (325 feet) in the first part of the longer trail.

Cascade Trail (Map 14/G1, 15/A1, 20/G7) is an easy but long backcountry trail follows the gated Lake Minnewanka Road for a few kilometres, and then turns up the Cascade valley on an old fire road. The trail is groomed, and is usually in good condition. A return trip to the ranger station is 28 km (17.4 miles), with an elevation gain of 180 m (590 ft).

Castle Junction Trails (Map 20/B7) provide 8.7 km (5.4 miles) of track set trails in the forests surrounding the Castle Junction. These are easy trails, with little elevation gain, and the occasional view of the surrounding mountains.

Fairview Loop (Map 19/G5) starts from Moraine Lake Road and follows the Tramline Trail to the Lake Louise parking lots, where it takes a left into the trees. The trail loops back and down to the Moraine Lake Road. There is one steep hill on this loop, which makes it a route for better skiers. Due to the hill, doing this loop in reverse is not recommended.

Forty Mile Creek (Map 14/G1–20/E7) provides access to several great backcountry options. A good half-day trip is to follow the moderate ungroomed 5 km (3 mile) trail from the Mount Norquay Parking Lot to Edith Pass, losing 150 m (488 ft) along the way. If it is not quite long enough for you, you can continue another 15 km (9.3 miles) on to Mystic Lake by climbing 270 m (878 ft). This winds up being a 40 km (24.8 mile) round trip, and some skiers may have difficulty doing it on one of the short winter days, especially if they are breaking trail. Branching from the Forty Mile Creek Trail is a route up to Elk Lake. Following the Elk Pass Trail down to the Cascade River Valley can extend this route. Another option is to return via Johnson Creek (see below). A second vehicle is ideal recommended for these alternatives.

Great Divide Trail (Map 19/F5) is an easy groomed and track set trail that follows the route of the old Highway 1A to the BC Alberta boundary. There is an exhibit here about the divide, and you can continue into Yoho National Park along the Ross Lake Trail, which is an old road that is not groomed. From the parking lot to the divide is 7.5 km (4.7 miles).

Healy Creek Trail (Map 14/D4) starts from the top of the Wa-Wa Chairlift at Sunshine Village Ski Area. Head northeast towards a notch in the ridge, then head west across an open meadow to the top of a long descent through an open forest. Watch out for a cliff band as you head down! If you keep right, you will eventually hook up with the Healy Creek Trail, which is a steep, tricky descent. This 10 km (6.2 mile) trip is best left to advanced backcountry skiers.

Healy Pass Trail (Map 14/C3) is a popular day trip from the Sunshine Road up to Healy Pass, and then down to Egypt Lake. The 10 km (6.2 mile) trail climbs 640 m (2,080 ft) to the pass before dropping 340 m (1,105 ft) to the lake. The pass provides some good backcountry skiing (downhill) options. This is a good trip for strong intermediate skiers.

Johnson Lake Trails (Map 15/A1) provide a series of ungroomed trails around the lake. There is one moderate section, but the majority of the 11.4 km (7 miles) of trails are easy. The longest trail is 8.2 km (5 miles) long.

Johnston Creek Trail (Map 14/B1–20/B7) begins from the Johnston Canyon Parking Lot. It is a long day trip (34 km/21.1 miles) to Luellen Lake, gaining 520 m (1,690 ft). A shorter option along the same trail is the Inkpots, which are only 10 km (6.2 miles) return. It is also possible to head over Mystic Pass and return via Forty Mile Creek (see above).

Lake Louise (Map 19/G5) is a popular area for people to get out and experience some of the charm that winter brings. From the resort, most people follow the moderate track-set ski trail along the lakeshore or snowshoe across the lake to Louise Falls to the southwest end of the lake. It is a 2.4 km (1.5 miles) one-way trip to the end of the lake. Travel beyond here is not recommended without appropriate avalanche safety equipment and knowledge.

Moraine Lake Road (Map 19/G7) provides an easy 16 km (9.6 mile) one-way trip along the unplowed road in winter. Although there is some elevation gained on the way to the lake, the chance to see this amazing scenery in the winter is worth the effort. The first few kilometres are wooded, but the last few are absolutely phenomenal. Besides, coming back is a lot easier.

Paradise Valley Trail (Map 19/G6) begins from the Moraine Lake Road. This is an ungroomed (but often tracked) touring trail that climbs 410m (1,333 ft) to the spectacular Paradise Valley Meadows. Give yourself the better part of a day to ski the popular 20 km (12.4 mile) return trip.

Pipestone Loops (Map 19/G5) consist of five different loop trails in the Pipestone area of Lake Louise. The shortest trail is a difficult 1.5 km (1 mile) loop, while the longest is 12.6 km (7.8 miles). The rest of the trails are less than 3 km (1.8 miles), and are mostly easy, but watch out for the occasional steep hill. Check at the Visitor Centre for information on grooming and snow conditions.

Plain of the Six Glaciers (Map 19/F6) is a spectacular backcountry trip that takes you past some of the best scenery that Banff has to offer. From the postcard-perfect Lake Louise, the 10 km (6.2 mile) return trail climbs 200 m (650 ft) into the gorgeous meadows that make up the Plain of the Six Glaciers. This trip takes you through avalanche country and is recommended for experienced backcountry skiers only.

Rock Isle Lake Trail (Map 14/D4) lies in British Columbia, but the easiest access to it is from the Sunshine Ski Village. It is only 4 km (2.4 miles) return to the lake, gaining 110m (358 ft). Almost all of it at the beginning of the run as you climb up from the Strawberry Chairlift to the top of Rock Isle Road. This is a perfect place for getting the feel for touring skis. From here, it is possible to continue on up Quartz Ridge (10 km/6 miles return), to Citadel Pass (20 km/12.4 miles return) or even on through Mount Assiniboine Park to Highway 93.

Rockbound Lake Trail (Map 20/B7) is a difficult 14 km (8.7 mile) trip that climbs steeply up to a beautiful open valley and Rockbound Lake. You will gain 760 m (2,470 ft) on your way to the lake, but the real trick is coming down the fairly narrow, sometimes icy trail.

Shadow Lake Trail (Map 14/B2–D1) begins from the trailhead on the Trans-Canada, 20 km (12.4 miles) west of Banff. This moderate track set trail takes you 14.5 km (9 miles) to the Shadow Lake Lodge, climbing 325 m (1,050 ft) along the way. From here it is possible to continue on to Haiduk Lake (14 km/8.7 miles return to the lodge) or Ball Pass (12 km/7.5 miles return).

Skoki Valley Trail (Map 19/G5) is a moderate 11 km (6.8 mile) trip that takes you from the Lake Louise Ski Area to the Skoki Lodge. While this trip can easily be done in a day, many prefer to book overnight accommodations at the heritage lodge. Built in the 1930s it is situated in a perfect valley for backcountry touring. Routes include the **Skoki Mountain Loop** (an easy 9 km/5.6 mile return), the Natural Bridge (an easy 16 km/10 mile return), Fossil Mountain (a moderate 11 km/7 mile return), Oyster Lake (a moderate 12 km/7.5 miles return), and Merlin Valley (a difficult 6 km/3.6 miles return). There are also a number of great slopes to sample, including Packers Peak, Merlin Ridge and the Wolverine Slopes.

Spray River Loop (Map 14/G2) begins from the Bow Falls Parking Lot. It is an easy 12.5 km (7.8 mile) loop through the rolling, forested terrain around the Banff townsite. The trail is groomed and track set, with an elevation gain of 200 m (660 ft).

Sundance Canyon Trail (Map 14/G2) begins from the Cave and Basin Historic Site. It is an easy trail that climbs 3.7 km (2.3 miles) up to the

Sundance Canyon. Well. It climbs, but only 30 m (100 ft). The route is track set, but lack of snow and sometime high winds can make the conditions sketchy. Hikers/snowshoers also use this route, and not all of them stay off the groomed trail. Also in the area is the **Healy Creek Connector**. The 4.8 km (3 mile) one-way trail follows the same route as Sundance Canyon but branches off, ultimately connecting with the Sunshine Road.

Telemark Loop (Map 19/F5) is divided into two sections. The upper trail runs above the Great Divide Trail, while the lower trail runs below. That's not the only difference, though. The upper trail is also much more difficult to ski. The Lower Telemark Loop is an 8.3 km (5.2 mile) track set trail that meanders through the forest near the Great Divide, while the upper section is a 9.3 km (5.8 miles) trip.

Tramline (Map 19/F5) is an easy 4.5 km (2.7 mile) trail that follows an old railbed from Lake Louise the town to Lake Louise the lake. The route begins at The Station Restaurant on Sentinel Road and climbs steadily, gaining 200 m (655 ft). The Louise Creek Trails can be added on to make a 7 km (4.3 mile) loop.

Wapta Icefield (Map 19/A1-B2) is one of the prime destinations for backcountry skiers and mountaineers in Canada. There are many advanced routes in this area that require good route finding skills and the ability to cross glaciers. If you are interested in exploring this area, contact the Alpine Club of Canada, who maintains a number of huts in the area.

Beauvais Lake Provincial Park (Map 2/D1)
Ranging from easy to difficult, Beauvais Lake Provincial Park provides 13 km (8.1 miles) of groomed ski trails and many more ungroomed trails. The trails are snowmobile packed, but not track set and can be used by snowshoers. The Beaver Creek warm-up shelter is supplied with firewood and available for use in the winter. The park also has 17 designated winter campsites.

Bighorn Wildland Recreation Area (Maps 20, 21, 26, 27, 32, 33)
This huge recreation area (covering 2,463 square km of rugged alpine terrain) contains breathtaking mountainous backcountry terrain with very few facilities or services, especially in winter. There are about 700 km (435 miles) of trails, which are a combination of the old forestry pack trails established in the early 1900s and a number of mineral exploration roads and trails. The trail system is not maintained or groomed. Because there is so much space here, do not expect to find much in the way of broken trail to follow, although snowmobilers also use many of the trails. All backcountry skiers/snowshoers need to know what they're doing, how to travel in avalanche country, and be prepared for difficult conditions. Access to the recreation area is provided via Highway 11 and the all weather, gravel Forestry Trunk Road (734) and Red Deer River Roads.

Burstall Pass Trail (Map 10/A1–C1)
It is 7.5 km (4.7 miles) one-way to the pass from the trailhead on the Smith-Dorrien Spray Trail in Peter Lougheed Provincial Park. The trail provides an excellent backcountry ski/snowshoe as it leads past glaciers and across (hopefully frozen) streams to the pass. From here, can you descend to the Upper Spray Valley for further exploration.

Calgary Parks & Golf Courses (Map 17)
Many of Calgary's city parks have ungroomed cross-country and snowshoe trail systems when it snows. Parks include Bowness, Edworthy, River Park, Sandy Beach and South Glenmore. More developed options are described below:

Canada Olympic Park (Map 17/C3) was developed for the 1988 Winter Olympics and is easily spotted from a distance, sporting a pair of ski jumping towers (the tallest is 90 m/290 ft high). While tourists flock here year-round, it is better known for its downhill skiing and snowboarding, the park is also home to a 1.8 km (1.1 mile) groomed and track set cross-country loop. Other activities in the area include the aforementioned ski jumping, biathlon ski jumping, winter mountain biking, luge, skeleton and bobsledding.

Confederation Park Golf Courses (Map 17/E3) is located at 3204 Collingwood Dr NW (between 6th and 14th Streets NW and north of 21st Ave NW). If the gates are open, then the golf course is groomed.

Maple Ridge Golf Course (Map 17/E6) is located at 1240 Maple Glade Dr. SE in Calgary. This golf course has groomed cross-country trails in the winter.

Shaganappi Point Golf Course (Map 17/D5) becomes a cross-country ski haven in the winter. There are 5 km (3 miles) of groomed and track set trails here, and 7 km (4.3 miles) groomed for skate skiing. The area can be busy on weekends and is located at 1200 26 St. SW.

Canmore Nordic Centre Provincial Park (Map 15/B3)

The Canmore Nordic Centre is one of the world's premier Nordic skiing centres. It has 72 km (44.7 miles) of cross-country ski trails including 2.5 km (1.6 miles) of lit trails. The trails are groomed daily to accommodate both classic and skate styles of skiing. There is even snowmaking on 12 km (7.4 miles) of trail. The area appeals to both competitive skiers (there are 32 km/19.9 miles of competitive cross-country trails and 20 km/12.4 miles of biathlon trails) and recreational skiers (approximately 50 km of the trails are groomed and track set). Facilities include a day lodge that can cater up to 250 people, meeting rooms, biathlon facilities, rentals, repairs and lessons as well as the Bill Warren Training Centre, an on site athlete training building.

Chester Lake Trail (Map 10/C1)

Found off the Smith-Dorrien Spray Trail, this 5 km (3 mile) one-way trail leads through the forest up to Chester Lake. It is an ungroomed trail that can be used by snowshoers and backcountry skiers.

Crimson Lake Provincial Park (Map 35/G3)

Located northwest of Rocky Mountain House off Secondary Highway 756, this popular provincial park is situated where the foothills of the western Rockies meet the northern boreal forest and the eastern aspen parkland. In the winter, two group camping areas are cleared and can be used for a fee. Cross-country skiers will find 10 km (6.2 miles) of groomed trails and 10 km (6.2 miles) of non-groomed trails. Snowshoers often explore the ungroomed trails.

Evans-Thomas Creek Trail (Map 15/F7)

This ungroomed backcountry route starts at a trailhead on Highway 40 near Kananaskis Village. From here, it is 14 km (8.7 miles) to Evans-Thomas Pass, gaining a grueling 760 m (2,470 ft) en route.

Fish Creek Provincial Park (Map 17/E6)

Fish Creek Park, at the south end of Calgary, is one of the largest urban parks in North America. There are 20 km (12.4 miles) of ungroomed, but usually well-tracked, cross-country ski trails, as well as snowshoeing, tobogganing and ice-skating. The most consistent snow conditions are in the west end of the park.

Fish Lake Recreation Area (Map 33/G3)

Also called Shunda Lake, Fish Lake is located 8 km (4.8 miles) west of Nordegg on Highway 11. There is a series of trails in the area that link with Goldeye Lake that can be used for cross-country skiing or snowshoeing during the winter.

Goat Creek Trail (Map 14/G2–15/A4)

This is an interesting backcountry ski/snowshoe trip that is not too challenging. However, it is still a daunting 18.3 km (11.4 miles) from the trailhead on the Smith-Dorrien Spray Trail to the Banff townsite. The first part of this trail is rougher than the last, which follows the Spray River Fire Road into town. You can arrange for a shuttle, return the way you came, or do this route in reverse by starting in Banff.

Ghost Airstrip Recreation Area (Map 21/G6)

Located 50 km (31 miles) northwest of Cochrane on Forestry Trunk Road (Highway 40), there are a number of trails at nearby Waiparious Creek. This is a popular snowmobiling area that also makes a fine place to ski or snowshoe.

Goldeye Lake Recreation Area (Map 33/G3)

Linking with nearby Shunda Lake, there are a lot of trails to explore in the Goldeye Lake area. The trails are not groomed but usually track set by previous skiers. If snowshoeing please stay off the cross-country tracks. Ice fishing on Goldeye Lake is also possible.

Kananaskis Lakes Trail (Map 10/E3)

The road leading to the Kananaskis Lakes offers a number of a number of ungroomed backcountry ski/snowshoe trails. All together, there are more than 75 km (47 miles) of trails to explore. Most are easy or intermediate routes, although there are a few difficult sections to be wary of.

Mount Shark Racing Trails (Map 15/B7)

The Mount Shark Racing Trails were developed for organized races, as well as training. When not being used for races, the 18 km (10.8 miles) of trails are open to the public. If a race is in progress, it is possible to follow the Watridge Lake Trail (see below).

North Ghost Recreation Area (Map 21/G6)

This huge recreation area is located next to Waiparous Creek. The trails in the area are popular with cross-country skiers, snowshoers and snowmobilers in the winter.

Police Outpost Provincial Park (Map 3/F7)

Alberta's southern most provincial park is situated where the foothills parkland and grasslands meet. The rolling hills are perfect for cross-country skiing/snowshoeing. Seven kilometres (4.3 miles) of trails lead south from the park and circle the southern shores of the lake.

Ribbon Creek Area (Map 15/E6)

Found 20 km (12.4 miles) south of Barrier Lake Information Centre on Kananaskis Trail (Highway 40), near the Nakiska Ski Area (Marmot Basin), Ribbon Creek offers a series of ungroomed cross-country ski/snowshoe trails. Ranging from easy to difficult, the 58 km (34.8 miles) of trails that wind their way through the forests and meadows along Ribbon Creek and through Marmot Basin.

Sandy McNabb Recreation Area (Map 11/G3)

Located 18 km (10.8 miles) west of Turner Valley on Sheep River Trail (Secondary Hwy 546), there are about 37 km (23 miles) of cross-country ski/snowshoe trails here. Most of the trails are rated easy, but there are a few intermediate and difficult sections. The longest trail is 6 km (3.6 miles) long, the shortest, less than a kilometre. The road is closed beyond the Sandy McNabb Recreation Area in the winter.

Siffleur Wilderness Area (Map 26/C2-C6)

This 255 square km wilderness area contains picturesque valleys, high peaks and alpine meadows. In the winter, it is the domain of snowshoers and backcountry skiers. As with all remote mountainous areas, people who travel here should be self-reliant and know how to handle themselves in avalanche country.

Smith-Dorrien Trails (Map 10/D1)

There are 33 km (19.8 miles) worth of track set intermediate and difficult cross-country ski trails here. The trails are not recommended for beginners.

Snow Creek Recreation Area (Map 33/F3)

Found next to Highway 11 about 17 km (10.5 miles) west of Nordegg, this group site is open year-round. In the winter, cross-country skiers use the area. Reservations for camping can be made by calling (403) 845-2781.

Spray Valley Provincial Park (Map 15/B6)

Bordering on Banff National Park, the hub of this area is found 18 km (11.2 miles) south of Canmore on a good gravel road called the Smith-Dorrien Spray Trail. Many of the trails provide backcountry skiing, snowshoeing and snowmobiling opportunities in the winter.

Strubble Lake Recreation Area (Map 35/G7)

To the southeast of Strachan off Strubble Road, this recreation area is open year-round. In the winter, the area is popular with cross-country skiers and snowshoers with Terratima Lodge providing accommodation.

Sundre Area (Map 29/E6)

Located in the northeast corner of Sundre, there are a few kilometres of easy/intermediate trails circling around Snake Hill. There is also a short (less than 500 m), difficult trail on the north side of the area.

Syncline Cross-Country Ski Area (Map 2/A1)

Located 28 km (17.4 miles) southwest of Crowsnest in the rolling terrain of the Castle River Valley, Syncline Cross-country Ski Area contains 17 km (10.6 miles) of ungroomed trails that can also be used by snowshoers. These trails are easily accessible by following Secondary Highway 774 southwest for 15 km (9.3 miles) from Beaver Mines.

Upper Shunda Creek Recreation Area (Map 34/A2)

Situated close to intersections of several historic aboriginal trails, this recreation area is on a terrace overlooking Shunda Creek. Nearby Coliseum Mountain offers a series of trails at the foot of the mountain that are groomed for cross-country skiing and snowshoeing.

Waterton Lakes National Park (Maps 2&3)

Waterton has two designated cross-country ski trails, both located along the upper Akamina Parkway. The **Dipper Ski Trail** is a moderate 6.5 km (4 mile) return trip that begins at the Rowe Lakes Trailhead (Map 3/F7). The **Cameron Ski Trail** is an easy 5 km (3 mile) round trip that begins at the Little Prairie Picnic Site (Map 3/G7). In addition to these designated trails, ski touring and snowshoeing can be done on (or off) many of the park's trails. Popular snowshoeing destinations are Bertha Falls and Crandell Lake. Skiers looking for easier backcountry ski routes should try the trails to Crandell Lake or Akamina Pass. Rowe Trail, Summit Lake and Wall/Forum Lake are much more difficult backcountry ski routes.

Watridge Lake Trail (Map 15/A7)

From the trailhead at the end of Mount Shark Road to Watridge Lake is a moderate 3.2 km (2 miles).

West Bragg Creek (Map 16/D6)

Found 10 km (6 miles) west of Bragg Creek, there are about 45 km (28 miles) of mostly easy groomed cross-country ski trails in the area. The longest trail, which is 16 km (10 miles) long, will challenge most skiers.

White Goat Wilderness Area (Maps 25, 26, 32, 33)

This 445 square km wilderness area contains hanging glaciers, tarns, alpine meadows, waterfalls and beautiful mountain lakes. In the winter, experienced backcountry skiers and snowshoers will find this wonderful area to visit. To access the southeastern portion of the wilderness area, take the **Pinto Lake Trail** from the David Thompson Highway (Hwy 11) were it meets the Cline River west of Abraham Lake (Map 33/C7). If you want to access the southwestern portion of the wilderness area, followed Norman Creek on the **Sunset Pass Trail** from the Icefield Parkway (Highway 93) in Banff National

Park (Map 25/E1). To reach the more rugged northern portion of the wilderness area requires a trek up the **Nigel Creek Trail** from the Icefield Parkway (Map 32/B7).

Wyndham-Carseland Provincial Park (Map 18/F7)

There are 2.4 km (1.5 miles) of ungroomed but usually tracked cross-country trails in this provincial park, which is located southeast of Calgary. There are also 56 winter campsites.

Snowmobiling

It has long been held that snowmobiles could go just about anywhere. As more and more terrain is being closed to snowmobilers, that is no longer the case. Areas get closed for a number of reasons. Sometimes it is to protect fragile nature. That's a good thing. Sometimes it's because of stupid snowmobilers damaging the environment and landscape, or just acting like buttheads in relation to other users. That's a bad thing. If you don't want to see the mountains entirely closed to snowmobiles, be responsible.

Even with a large chunk of the mountains closed (National parks have traditionally been closed to motorized recreation, as have most provincial parks), there are some great places to ride. Much of the Bighorn remains open to snowmobilers, as does a large area around the Crowsnest Pass. There are lots of old roads to be explored in the foothills, and there is a lot of prairie landscape that can be explored, too. But, please respect private property.

Below we have provided write-ups on the more popular areas in Southwest Alberta. This is not an exhaustive list. If you are new to an area, we suggest you contact the local club to get more details on a route. Most clubs are more than willing to set you up with a guide. Call the Alberta Snowmobile Association at (780) 427-2695 for more information.

As always, avalanches are a hazard when travelling through the mountains in the winter. Always carry an avalanche beacon, and never travel alone. When in doubt, stick to groomed routes.

Atlas Snowmobile Trails (Map 4/E4)

Located 11 km (6.8 miles) northwest of Crowsnest, the Atlas Road Recreation Area provides access to 18.7 km (11.6 miles) of designated snowmobile trails. Add in the extra 600 km (375 miles) or so of backroad/alpine riding nearby and you can see why this is a popular area. A 35 unit parking lot and pit toilets are found at the recreation area. An alternate access point to this area is found further south at the Allison Lake Recreation Area. Snowmobilers are able to use the 6 km (3.6 mile) multi-use trail on the western edge of the ski area.

Bighorn Wildland (Maps 20, 21, 26, 27, 32, 33)

This huge 2,463 square km area is subdivided into six separate forestland use zones. Snowmobiling is allowed in four of these zones, providing access to more than 1,000 km (600 miles) of trails. It is a big, area that provides access to spectacular mountainous terrain but offers little in the way of facilities or services. The trails, which are open to snowmobilers from December 1 to April 30, are monitored closely. Check http://www3.goc.ab.ca/srd/regions/southwest/bighorn/index.html for the most up-to-date information on trail closures and openings. The four main sledding areas are:

Onion Lake Sledding Area (Map 26/G2) is accessed along the Onion Lake Trail or the Hummingbird Creek Trail from the Forestry Trunk Road.

Ranger Creek Sledding Area (Map 27/A5) is located on the Banff boundary at the end of the Ranger Creek Trail. This random sledding area is a popular destination.

Scalp Creek Sledding Area (Map 27/D7) is located near the Banff boundary, just north of Ya-Ha Tinda Ranch. The area incorporates the slopes of Tomahawk Mountain, which is a fairly important wildlife habitat area. Please do not do anything to scare wintering elk and bighorn sheep.

Sugarbowl Sledding Area (Map 33/A6) is indeed sweet riding. It is a large area located at the junction of the Bighorn, Littlehorn and Whitegoat Trails.

Bluehill Snowmobile Trails (Map 28/G6, 29/A6)

The staging area for this riding area is found 5 km (3 miles) due west of Bearberry. There are three ungroomed loops, with a total of 90 km (56 miles)

of trail, maintained by the Olds Snowmobile Club. The area is sometimes inaccessible due to logging.

Carbondale Recreation Area (Map 2/A1)
Located between Carbondale and West Castle Rivers about 25 km (15.5 miles) southwest of Crowsnest, this is a winter recreation area with 40 km (24.8 miles) of brushed and groomed snowmobiling trails. This area is located in the Castle Mountain Management Area, and off-trail riding is not allowed. There is a 35 unit parking lot with pit toilets at the trailhead off Secondary Highway 774.

Caroline Area (Map 29/C2)
The Caroline Snowmobile Club maintains over 65 km of trails in the foothills around the Clearwater River. The Phylis Lake Recreation Area is a popular staging area. Contact the Caroline & District Chamber of Commerce (403-722-4066) for more information.

Cataract Creek Snowmobile Area (Map 7/D1-D3)
In the Cataract Creek area, there are 123 km (76.5 miles) of groomed trails, signed for two-way traffic. Winter camping is available at Etherington Creek and Cataract Creek staging areas. In addition to these two, there are a few other snowmobiling staging areas, all with picnic tables, group fire circles, garbage receptacles and toilet facilities. The Cataract Creek staging area also has a picnic shelter.

Chambers Creek (Map 35/C4)
Staging for this area, one of the main snowmobiling areas for Rocky Mountain House sledders, is found at the Chambers Creek Recreation Area on Highway 11. There are 89 km (55.3 miles) of signed but unmaintained trails in the area. There are no fees. Winter camping is allowed at the recreation area; contact the operator at (403) 845-2781 to set up.

Crowsnest Pass Area (Maps 1, 2, 4, 5)
There are 1,200 km (745 miles) of groomed and signed trails in the Crowsnest Pass area, including areas like Atlas and Carbondale (both above), with another 1,000 km (621 miles) of ungroomed trails. This area is easily the most popular snowmobiling area in Alberta, possibly in all of Canada. It is also one of the most beautiful. Trail maps are available in any of the small towns off the Crowsnest Highway (Hwy 3).

Eagle Mountain Trail (Map 34/C3)
Accessed from the Old Alberta Forestry Woodlot on Highway 11, this is a 15 km (9.3 mile) route that climbs up a slope to the summit of Eagle Mountain. There are excellent views of the Brazeau Range throughout the area.

Fallen Timber Creek Area (Map 21/D4-G7)
Located 70 km (43.5 miles) northwest of Cochrane off the Forestry Trunk Road, the Fallen Timber South Recreation Area is a popular staging area for snowmobilers. There is a total of 183 km (113.7 miles) of trails that link Burnt Timber, Fallen Timber and Waiparous Creeks.

Fisher Creek Area (Map 11/F1)
Accessed off Secondary Highway 549 west of Millarville, the Fisher Creek Recreation Site is used as a staging area for snowmobiles in the winter. There are 20 sites for camping. Between Fisher, McLean Creek, and Sibbald Flats (both below) there are 209 km (130 miles) of trails.

Ghost Snowmobile Area (Map 22/A7)
The South Ghost Recreation Area is located 43 km (26.7 miles) northwest of Cochrane on the Forestry Trunk Road (Highway 40). It is one of the main staging areas for trips into the Ghost Snowmobile Area. (Other staging areas include Fallen Timber and Ghost Air Strip Recreation Areas. Winter campers can stay at the latter area.) There are 183 km (113.7 miles) of trails in the area.

Gull Lake (Map 37/F3)
Snowmobilers looking for a wide open play area will find Gull Lake a lot of fun to cruise over. The boat launch at Aspen Beach Provincial Park is a popular staging area to access the lake (although snowmobiling is not allowed elsewhere in the park). Please be wary of ice conditions.

McLean Creek Area (Maps 16/D7)
McLean Creek is one of the biggest and best-known off-roading areas in the province. In the winter, this area becomes a snowmobile haven. Between McLean Creek, Fisher Creek (above), and Sibbald Flats (below) there are 209 km (130 miles) of trails. ATVs are also active in this area in the winter.

Prairie Creek Recreation Area (Map 35/C7)
Prairie Creek is located on Secondary Highway 752 about 41 km (25.5 miles) southwest of Rocky Mountain House. In the winter, cross-country skiing and snowmobiling are popular.

Red Deer River (Map 38/A6)
Snowmobilers access the Red Deer River from the boat launch at Great West Adventure Park in town. From here, they head up or downstream along the frozen river. Caution is needed.

Rocky Mountain House/Nordegg Area (Maps 33-36)
In addition to the trails around Chamber's Creek (see above) and Upper Shunda Creek (below), there are hundreds of kilometres of ungroomed backroads, old fur trading trails, oil and gas cutlines and frozen lakes to explore. All tolled, there are about 1,000 km (600 miles) of trails in the Rocky Mountain House/Nordegg area.

Sibbald Flats Snowmobile Area (Map 16/A5)
To reach the Sibbald Flat Staging Area, take the signed turn-off for the Sibbald Creek Trail, (off the Trans-Canada Hwy), about 35 km (22 miles) west of Calgary. Turn south on Powderface Trail, and watch for the Dawson Staging area, 3 km (1.8 miles) down. There are ten sites for winter campers. Between McLean Creek, Fisher Creek (above), and Sibbald Flats, there are 209 km (130 miles) of trails. ATVs are also active in this area in the winter.

Upper Shunda Creek Recreation Area (Map 34/A2)
Situated close to intersections of several historic aboriginal trails, Upper Shunda Recreation Area is on a terrace overlooking Shunda Creek. Coliseum Mountain, found nearby offers a series of trails at the foot of the mountain. Snowmobiling and cross-country skiing are popular winter activities.

Wildhorse Recreation Area (Map 21/C1)
Located next to Wildhorse Creek, as it flows into the Red Deer River, this group recreation area is used as a staging area for snowmobilers in winter.

Southwestern Alberta Mapkey

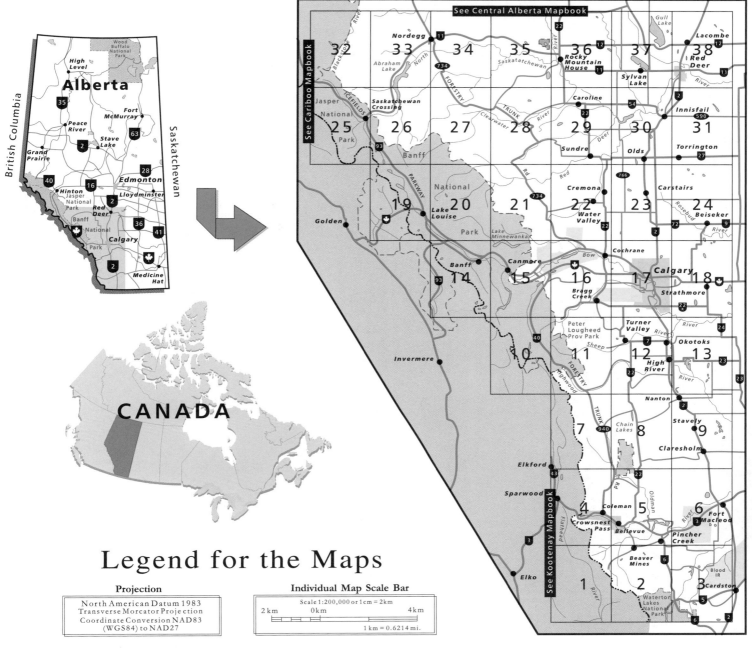

Legend for the Maps

Projection

North American Datum 1983
Transverse Morcator Projection
Coordinate Conversion NAD83
(WGS84) to NAD27

Individual Map Scale Bar

Scale 1:200,000 or 1cm = 2km

2 km   0 km   4 km

1 km = 0.6214 mi.

Recreational Activities:

Anchorage . . . .
Boat Launch . . . .
Beach . . . .
Campsite / Limited Facilities . . . .
Campsite / Trailer Park . . . .
Campsite (trail / water access only) . . . .
Canoe Access Put-in / Take-out . . . .
Cross Country Skiing . . . .
Diving . . . .
Downhill Skiing . . . .
Fishing . . . .
Golf Course . . . .
Hang-gliding . . . .
Hiking . . . .
Horseback Riding . . . .
Mountain Biking . . . .
Motorbiking / ATV . . . .
Paddling (canoe-kayak) . . . .
Picnic Site . . . .
Portage . . . .
Rock Climbing . . . .
Snowmobiling . . . .
Snowshoeing . . . .
Wildlife Viewing . . . .

Miscellaneous:

Airport / Airstrip . . . .
Beacon . . . .
Cabin / Lodge / Resort . . . .
Float Plane Landing . . . .
Forestry Lookout (abandoned) . . . .
Gate . . . .
Highways
    Trans-Canada . . . .
    Secondary Highway . . . .
Hospital . . . .
Interchange . . . .
Lighthouse . . . .
Marsh . . . .
Microwave Tower . . . .
Mine Site (abandoned) . . . .
Parking . . . .
Point of Interest . . . .
Portage (metres) . . . .
Ranger Station . . . .
Town Village, etc . . . .
Travel Information . . . .
Viewpoint . . . .
Waterfalls . . . .

Line Definition:

Highways . . . .
Paved Secondary Roads . . . .
Main Industry Roads . . . .
Active Industry Roads (2wd) . . . .
Industry Roads (2wd / 4wd) . . . .
Long Distance Trail . . . .
Unclassified / 4wd Roads . . . .
Deactivated Roads . . . .
Trail / Old Roads . . . .
Routes (Undeveloped Trails) . . . .
Seismic Lines . . . .
Snowmobile Trails . . . .
Paddling Routes . . . .
Powerlines . . . .
Pipelines . . . .
Railways . . . .
Wildlife Management Units . . . .

Provincial Park

Recreation Area/
Ecological Area

City

Restricted Area /
Private Property

Glaciers/
Swamps

Indian Reserve

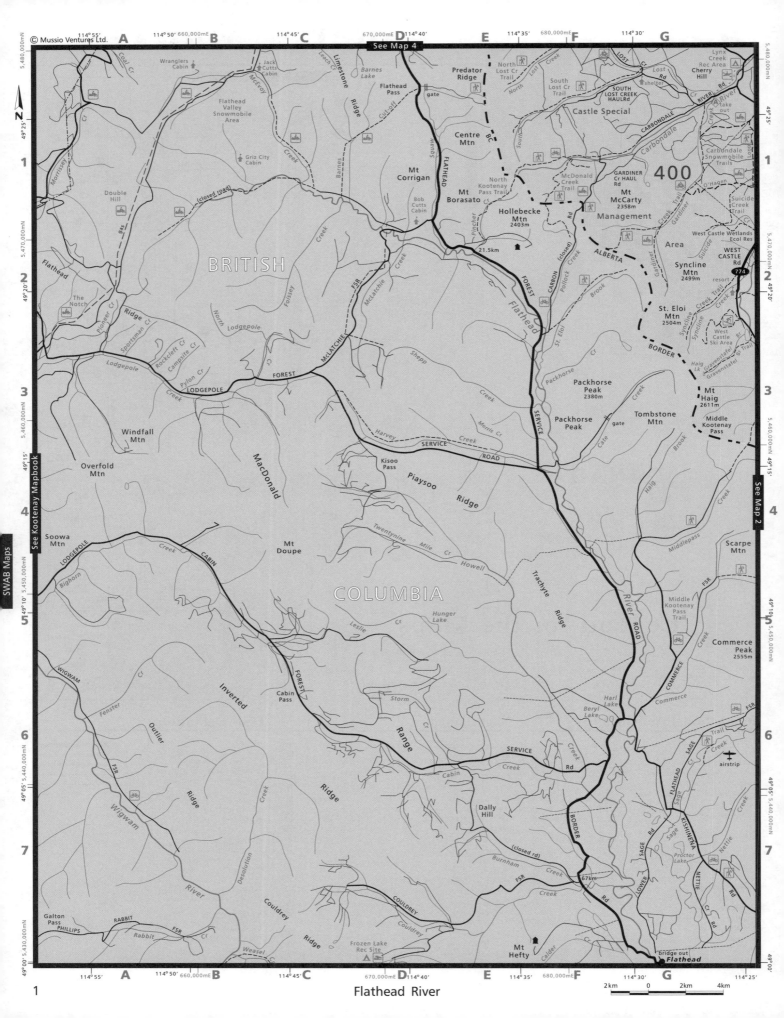

BRITISH

COLUMBIA

400

SWAB Maps

See Kootenay Mapbook

See Map 2

Flathead River

1

2km   0   2km   4km

© Mussio Ventures Ltd.

114°25' 690,000mE · A · 114°20' · B · 114°15' 700,000mE · C · 114°10' · D · 710,000mE · 114°05' · E · F · 114°00' · G · 113°55' 300,000mE

49°25'
49°20'
49°15'
49°10'
49°05'
49°00'

5,480,000mN
5,470,000mN
5,460,000mN
5,450,000mN
5,440,000mN

SWAB Maps

See Map 1

See Map 3

110

302

400

Beaver Mines

Carbonale put in
Castle Falls Rec Area
Castle Rd
Castle River Route
Seven Gates Rd
Carbondale Hill 1802m
Mt Backus 1815m
Beaver Mines Rd
BEAVER MINES Rd
GLADSTONE VALLEY Rd
775
Pincher
Kettles
Creek Rd
RGE 302
CHIEF
Mill Creek Rd
Marna Lake
Chipman
TWP Rd 54
6 Mtn
Hwy
Syncline in Rec Area
take out
CASTLE
Gladstone Mtn Ranch Resort
Mill Creek Rd
Gladstone Valley
Beauvais Lake Prov Park
Daigle Lake
Lynch Lakes
774
Castle River Bridge Rec Area
Beaver Mines Lake
WEST
BEAVER
Christie
Mine
Ridge
Fish Lake
505
Castle Mtn
MINES
Beaver Mines Lake Rec Area
Camp Impeesa
Table Mtn 2232m
Table Mtn Trail
Whitney Creek Trail
FRONT
RANGE
Pecten
SHELL WATERTON GAS PLANT Rd
West Castle
Wetlands Ecol Res
Barnaby (Southforks) Lakes
Whistler Mtn Lookout Trail
Whistler Mtn
Mt Gladstone 2370m
Victoria Peak
Prairie Bluff
Prairie Bluff Trail
RGE Rd 303
SPREADEAGLE
Southfork Mtn
Castle Special
Castle Peak
Windsor Mtn 2544m
Windsor Ridge
Pincher Ridge
Drywood Ridge
Drywood Mtn
Yarrow Cr
Margaret Lakes
Spread Eagle Rd
TWP Rd 40
Barnaby Ridge
SOUTH
Management
Lys Lake Trail
Castle Rd
ACCESS
DRYWOOD CREEK Rd
TWP Rd 34
Middle Kootenay Pass Trail
Grizzly Creek
Ruby Lake
Lys Lake
Tank Trap
Jutland Brook Trail
Area
Big Sagebrush Wildlife Viewing
Victoria Pincher Ridge
Drywood
South Drywood
Spionkop
Kesler Lake
TWP Rd 28
Rainy Ridge
Grizzly Lake
North Scarpe Lake
Scarpe
South Scarpe Lake
River
Font
Sage Mtn 2376m
Bovin Lake
Loaf Mtn 2630m
Spionkop Ridge
Canyon
Yarrow
Oil Basin Warden Cabin
Park Line Trail
Rainy Ridge Lk
Rainy Lakes
La Coulotte Peak
Jutland Mtn 2408m
Mt Matkin
Font Mtn 2353m
Coulotte Ridge
Newman Peak 2515m
Spionkop
Avion Ridge Route
Mt Glen Cowan 2653m
Yarrow
Dungarvan
Cottonwood
Jake Smith Lake
BRITISH
BC
Avion Ridge
Goat Lake
Goat Lake Trail
Mt Dungarvan 2566m
Waterton
Sunkist Ridge
Roche Ridge
ALBERTA
Lost Lake
Snowshoe
Twin Lakes
Snowshoe Warden Cabin
Mt Bauerman 2409m
Anderson Peak 2698m
Lost Mtn 2509m
Rock Canyon
Red
Lakes
Mt Galway 2348m
Sunkist Mtn 2348m
FSR
Sage Creek
Flanders Brook
South Kootenay Pass 2104m
Blakiston Creek
Lone Mtn 2420m
Mt Blakiston 2940m
Blakiston Falls
Red River
Lost Horse Cr
Coppermine Cr
PARKWAY
Crandell Campground
FLATHEAD
SAGE
Flanders Mtn
South Kootenay Pass Trail
Tamarack Trail
Lone Lake
Ruby Lake
Canyon Camp
Crandell Lake
Cameron Creek Trail
Langemark Mtn
Nettle Cr
COLUMBIA
Kenow Mtn
Mt Yarrell
8.5km
Festubert Mtn 2522m
BORDER
Lone Creek
National
Lineham Lakes
Mt Lineham 2728m
Cameron Cr
PARKWAY
Prairie Picnic Area
McNeally's Picnic Area
Bertha Peak 2440m
Mt Crandell 2378m
Park
Lonesome Lake
Waterton Park
5
Miskwashi Peak 2594m
FSR
Beaver Mines Creek
Akamina
Grizzly Gulch
Festubert Trail
Rowe Lakes Trail
Rowe Lakes
Rowe Lake
AKAMINA
Buchanan Ridge
Carthew Summit
take out
Upper Bertha Lake
Lower Bertha Lake
Bertha Campsite
Shoreline Trail
Waterton Lake
Wishbone Trail
KISHINEA
Starvation Peak
Akamina Ridge
Kishinena Ridge
Kishinena Creek
Akamina Pass 1779m
Akamina Cr
Wall Lake
Rec Area
Mt Rowe 2452m
Cameron Lk
Summit Lake
Alderson Lake
Carthew Lakes
Mt Alderson 2692m
Crypt Landing
Upper Waterton Lake
Middle Waterton Lake
To Flathead
Well Site
King Edward Peak
Starvation Creek
N. Kintla
Provincial
Akamina Ridge
Forum Lake
Boundary Trail
Mt Richards 2416m
Bertha Lake Trail

2km 0 2km 4km

Waterton Park

2

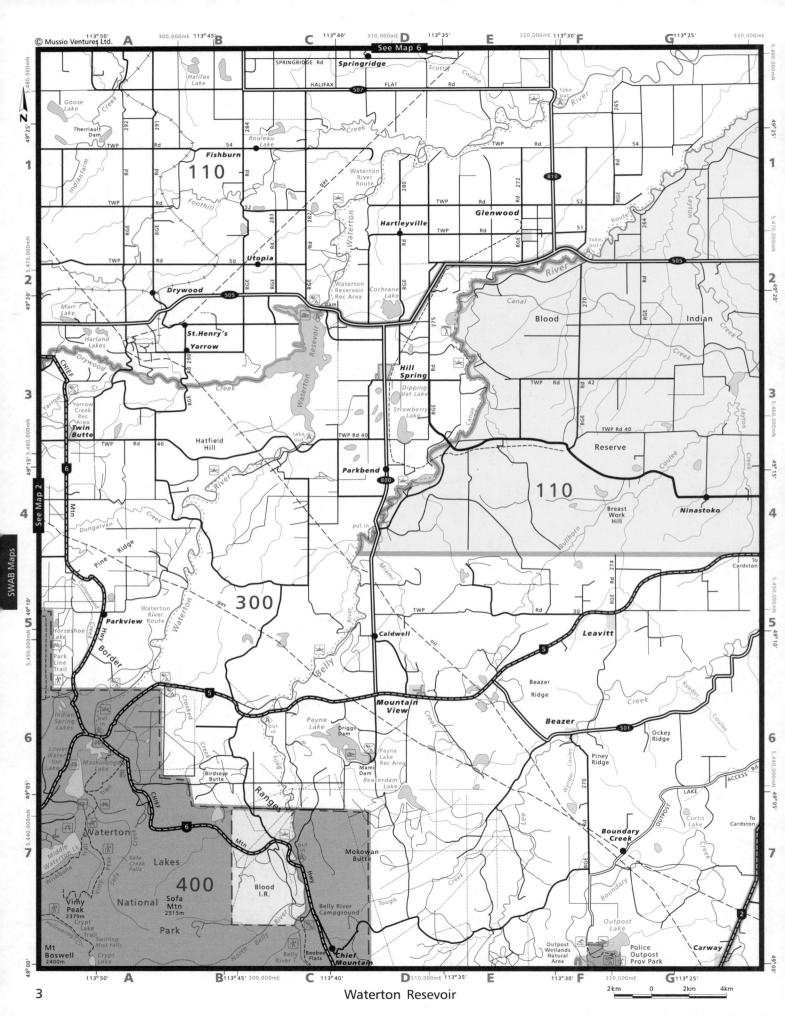

© Mussio Ventures Ltd.

650,000mE 114° 55' 114° 50' 660,000mE 114° 45' 114° 40' 670,000mE 114° 35' 114° 30' 680,000mE 114° 25'

N

A **B** **C** **D** **E** **F** **G**

DUTCH Cr Rd
Dutch Trail
Dutch
shelter
Station
Fly Cr

49° 50'
BRULE Cr
Cr
LINE CREEK MINE Rd
Line Creek
Mt Salter 2540m
Grave Lake
Harriet Lake
Sheep Mtn
Mt Erris 2841m
N Racehorse
Wintering
Racehorse Roundabout Trail
Racehorse RACEHORSE CREEK Rd
Racehorse Creek Rec Area

1

Nordstrom
Harmer
Natal
Dalzell
BRITISH
Erickson
West Alexander Creek
Mt Secord 2652m
Mt Domke
shelter
put in
Salt Cr
Victry Creek DAISY Rd
402
940

2

49° 45'
CUMMINGS CREEK FSR
Elk Prarie
open pit
BC
Racehorse Pass Trail
Racehorse Pass
Window Mountain Lake
Mt Ward 2530m
Allison Peak 2643m
Seven Sisters Mtn 2591m
McGillvray Ridge Trail
RESOURCE
ROAD
Daisy
49° 45'

3

Sparwood
ALEXANDER (4wd)
Alexander Creek #2 Rec Site
ALBERTA
Alexander Creek #1 Rec Site
Deadman
Ma Butte
Crowsnest Mtn Trail
Crowsnest Mtn 2786m
McGillvray Creek
Grassy Mtn 2065m
Grassy Mtn Trails
See Map 5

4

Natal
Michel
dump
Baldy Mtn
Ridge
Mt Erickson 2485m
4-23
CROWSNEST FSR
Deadman Pass
Atlas Snowmobile Trails
Chinook Lake Rec Area
Allison X-C Ski Trail
Wedge Mtn 1870m
Saskatoon Mtn
Nez Perce Trail
FORESTRY
49° 40'

5

McGillivray
FIR-ROBETS
CROWSNEST
Phillips Pass Trail
Phillips Peak 2500m Crowsnest Prov Park
Mt Tecumseh 2549m
Tecumseh Rd
Phillips Lake Crowsnest Lake
Hwy 3
Coleman
306
Bluff Mtn
Blairmore

Crowsnest
Hazell
Sentinel
Emerald Lake
Island Lake Rec Area
Crowsnest Trail
falls
Star Creek Trail
Star Cr Falls
Three Cabin Trail
16th Ave
York Cr
BLAIRMORE
Lyons Cr Ravine Trail
49° 35'

6

Hosmer Ridge
Wheeler Creek
OLD LOOKOUT Rd
CORBIN
Trail Hill
CHINOOK
Ptolemy Pass Trail
Trail of Seven Bridges
Sentry Mtn 2435m
Chinook Peak 2591m
Mt Parrish 2530m
Mt McLaren 2286m
Coulthard Mtn Meadows Trail
North York Cr
Ironstone Lookout Trail
Ironstone Lookout
Drum Creek Trail
Turtle Mtn

Marten
Carbon
Tent Mtn Trails
Ptolemy Pass
Trail to the Promised Land
Mt Ptolemy 2815m
Andy Good Peak 2621m
Mt Coulthard 2642m
Lynx Cr Trails
400

7

49° 30'
COAL
MATHESON Cr
Coal Cr
Coal Creek Pass Ridge
Mt Taylor 2243m
Michel Ridge
Michel Creek
Limestone Ridge
Corbin
FLATHEAD
Coal Mtn
BORDER
Mt McGladrey
Castle Special
Mt Pengelly 2560m
GOAT CREEK Rd
Goat Creek Loop
Mt Darrah 2754m
LOST CREEK Rd
Management
Area
LYNX
Adanac Ridge Trail
take out
49° 30'

COLUMBIA

650,000mE 114° 55' 114° 50' 660,000mE 114° 45' 114° 40' 670,000mE 114° 35' 114° 30' 680,000mE 114° 25'

A **B** **C** **D** **E** **F** **G**

2km 0 2km 4km

Crowsnest

4

SWAB Maps

See Kootenay Mapbook

© Mussio Ventures Ltd.

690,000mE 114° 20' 114° 15' 700,000mE 114° 10' 114° 05' 710,000mE 114° 00' 290,000mE 113° 55'

N

402
306
308
305
400
302

Bob Creek Wildland
Lower Camp Creek Trail
Upper Camp Cr Trail
Whaleback Ridge Trails
Beaverdam Creek Trail

Dutch Creek Rec Area
Gap Pond Picnic Area
Livingstone Ranger Station

Oldman River
The Gap
Gap Falls
The Gap Pass
22.5km
15km
MAYCROFT Rd

Thunder Mtn 2352m

Oldman
Maycroft
Tetley

Willow Valley
WILLOW
Tod Creek

Center Peak
Caudron Peak 2547m

Livingstone Range

Chapel Rock
CHAPEL ROCK Rd

Skyline Rd
Skyline Ranger Station
Porcupine Lookout
East Porcupine Wildlife Viewing

Porcupine Hills

Beaver Creek Rec Area

Waldron Flat
Maycroft Rec Area
Maycroft Rapids
Waldron Falls

Oldman River Route

Antelope Butte
Unnecessary Mtn
Chapel Butte

Longview Rd

Peigan IR

North Fork
Olin Creek
Olin

Tanner

Lille (ghost town)
Lille Trail
Livingstone Ridge Trail

Hudson Bay Lake
Ross Lake
Lee
Connelly

Frank Slide
Robertson Peak
Frank
Bellevue
Two Mine Trail
Tallon Peak
Hillcrest Mines
Burmis
BURMIS Rd
Leitch Collieries Historical Site
Crowsnest River Route
Lundbreck Falls
Lundbreck Falls Rec Area
Lundbreck

Crowsnest River
Castle River Rec Area

Cowley
TWP Rd 74
TWP Rd 73
TWP Rd 72

Massacre Butte
Oldman Dam (Three Rivers Reservoir)
Oldman Dam Rec Area
Reservoir

Pincher Station

Hillcrest Mtn
Byron Creek Falls
Byron Hill Trail
Byron Hill 1839m
Byron

Lee's Lake
Burmis Mine Ridge Trail

Pincher Creek
MAIN ST

Castle Special Management Area
Ginger Hill
Carbondale River Route
Maverick Hill

Beaver Mines
SEVEN GATES Rd
BEAVER MINES Rd

Riverside Ranch
Screwdriver Cr
Wind Valley

Waterton River

2km 0 2km 4km

SWAB Maps
See Map 4
See Map 6

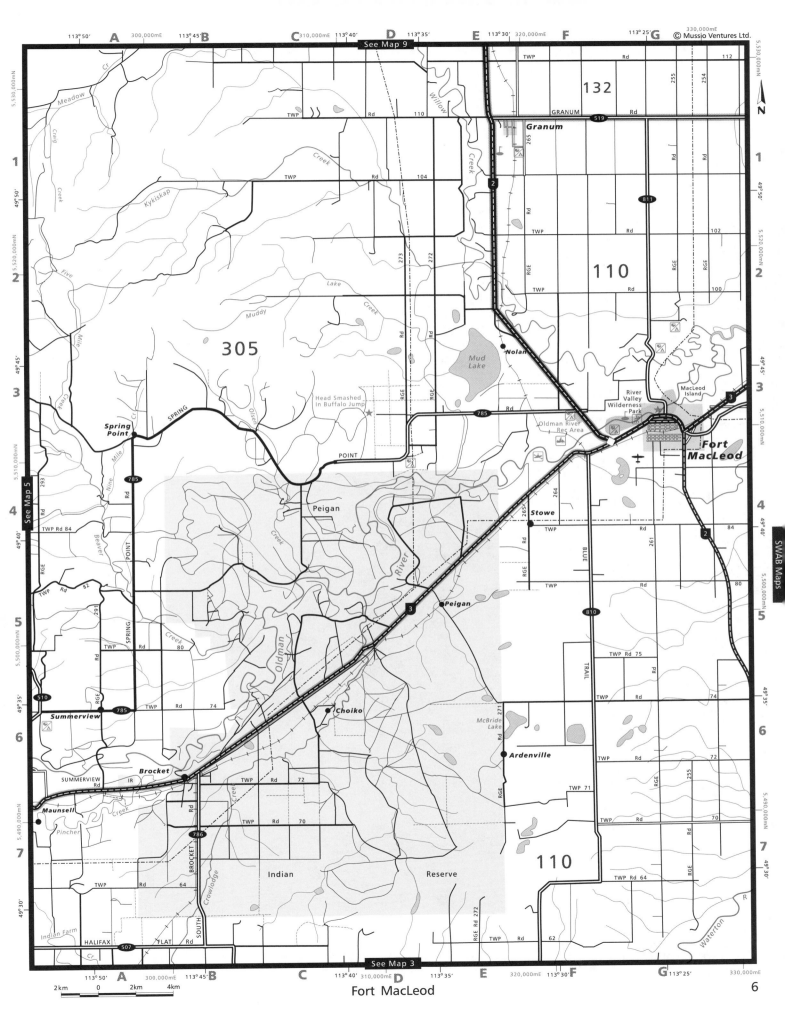

See Map 5

SWAB Maps

132

110

305

110

Granum

Nolan

Mud Lake

Head Smashed In Buffalo Jump

Spring Point

SPRING

POINT

Peigan

River Valley Wilderness Park

MacLeod Island

Oldman River Rec Area

Fort MacLeod

Stowe

Peigan

BLUE

TRAIL

Choiko

McBride Lake

Ardenville

Brocket

Summerview

SUMMERVIEW

Maunsell

Indian Reserve

BROCKET

Crowlodge

SOUTH

HALIFAX

Indian Farm

2km 0 2km 4km

Fort MacLeod

6

© Mussio Ventures Ltd.

650,000mE 660,000mE 670,000mE 680,000mE

BRITISH COLUMBIA

ALBERTA

310

404

402

4-23

See Kootenay Mapbook

Mt Bleasdell 2590m
Mt Veits
Mt MacLaren
Mt Armstrong 2823m
Coyote Hills
Don
Getty
Don
Getty Wildland Prov Park
Mt Burke 2542m
Miller Creek Road
Devil's Bite
Pictographs
Fitzsimmons Creek Trail
Lower Etherington Creek Trail
Middle Falls
Weeping Wall
Upper Falls
Zephyr Creek Trail
Zephyr/Bear Pass
Bear Creek Trail
Mt Bolton 2706m
Fording River Pass 2299m
Fording Pass Trail
Baril Peak 2998m
Mt Cornwell 2972m
Courcelette Peak 3044m
Gill Peak
BC High Rock Border
Mt Etherington 2877m
Mt Schinger 2755m
Wildland
Raspberry Ridge Lookout
Mosquito Hill
Cataract Creek Rec Area
Plateau Mountain
Sentinel Peak 2340m
Corral Cr Trail
Mt Tuxford 2550m
Mt Turnbull
Mt Holcroft 2713m
Mt Acrimger
Cataract Prov Park
Plateau
Ecological Reserve
Sentinel Pass
Hailstone Butte Lookout
Bear Pond Trail
Bear Pond
Mt Farquhar 2895m
(Closed Dec - April)
Plateau Mtn Trail
restricted access
Plateau Mtn 2438m
Twin Summit Trail
Hailstone Butte Fire Lookout
Twin Peaks Trail
The Hump
Mt Pierce
Divide Trail
Sentinel Pass & Peak Trail
Teardrop Lake
Windy Peaks Trail
Timber Cr Trail
(restricted road access)
Fording Coal
Mt O'Rouke
Pasque Mtn Route
Prov
Great Divide
Pasque Mtn 2541m
Greenhills Range
Park
Mt Gass 2866m
Memory Lake
Oldman Headwaters Trail
Isolation Creek Trail
Isola Peak 2494m
Isolation
Slacker Creek Trail
Livingstone Falls Rec Area
Beaver Creek Trail
Beehive
Mt Lyall 2952m
Beehive Mtn Trail
Lyall Range
Windy Pass
Beehive Mountain 2281m
Natural
Area
Cyclamen Ridge
Twin Peaks
Spears Creek Trail
Spears
Cabin Ridge Trail
Cabin Ridge
Round Prairie
River Walk
ELK RIVER FSR
dump
Cache Creek Trail
Honeymoon Creek Group Camp
Shale Creek Trail
Livingstone River Route
Elkford
Lost Lily Lakes Trails
Lost Lily Lake
Josephine Falls
Fording Mtn 1769m
Mt Lyne 2702m
Tornado Pass 2163m
Tornado Mtn
Sugarloaf Lookout 2515m
Sugarloaf Lookout Trail
Oldman River Route put in
Oldman River North Rec Area
Northfork Pass 1992m
Great Divide Trail
Tornado Pass Trail
Grassy Ridge
DUTCH CR Rd

Oldman River

2km 0 2km 4km

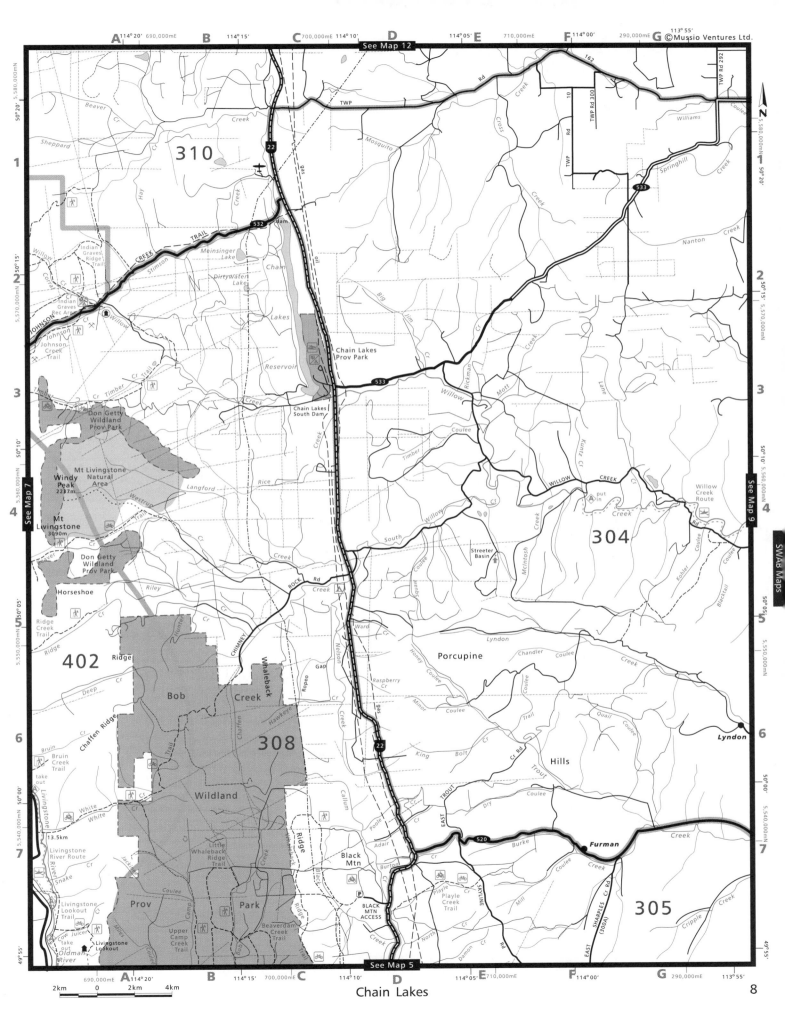

© Mussio Ventures Ltd.

A 114°20' 690,000mE B 114°15' C 700,000mE 114°10' D E 114°05' 710,000mE F 114°00' 290,000mE G 113°55'

310

532

22

Beaver Cr

Sheppard

Willow

Corral

JOHNSON

Indian Graves Ridge Trail

TRAIL

CREEK

Stimson

Hay

Creek

Meinsinger Lake

DirtyWater Lake

dam

Chain

Lakes

Reservoir

Indian Graves Rec Area

Johnson Creek Trail

Cr Trail

Willow

Timber

Cr Timber

Creek

Chain Lakes South Dam

Chain Lakes Prov Park

gas

oil

Creek

TWP

Mosquito

Cross

Creek

Creek

Creek

Big Jim

Cr

Willow

Rickman

Mott

Cr

162

TWP Rd 300

TWP Rd

10

TWP Rd 292

Springhill

Nanton

Creek

Williams

Coulee

533

Creek

533

N

1

2

3

50°20'

50°15' 5,570,000mN

50°10' 5,560,000mN

5,580,000mN

SWAb Maps

See Map 7

See Map 9

Don Getty Wildland Prov Park

Windy Peak 2237m

Mt Livingstone Natural Area

Mt Livingstone 3090m

Don Getty Wildland Prov Park

Horseshoe

Timber

Westrup Trail

Langford

Rice

Creek

South

Willow

Coulee

Streeter Basin

put in

McIntosh

Kuntz Cr

WILLOW

CREEK

Willow Creek Route

Kohler Coulee

Blacktail

Coulee

304

4

5

50°10' 5,560,000mN

50°05'

5,550,000mN

402

Ridge

Ridge Creek Trail

Ridge

Deep

Cr

Bruin Cr

Bruin Creek Trail

Chaffen Ridge

Hunter

Cr

Chaffen

Cr

Bob

Creek

Whaleback

Gap

Ropeo

Hawkeye Cr

308

Wildland

Nelson

Creek

Ward Cr

Raspberry Cr

Chimney

Rock

Creek

Rd

Cr

Porcupine

Lyndon

Honey Coulee

Chandler Coulee

Menby

Coulee

Minor

Coulee

King Bolt

Cr

Trail

Creek

Hills

Quail Coulee

Lyndon

6

50°00' 5,540,000mN

White

White

Cr

Cr

Jack

Snake

Camp

Miles

Coulee

Coulee

Cr

Park

Little Whaleback Ridge Trail

Upper Camp Creek Trail

Beaverdam Creek Trail

Black Ridge

Whaleback

Ridge

Black Mtn

BLACK MTN ACCESS

P

Callum

Adair

Poole

Burton

Cr

Playle Creek Trail

SKYLINE

Damon

North

Creek

Rd

Cr

EAST

TROUT

520

Burke

Coulee

Mill

Dry

Coulee

Furman

SHARPLES Cr Rd (300A)

EAST

Creek

Cripple

305

7

49°55'

Livingstone

13.5km

Livingstone Lookout Trail

Livingstone River Route

take out

Oldman River

Cow Juicer take out

Livingstone Lookout

Prov

22

520

7

A 114°20' 690,000mN 0 B 114°15' 700,000mE C 114°10' D E 114°05' 710,000mE F 114°00' G 290,000mE 113°55'

2km 0 2km 4km

Chain Lakes

8

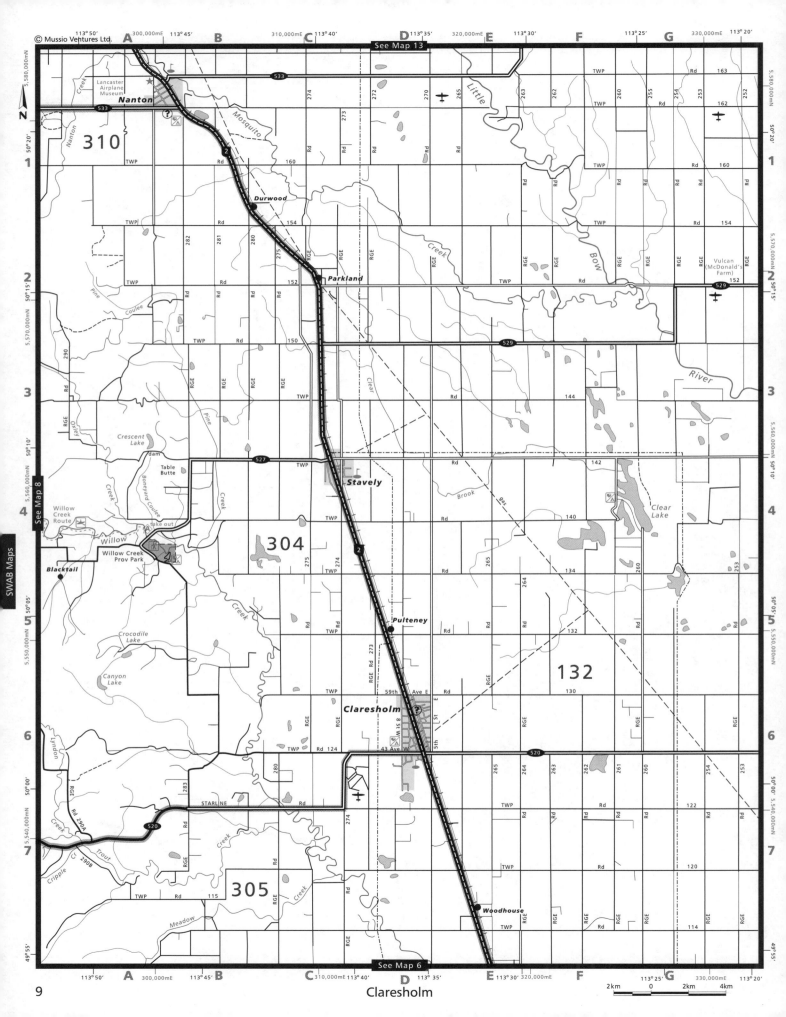

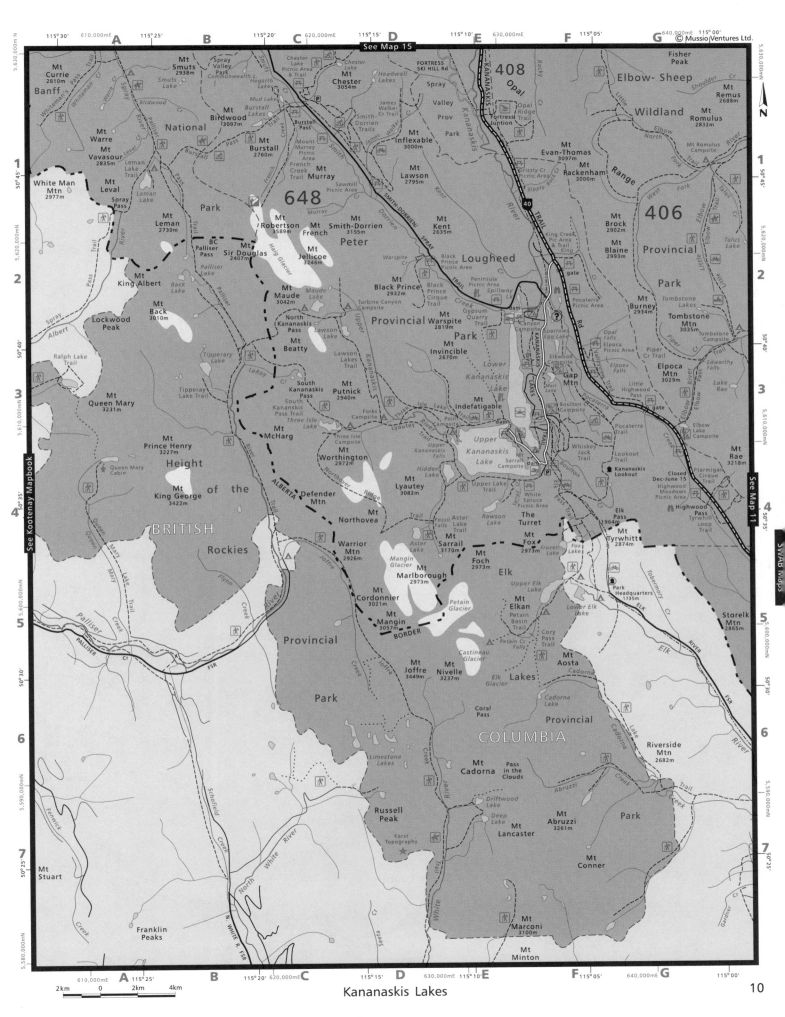

Kananaskis Lakes

10

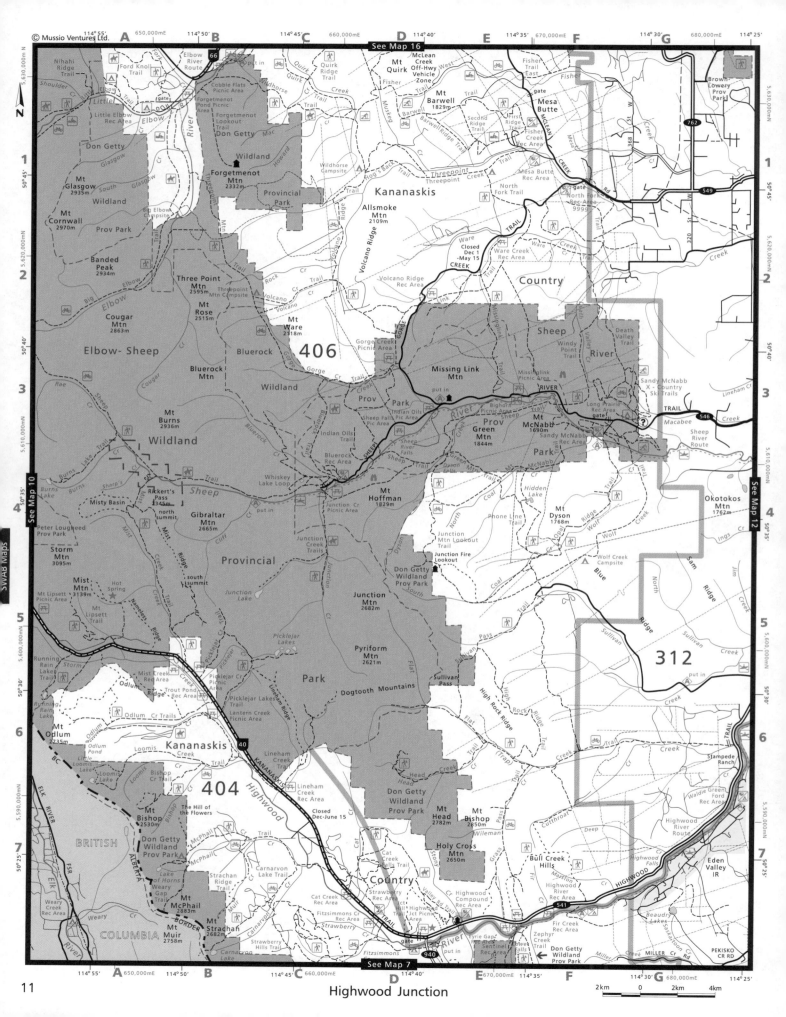

See Map 10

See Map 12

11

Highwood Junction

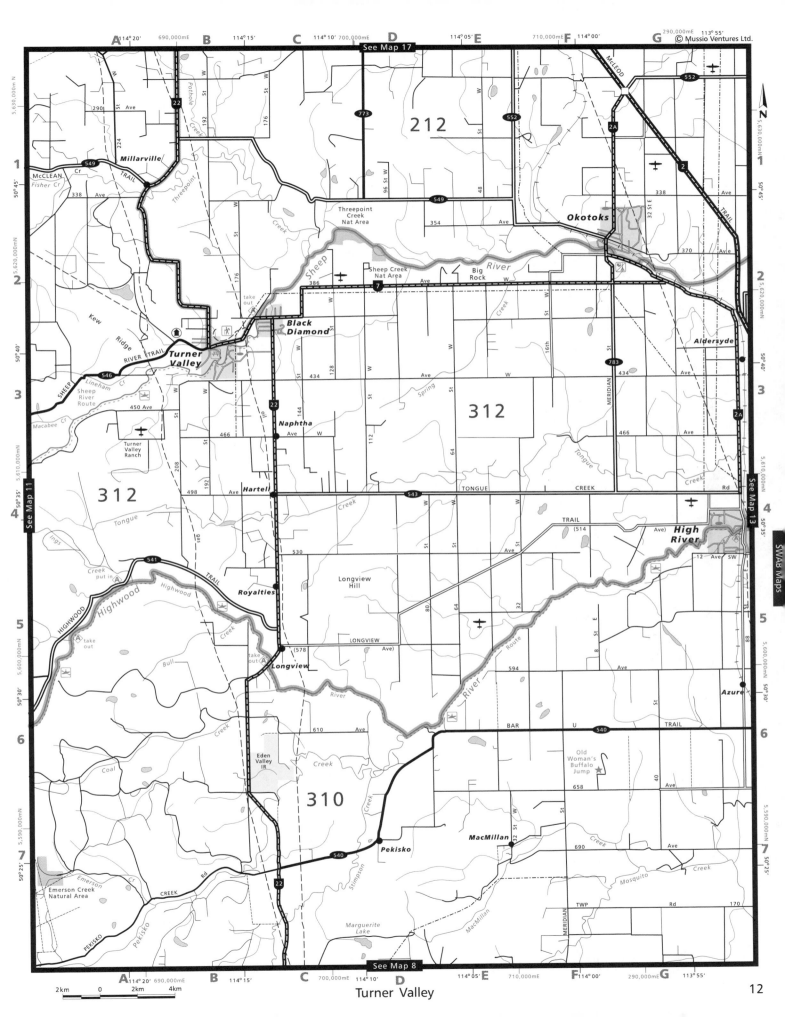

SWAB Maps

See Map 11

See Map 13

212

312

312

310

Millarville

McCLEAN

Fisher Cr

Threepoint Creek Nat Area

Sheep Creek Nat Area

Big Rock

Okotoks

Aldersyde

Turner Valley

Black Diamond

Kew

Ridge

Sheep

Lineham Cr

Macabee Cr

Turner Valley Ranch

Naphtha

Hartell

Tongue

CREEK

Spring

Tongue

CREEK

Tongue

High River

Highwood

Highwood

Royalties

Longview Hill

LONGVIEW

Longview

Azure

Bull

River

Route

Eden Valley IR

BAR

U

TRAIL

Old Woman's Buffalo Jump

Coal

Emerson Creek Natural Area

Emerson Cr

PEKISKO

Pekisko

Stimpson

Marguerite Lake

MacMillan

MacMillan

Mosquito

MERIDIAN

TWP

Turner Valley

2km 0 2km 4km

12

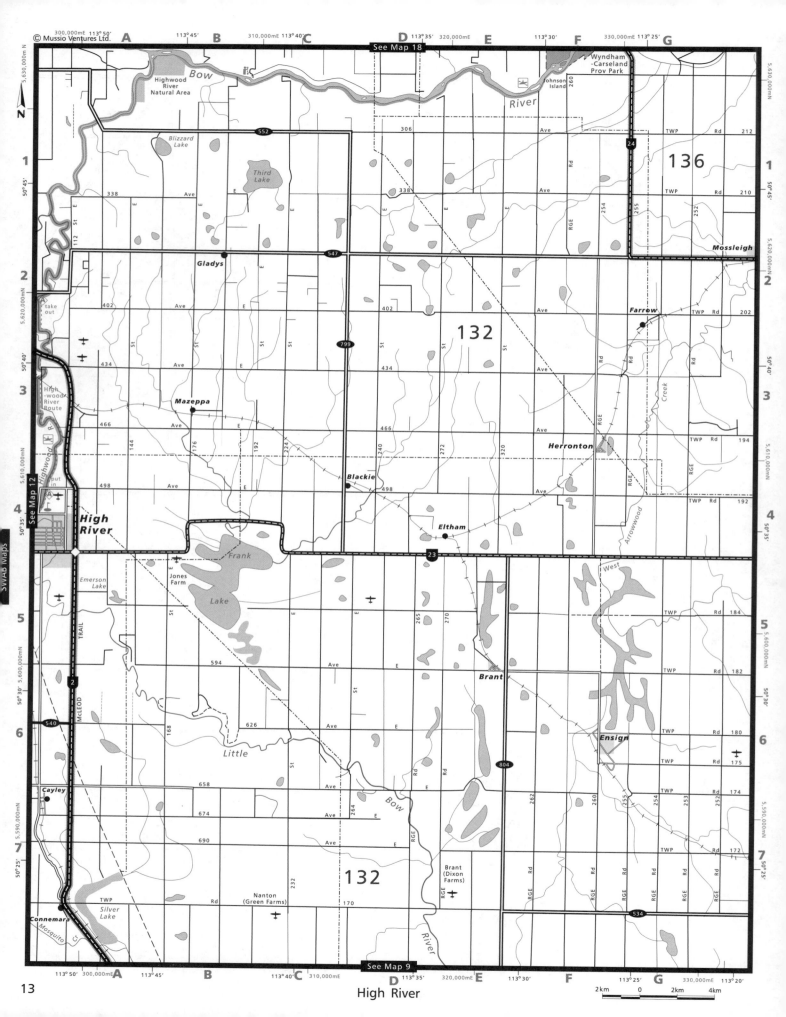

See Map 18

See Map 9

High River

13

136

132

132

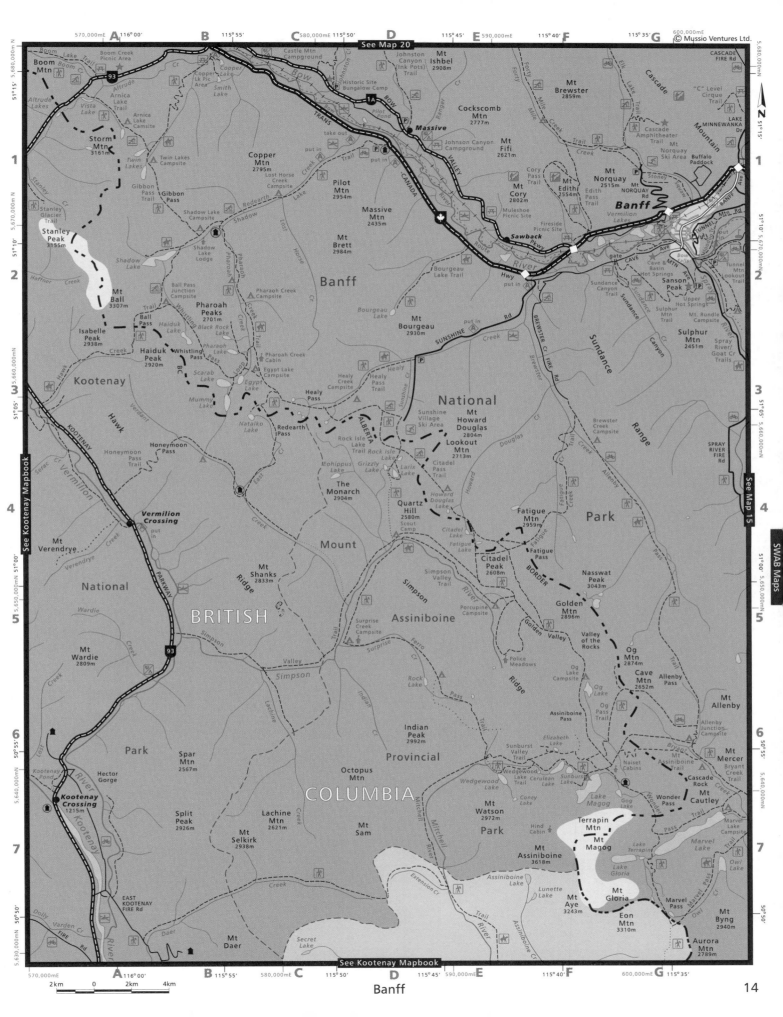

See Kootenay Mapbook

See Map 15

SWAB Maps

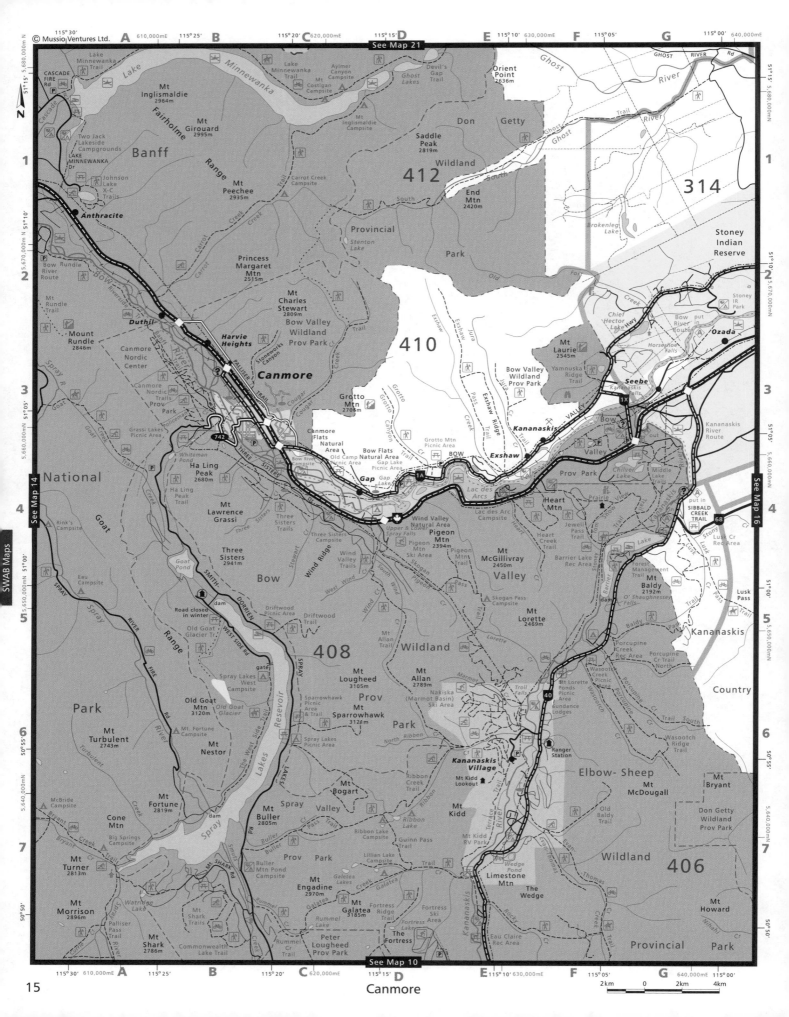

See Map 21

412

314

410

408

406

See Map 14

See Map 16

See Map 10

15

Canmore

2km 0 2km 4km

© Mussio Ventures Ltd.

314

312

406

212
Sarcee
Indian Reserve
(Tsuut'ina Nation)

312

Cochrane Lake

Cochrane

Mitford

Wildcat
Wildcat Island Nature Area

Radnor

Ghost Lake

Ghost Reservoir Rec Area

Stony IR

Stony IR

Spencer Hills

Irwin Hill

Cheneka

Morley

Stoney Indian Reserve

Potts Lake

McLennan

Bow

Indian

Reserve

Chiniki Lake

Eagle

Old Buck Mtn Natural Area

Westover Lake

Frederick Lake

Darnell Lake

Ole Buck Mtn 1905m

Ole Buck Trails

Bateman

Sibbald Lake Rec Area

SIBBALD

Pine Grove Rec Area

Jumpingpound Trail West

Little Jumpingpound

Sibbald Lakes

Livingstone Ridge

Barnes Ridge

Logan Ridge

Norman Lake

Hermitage

Sarcee Butte

Kananaskis

Cox Hill

Jumpingpound Mtn 2225m

Coxhill Ridge

Moose Mtn 2210m

LOOKOUT

Pinetop Hill

West Bragg X-C Ski Trails

West Bragg Picnic Area

Hostel Loop

Sundog Loop

Bragg Creek Prov Park

Bragg Creek

Foothills Natural Area

Redwood Meadows

Robinson Hill

Lusk Pass Trail

POWDERFACE

Moose Mtn Trail

Ranger

Fullerton Loop Trail

Gooseberry Rec Area

Allen Bill Pond & McLean Pond Picnic Areas

McLean Creek Rec Area

McLean Hill

Ice Caves (access closed)

Ing's Mine Picnic Area

Diamond T Loop
Elbow River Rec Area

Prairie Mtn 2210m

Country

Elbow Falls Rec Area

Beaver Flats Rec Area

Elbow River Launch

Elbow River Route

Quirk Cr Trail

Quirk Ridge Trail

Silvester Trail

Muskeg Link Trail

McLean Creek Off-Hwy Vehicle Zone

Stallion Run Trail

Whiskey Hill Trail

Valley Trail

Brown Lowery Prov Park

Compression Ridge

Don Getty Wildland Prov Park

Nihahi Ridge

Powderface Ridge

Powderface Picnic Area

Powderface Trail

Paddy's Flat Rec Area

Springbank

Prairie

SWAB Maps

See Map 15

See Map 17

2km 0 2km 4km

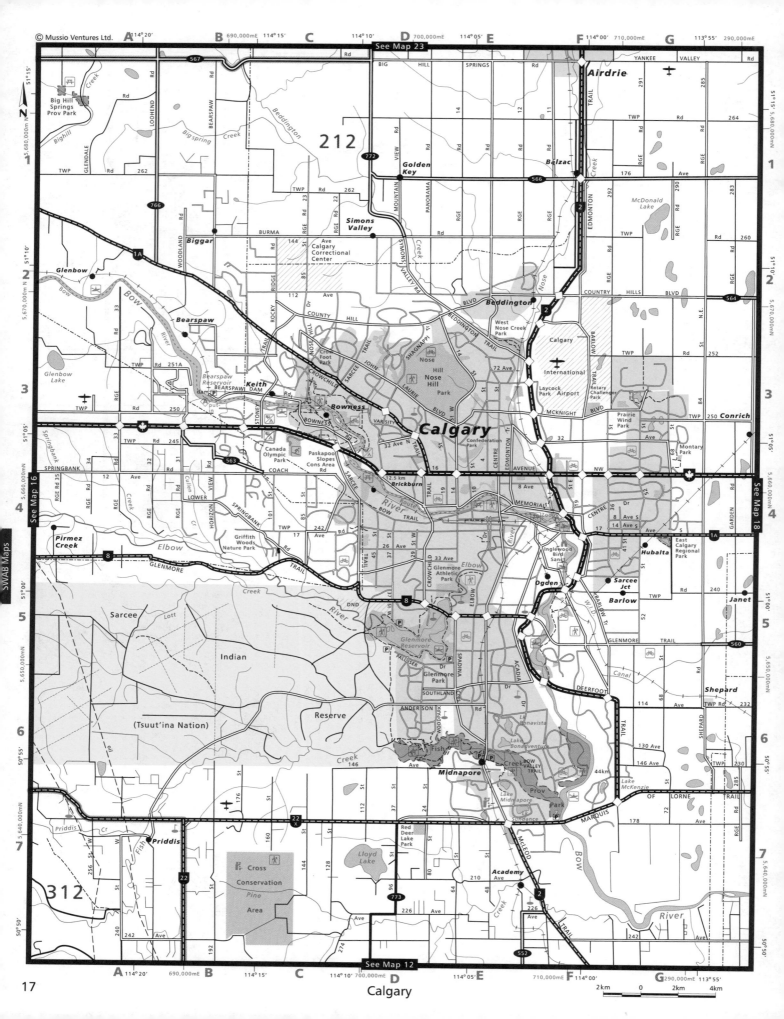

© Mussio Ventures Ltd.

See Map 23
See Map 16
See Map 18
See Map 12

SWAB Maps

Calgary

17

Top border coordinates: 300,000mE · 113°50' · A · 113°45' · B · 310,000mE · 113°40' · C · 320,000mE · D · 113°35' · E · 113°30' · F · 330,000mE · 113°25' · G

N

51°15'

Brush Lake

Gaylord

abandoned

railway

Long Lake

Twin Lakes

Kathryn · **Keoma**

270 · 264 · 261 · 254 · 252 · 245

566

51°10'

791

Delacour

Serviceberry

564

Dalroy

Nightingale

Ardenode

Creek
Dawson Lake

9

Lyalta

Bruce Lake

156

817

McElroy Slough

51°05'

INVERLAKE (TWP

Chestermere

Norfolk · **Inverlake**

CANADA

Caruso

Strathmore

SWAB Maps

1A

TRANS-

791

Willow

797

Cheadle

Eagle Lake

51°00'

GLENMORE

560

TRAIL

VALLEYVIEW

Weed Lake

Langdon

Carcass

DEADHORSE Rd

Bennett

24

Hill

Dalemead Lake

817

50°55'

Indus

901

Alkaline Lake

22X

212

Dalemead

Strangmuir

De Winton South Calgary

McKinnon Flats Wildlife Viewing

797

West Carseland

Carseland

Bow River

Wyndham-Carseland Prov Park

Bow

Willow Island

50°50'

242 Ave

Bow River

24

Bottom border coordinates: 300,000mE · 113°50' · A · 113°45' · B · 310,000mE · 113°40' · C · 320,000mE · D · 113°35' · E · 113°30' · F · 330,000mE · 113°25' · G

Strathmore

© Mussio Ventures Ltd.

BRITISH COLUMBIA

ALBERTA

Yoho National Park

Banff National Park

Kootenay National Park

Mistaya Mtn

Mt Baker 3172m
Peyto Peak 2970m
Peyto Hut
Peyto Glacier
Baker Glacier
Caldron Lake
Bow Summit Lookout Trail

Mt Jimmy Simpson
Mt Thompson 3084m
Portal Peak 2911m

Historic Num-Ti-Jah Lodge
Bow Lake
Bow Pass 2070m

Cirque Peak 2993m
Lake Helen
Dolomite Pass
Dolomite Peak 2782m

Devon Mtn 3004m
Dip Slope Mtn 3125m
Pipestone Pass

Ayesha Glacier
Ayesha Peak
Mt Collie
Wapta Icefield

Crowfoot Mtn 3050 m
Crowfoot Glacier
Bow Hut
Wapta Traverse

Helen Creek Trail

Mosquito Creek Campsite
Mosquito Lake
Mosquito Creek Trail

North Molar Pass
Fish Lakes Campsite
Upper Fish Lake
Lower Fish Lake
Deer Lake

Mont des Poilus 3161m
Amiskwi Lake
Amiskwi Falls

St Nicholas Peak 2970m
Mt Gordon 3153m
Mt Olive 3130m
Balfour Hut

Yoho Glacier
Yoho Peak
Diableret Falls
Fall of the Waves
Balfour Pass
Mt Balfour 3272m

Lilliput Mtn
Waputik Icefield

Bow Peak 2868m
Noseeum

Molar Pass
Molar Glacier
Molar Mtn 3022m
Molat Creek Campsite

Mt Hector 3394m
Hector Glacier

Molar Creek

Little Pipestone Cr Trail
Little Pipestove Cr
Lake Merlin
Lake Merlin Trail
Castilleja Lake

Mt McArthur 3015m
Kiwetinok Peak
Kiwetinok Lake
Little Yoho Valley Trail
Yoho Skyline Trail
Twin Falls
Marpole Lake
Laughing Falls
Fairy Lake
Lake Celeste
Lake Duchesnay

Mt Daly 3152m
Daly Glacier
Bath Glacier

Hector Lake Campsite
Lake Margaret
Turquoise Lake
Hector Lake
Hector Lake Trail

Pulpit Peak 2725m

Waputik Range

Pipestone River

Mt Richardson 3086m
Boulder Pass
Hidden Lake
Hidden Lake Campsite

The President
President Range

Takakkaw Falls
Takakkaw Falls Campsite

BRITISH COLUMBIA

Mt Carnarvon
Emerald Basin Trail
Hamilton Lake
Hamilton Lake Trail
Emerald Lake
Emerald Lake

Mt Ogden 2684m
Sherbrooke Lake Trail
Sherbrooke Lake
Paget Peak

Mt Bosworth 2771m
Kicking Horse Pass
Wapta Lake

Lost Lake Trail
Lost Lake
Missing Lake

put in
Herbert Lake
Mud Lake

Mt Whitehorn 2637m
Lake Louise Ski Area
Skoki Valley Trail
Temple Fire

Lipalian Mtn 2672m
Island Lake
Island Lake

Horse Trail
Burgesspass Trail
Wapta Mtn
Yoho River
Highline Trail

Kicking Horse Campsite
Mt Field 2638m
Mt Burgess

TRANS CANADA

Mt Stephen 3199m
Field
Tally Ho Trail

Park

Cathedral Mtn 3189m

Narao Lakes
Lake O'Hara
Ross Lake
Ross Lake

Lake Agnes
Plain of Six Glaciers
Chateau
Lake Louise

Lake Louise
put in
Fish Cr Parking Lot
chalet

Narao Peak
Mt Niblock 2976m
Mt Whyte 2982m

Fairview Mtn 2743m
Tramline Trail
Saddleback Trail

BOW VALLEY PARKWAY

Mt Dennis 2541m
Natural Bridge

Duchesnay Basin Trail
Cathedral Lakes
Vera Lake
Odaray Mtn
Morning Glory
Lake O'Hara Lodge & Campsite
Lake O'Hara

Abbot Pass Hut
Mt Victoria 3459m
Victoria Glacier

Mtn Aberdeen 3151m
The Mitre 2889m
Paradise Creek Campsite
Lake Annette
Paradise Valley Trail

Mt Duchesnay
Linda Lake
Lake Linda
Linda Lake Circuit
McArthur Pass
Lake McArthur
Lake McArthur

Lake Oesa
Hungabee Lake
Opabin Plateau Circuit
Opabin Lake

Mt Lefroy 3423m
Sentinel Pass
The
Horseshoe Glacier
Eiffel Lake Trail
Eiffel Lake

Mt Temple 2543m
Sentinel Pass Trail
Paradise Valley

Larch Valley Trail
Moraine Lake
Moraine Lake Rd
Valley of the Ten Peaks
Bow River Route

Mt Owen
Park Mtn

Mt Biddle
Pinnacle Mtn 3067m
Wenkchemna Pass
Deltaform Mtn 3424m

Mt Hurd
Ottertail
Float Creek Campsite

Misko Mtn
Misko Pass

Mt Allen 3301m
Mt Little 3088m
Mt Fay 3235m
Mt Quadra 3173m
Consolation Lakes
Taylor Lake
Taylor O'Brien Lake Campsite
Mt Bell 2922m

Mt Vaux
Hanbury Glacier
Fulmen Mtn
Ottertail Falls
Mt Oke

Misko

19

Lake Louise

See Kootenay Mapbook

SWAB Maps

See Map 20

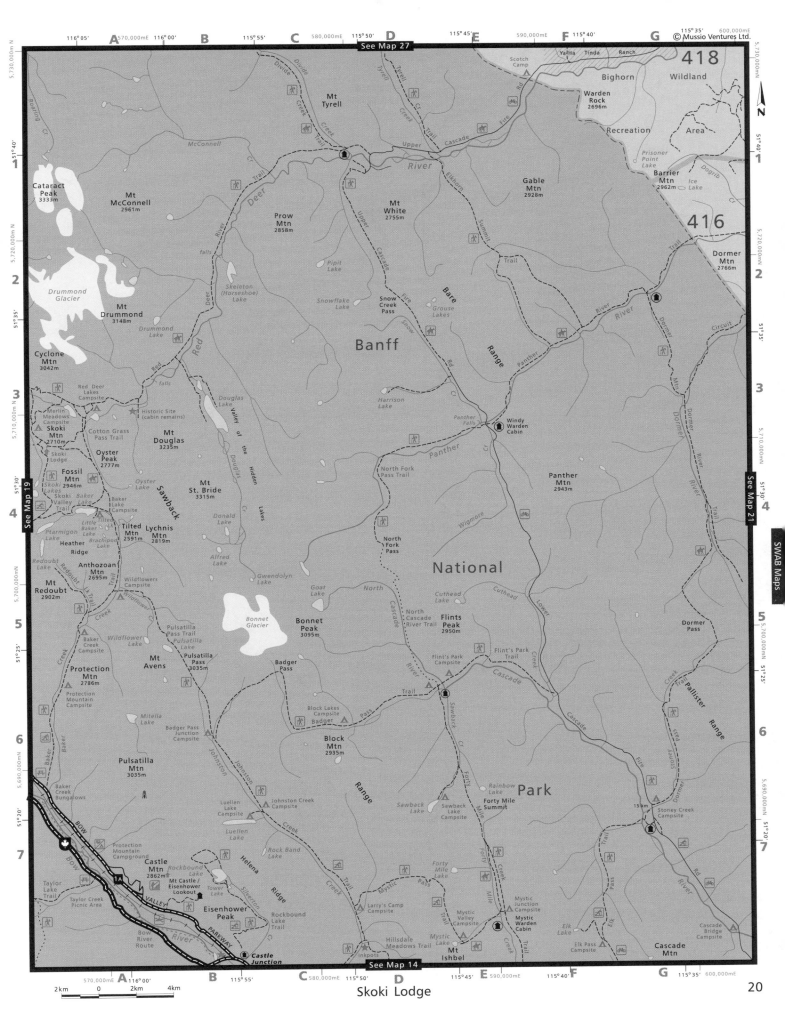

© Mussio Ventures Ltd.

N

418

Bighorn

Wildland

Warden
Rock
2696m

Recreation   Area

Prisoner
Point
Lake

Barrier
Mtn
2962m

Ice
Lake

Dogrib

416

Dormer
Mtn
2766m

Scotch
Camp

YaHa   Tinda   Ranch

Cataract
Peak
3333m

Mt
McConnell
2961m

McConnell

Roaring

Divide
Creek

Divide
Creek

Mt
Tyrell

Tyrell
Creek

Tyrell
Trail

Upper   Cascade   Trail

Elkhorn

Fire

Rd

River

Gable
Mtn
2928m

Mt
White
2755m

Prow
Mtn
2858m

Deer

River

River

falls

Pipit
Lake

Snowflake
Lake

Upper

Cascade

Summit

Trail

Bare

Range

Fire

Grouse
Lakes

Snow
Creek
Pass

Dormer

River

River

Drummond
Glacier

Mt
Drummond
3148m

Drummond
Lake

Red

Red

falls

Douglas
Lake

Valley

Skeleton
(Horseshoe)
Lake

Snow
Creek
Pass

Harrison
Lake

Snow

Rd

Panther

Cr

Dormer

River

Dormer

Mtn

Cyclone
Mtn
3042m

Red Deer
Lakes
Campsite

Merlin
Meadows
Campsite

Skoki
Mtn
2710m

Historic Site
(cabin remains)

Cotton Grass
Pass Trail

Mt
Douglas
3235m

of

the

Panther
Falls

Windy
Warden
Cabin

Panther
Mtn
2943m

Skoki
Lodge

Fossil
Mtn
2946m

Skoki
Lakes

Skoki
Valley
Trail

Baker
Lake
Campsite

Oyster
Peak
2777m

Oyster
Lake

Sawback

Mt
St. Bride
3315m

Douglas

Hidden

North Fork
Pass Trail

Panther

Little
Baker
Lake

Tilted
Mtn
2591m

Lychnis
Mtn
2819m

Donald
Lake

Lakes

Cr

North
Fork
Pass

National

Ptarmigon
Lake

Heather
Ridge

Anthozoan
Mtn
2695m

Alfred
Lake

Gwendolyn
Lake

Wigmore

Cuthead
Lake

Cuthead

Redoubt
Lake

Brachipod
Lake

Wildflowers
Campsite

Goat
Lake

North

North Cascade
River Trail

Flints
Peak
2950m

Dormer
Pass

Mt
Redoubt
2902m

Redoubt

Creek

Bonnet
Glacier

Bonnet
Peak
3095m

Cascade

Flint's Park
Campsite

Flint's Park
Trail

Lower

Cascade

Pallister

Range

Wildflower
Lake

Wildflower
Trail

Pulsatilla
Pass Trail

Pulsatilla
Lake

Pulsatilla
Pass
3035m

Badger
Pass

River

North Cascade
River Trail

Cuthead

Dormer
Pass

Baker
Creek
Campsite

Mt
Avens

Protection
Mtn
2786m

Mitella
Lake

Badger Pass
Junction Campsite

Block Lakes
Campsite

Badger

Sawback

Pass

Trail

Stoney

Creek

Creek

Baker

Baker

Pulsatilla
Mtn
3035m

Block
Mtn
2935m

Range

Rainbow
Lake

Park

Dormer

Johnston

Creek

Forty Mile

Sawback
Lake

Forty Mile
Summit

15 km

Stoney Creek
Campsite

Baker Creek
Bungalows

Protection
Mountain
Campground

Luellen Lake
Campsite

Johnston Creek
Campsite

Johnston

Creek

Rock Band
Lake

Sawback
Lake

Sawback
Campsite

Cascade

Fife

Taylor
Lake
Trail

1A

Castle
Mtn
2862m

Rockbound
Lake

Helena

Ridge

Silverton

Luellen
Lake

Tower
Lake

Mt Castle /
Eisenhower
Lookout

Mystic
Pass

Forty
Mile
Lake

Larry's Camp
Campsite

Forty
Mile

Mystic
Junction
Campsite

Mystic
Warden
Cabin

Elk
Pass

Cascade
Bridge
Campsite

Taylor Creek
Picnic Area

Protection
Mountain
Campground

Bow
River
Route

Eisenhower
Peak

Rockbound
Lake Trail

VALLEY

PARKWAY

Bow

River

Creek

Trail

Mystic

Mystic
Valley
Campsite

Mt
Ishbel

Elk

Pass

Trail

Elk
Lake

Elk Pass
Campsite

Cascade
Mtn

Castle
Junction

Hillsdale
Meadows Trail

SWAB Maps

2km   0   2km   4km

Skoki Lodge

20

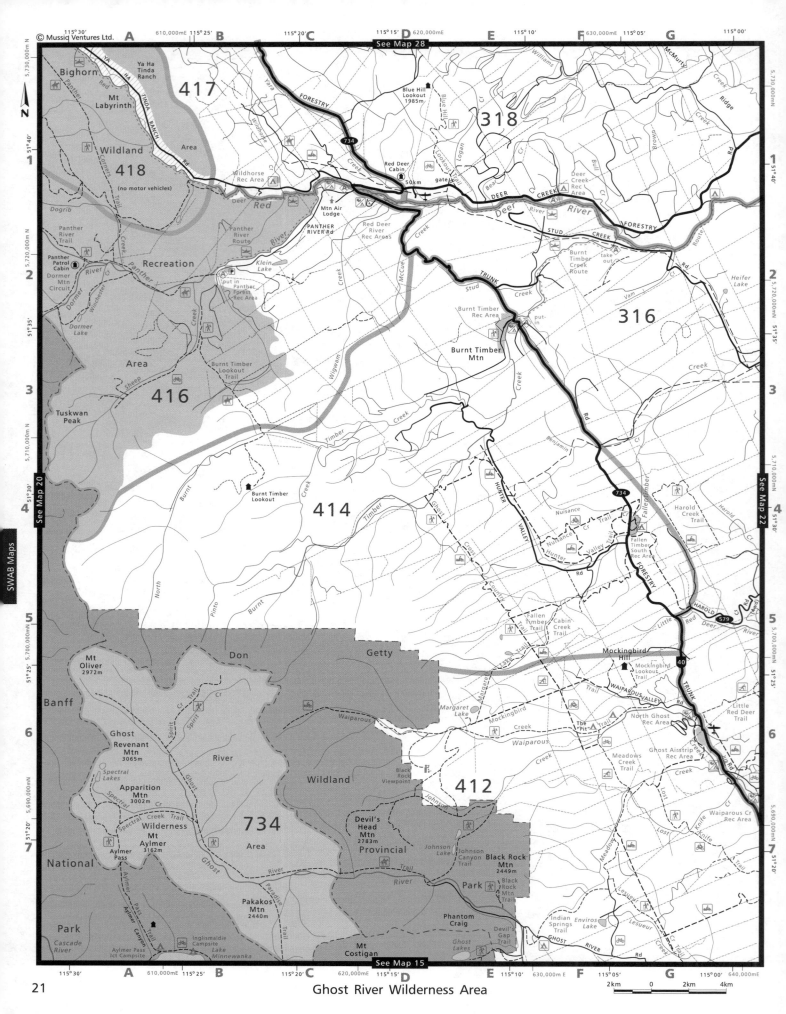

Ghost River Wilderness Area

© Mussio Ventures Ltd.

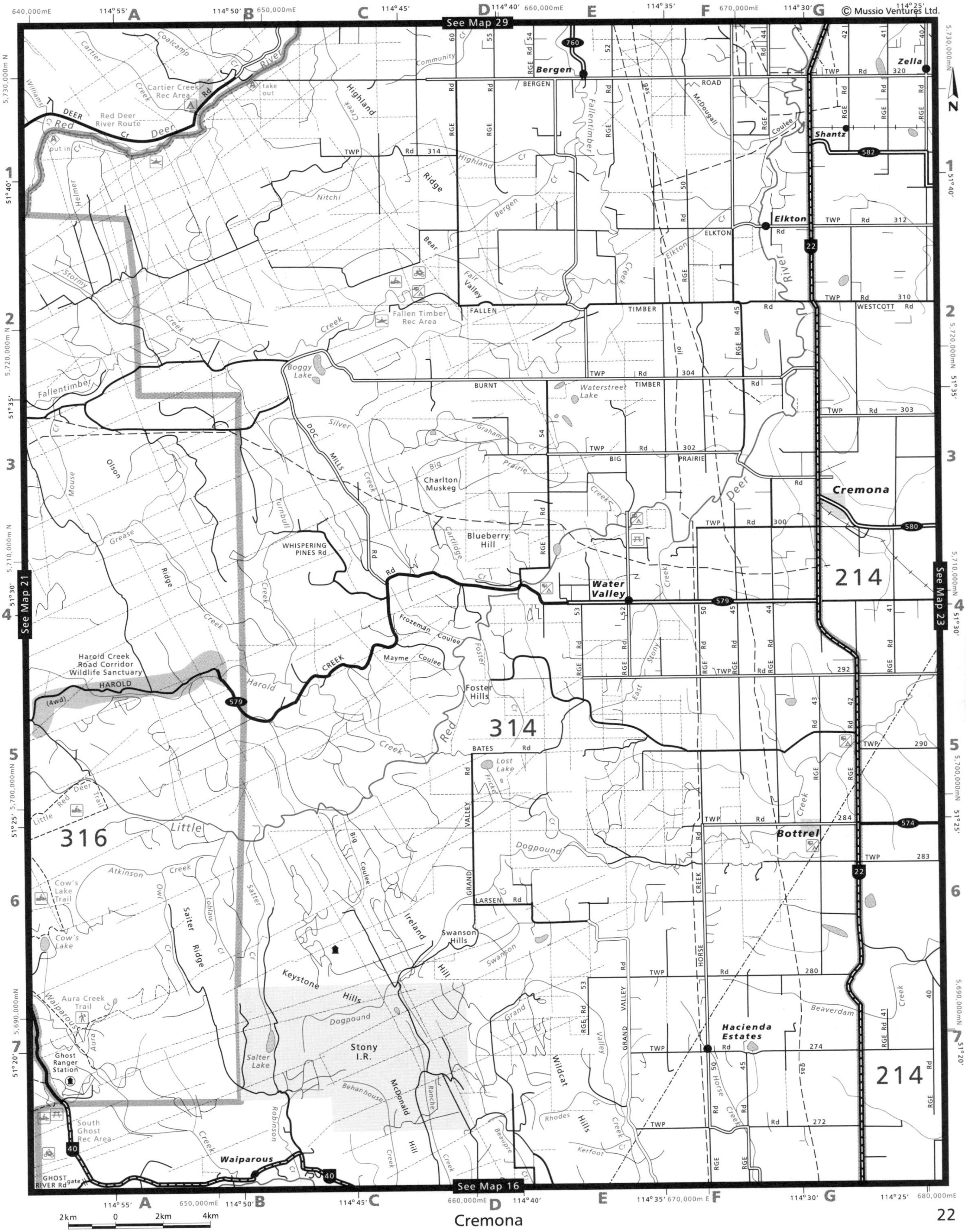

SWAB Maps

640,000mE 114°55' 114°50' 650,000mE 114°45' 114°40' 660,000mE 114°35' 670,000mE 114°30' 114°25' 680,000mE

5,730,000mN

Coalcamp Rd

Cartier Creek Rec Area

Red Deer River Route

Cartier Cr

Deer

Red Deer River

take out

put in

Williams Cr

Helmer Cr

Community Rd

Bergen

BERGEN

Zella 320

Shantz

ROAD

McDougall

582

Highland Creek

Ridge

Nitchi

Highland Cr

Bergen Cr

Fallentimber Creek

Elkton

ELKTON

TWP Rd 312

22

River

Stormy Creek

Bear Cr

Fair Valley

Fall Valley Cr

Fallen Timber Rec Area

FALLEN

Creek

Fallentimber

Creek

Mouse Cr

Olson Cr

Grease Creek

Ridge Creek

Turnbull Creek

Silver Creek

DOC MILLS Creek

Boggy Lake

WHISPERING PINES Rd.

Charlton Muskeg

Cartridge Cr

Blueberry Hill

BURNT

TIMBER

Graham Cr

Waterstreet Lake

Big Prairie Creek

TIMBER

BIG PRAIRIE

Cremona

580

214

WESTCOTT

TWP Rd 310

TWP Rd 304

TWP Rd 303

TWP Rd 302

TWP Rd 300

Water Valley

579

316

Harold Creek Road Corridor Wildlife Sanctuary

HAROLD (4wd)

Harold Creek

579

CREEK

Frozeman Coulee

Mayme Coulee

Foster Creek

Foster Hills

314

Red Creek

Little Red Deer Trail

Little Deer Creek

Atkinson Creek

Cow's Lake Trail

Cow's Lake

Salter Ridge

Loblaw Cr

Salter Cr

Big Coulee Cr

Keystone Hills

Salter Lake

Ireland Hill

BATES Rd

Lost Lake

Cr

Valley Rd

GRAND

LARSEN Rd

Dogpound Creek

Swanson Hills

Swanson

Dogpound

Stony I.R.

Behanhouse Cr

Robinson Creek

McDonald Hill

Ranche Cr

Beaupre Creek

Wildcat Hills

Grand Valley Cr

Rhodes Hills

Kerfoot Creek

East Stony Creek

HORSE CREEK

GRAND VALLEY Rd

Bottrel

574

22

Hacienda Estates

214

Beaverdam Creek

Ghost Ranger Station

South Ghost Rec Area

40

GHOST RIVER Rd gate

Aura Creek Trail

Waiparous Creek

Aura Cr

Waiparous

40

2km 0 2km 4km

Cremona

22

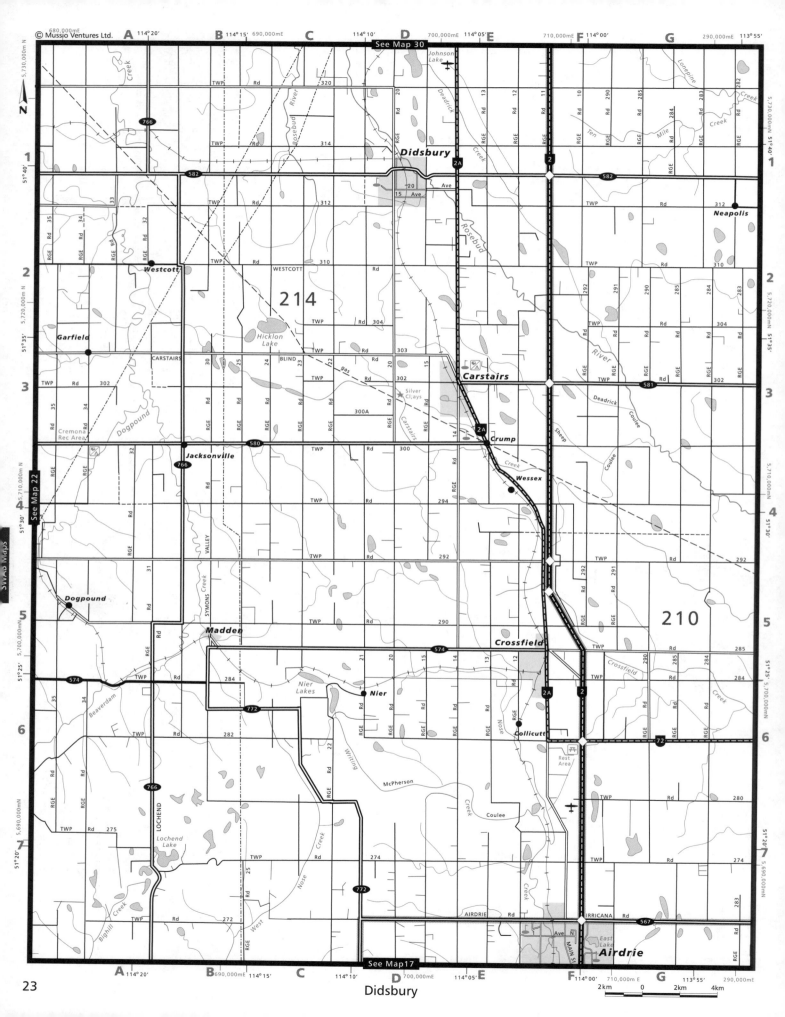

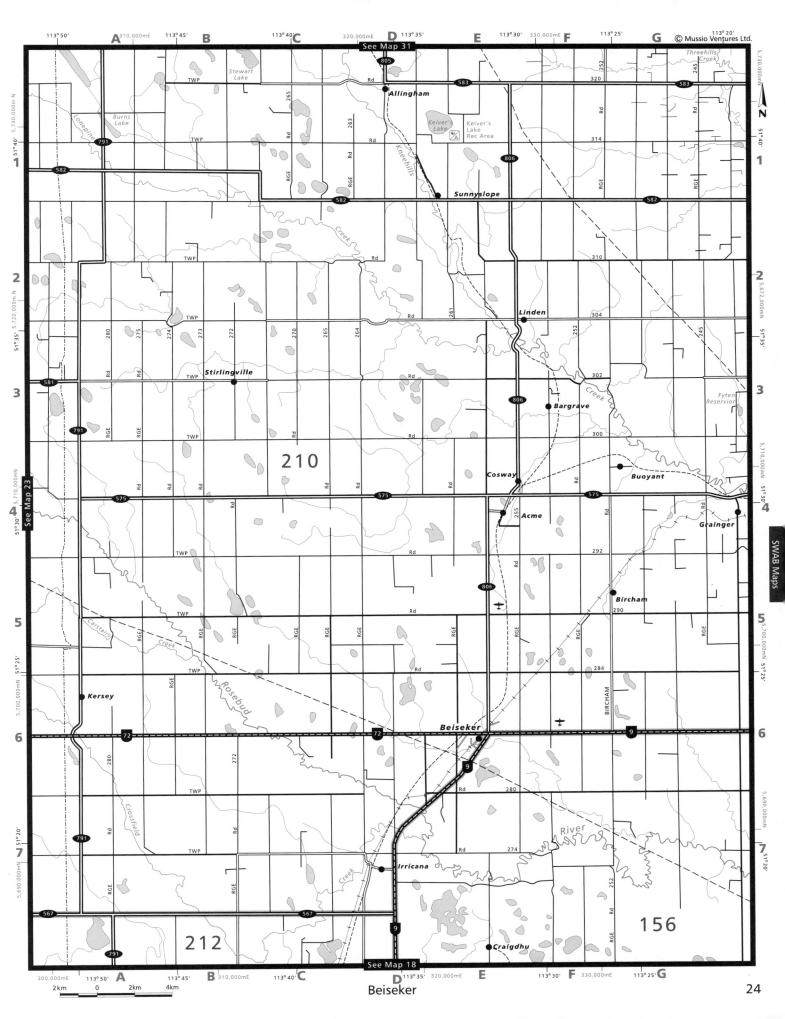

© Mussio Ventures Ltd.

See Map 23

210

212

156

See Map 18
Beiseker

24

2km 0 2km 4km

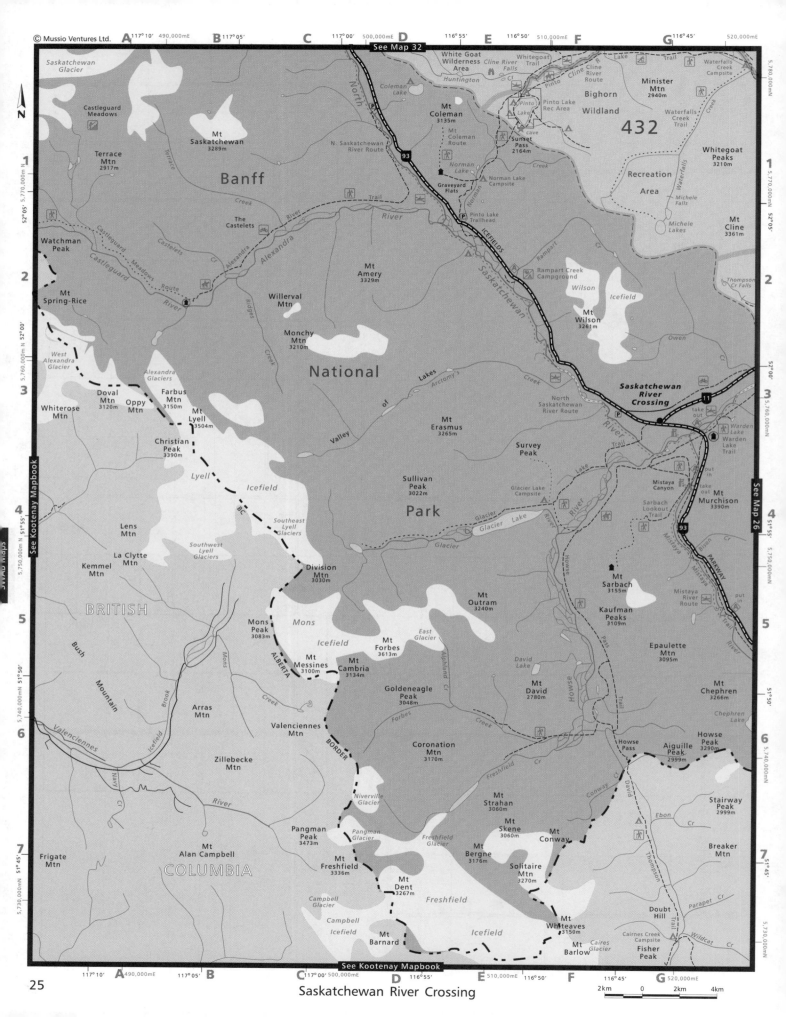

A 117°10' 490,000mE   B 117°05'   C 117°00' 500,000mE D   116°55' E   116°50' F 510,000mE   G 116°45'   520,000mE

See Map 32

Saskatchewan Glacier

Castleguard Meadows

Terrace Mtn 2917m

Mt Saskatchewan 3289m

Banff

White Goat Wilderness Area

Cline River Falls

Whitegoat Trail

Coleman Lake

Mt Coleman 3135m

Mt Coleman Route

Huntington

Pinto Lake Rec Area

cave

Bighorn Wildland

Minister Mtn 2940m

Waterfalls Creek Campsite

432

Watchman Peak

Mt Spring-Rice

The Castelets

Castleguard Creek

Alexandra River

N. Saskatchewan River Route

93

Sunset Pass 2164m

Norman Lake

Norman Lake Campsite

Graveyard Flats

Recreation Area

Whitegoat Peaks 3210m

Michele Falls

Michele Lakes

Mt Cline 3361m

Whiterose Mtn

Doval Mtn 3120m

Oppy Mtn

Farbus Mtn 3150m

Mt Lyell 3504m

Willerval Mtn

Mt Amery 3329m

Monchy Mtn 3210m

Pinto Lake Trailhead

ICEFIELDS

Saskatchewan

Rampart

Rampart Creek Campground

Mt Wilson 3261m

Wilson Icefield

Thompson Cr Falls

National

Lakes

Arctomy's Creek

North Saskatchewan River Route

Saskatchewan River Crossing

11

take out

Christian Peak 3390m

Lyell Icefield

BC

Southeast Lyell Glaciers

Southwest Lyell Glaciers

Alexandra Glaciers

Castelets Ridges

Castleguard Meadows Route

West Alexandra Glacier

Valley of

Mt Erasmus 3265m

Survey Peak

Sullivan Peak 3022m

Park

Glacier Lake Campsite

Glacier Lake

Mistaya Canyon

Sarbach Lookout Trail

Warden Lake

Warden Lake Trail

Mt Murchison 3390m

93

Lens Mtn

La Clytte Mtn

Kemmel Mtn

BRITISH

Bush Mountain

Division Mtn 3030m

Mons Peak 3083m

Mons Icefield

ALBERTA

Mt Messines 3100m

Mt Cambria 3134m

Mt Forbes 3613m

East Glacier

Mt Outram 3240m

Highland Cr

David Lake

Mt David 2780m

Mt Sarbach 3155m

Kaufman Peaks 3109m

Epaulette Mtn 3095m

Mt Chephren 3266m

put in

Mistaya River Route

take out

PARKWAY

BISON

Arras Mtn

Zillebecke Mtn

Mons Brook

BORDER

Valenciennes Mtn

Goldeneagle Peak 3048m

Coronation Mtn 3170m

Forbes Creek

Howse Pass

Howse Pass

Howse River

Aiguille Peak 2999m

Howse Peak 3290m

Chephren Lake

Valenciennes River

Navy Creek

Icefield Brook

Frigate Mtn

Mt Alan Campbell

COLUMBIA

Pangman Peak 3473m

Niverville Glacier

Pangman Glacier

Mt Freshfield 3336m

Freshfield Cr

Freshfield Glacier

Mt Strahan 3060m

Mt Skene 3060m

Mt Bergne 3176m

Mt Conway

Solitaire Mtn 3270m

Conway Cr

Stairway Peak 2999m

Ebon Cr

Breaker Mtn

David Thompson Trail

Mt Dent 3267m

Mt Barnard

Campbell Glacier

Campbell Icefield

Freshfield

Mt Whiteaves 3150m

Freshfield Icefield

Mt Barlow

Caires Glacier

Doubt Hill

Cairnes Creek Campsite

Fisher Peak

Parapet Cr

Wildcat Cr

See Map 32
See Map 26
See Kootenay Mapbook

A 490,000mE   B 117°05'   C 117°00' 500,000mE   D 116°55'   E 510,000mE   F 116°50'   G 116°45'   520,000mE

Saskatchewan River Crossing

2km   0   2km   4km

52°05'N   5,770,000mN   52°05'   52°00'   5,760,000mN   51°55'   5,750,000mN   51°50'   5,740,000mN   51°45'   5,730,000mN

See Kootenay Mapbook

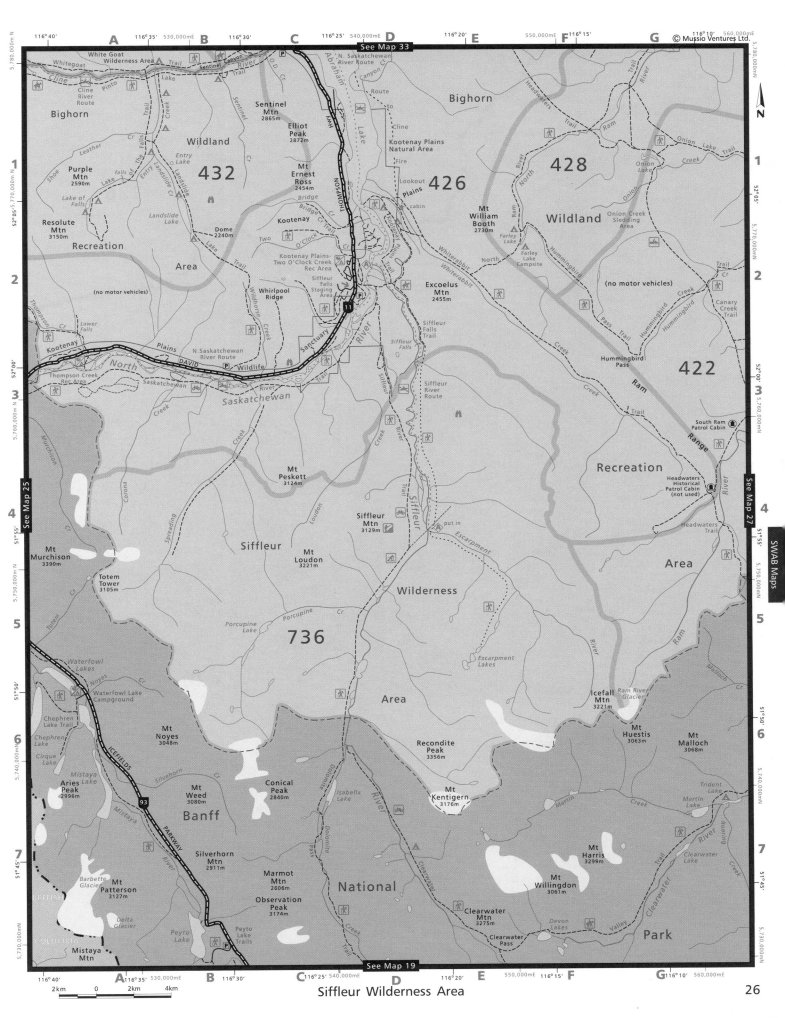

© Mussio Ventures Ltd.

N

SWAB Maps

See Map 25

See Map 27

White Goat Wilderness Area

Bighorn

Wildland

432

Bighorn

428

Wildland

426

422

Recreation

Area

(no motor vehicles)

(no motor vehicles)

Recreation

Area

Siffleur

Wilderness

736

Area

Banff

National

Park

BRITISH
COLUMBIA

Purple
Mtn
2590m

Resolute
Mtn
3150m

Sentinel
Mtn
2865m

Elliot
Peak
2872m

Mt
Ernest
Ross
2454m

Dome
2240m

Kootenay

Whirlpool
Ridge

Kootenay Plains-
Two O'Clock Creek
Rec Area

Kootenay Plains
Natural Area

Mt
William
Booth
2730m

Excoelus
Mtn
2455m

Siffleur
Falls

Siffleur Falls
Staging
Area

Hummingbird
Pass

South Ram
Patrol Cabin

Mt Murchison
3390m

Totem
Tower
3105m

Mt Peskett
3124m

Siffleur
Mtn
3129m

Mt
Loudon
3221m

Headwaters
Historical
Patrol Cabin
(not used)

Headwaters
Trail

Icefall
Mtn
3221m

Ram River
Glacier

Mt
Huestis
3063m

Mt
Malloch
3068m

Waterfowl
Lakes

Waterfowl Lake
Campground

Chephren
Lake Trail

Chephren
Lake

Cirque
Lake

Mistaya
Lake

Aries
Peak
2996m

Mt
Noyes
3048m

Mt
Weed
3080m

Conical
Peak
2840m

Recondite
Peak
3356m

Mt
Kentigern
3176m

Trident
Lakes

Mt
Harris
3299m

Mt
Willingdon
3061m

Martin
Lake

Mt
Patterson
3127m

Barbette
Glacier

Silverhorn
Mtn
2911m

Marmot
Mtn
2606m

Observation
Peak
3174m

Clearwater
Mtn
3275m

Clearwater
Pass

Devon
Lakes

Clearwater
Lake

Mistaya
Mtn

Delta
Glacier

Peyto
Lake

Peyto Lake
Trails

Escarpment
Lakes

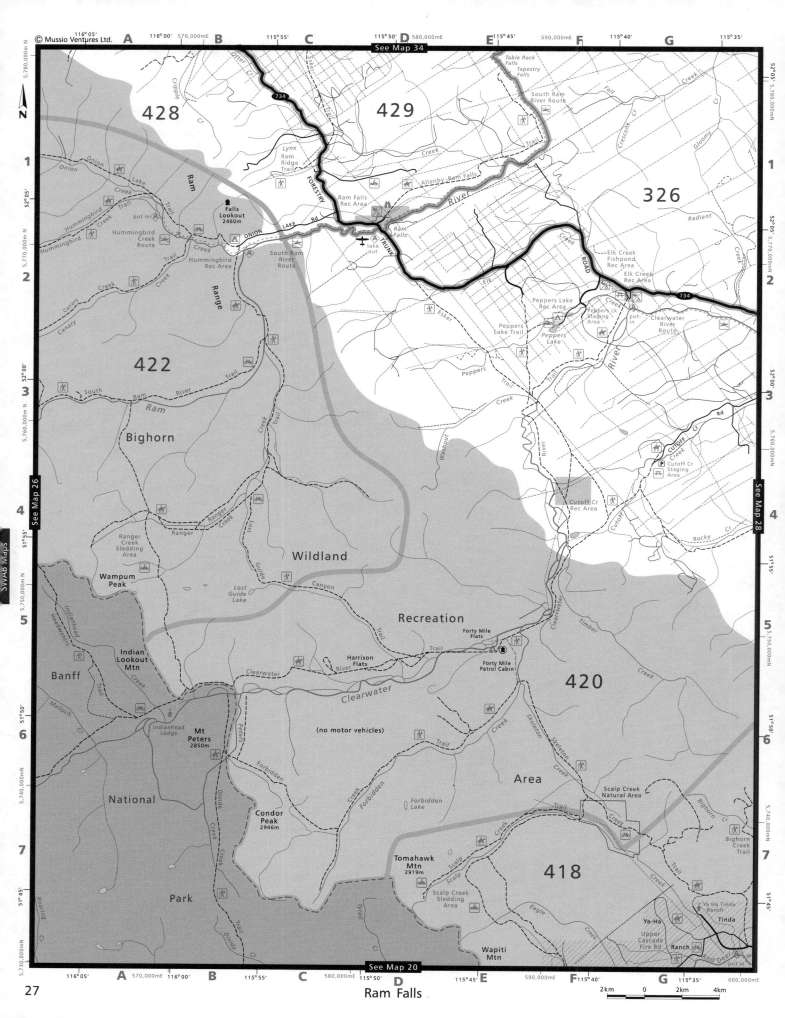

N

116° 05'   116° 00'   570,000mE   115° 55'   115° 50'   580,000mE   115° 45'   590,000mE   115° 40'   115° 35'

A   B   C   D   E   F   G

428

429

326

Otter Cr

Cripple Cr

Onion Lake Trail

Onion Creek

Hummingbird Creek Route

Hummingbird Creek Trail

Hummingbird Rec Area

Canary Creek

Canary Creek

Lynx Ram Ridge Trail

FORESTRY

LAKE Rd

ONION

Falls Lookout 2460m

put in

South Ram River Route

Ram Falls Rec Area

Ràm Falls

take out

TRUNK

Allenby Ram Falls

River

Ram

Table Rock Falls

Tapestry Falls

South Ram River Route

Crescent Cr

Fall Creek

Gloomy Creek

Radiant

ROAD

734

Elk Creek Fishpond Rec Area

Elk Creek Rec Area

Peppers Lake Rec Area

Peppers Lake Trail

Peppers Lake

Peppers Lk Staging Area

put in

Clearwater River Route

Esker Trail

Peppers Creek

Washout

Elk Creek

422

326

Ram Range

Bighorn

South Ram River Trail

Ranger Creek Sledding Area

Ranger Creek

Ranger

Lost Guide Lake

Wampum Peak

Lost Guide Trail

Canyon

Wildland

Peppers Creek Trail

Clearwater River

CUTOFF Cr Rd

Cutoff Creek

Cutoff Cr Staging Area

Cutoff Cr Rec Area

Cutoff

Rocky Cr

Indianhead Headwaters

Indian Lookout Mtn

Banff

Indianhead Lodge

Indianhead Creek

Malloch Cr

National

Mt Peters 2850m

Peters Creek

Forbidden Creek

Recreation

Harrison Flats

Clearwater River

Clearwater

(no motor vehicles)

Forbidden Lake

Forty Mile Flats

Forty Mile Patrol Cabin

Clearwater River

Clearwater Creek

Skeleton Creek

Timber Creek

420

Area

Scalp Creek Natural Area

Bighorn Cr

Bighorn Creek Trail

Park

Condor Peak 2946m

Divide Creek Trail

Tyrell Creek

Tomahawk Mtn 2919m

Scalp Creek

Scalp Creek Sledding Area

Scalp Creek

Eagle Creek

418

Wapiti Mtn

Ya-Ha

Upper Cascade Fire Rd

Ranch

Ya-Ha Tinda Ranch

Tinda

Red Deer River

put in

Roaring Cr

1   2   3   4   5   6   7

5,780,000mN   5,770,000mN   5,760,000mN   5,750,000mN   5,740,000mN   5,730,000mN

52° 05'   52° 00'   51° 55'   51° 50'   51° 45'

See Map 34

See Map 26

See Map 28

See Map 20

SWAB Maps

27   Ram Falls

116° 05'   116° 00'   570,000mE   115° 55'   115° 50'   580,000mE   115° 45'   590,000mE   115° 40'   115° 35'   600,000mE

2km   0   2km   4km

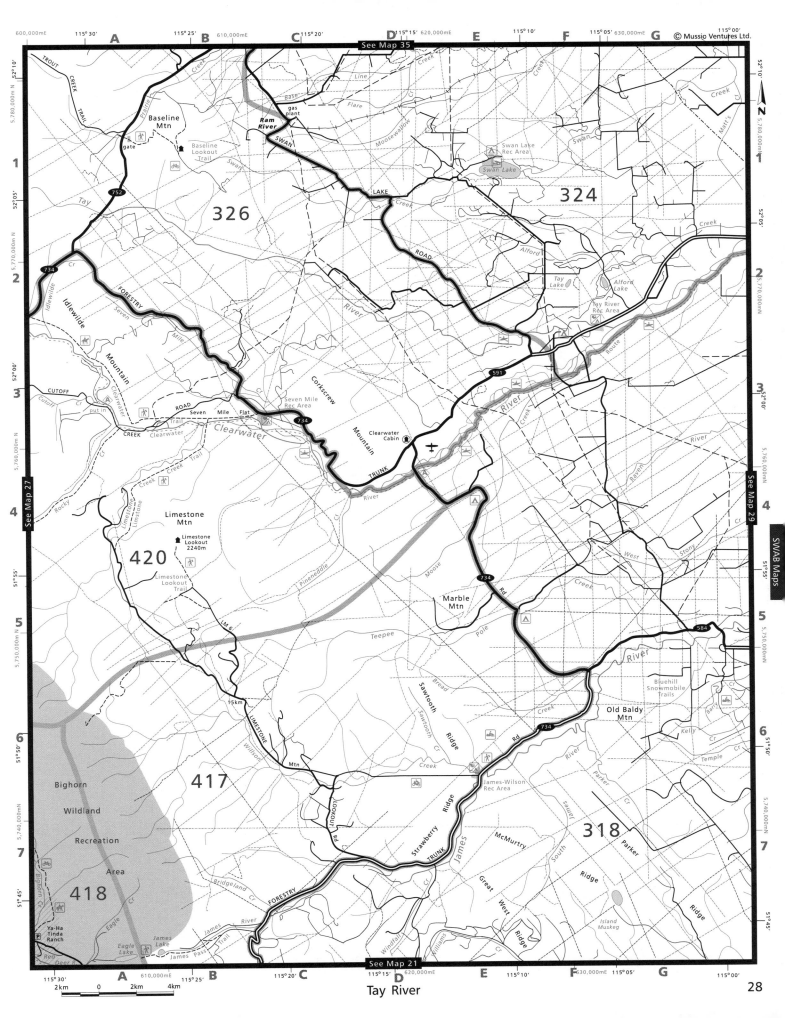

See Map 35

326

324

420

417

418

318

See Map 27

See Map 29

See Map 21

Tay River

28

© Mussio Ventures Ltd.

A · 114° 55' · 640,000mE
B · 114° 50' · 650,000E
C · 114° 45'
D · 114° 40' · 660,000mE
E
F · 114° 35' · 670,000mE
G · 114° 30'
114° 25'

52° 10'

Prairie Creek

Chedderville
Chedderville Natural Area

Stauffer
TWP Rd · 372
43
761

5,780,000m N

COPPERHEAD Rd

324

322

Hale Lake

1

Raven River

North

TWP Rd · 370
45

TWP Rd · 364

52° 05'

Phyllis Lake Rec Area

Alford
Ricinus · 591

take out

Caroline

Clearwater Rincinus Natural Area

54

Raven

Raven Rec Area

Clearwater River Route

Clearwater

Raven

River

2

MARSHMELLOW Rd

318

BURNSTICK LAKE Rd

Beaver

Crammond
TWP Rd · 354

River

TWP Rd · 360

320

Kevisville

52° 00'

Hurchimen Trail

Birch Lake

Beaver Lake

5,770,000m N

Summer Village of Burnstick Lake

Burnstick Lake

Stony Cr

Lower

East

Stony

Crooked Creek

Creek

TWP Rd · 352

3

Butcher Creek Natural Area

Stony Creek

Teksep Cr

TWP Rd · 350

Schrader

Creek

4

See Map 28

West

James River Bridge
James River Bridge Rec Area
587

gas plant

River

51° 55'

Garrington

See Map 30

James

TWP Rd · 342

River

5,750,000m N

Bearberry Nordic Centre

Barry

RGE Rd · 74

RGE Rd · 73

Bearberry

James River

Deer

22 · TWP Rd · 340

Snake's Head Natural Area

Eagle Hill

216

5

Kelly Cr

Temple

584

RGE Rd

RGE Rd · 70

BEARBERRY Rd

320

Jackson

Creek
TWP Rd · 334

Snake Hill Trails

Mound

6

51° 50'

Schott's Lake

Hill Twelve
Bentz Lake Natural Area

Walton

Bentz Lake

Sawmill Hill · dam

Creek

TWP Rd · 332

Sundre North Natural Area

McDougall Flats

TWP Rd · 330 · 584

Sundre

Sundre Red Deer Nat Area

Red

27

Deer River

Westward Ho

7

5,740,000m N

Stafne

Ridge

Smith

Bearberry

Prairie

Bearberry Prarie Natural Area

TWP Rd · 324

Red

Sundre Prov Natural Area

Fallentimber Cr

760

Mound

Harmattan

TWP Rd · 324

214

318

314

Coalcamp Cr

Community Rd · 322

TWP Rd · 322

51° 45'

A · 114° 55' · 640,000mE
B · 114° 50' · 650,000mE
C · 114° 45'
D · 114° 40' · 660,000mE
E
F · 114° 35' · 670,000mE
G · 114° 30'
114° 25'

29

Sundre

2km · 0 · 2km · 4km

SWAB Maps

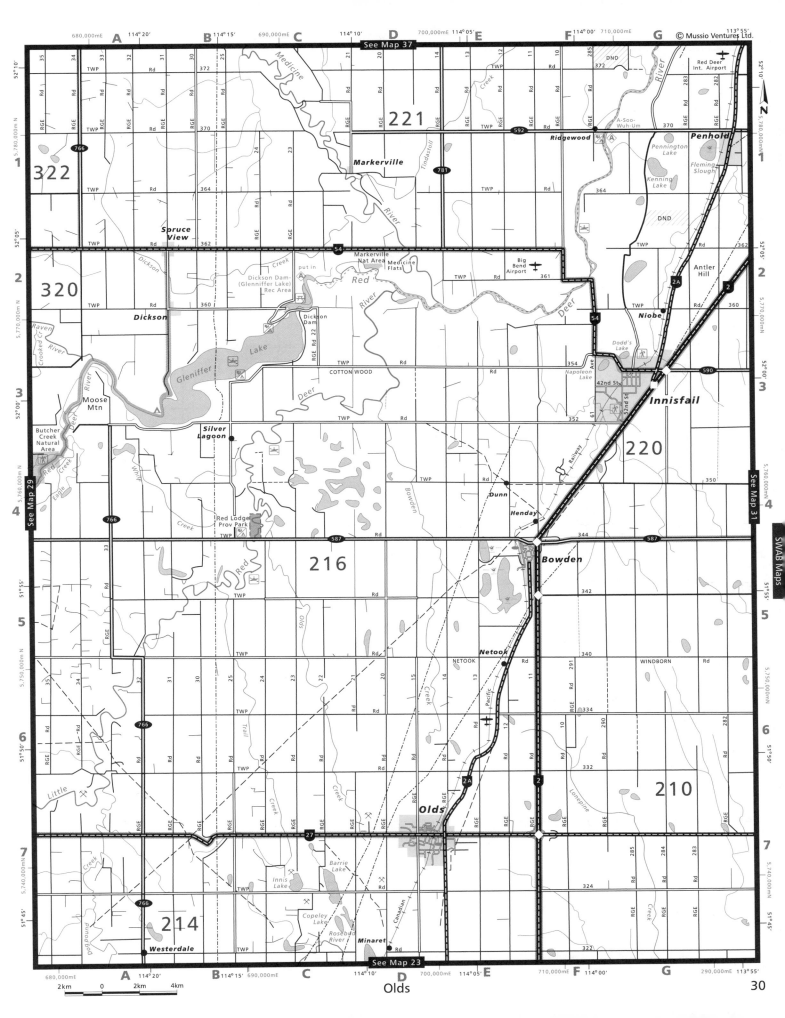

© Mussio Ventures Ltd.

Red Deer
Int. Airport

Penhold

N

221

322

320

Markerville

Spruce
View

Dickson Dam-
(Gleniffer Lake)
Rec Area

Markerville
Nat Area

Medicine
Flats

Red

Deer

Big Bend
Airport

Ridgewood

A-Soo-
Wuh-Um

Pennington
Lake

Fleming
Slough

Kenning
Lake

Antler
Hill

Dickson

Dickson
Dam

Gleniffer
Lake

put in

COTTON WOOD

Niobe

Dodd's
Lake

Napoleon
Lake

Innisfail

Moose
Mtn

Butcher
Creek
Natural
Area

Silver
Lagoon

Deer

220

Red Lodge
Prov Park

216

Dunn

Henday

Bowden

Netook

NETOOK

WINDBORN

210

Little

Olds

Innis
Lake

Barrie
Lake

Copeley
Lake

Rosebud
River

Minaret

214

Westerdale

See Map 29

See Map 31

SWAB Maps

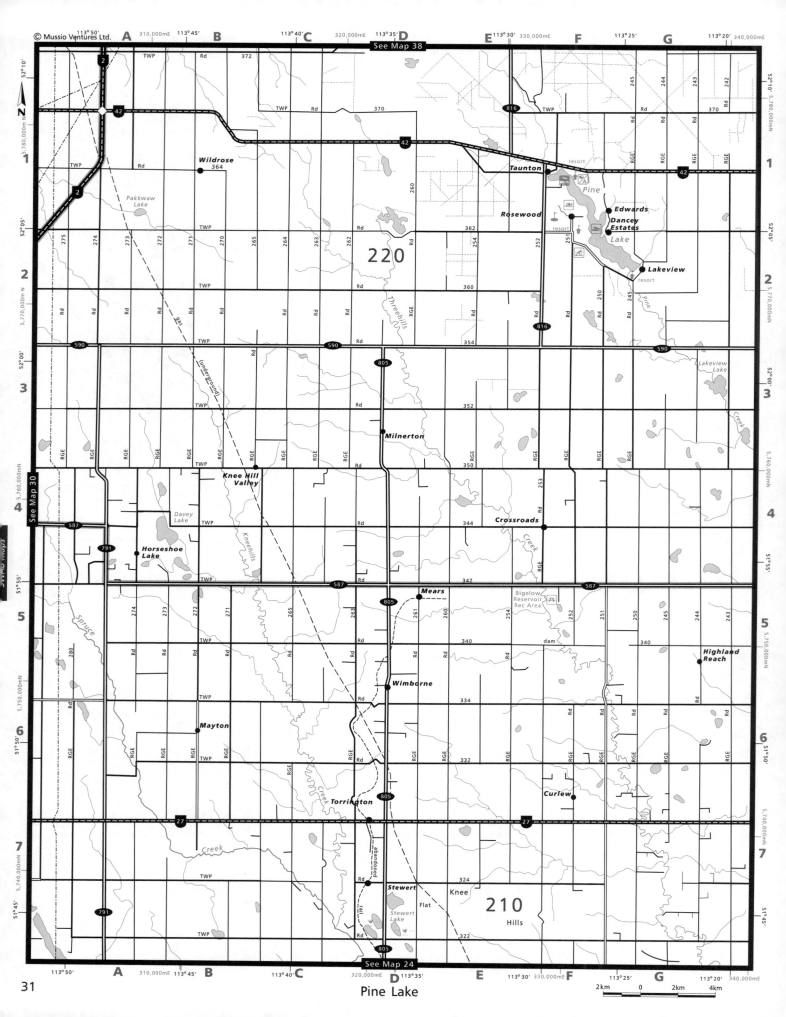

See Map 38

See Map 30

See Map 24

Wildrose
364

Pakkwaw Lake

220

Taunton

Pine

Rosewood

Edwards

Dancey Estates

Lake

Lakeview

resort

resort

Threehills

Milnerton

Lakeview Lake

Knee Hill Valley

Davey Lake

Crossroads

Kneehills

Horseshoe Lake

Spruce

Mears

Bigelow Reservoir Rec Area

dam

Highland Reach

Wimborne

Mayton

Curlew

Torrington

Creek

Stewert

Stewert Lake

abandoned rail

Knee Flat

210

Hills

31

Pine Lake

2km   0   2km   4km

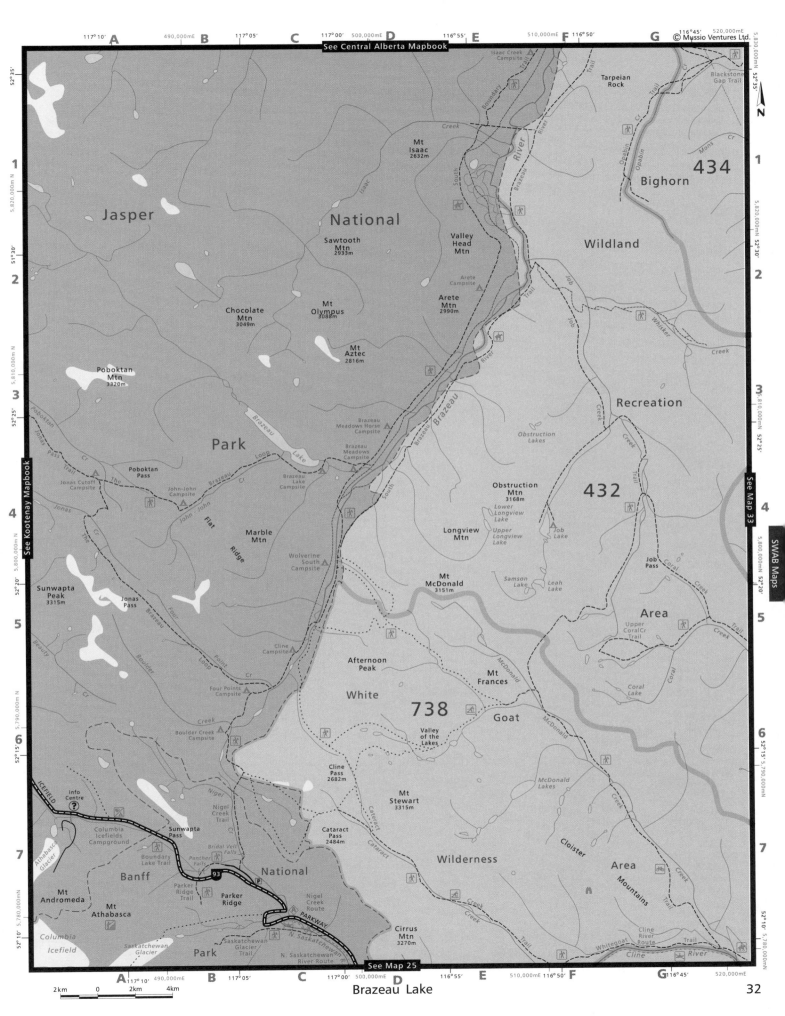

© Mussio Ventures Ltd.

N

117° 10' A 490,000mE B 117° 05' C 117° 00' 500,000mE D 116° 55' E 510,000mE F 116° 50' G 116° 45' 520,000mE

5,830,000mN
52°35'

1

5,820,000m N
52°30'

2

5,810,000m N
52°25'

3

5,800,000m N
52°20'

4

5,790,000m N
52°15'

5

5,780,000mN
52°10'

6

7

Jasper

National

Park

Mt Isaac
2632m

Sawtooth
Mtn
2933m

Valley
Head
Mtn

Chocolate
Mtn
3049m

Mt
Olympus
3088m

Arete
Campsite

Arete
Mtn
2990m

Mt
Aztec
2816m

Poboktan
Mtn
3320m

Brazeau
Lake

Isaac Creek
Campsite

Tarpeian
Rock

Blackstone
Gap Trail

Bighorn

434

Wildland

Mons Cr

Opabin Cr

Whisker Creek

Job Trail

Job River

Recreation

432

Obstruction
Lakes

Obstruction
Mtn
3168m

Lower
Longview
Lake

Longview
Mtn

Upper
Longview
Lake

Job
Lake

Coral Creek Trail

Job
Pass

Area

Upper
CoralCr
Trail

Coral Creek

Brazeau Meadows Horse Campsite

Brazeau
Meadows
Campsite

Poboktan
Pass

Jonas Cutoff
Campsite

John-John
Campsite

Jonas
Pass Trail

The

Jonas

The

Poboktan Cr

Brazeau
Loop

Cr

Flat

Ridge

John John

Marble
Mtn

Wolverine
South
Campsite

Brazeau Lake
Campsite

South

Brazeau

Brazeau

River

Creek

Samson
Lake

Leah
Lake

Coral
Lake

Sunwapta
Peak
3315m

Jonas Pass

Four
Point
Loop

Boulder

Cline
Campsite

Mt
McDonald
3151m

Mt
Frances

Area

Four Points
Campsite

Creek

Boulder Creek
Campsite

Afternoon
Peak

White

738

Valley of
the Lakes

Goat

Mt
McDonald

McDonald Creek

McDonald
Lakes

Coral

Cloister

Beauty

Nigel

Cline
Pass
2682m

Mt
Stewart
3315m

Wilderness

Area

Mountains

Info Centre
(?)

Columbia Icefields
Campground

Sunwapta
Pass

Nigel Creek
Trail

Bridal Veil
Falls

Panther
Falls

Boundary Lake Trail

93

Parker Ridge
Trail

Parker
Ridge

Nigel Creek
Route

Cataract
Pass
2484m

Cataract

Cataract

Creek

Cline
River
Route

ICEFIELD

Mt
Andromeda

Athabasca
Glacier

Mt
Athabasca

Banff

National

Park

PARKWAY

Saskatchewan
Glacier

Saskatchewan Glacier
Trail

N. Saskatchewan
River Route

N. Saskatchewan
River Route

Cirrus
Mtn
3270m

Cline

Creek

Trail

Whitegoat

Cline
River
Route

Cline River

Columbia
Icefield

Brazeau Lake

1

2

3

4

5

6

7

52°35'

52°30'

52°25'

52°20'

5,810,000mN

52°15' 5,790,000mN

52°10' 5,780,000mN

See Kootenay Mapbook

See Map 33

SWAB Maps

117° 10' 490,000mE A 117° 05' B 117° 00' C 500,000mE D 116° 55' E 510,000mE F 116° 50' G 116° 45' 520,000mE

2km 0 2km 4km

32

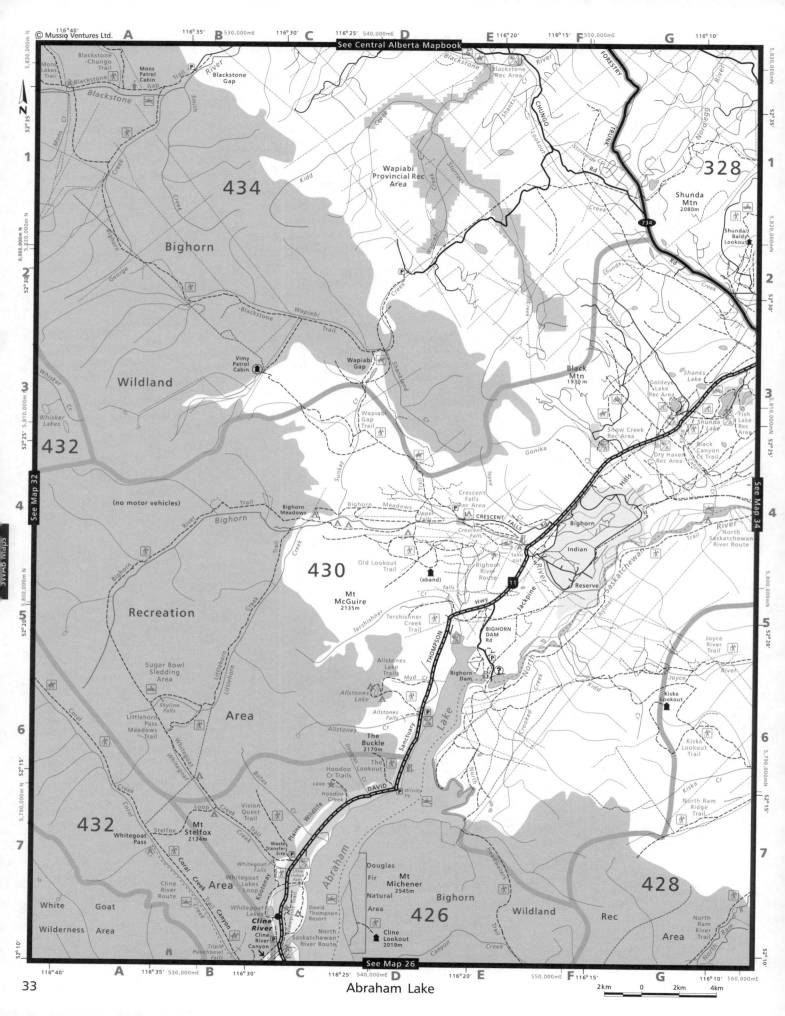

© Mussio Ventures Ltd.

A 116°40' **B** 116°35' 530,000mE **C** 116°30' **D** 116°25' 540,000mE **E** 116°20' **F** 116°15' 550,000mE **G** 116°10'

52°35'

1

Mons Lakes Trail
Blackstone-Chungo Trail
Blackstone
Mons Patrol Cabin
Blackstone Gap
Blackstone Gap

Blackstone
River

Smith

Mons Cr
Blackstone

Kidd Cr

Bighorn Cr

434

Bighorn

Wapiabi Provincial Rec Area

Blackstone Rec Area

Chungo

Shanks Cr

Surrock Creek

Wapiabi Creek

FORESTRY TRUNK

Stovepipe Cr Rd

Shunda Cr

Nordegg River

328

Shunda Mtn 2080m

734

Shunda Rd

Shunda // Baldy Lookout

52°35'

52°30'

2

6,060,000 N
5,820,000 N

George Cr

Wildland

Blackstone
Wapiabi Trail

Vimy Patrol Cabin

Wapiabi Gap

Shankland Cr

Lookout

Black Mtn 1930m

Shanks Lake

Goldeye Lake Rec Area

Shunda Lake

Fish Lake Rec Area

52°30'

52°25'
5,810,000 N

3

Whisker Cr

Whisker Lakes

432

Wapiabi Gap Trail

Sunkay

Gonika Cr

Tepee Cr

Snow Creek Rec Area

Dry Haven Rec Area

Black Canyon Cr Trail

Hills

52°25'

4

(no motor vehicles)

Recreation

Bighorn River
Bighorn Creek
Trail

Bighorn Meadows

Bighorn Meadows

Upper Falls

Crescent Falls Rec Area

Crescent Falls

CRESCENT FALLS

Crescent Falls Rd

take out

Bighorn River Route

Bighorn Indian Reserve

North Saskatchewan River Route

River

52°20'
5,800,000 N

5

Littlehorn Creek

Sugar Bowl Sledding Area

Skyline Falls

Littlehorn Pass Meadows Trail

Area

430

Mt McGuire 2135m

Old Lookout Trail

(aband)

falls

Tershishner Creek Trail

Tershishner Cr

falls

Hwy

Jackpine

11

THOMPSON

BIGHORN DAM Rd

Bighorn Dam

?

North Saskatchewan

Jackpine Creek

Aylmer Cr

Joyce River Trail

Joyce River

52°20'

52°15'

6

Coral Cr

Whitegoat Creek

Littlehorn Creek

Allstones Lake Trails

Allstones Lake

Allstones Falls

Allstones Cr

The Buckle 2170m

Sanctuary

Lake

Mud Cr

Crooked Creek

North Cr

Kiske Lookout

Kiska Lookout Trail

Kiska Cr

52°15'

5,790,000 N

7

432

Coral

Stelfox

Whitegoat Pass

Mt Stelfox 2134m

Loop
Coral Creek Trail Canyon

Coral Creek

Whitegoat Creek

Barus Cr

Vision Quest Trail

Waste Transfer Site

Douglas Cr

The Lookout

Hoodoo Cr Trails

cave

Hoodoo Creek

DAVID

Windy Pt

Douglas Fir Natural Area

Mt Michener 2545m

426

Bighorn

Wildland

Headwaters

North Ram Ridge Trail

Rec

North Ram River Trail

North Ram R

428

52°10'

White

Goat

Wilderness

Area

Whitegoat Lakes Loop

Kootenay

Whitegoat Lakes

Cline River Route

Little Indian Falls

Plains Wildlife

Cline River

Cline River Canyon

Triple Punchbowl Falls

David Thompson Resort

North Saskatchewan River Route

Area

Cline Lookout 2019m

52°10'

116°40' **A** 116°35' 530,000mE **B** 116°30' **C** 116°25' 540,000mE **D** 116°20' **E** 116°15' 550,000mE **F** **G** 116°10' 560,000mE

33

See Map 32

See Map 34

2km   0   2km   4km

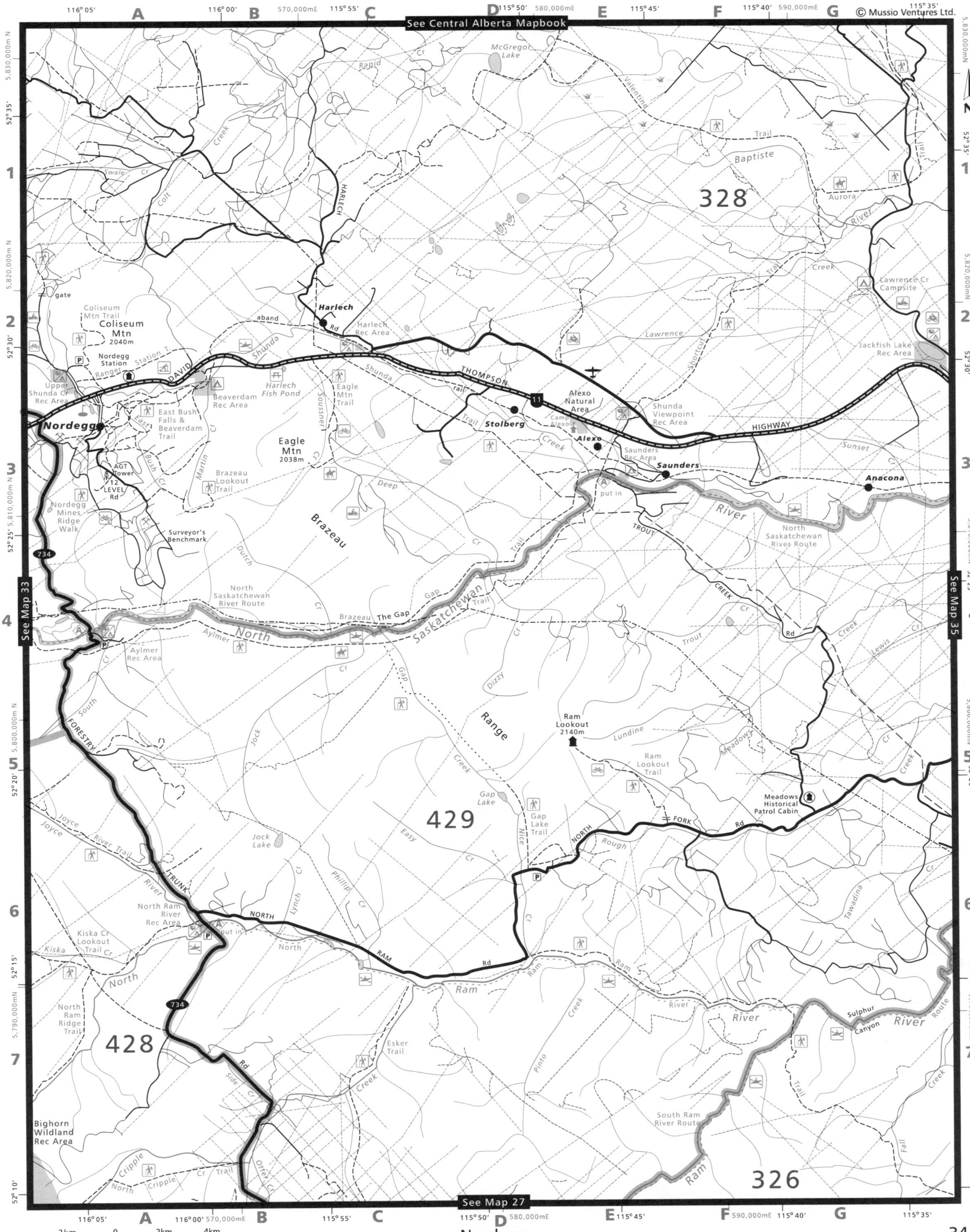
© Mussio Ventures Ltd.
See Central Alberta Mapbook
See Map 33
See Map 35
See Map 27
116° 05'
116° 00'
115° 55'
115° 50'
115° 45'
115° 40'
115° 35'
570,000mE
580,000mE
590,000mE
5,830,000m N
5,820,000m N
5,810,000m N
5,800,000m N
5,790,000mN
52° 35'
52° 30'
52° 25'
52° 20'
52° 15'
52° 10'
A
B
C
D
E
F
G
1
2
3
4
5
6
7
328
429
428
326
McGregor Lake
Rapid Cr
Valentine
Trail
Baptiste
Aurora
River
Creek
Lawrence Cr Campsite
Lawrence
Shortcut
Jackfish Lake Rec Area
Swale Cr
Colt
Creek
HARLECH
Harlech
Rd
Harlech Rec Area
aband
gate
Coliseum Mtn Trail
Coliseum Mtn
2040m
Nordegg Station
Ranger Station T.
DAVID
Shunda
THOMPSON
11
HIGHWAY
Upper Shunda Cr Rec Area
Beaverdam Rec Area
Harlech Fish Pond
Eagle Mtn Trail
Trail
Alexo Natural Area
Shunda Viewpoint Rec Area
Nordegg
East Bush Falls & Beaverdam Trail
East
Bush
Cr
Martin
Cr
Soussner
Cr
Eagle Mtn
2038m
Stolberg
Camp Alexo
Alexo
Saunders Rec Area
Saunders
Sunset
Cr
Anacona
AGT Tower
12 LEVEL Rd
Brazeau Lookout Trail
Deep
put in
River
North Saskatchewan River Route
TROUT
CREEK
Nordegg Mines Ridge Walk
Brazeau
Dutch
Cr
Surveyor's Benchmark
734
North Saskatchewan River Route
Gap
The Gap
Brazeau
Saskatchewan
North
Trail
Aylmer
Aylmer Rec Area
Cr
Trout
Rd
Creek
Lewis
Cr
Gap
Dizzy
Cr
Range
South
FORESTRY
Jock
Creek
Ram Lookout
2140m
Lundine
Meadows
Ram Lookout Trail
Cr
Creek
Meadows Historical Patrol Cabin
Gap Lake
Gap Lake Trail
Nice
FORK
Rd
NORTH
Rough
Joyce
Joyce
River Trail
Jock Lake
Easy
Cr
Phillip
Cr
Lynch
Cr
TRUNK
River
North Ram River Rec Area
put in
NORTH
RAM
Rd
North
Cr
Tawadina
Cr
Kiska Cr Lookout Trail
Kiska
Cr
North
Ram
Ram
Ram
River
River
Sulphur
Canyon
River
Route
North Ram Ridge Trail
Esker Trail
Pinto
Creek
Trail
Creek
Rd
Side
Cr
Creek
Bighorn Wildland Rec Area
South Ram River Route
Cripple
Cripple
Cr
Trail
North
Otter
Cr
Fall
Ram
2km
0
2km
4km

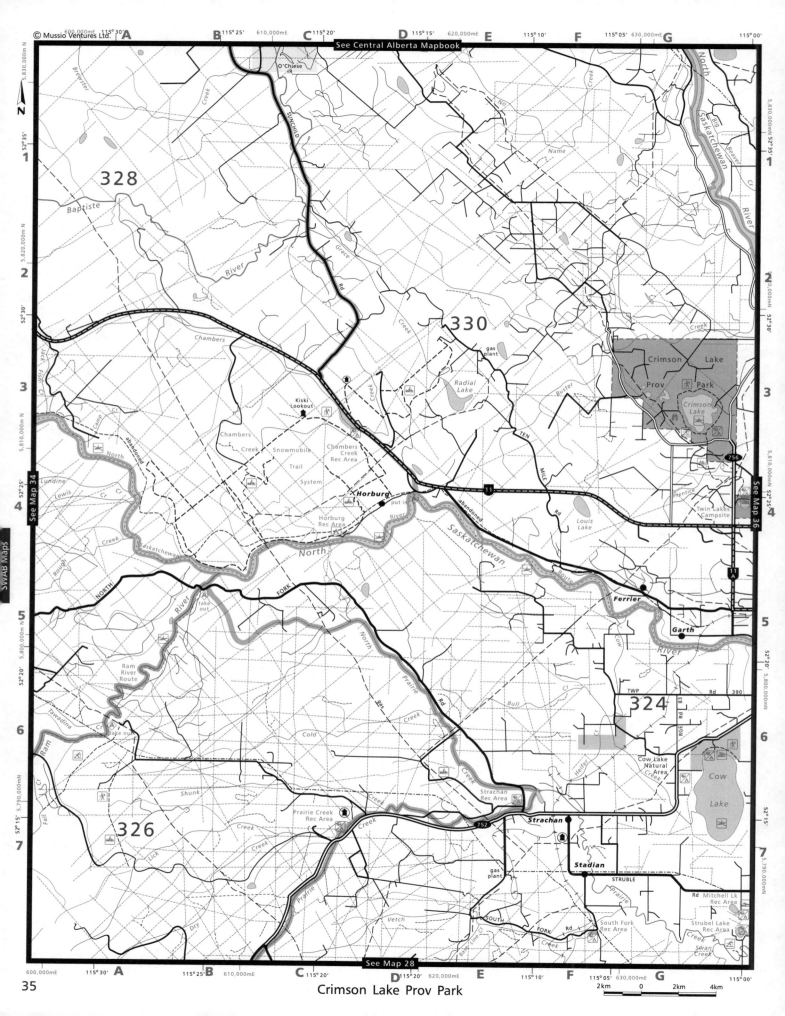

600,000mE 115°30'   115°25'   610,000mE   115°20'   115°15'   620,000mE   115°10'   115°05' 630,000mE   115°00'

A   B   C   D   E   F   G

N

328

Brewster
Creek

Baptiste

5,830,000mN

52°35'

1

5,820,000mN

Grace

River

52°30'

2

O'Chiese
IR

SUNCHILD

Chambers

330

gas
plant

Name Creek

Crimson   Lake

Prov   Park

3

Chambers
Rd

Radial
Lake

Crimson
Lake

52°25' 5,810,000mN

Kiski
Lookout

Chambers
Creek Rec Area

Buster

756

Creek

Chambers
Creek

Snowmobile

Trail

System

TEN

MILE

11

abandoned

Rd

Prentice

See Map 36

4

Camp Cr

North

abandoned

Lundine
Lewis
Cr

See Map 34

SWAB Maps

Horburg

put in

Horburg
Rec Area

North

River

Saskatchewan

Louis
Lake

Twin Lakes
Campsite

**11
A**

5,810,000mN

Rough

Creek

Saskatchewan

North

FORK

take
out

River

Route

Ferrier

Garth

52°20'

5

5,800,000mN

Ram
River Route

North

Prairie

Rd

Creek

Cow

Bull

Cr

River

324

TWP   Rd   390

RGE Rd 83

52°20' 5,800,000mN

6

Fall
Cr

Ram

Tawadina
Cr

take out

gas

Cold

Creek

Creek

Helfer

Cow Lake
Natural
Area

Cow
Lake

326

Shunk

Creek

Creek

Prairie Creek
Rec Area

Creek

Strachan
Rec Area

52°15' 5,790,000mN

7

Lick

Creek

752

Strachan

Stadian

STRUBLE

Prairie

Rd Mitchell Lk
Rec Area

Dry

Prairie

FORK

Creek

gas
plant

SOUTH

Vetch

FORK

Rd

South Fork
Rec Area

Strubel Lake
Rec Area

Swan
Creek

5,790,000mN

See Map 28

600,000mE   115°30'   115°25'   610,000mE   115°20'   115°15' 620,000mE   115°10'   115°05' 630,000mE   115°00'

A   B   C   D   E   F   G

35   Crimson Lake Prov Park

2km   0   2km   4km

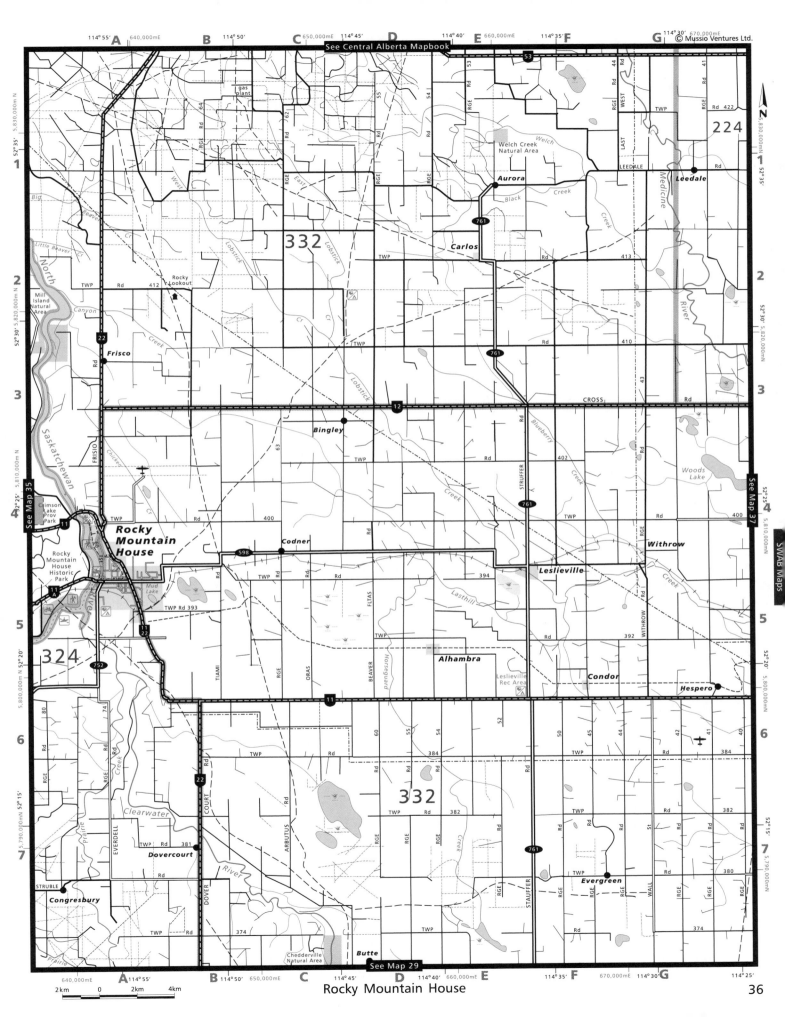

© Mussio Ventures Ltd.

224

332

332

324

Rocky Mountain House

See Map 35
See Map 37
See Map 29

SWAB Maps

2km 0 2km 4km

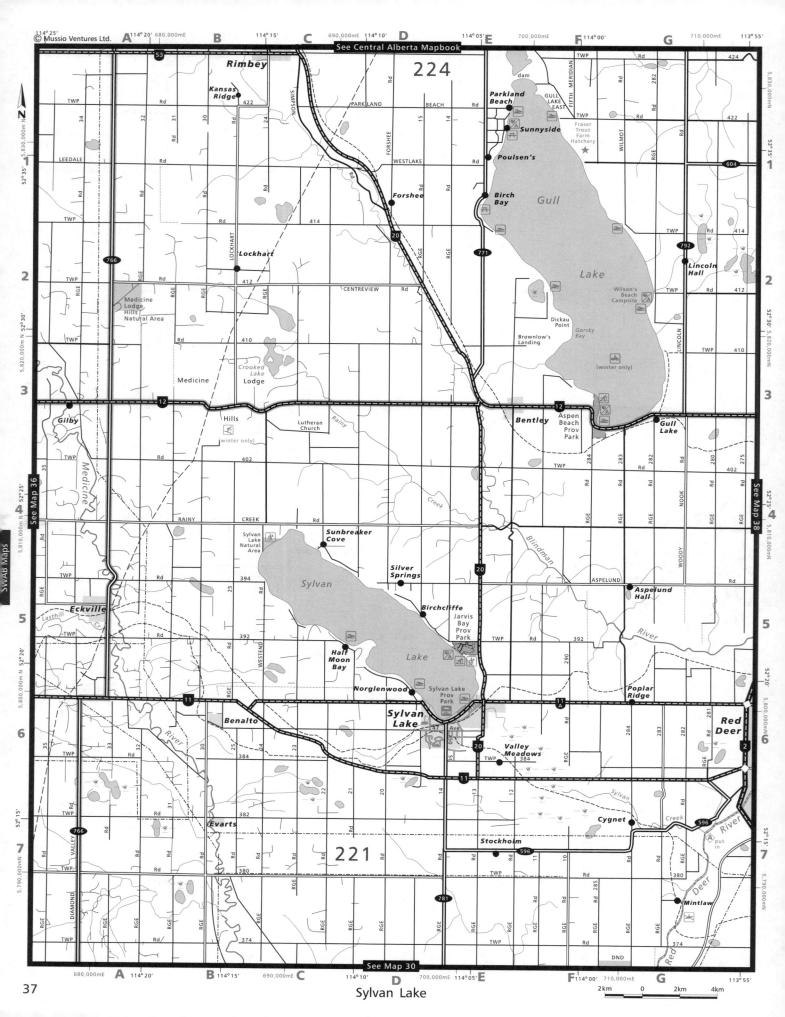

Rimbey

Kansas
Ridge

Parkland
Beach

GULL
LAKE
EAST

Sunnyside

Fraser
Trout
Farm
Hatchery ★

Poulsen's

Gull

Forshee

Birch
Bay

Lincoln
Hall

Lake

Lockhart

Wilson's
Beach
Campsite

Medicine
Lodge
Hills
Natural Area

Dickau
Point

Gorsky
Bay

Crooked
Lake
Lodge

Brownlow's
Landing

Medicine

(winter only)

Gilby

Bentley

Aspen
Beach
Prov
Park

Gull
Lake

Hills

Lutheran
Church

(winter only)

Rainy

See Map 36

Medicine

Creek

See Map 38

Eckville

RAINY   CREEK

Sunbreaker
Cove

Sylvan
Lake
Natural
Area

Silver
Springs

Blindman

Aspelund

Aspelund
Hall

Sylvan

Birchcliffe

Jarvis
Bay
Prov
Park

River

Half
Moon
Bay

Lake

Poplar
Ridge

Norglenwood

Sylvan Lake
Prov
Park

Red
Deer

Benalto

Sylvan
Lake

Valley
Meadows

Evarts

Sylvan

Cygnet

Stockholm

221

Creek

Mintlaw

DND

Red   Deer   River

put
in

See Map 30

37

Sylvan Lake

2km   0   2km   4km

SW AB Maps

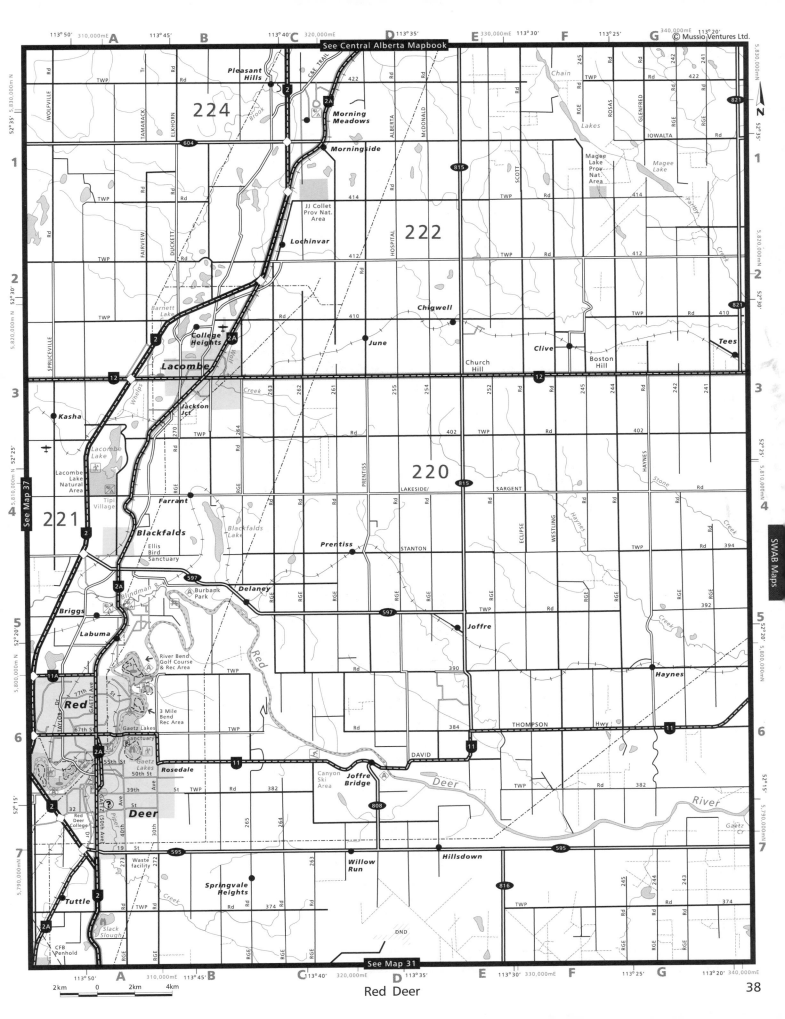

© Mussio Ventures Ltd.

N

See Map 31

Red Deer

38

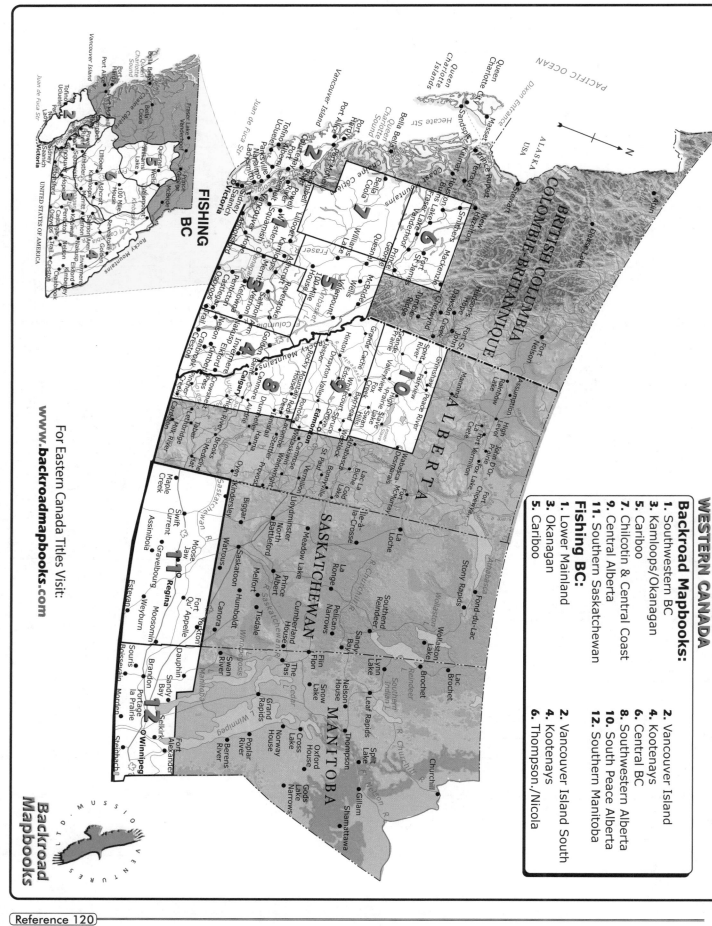

SERVICE PROVIDERS DIRECTORY

Accommodations

Sales/Service

Tours/Guides

Backroad Mapbooks service providers directory is a list of services in the area covered in our books. They consist of Accomodations, Sales/Services, and Tours/Guides. They are arranged alphabetically by City/Region, then by Business name. They flow from left to right.

To advertise your business in this section, call 1-877-520-5670 or 905-342-1169

Buffalo Plains Rv Park & Campground

Park is just 4km from Head Smashed in Buffalo Jump. Large Pull thrus & Back ins. Sheltered tent sites, playground, laundry, showers, dump station. Pets welcome. Open May-October.

Fort Maclead, AB (Call for directions)

403-553-2592

anne@buffaloplains.com

www.buffaloplains.com

Kountry Aire Campground

Tea house- Home cooking & crafts
Near by: Fishing, boating, horseback riding, golfing, ATV trails.

29 km West of Caroline, AB
on HWY #54 & 591

(403) 722-2922

Mountain Valley Sports Fishing & Tours

Dwayne D'Andrea

Castlegar, BC, V1N 2R9

1-800-554-5684

Professional Flyfishing Guide Service Specializing on the Columbia River

mtvalley@telus.net
kootenayflyfishing.com

Pioneer Supply Company

Apple Pie Cafe- Home Cooking, Friendly Service, Jewelry & Giftware

Gas West- Gas, Diesel, **Superior** Propane, Tire repairs-Balancing
Wide Variety of Camping Supplies.

Coming Spring 2006
Guided Tours of the Eastern Slopes of the Rokies & the Drumhellar Badlands.

Located at 1st Ave & 6th St. Beiseker

(403)947-3200

TJD Guiding Services Ltd

Based out of Sheridan Lake, BC, we are your guide to the beautiful secluded lakes of the Cariboo region of BC. All-inclusive fishing packages provided for your convenience.

Office Address: 15617 - 83 Ave, Edmonton, AB. T5R 3T6
780-489-7768
tjguiding.hypermart.net

Invermere

Deere Ridge Luxury Cabins- B&B

Deluxe Rustic honeymoon, family, group log cabins. Hot-Tub, fireplaces, decks, BBQ, kitchenettes, breakfast avail, non-smoking. Nearby, Hot Springs, beaches, hiking, golfing. Dogs on advanced approval.

Invermere, BC (Call for direction)

250-341-3477

www.deereridge.com

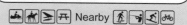 Nearby

Highlight Your City or Region
(20 Characters)

Basic Service Provicer Ad
(350 Characters)

www.deereridge.com

Option 1
Ad Symbols (8 Total)

Option 2
Highlight your website

Vendors

Option 3
Ad Vendors

For more information and pricing on this and other advertising oppertunities in this book please call 1-877-520-5670 or 905-342-1169

IMPORTANT NUMBERS

General

Alberta Camping Association	(403) 453-8570
Alberta Resort & Campground Association	(403) 963-3993
Campground Reservations	1-800-661-8888
Alpine Club of Canada	(403) 678-3200
Updates	http://www.backroadmapbooks.com

Alberta Forest Service (www3.gov.ab.ca/srd/forests/)

Blairmore	(403) 562-3210
Calgary	(403) 297-8800
Drayton Valley	(403) 542-6616
Nordegg	(403) 721-3965
Rocky Mountain House	(403) 845-8272
Southern East Slopes	(403) 845-8250
Sundre	(403) 638-3805
Turner Valley	(403) 933-4381

Natural Resources Services

Canmore	(403) 678-5508
Environmental Protection	(403) 944-0313
Fish & Wildlife Services	(403) 427-3574

Parks

Provincial Parks Information Line	1-866-427-3582
	www.cd.gov.ab.ca/gateway
Recreation & Protected Areas	(403) 427-7009
Kananaskis Country	

www.cd.gov.ab.ca/enjoying_alberta/parks/featured/kananaskis/

Barrier Lake Visitor Centre	(403) 673-3985
Calgary	(403) 297-3362
Peter Lougheed Park	(403) 591-6322
	(403) 678-5508

National Parks

Banff National Park	(403) 762-1550
Heritage Canada (National Parks)	1-800-651-7959
	www.parkscanada.ca
Kootenay National Park	(250) 347-9615
Waterton National Park Administration	(403) 859-2224
Visitor Information (summer)	(403) 859-5133
Yoho National Park	(250) 343-6783

Index

Notes

**Backroad
Mapbooks**

Information Wanted:

We would appreciate a copy of your notes pages to help us update your mapbook. Any information on road conditions or places you visit is invaluable in helping us make a better guide-book. If you are GPS user, please send us tracks of the area. These tracks will help us keep the guidebook the most up to date source for outdoor recreation.

Please contact us at:
Mussio Ventures Ltd.
5811 Beresford St,
Burnaby, B.C. V5J 1K1

Email: updates@backroadmapbooks.com

P: 604-438-3474 toll free 1-877-520-5670 F: 604-438-3470
www.backroadmapbooks.com

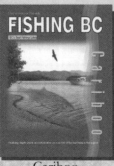